Harvests of Liberation

HARVESTS OF LIBERATION

Cotton, Capitalism, and the End of Empire in Egypt

Ahmad Shokr

Stanford University Press
Stanford, California

Stanford University Press
Stanford, California

Library of Congress Cataloging-in-Publication Data
Names: Shokr, Ahmad, author.
Title: Harvests of liberation : cotton, capitalism, and the end of empire in Egypt / Ahmad Shokr.
Description: Stanford, California : Stanford University Press, 2025. | Includes bibliographical references and index.
Identifiers: LCCN 2024056800 (print) | LCCN 2024056801 (ebook) | ISBN 9781503640085 (cloth) | ISBN 9781503642799 (paperback) | ISBN 9781503642805 (ebook)
Subjects: LCSH: Cotton trade—Egypt—History—20th century. | Agriculture and state—Egypt—History—20th century. | Capitalism—Egypt—History—20th century. | Nationalism—Egypt—History—20th century. | Egypt—Politics and government—1919–1952. | Egypt—Politics and government—1952–1970. | Egypt—Economic policy.
Classification: LCC HD9087.E42 S43 2025 (print) | LCC HD9087.E42 (ebook) | DDC 381/.413510962—dc23/eng/20250131
LC record available at https://lccn.loc.gov/2024056800
LC ebook record available at https://lccn.loc.gov/2024056801

Cover design: Susan Zucker
Cover image: Political cartoon by Zuhdī al-ʿAdawī in *Rūz al-Yūsuf* vol. 1993, August 22, 1966

The authorized representative in the EU for product safety and compliance is: Mare Nostrum Group B.V. | Mauritskade 21D | 1091 GC Amsterdam | The Netherlands | Email address: gpsr@mare-nostrum.co.uk | KVK chamber of commerce number: 96249943

CONTENTS

	Acknowledgments	vii
	Introduction	1
ONE	Anatomy of a Global Plantation	25
TWO	Cotton Nationalism and the Crisis of Empire	52
THREE	Global Depression in the Nile Valley	87
FOUR	Rural Reconstruction and the New Peasant	128
FIVE	Reimagining Development	156
SIX	Growth Politics and the Officers' Republic	189
	Epilogue	228
	Notes	235
	Bibliography	275
	Index	301

ACKNOWLEDGMENTS

The genesis of this book goes back to the Egyptian revolution of 2011. At the time, I was working as a journalist in Cairo. For years, I had wanted to bring my long-standing interests in decolonization, on the one hand, and the history of capitalism, on the other, to the study of twentieth-century Egypt. The revolution solidified that conviction. In discussions with my friends and comrades, we often invoked history as a way to make sense of the extraordinary moment in which we lived. What were Egyptians in 2011 revolting against? Were they revolting against one autocrat who had ruled the country for 30 years? Or against a neoliberal transformation that had unfolded, albeit inconsistently, for 40 years? Or against an officers' republic that had existed for nearly 60 years? Or against a modern state as it had emerged since the nineteenth century? In these conversations, the worlds of activism, academia, and journalism that I inhabited came together and underscored the importance of grappling with our political present through a study of the past. Understanding the origins of the postcolonial state, the legacy of which had cast a long shadow over Egyptian politics, seemed ever more urgent.

Just as the revolution was a collective endeavor in which I constantly engaged with and learned from those around me, so too was the experience of writing this book. It would not have been possible without the generous support of many teachers, friends, colleagues, and institutions. I am fortunate to have had the opportunity to work with Kate Wahl, Chris Peterson, and Catherine Mallon at Stanford University Press who helped me bring this book from the initial stages of its conception into the form in which it now exists.

Zachary Lockman helped me conceive this project and remained a remarkable source of guidance, encouragement, and inspiration. Timothy Mitchell encouraged me to expand my research in innovative directions and offered critical insights that urged me to challenge conventional ways of thinking. Khaled Fahmy helped me to enter the Egyptian National Archives, to think about the politics of archival accessibility and organization, and to appreciate the importance of publicly engaged history. David Ludden devoted countless hours to discussing my research and helped me think about where it fits into the larger picture of global history. Manu Goswami guided me in thinking through the theoretical and political stakes of my work. Karl Appuhn offered critical and constructive insights from which I have benefited greatly. I am grateful for funding from the Social Sciences and Humanities Research Council of Canada's Doctoral Fellowship. The completion of the manuscript was supported by a fellowship at Crown Center for Middle East Studies, Brandeis University in 2016–17 as well as various grants and funds from Swarthmore College.

This book project was made possible by years of conversations with many close friends, colleagues, and interlocutors. I have benefited enormously from countless discussions and collaborations with Aaron Jakes who has helped shape the way I think about the history of capitalism and the field of Middle East history. Samantha Iyer has been a careful and incisive reader of my work; many insights in this book, especially about agrarian history and global political economy, have developed through discussions with her. My friendship with Amr Abdelrahman has had a lasting impact on the way I think about Egyptian history and politics as well as the significance of various currents in leftist thought in Egypt; his extensive knowledge and generosity helped get me through the final stages of this project. My friendship with Shehab Ismail has likewise shaped many aspects of the way I think about the history of decolonization in Egypt, and conversations with him helped steer this project in the direction that it ultimately took. Andrew Liu and I had many conversations about our respective research interests that helped me think about how to study capitalism in a non-Western context. Many other people have shaped the trajectory of this project. For their friendship, support, and feedback, I would like to thank Laura Abaza, Mona Abaza, Ziad Abu-Rish, Ali al-Adawy, Waiel

Ashry, Lina Attalah, Joel Beinin, Ritu Birla, Allison Brown, Megan Brown, John Chalcraft, Ebony Coletu, Jennifer Derr, Beshara Doumani, Nihal El Aasar, Mohammed Ezzeldin, Wael Gamal, Farha Ghannam, Laura Gribbon, Serra Hakyemez, Hanan Hammad, Jens Hansen, Toby Jones, Ezzeldin Kamel, Arang Keshavarzian, Konstantin Kilibarda, Chihab El-Khashab, Malak Labib, Julie Livingston, Mohamed Mabrouk, Samia Mehrez, Pascal Menoret, Alaina Morgan, Donna Murch, Andrew Needham, Hussein Omar, Hassan Rashad, Galal al-Rifa'i, Sarah Rifky, Reem Saad, Rawia Sadek, Sherene Seikaly, and Abdel Razzaq Takriti. I would also like to thank my former student researcher, Grayson Mick, who helped me compile some of the materials for chapter 3.

I am heavily indebted to many friends who read the book manuscript, either in part or in whole, and offered feedback and encouragement. They include Amr Abdelrahman, Sabeen Ahmed, Alia Ayman, Noura Erakat, Joan Flores-Villalobos, Adam Hanieh, Shehab Ismail, Samantha Iyer, Aaron Jakes, Hazem Jamjoum, Anjali Kamat, Amr Khairy, Mohamed Naeem Kinawy, Andrew Liu, Zachary Lockman, Sangina Patnaik, Andrew Sartori, Matthew Shutzer, and Gabriel Young. The completion of this book would not have been possible without the kind assistance of staff members at the National Archives (United Kingdom), the Egyptian National Archives, the Egyptian National Library, and Swarthmore College. I would like to thank the former directors of the Egyptian National Archives, Dr. Muhammad Sabir 'Arab and Dr. 'Abd al-Wahid al-Nabawi, as well as the employees who helped facilitate my research, including Madame Nadia Mustafa. I would also like to extend my gratitude to Kerry Kristine McElrone and Simon Elichko at Swarthmore College.

Over the years, I have had the opportunity to present portions of the book manuscript at several workshops and conferences. I am grateful to the organizers and participants of the New Directions in Political Economy workshop at the Hagop Kevorkian Center for Near Eastern Studies, New York University (2014); the Post-1945 Seminar at the History Department, New York University (2015); the Worlds of World War I workshop at NYU London (2016); the Ecologies of Capital in the Middle East workshop at the Watson Institute for International and Public Affairs, Brown University (2017); the Histories of Economy in the Middle East workshop at the University of California, Santa Barbara (2018); the Annual Conference of the British Society for Middle Eastern Studies (2018); the Annual Conference of the Middle East Studies Association (2016 and 2019); Swarthmore College's Aydelotte Foundation Faculty Dinner (2019) and Faculty Lecture (2021); and the Rethinking Land, Labor, and Capital in Egypt workshop at the Crown Center for Middle East Studies, Brandeis University (2022).

Finally, I would like to thank Mohammed Shokr, Amira Shokr, Alia Ayman, Tarek Shokr, Hisham Shokr, and Reshana Singh for their unwavering love and support. Our innumerable conversations about Egyptian politics and history have been a crucial part of my own political and intellectual journey. No words can express the depth of my gratitude and respect towards them.

INTRODUCTION

IF BREAKING WITH THE COLONIAL past was the foundational claim of the Egyptian military officers who seized power in 1952, then Rashid al-Barrawi was its principal theorist. A self-fashioned thinker from Daqahliyya, a major cotton-growing province in the Nile Delta, he was one of the few people to be chosen by the army to oversee the earliest projects that established its political legitimacy. His status as a widely respected intellectual who was vocally critical of the old order captured the attention of the new revolutionary leadership. The head of the Free Officers, Major General Muhammad Naguib, described him as "a veteran leftist" who wrote prolifically about socialism in Egypt, while the future culture minister, Tharwat 'Ukasha, praised him for being a "distinguished professor of economics."[1] After the coup, al-Barrawi was promptly recruited into the nerve center of the nascent republic where he was tasked with revolutionizing the country's economic system. At the time, he maintained a personal relationship with Colonel Gamal Abdel Nasser, a leader in the officers' movement who would, in a few years, win an internal struggle to become the president of Egypt. Al-Barrawi convinced the officers to urgently adopt an initiative that would "draw the masses around [them] and gain their support."[2] In a matter of days, they asked him to draft a land reform law, which allowed the officers to redistribute properties that belonged to the country's largest estate owners, and soon afterwards they placed him on the Permanent Council for the Development of National Production (PCDNP), which became a forum for major debates and decisions on economic policy.[3] Six months after the officers overthrew the royal family, al-Barrawi published one of the first historical accounts of their rise to power, an event that would soon be renamed the July Revolution. He argued that the removal of the old regime had become necessary to realize the overlapping imperatives of achieving national independence, eliminating autocratic rule, destroying the feudal apparatus, expunging corruption from public life, and raising the living standards of the Egyptian masses.[4] Three years later, al-Barrawi developed these broad aims into a comprehensive philosophy that rested on the principles of scientific management, central planning, and social redistribution.[5] More than anything, he believed in wielding state power for the purpose of bringing about a complete transformation of society, and the revolution led him to discover a group of protagonists that could credibly pursue this mission. The arrival of the officers, he believed, would inaugurate a new era marked by efficiency, industrial development, and modernization.

By the time the officers deposed the monarchy, al-Barrawi already had a reputation that preceded him. He stood out among a generation of ascendant middle-class Egyptians who had studied abroad and returned home to join the ranks of a nationalist intelligentsia that was engulfed by a surge of anticolonial mobilization.[6] He began his career as a schoolteacher before traveling to Britain in the 1930s to earn his undergraduate and graduate degrees. In 1940, he was appointed to Egypt's leading institution of higher education, Fu'ad I University, first as a history lecturer then as a professor in the Faculty of Commerce. By the end of the decade, al-Barrawi had firmly established himself as an outspoken voice for social change. He played a central role in fashioning what became the authoritative lexicon of the July Revolution. A prolific writer who published more than a dozen books, his oeuvre covered many different places and time periods, and it included one of the first economic histories of Egypt to be written by an Egyptian.[7] In this body of work, he helped introduce concepts like "monopoly capitalism," "the alliance between colonialism and feudalism," and "economic backwardness" into the glossary of what would become the officers' republic. He condemned the British occupation for turning the country into a vast cotton plantation—or what he called the "dominance of economic specialization"—with almost no horizon for industrial development.[8] Overcoming this status required an agenda for social transformation that would be directed from the upper echelons of state power. Like many future postcolonial leaders, al-Barrawi was heavily influenced by Fabian socialism. He preached an agenda for gradual reform that did not spill over into complete revolution. He translated many classics from the socialist tradition into Arabic—including Marx, Engels, and Lenin—yet declined to affiliate himself with any political party or current.[9] He adopted a materialist conception of history, but rejected any program for the violent overthrow of one class by another. He admired the Soviet experiment in creating a planned economy, but disregarded its rhetoric of proletarian revolution. According to his biographer, al-Barrawi's unyielding faith in technocratic rationality as a pathway towards independence made him "one of the most important precursors of the Nasserist state."[10]

Many accounts of the origins of Nasserism assume the project to have either been a predictable response to a colonial economy that privileged a handful of royal family members, landed magnates, and powerful merchants since the nineteenth century, or a haphazard phenomenon that could not have been anticipated in advance. In reality, however, Nasserism emerged from the profound social disruptions of depression and war in the 1930s and 1940s. The developmentalist phraseology employed by al-Barrawi was born in that historical moment, and it provided the basis for claims to independence that were very different from those that his predecessors, who were trying to address a different set of problems, had made two or three decades earlier. Cotton was at the center of this transformation. In the 1910s and 1920s, Egyptian nationalists consistently warned about the exposure of Egyptian cultivators, especially those who grew cotton, to the perilous volatilities of foreign markets and capital.[11] Independence could only be complete when cultivators were insulated from such intractable forces so that they could enjoy a greater share of the wealth they produced. For these thinkers, then, sovereignty meant the ability to exercise political authority without interference from impersonal compulsions that they had increasingly associated with living under colonial rule. Whereas their main preoccupation was how to escape domination by foreign capital and markets, the concern of nationalists in the postwar period was how to overcome what they understood to be the sluggish productive capacities of a country that continued to supply raw materials to industrialized nations. The divergent aims of these two generations were rooted in different understandings of what constituted imperialism. For an earlier generation of nationalists, the central problem that imperial domination had introduced into the country was the dependence of millions of Egyptians on recurring and unpredictable movements of goods, capital, and prices over which they had little or no control. In their view, Egypt's colonial condition emanated from its lopsided insertion into uneven relations of exchange in an imperial world economy. For that reason, they had more to say about the unequal terms of trade that diminished the control of rural producers over their own lives and less to say about their productive efficiency or unequal access to land. For postwar nationalists, however, the problem with imperial domination was that it collaborated with reactionary local allies to impose stagnation on Egyptian society. The perceived locus of imperial domination therefore shifted from the realm of circulation to the realm of production. After seizing power, the Free Officers understood their central task to be the triumph over economic backwardness that required a transition from an agrarian to an industrial economy.

Writing in the throes of global decolonization, al-Barrawi lived in a world that was rapidly changing. In the 1950s, many observers tried to make sense of the proliferation of newly independent countries that did not yet appear to fit existing archetypes of development and social change. As the Cold War unfolded, political leaders, intellectuals, and activists around the world began to grapple with the emergence of postcolonial states in the Middle East, Africa, and Asia that did not seem to be straightforwardly capitalist or communist. In his writings, for example, al-Barrawi described the system that would underpin an independent Egypt using a variety of terms, like "economic democracy," "mixed economy," and "new society."[12] If postcolonial societies were theorized in ways that acknowledged their divergence from the West so, too, was the past from which they emerged. In his diagnosis, al-Barrawi disseminated two principal categories through which Egyptian political economy and, by extension, Egyptian history came to be understood under the Free Officers: monopoly and feudalism. Having translated Lenin's treatise *Imperialism, The Highest Stage of Capitalism*, he argued that Western monopoly capital had expanded into Egypt by allying with local feudalists who allowed it to exercise control over agricultural lands.[13] It was this set of imperial arrangements that needed to be eradicated. "The feudal system is fully aware that it is the object of hatred by the people," he wrote, "and that the justification for its survival no longer exists after it has actually become a fetter on the progress of industrial and agricultural production."[14] To vindicate the creation of the officers' republic, then, al-Barrawi determined that the pre-revolutionary social order had fallen into obsolescence and that its persistence frustrated the country's indubitable entry into modernity. Revolution was therefore historically inevitable. Al-Barrawi's verdict would be faithfully reproduced for years. In his own account of the July Revolution, Nasser concluded that it was not the army that dictated the course of history, but rather "the events and their evolution that determined the army's role in the mighty struggle for the liberation of the homeland."[15] The 1956 constitution and the 1962 National Charter, arguably the two most foundational documents of the Nasserist period, both identified six principles of the revolution that included the elimination of imperialism, feudalism, and monopoly capital. While these categories existed in temporal tension with one another—feudalism implied an archaic social form while monopoly suggested an advanced stage of capitalism—they ultimately sought to capture something abnormal about the country's historical development that the inescapable emergence of the officers promised to rectify.

To insist that the experience of colonialism had set the country on a path of deviant development was to grasp Egypt's relationship to world history through its ostensibly anomalous status. This book explains how the country's past became apprehended in this way. It offers both a history of the circumstances that led to the rise of Nasserism as well as a reflexive account of the historiography of modern Egypt. Understanding why the Free Officers embraced a program of national development, and why the history of modern Egypt became told in stagist terms, requires an investigation into their conditions of possibility. Rather than being a generic expression of national liberation, Nasserism was a historically situated phenomenon. It emerged on a restive cotton frontier that was on the precipice of change, including in its relation to a world economy that was gradually disarticulating from the British Empire. Tracing the roots of Nasserism, then, requires that we examine the layered transformation of Egypt's cotton economy between the 1920s and the 1960s. The following pages illustrate how the historical conjuncture of decolonization, agricultural depression, wartime instability, and postwar development ideology ultimately gave rise to Nasserism and allowed it to assume the quintessential form of a national liberation project by the middle of the twentieth century.

NASSERISM AND "LONG" DECOLONIZATION

Nasserism was the main ideology in which Egypt's leaders anchored their political legitimacy during the first two decades of the postcolonial republic. It represented an eclectic project that aimed to achieve national independence by harnessing the powers of the state to promote rapid growth, anti-imperialism, and pan-Arab solidarity while socializing many of the costs of reproducing Egyptian labor.[16] Its official proponents pursued a program of centrally planned industrialization and social welfare, while distributing a large portion of its financial burden to actors that did not form an essential part of Nasser's political base. At the same time, they captivated the minds of millions of Egyptians by convincing them that the country's march to modernity would usher in an era of unprecedented progress. Glowing paeans by artists and intellectuals, filmmakers and singers, journalists and poets inscribed the project into cultural life and aroused a sense of collective agency and achievement. Of course, the Free Officers' regime went through different phases under Nasser, culminating with its most radical turn in the early 1960s. From early on, however, Nasserism coalesced around a central tenet that would guide Egyptian leaders for almost two decades: that national liberation should primarily take the form of national development.

The historiography of Nasserism is remarkably extensive. The scholarship from the last half century or so may be divided into several groups that are not mutually exclusive. The first cluster comprises works that have devoted attention to the actions of political and military leaders in the 1950s and 1960s. These include numerous biographies that focus on the personality of Nasser himself as well as accounts that examine the formation and organization of Egyptian officers, administrators, and technocrats who steadily replaced landowners, professionals, businessmen, and royal family members at the helm of state power.[17] A second cluster includes studies that examine the social structures that both produced Nasserism and that it subsequently refashioned. Egyptian Marxists have understood Nasserism in terms of the class interests and coalitions to which it gave voice, as well as the historical phase to which it appropriately belonged. Adopting an orthodox view of historical stagism, many Egyptian communists in the 1950s and 1960s understood prerevolutionary Egypt to be a feudal society, or at least one with unmistakably feudal features, and believed the officers to be a historically progressive force that deserved some degree of support. Among the few Marxists who broke with established dogma, some of them argued that Egypt's transition to capitalism since the 1880s had rid it of any feudal elements and transformed its ruling classes, whether landed estate owners or urban bourgeoisies, into compradors that were dependent on the world capitalist system.[18] Others began to challenge the premise that Egyptian history unfolded within a sequence of predetermined stages—from feudalism, to capitalism, to socialism—that possessed universal validity, and instead they introduced new sociological categories to understand the character of the ruling class in Egypt.[19] A third cluster of books, which appeared in the last 30 years, has focused principally on the Nasserist state's ability to exercise ideological control and to produce modern political subjects.[20] These methods of domination had the combined effect of circumscribing the political alliances that the officers could forge, inviting novel forms of government intervention into the everyday lives of Egyptians, effacing any cleavages within the national body politic, and raising Nasser to the status of undisputed spokesman.

What this voluminous body of scholarship has done less intently is inquire into the conditions that made the underlying precepts of Nasserism conceptually plausible. To the extent that these works do try to excavate the historical origins of the project, they usually present the emergence of Nasserism either as a historical necessity or an unforeseeable contingency. On the one hand, the July Revolution is understood in much of the literature to have emerged from slowly mounting pressures—monarchical decay, elite factionalism and corruption, and socioeconomic inequality and stagnation—that the previous regime could not contain. Egyptian Marxists and left-nationalists conventionally understood the July Revolution to be a corrective to the unsuccessful attempts at national-bourgeois revolution in the 1920s. Though his account is far less teleological, Kirk Beattie also concludes that the Free Officers were motivated in part by "frustration over the ability of corrupt feudalists, monopoly capitalists, and foreign interests to block reforms essential to socioeconomic development."[21] By presenting Nasserism as a necessary resolution to the long-standing contradictions of the colonial order these accounts reproduce some of the project's fundamental presuppositions about itself. This kind of developmentalist bias also pervades the historical scholarship on earlier periods. Since its publication more than half a century ago, Roger Owen's *Cotton and the Egyptian Economy, 1820–1914* has served as an authoritative study of the political economy of imperialism in the Middle East. Writing in the heyday of decolonization, Owen sought to provide a historical account of Egypt's underdevelopment that postcolonial leaders in the 1950s and 1960s were trying to overturn. He concluded that the country's shift towards large-scale cotton cultivation in the nineteenth century resulted in "growth but not development" as massive increases in agricultural production did not induce a transition from a primary-export to an industrial economy.[22] Writing about the three and a half decades before 1952, Robert Tignor similarly found that Egypt's industrial bourgeoisie "never gained an upper hand" in an economy that remained dominated by landed magnates.[23] Both of them assumed the central problematic of the postwar era—how newly independent nations could industrialize despite the entrenchment of powerful landowning classes that did not revolutionize their means of production—to be the logical outcome of the country's development under colonialism. In other words, they mistook a historically specific problem in the 1950s and 1960s to be an enduring feature of the country's political economy since the nineteenth century.[24]

On the other hand, some scholars have presented the emergence of Nasserism as a more fortuitous affair. The strongest version of this argument has been made by Robert Vitalis who criticized histories that are "written backward to deduce Nasserism as an outcome of the exceptionalist circumstances of colonial capitalist development."[25] Rather than treating the officers as agents of historical progress, Vitalis questioned the premise that land reform was necessary for industrialization, highlighted the role that U.S. officials and consultants played in shaping the officers' policies, and presented Nasserism as an outcome of the global spread of ideas about development.[26] If some scholars believe that Nasserism was born, at least in part, out of developmentalist diffusionism, others argue that when they seized power the officers did not stand on any firm intellectual foundations because they embodied a kind of pragmatism that was ultimately motivated by political gain. Taking aim at accounts that portray the July Revolution as historically inevitable, Joel Gordon has criticized scholars that "too often [take] for granted that Egypt stood on the brink of social revolution." Instead, he narrates the political ascent of officers who had "no clear vision of what they hoped to achieve except in the most abstract sense."[27] Sharif Yunis extends this argument further by insisting that because the officers sought to create a regime that appeared to stand above the sectional interests of any political faction, their existence as a "non-political force without any program, vision, or mass base became an advantage."[28] To the extent that they ascribe any distinctive ideas to Nasserism, these studies often locate their roots in the postwar period without explaining why they resonated with such a wide segment of people.

Although these accounts provide valuable insights into the character of the Nasserist state, many of them leave questions unaddressed about the origins of the project. Understanding Nasserism as a product of both the immediate historical circumstances that spawned it as well as the structural constraints within which that history unfolded requires a dynamic conception of capitalism. The system of generalized commodity production, which this term designates, has drawn people into fields of exchange in which the products of their own labor—and, in many cases, their labor itself—are bought and sold on markets for the purpose of endless accumulation. As William Sewell Jr. observes, the rhythms of social life under capitalism are both abruptly contingent and cyclically patterned.[29] They are filled with eventful ruptures and turning points—from business groups that rise and fall, to technological inventions that accelerate the pace of life, to governments that get overthrown by revolution—as well as monotonously repetitive processes—like the constant drive towards perpetual growth, or the recurrence of boom-bust cycles. The dual character of capitalist temporality—which is heterogeneously unique at the level of concrete events and occurrences yet homogeneously repetitive at the level of the system's abstract social logic—has a correlate in the workings of capitalist domination. To live in a capitalist world is to be subjected to two possible kinds of power. The first one stems from the direct actions of people and institutions, and can include extra-economic coercion, colonial plunder, and the promotion of racist and sexist ideologies.[30] The second one stems from the impersonal workings of the system of market competition itself in which people must continuously produce value at or above an average rate of efficiency determined by the level of skill, technology, and productivity that prevails in their society.[31] To build upon an analogy from Marx, personal domination is akin to somebody being physically pushed off the roof of a building while impersonal domination is like the force of gravity pulling them to the ground.[32] While the first kind of domination is not necessarily born from the imperatives of market competition, it can easily be repurposed to serve them. In short, then, people in capitalist society can be dominated either by other actors and institutions directly or by abstract compulsions that exceed them.

Approaching capitalist temporality and domination in this manner reveals the ways in which the character of socioeconomic life in Egypt was shaped by both historically specific conditions as well as abstract forms of interdependence. Over the course of the nineteenth and twentieth centuries, Egyptian peasants were physically abused by their landlords, they were targets of discipline and rehabilitation by government officials, and, by the postwar period, they were required to produce ever more cotton under the rubric of a modernization program that was sponsored by foreign aid and assistance. But these ostensibly contingent events, and the direct forms of political mediation upon which they depended, existed in constitutive tension with indirect forms of market mediation that linked the activities of Egyptian producers, traders, and bureaucrats to other parts of the world. Cultivators complained about having to endure an unremitting labor process to continuously produce ever larger amounts of cotton for distant markets. Landowners protested the seemingly intractable fluctuations in the price of the crop. Nationalists warned about financial crashes that were caused by unregulated flows of capital in and out of the country. All of these grievances underscored their exposure to impersonal compulsions that arose from being incorporated into a system of generalized commodity production that generated a variety of incoherent and contradictory developmental impulses.

Revisiting the experience of decolonization in Egypt through a history of capitalism might help us to overcome the problems that exist in the historiography of Nasserism. Doing so must begin from the premise that capitalism does not look the same everywhere, all the time. Although the Egyptian countryside has been part of an interdependent capitalist system for at least two centuries, its ongoing transmutations over that time have generated historically situated realities that different actors have had to navigate.[33] The distinctive shape that national development took under Nasser was not simply a response to contradictions that had long existed in the colonial economy. Rather, it grew out of the specific, if globally situated, conditions in Egypt during the middle of the twentieth century. These included material transformations in the late 1930s and 1940s—the devastation of cash crops, the impoverishment of peasantries, the collapse of rural credit, the spread of agrarian rentierism, and the wartime growth of urban industries and populations. It also included the interpretation of those conditions through transnationally circulating ideas about development after the war. The popular agitations that preceded 1952, the seizure of power by the Free Officers, and the overhaul of economic life after the revolution emerged from this conjuncture that transformed the foundations upon which Egyptian cotton had been produced and traded for almost a century. The ideas, programs, and narratives that formed the corpus of Nasserism were therefore a contextually specific expression of political-economic dynamics in this moment, rather than a reaction to developments in Egypt since the nineteenth century.

At the same time, the emergence of Nasserism reflected larger global patterns that cannot be understood simply in contingent terms. In the postwar period, internationally organized efforts to tame the incoherent and contradictory impulses of global capitalism as they existed in the previous three decades resulted in a political-economic reorientation around the world. Far from being bereft of an ideology, the officers embodied a set of ruling ideas from the start that informed many of their decisions and actions. The worldview within which they maintained their legitimacy was rooted in an ideology of postwar development. It emerged from the disruptions brought about by world markets and, by the 1950s and 1960s, had assumed the status of global common sense. The main ingredients of postwar development were nationally scaled growth, state-led industrialization, and the provision of social welfare that were managed within international networks of trade, finance, and expertise. As a political entity, Egypt had a long and identifiable history; for centuries, people living within that space had apprehended it as a unit that was ruled, more or less, by a single political authority. As a national economic space, however, Egypt was a much more recent invention. Only in the postwar period did it become a legible object of politics whose perpetual growth through industrialization was a principal goal of Egypt's leaders.[34] While the term "economic growth" was not widely used before the

1950s, it soon became a ubiquitous indicator of national prosperity and, according to historian John McNeill, its pursuit was "easily the most important idea of the twentieth century."[35] Any state that strove towards the realization of these objectives represented historical progress on a linear scale that could be observed, measured, and interpreted through the episteme of "development." The Nasserist project certainly had other important components—like its vision for social justice, non-alignment, and pan-Arab solidarity—and its ability to assert control over important assets and revenue streams, like the Suez Canal, that were previously kept out of the hands of Egyptians presented no small challenge to imperial powers. But the imperative towards industrial growth, including the international constraints within which that objective was pursued, often took precedence in shaping the trajectory of the project. Because many of the ideas that Nasserism drew upon became so widely established in the postwar period, few analysts perceived them to be distinctive because they, too, had internalized a similar perspective. In reality, however, the normative presuppositions about history and social change that came to define postwar development provided a standpoint from which the foundational claims of Nasserist leaders and intellectuals were habitually reproduced in their everyday utterances, initiatives, and practices.

This study will therefore historicize the emergence of Nasserism by looking closely at the sites in which the country's prized crop was produced and traded in the decades before the July Revolution. A few scholars have shown that there were discernible links between Nasserist policies and earlier kinds of knowledge, regulation, and institutions that moved through transnational circuits of experts and colonial administrators.[36] For that reason, the 1920s to the 1960s are best considered a period of "long decolonization" in which the basic structures of postcolonial life and politics were put together. As Omnia El Shakry has argued, the Nasserist state drew on an existing discourse of social reform that reveals "a continuity with the post-independence period, rather than the fundamental disjuncture usually presumed to have occurred with the 1952 revolution."[37] It is difficult to overestimate the impact of social scientists in the Ministry of Social Affairs, economists in the Faculty of Commerce at Fu'ad I University, and Marxist intellectuals from different parties across his period. As this study shows, these thinkers collectively established a repertoire of terms and ideas in the 1940s that would be appropriated by the Free Officers.

But the reason to situate Nasserism within a historical arc of long decolonization is not simply to question the originality of the project. Widening our temporal aperture undoubtedly reveals that the Free Officers activated ideas that were in circulation for years before the revolution. More importantly, however, it allows for a critical history of Nasserism that can explain why its own worldview and self-understanding came to be regarded as normal to so many observers by the 1950s and 1960s.

The postwar development ethos in which Nasserism was grounded shaped both its understanding of geopolitics and history. Embracing such a project meant that the Free Officers were compelled to abide by the written and unwritten rules of an international order that was not created on their own terms. As much as they imagined themselves to be achieving greater self-sufficiency, they also imposed undemocratic forms of political life on their population in order to meet the demands of ever-increasing growth, and they entered into new forms of political, economic, and technological reliance on foreign patrons. Rather than bring the country closer to genuine independence, the pursuit of national development locked Egypt into relations of uneven exchange on a world scale, and increased its need for support from global superpowers, in ways that were all too reminiscent of colonial subordination. By the mid-to-late 1960s, Nasserism had proven incapable of resolving the problem of national sovereignty with which Egypt's postcolonial leadership grappled. The politics of the Cold War resulted in the country's deepening entrenchment into forms of dependence that compromised the success of the project. These realities were concealed, however, by the way that Nasserist leaders, intellectuals, and hagiographers publicly reconceptualized the past from which they emerged. They often masked the project's limitations with an enduringly appealing way of narrating their own rise to power. The Free Officers understood themselves to be a political force that carried the weight of history on its shoulders. After overthrowing the monarchy, they began to revise conventional understandings of the country's past and to tell the story of modern Egypt in historicist terms. By presenting the July Revolution as a triumph over pre-capitalist forms of backwardness, a claim that was first elaborated by al-Barrawi, the officers advanced a revisionist narrative of Egyptian history in which the consolidation of their political authority simultaneously meant Egypt's ascent to a higher stage of development. Their account of the past obscured the country's subordinate position in global space by misconstruing its place in historical time. The July Revolution did not emerge to abolish feudalism or monopolies; rather, the leaders of the revolution appropriated these concepts from Egyptian thinkers in the 1940s and embellished them in order to legitimize their rule. What Nasserist renderings of the past concealed, then, was the reality that the July Revolution existed firmly within the history of capitalism in Egypt.

MONOPOLIES IN THE EGYPTIAN NILE VALLEY

The history of decolonization in the Egyptian Nile Valley is occasionally narrated as a transition from laissez-faire capitalism that prevailed under colonial rule to state capitalism that took hold in the age of national independence.[38] By contrast, this study tells the story of a transformation from one set of geographically scaled monopoly powers into another. The spatial unit that forms the basis of this study is the Egyptian Nile Valley, a zone of perennially irrigated agriculture around the Nile River that has existed under the successive authority of khedival, colonial, and national governments over the past two centuries. It was a vast hinterland in which monocrop agriculture, semi-free or unfree labor, and European technology and managerial skill combined to enable the mass production of raw commodities for English textile manufacturers. For that reason, we might analogize the Egyptian Nile Valley to a large plantation that acted as a crucial node in the geography of the British-centered imperial world economy.[39] Over the course of a century, it went from being an important territorial component in Britain's "empire of cotton" to a space in which economic life was increasingly organized through nationally scaled institutions and processes.[40] The multisited interactions between colonial advisors, nationalist leaders, agrarian reformers, merchant-financiers, landowners, and rural workers gradually moved the levers of the global cotton trade from the hands of groups and institutions that facilitated accumulation on an imperial scale to new sites of control within the postcolonial nation-state.

The principal institutions that were involved in the production and trade of Egyptian cotton across this unstable geography operated through various kinds of monopoly power. Many of them were not clearly situated inside or outside of the state, nor were they governed by people, processes, and epistemologies that were unambiguously colonial or national. For that reason, this study eschews any a priori distinction between the political and the economic; rather, it examines a variety of arrangements that fused together political and economic power, or what I call monopolistic domains. Before 1952, they included the landed oligarchy that owned large private estates (*'izbas*), the state railways administration, the powerful merchant families in Alexandria, and the handful of European mortgage banks that financed the purchase of land. Although they were not all monopolies in a strict sense—some of them were cartels, oligopolies, or oligarchies—they all fashioned politically determined arenas of accumulation in which competition was often circumscribed by overtly legal and/or political mechanisms that enabled a relatively small group of individuals or enterprises to make exorbitant profits. If the accumulation of capital in the Egyptian Nile Valley was to proceed through the production and trade of ever larger quantities of cotton, then doing so required as its pedestal the existence of extra-economic coercion, the political transfer of assets, and the construction of legal and physical infrastructures that benefited a handful of capitalists.

The monopolistic domains through which the production and trade of Egyptian cotton proceeded in the late nineteenth and early twentieth century were forged through preferential or concessionary arrangements of different sorts. The first domain comprised the large cotton estates (*'izbas*), particularly in the Nile Delta. In the 1820s and 1830s, the governor of Egypt, Mehmed Ali, established a monopoly over cotton production and export to increase the revenues of his modernizing state. Then, a worldwide economic crisis in 1836–37 prompted him to abandon this system in favor of direct land taxes. To promote the continued expansion of cash-crop cultivation, the governor and his successors seized village lands and granted them to rural notables and members of their extended family.[41] Over time, these proprietors formed the nucleus of a large landholding class that controlled much of the countryside and played a dominant role in Egyptian politics. The consolidation of large private estates in the hands of this landed oligarchy continued into the twentieth century. Between 1900 and 1906, for example, the government sold nearly half a million feddans of land that it had collateralized in the 1860s to guarantee its foreign loans (*daira saniyya*).[42] This massive privatization of land formerly owned by the state encouraged a greater concentration of property in the hands of a small number of large landholders. Estate owners did not act collectively as a monopoly. Within the walls of an individual *'izba*, however, an owner did possess arbitrary powers to abuse, starve, imprison, expel, and exploit those peasants working on his land.[43] In this way, the *'izba* functioned as a "hidden abode"—to borrow Marx's term—where forms of extra-economic violence and coercion continued to exist within its sovereign realm.[44]

The second domain was the state railways. The Egyptian State Railways (ESR) was created in the 1850s and acquired its monopoly powers through imperial arrangements that were put in place two decades later. After the khedival government faced the threat of bankruptcy in the 1870s, it created an international railway commission led by representatives from England, France, and Egypt. The commission ensured that most of the annual revenues of the state railways were used to repay interest on loans that the Egyptian government had borrowed from European banks.[45] This arrangement lasted until the first decade of the twentieth century when the state railways were again transformed from a debt-servicing institution into a state-run commercial enterprise. To safeguard the revenues (and later the profits) of the state railways, the managers of the ESR repeatedly sabotaged their competitors on roads and rivers. They ensured the imposition of heavy navigation tolls, they induced a reduction in maritime traffic by encouraging the neglect of existing canals and waterways, and they offered preferential freight rates for the transport of cotton and other vital commodities.

The third domain was the Alexandria General Produce Association (AGPA). The introduction of cotton cultivation into large parts of the Nile Valley in the nineteenth century attracted a cohort of Greek, Levantine, and Jewish immigrants who eventually formed a powerful merchant class. In 1883, these cotton traders created an association to regulate all transactions on the spot market, to establish grades for different types of cotton and cotton seed, and to arbitrate disputes between buyers and sellers.[46] As early as the 1910s, observers began to criticize the AGPA's monopoly over both the movement of cotton and the production of information about it. But its privileges relied as much on government activities as it did on ostensibly free markets. For example, the AGPA could not function without a state that built railways and roads to transport crops, that constructed irrigation works to expand cultivation, that promoted new cotton strains to increase yields, that enacted laws and regulations to enable trading activities, and that organized policing and security around the country.

The fourth monopolistic domain was mortgage banking. Between 1880 and 1907, a nascent land mortgage industry eventually came to be dominated by three British and French banks: the Crédit Foncier Égyptien, the Land and Mortgage Company of Egypt, and the Land Bank of Egypt.[47] They were established amidst the large-scale expansion of Western financial capital into the colonial world in the late nineteenth century. These banks catered almost exclusively to the minority of wealthy landholders in the country that owned large agricultural properties.[48] While they were not strictly monopolies, these banks did maintain some oligarchic qualities. For example, the Crédit Foncier rose to prominence in the early twentieth century by acquiring privatized khedivial estates from the government and flipping them for hefty profits in a high-demand land market.[49] The following year, in 1905, the value of its mortgage loans nearly doubled, and it would not return to its pre-1905 levels again until the Great Depression.[50] The bank became the most highly capitalized company in Egypt and dominated the mortgage sector more than any other institution.[51]

These kinds of monopoly powers persisted throughout the prolonged struggle for national independence. Writing in the late 1940s, one Egyptian economist complained that across the country "all forms of monopoly organization known to the capitalist world [were] represented."[52] After they seized power, the Free Officers, who claimed to be combatting monopolies, did not eliminate these domains, they simply reorganized them. The political and the economic continued to be entangled both in the way the officers extended their control over the management of agriculture and in the forms of international trade, aid, and loans upon which they relied. The *'izbas* gave way to a countrywide system of rural cooperatives that allowed for new kinds of government supervision over peasants; the mortgage companies were replaced by a state-run agricultural bank that managed the provision of seeds, fertilizers, and credit across the countryside; the state railways were subordinated to a program of road development; and the once powerful trading houses in Alexandria were merged into six public enterprises. Moreover, the central objectives of Nasserism—including national economic growth, industrialization, and the provision of social welfare—were not pursued through mechanisms that were purely internal to Egypt. Achieving these goals, even if provisionally, depended upon the country's position in the geopolitics of the Cold War, and specifically the extent to which the officers could leverage their relationships with global superpowers to acquire the necessary funds for development. Their accumulation strategy was supported and subsidized by forms of overt political intervention that often get forgotten in nostalgic accounts of Nasserism.

FROM CONCESSIONARY TO GOVERNMENTAL ACCUMULATION

The reconfiguration of these monopoly powers over decades signaled a deeper transformation in the regime of accumulation that underpinned the production and trade of Egyptian cotton. From the 1840s to the 1910s, an alliance of local rulers, landed oligarchs, wealthy traders, and Western powers transformed the Egyptian Nile Valley into a monocrop commodity frontier within the British Empire.[53] Two major turning points in that period were the U.S. Civil War (1861–65), which created supply shortages for Lancashire that were offset by increased exports of Egyptian cotton, and the decades-long occupation of the country by British military forces starting in 1882, which bolstered the production of Egyptian cotton for English textile manufacturers. As a result, larger numbers of Egyptians became dependent on distant markets over which they had little sway. Achieving this transformation depended on a concessionary regime of accumulation that created islands of exceptional authority through which landowners, merchant-financiers, and state administrators could earn profits with little or no competition. Creating an ostensibly open-market cotton economy over these 70 years did not obliterate the monopoly powers that were previously held by the state under Mehmed Ali. It transferred them to a new set of actors through concessionary arrangements of different sorts. In the interwar period, this regime began to wither away as depression and war led to a crisis of accumulation that unsettled many of the old centers of power in the Egyptian Nile Valley and prompted nationalists to embrace new visions for agrarian relief, reform, and reconstruction.

The genesis of the postcolonial state in Egypt was firmly situated within two larger historical dynamics that began after World War I. First, the arrangements that had sustained global capitalism since the nineteenth century were deeply unsettled. The four decades before the war are often described as a golden age of imperial globalization characterized by a dramatic growth of world trade, the expansion of international finance, increased migration, and massive overseas investments by European colonial powers in the production of raw materials.[54] The foundations of this British-centered imperial world economy were severely shaken by the war. Over the next two decades, as Eric Hobsbawm writes, "world capitalism retreated into the igloos of its nation-state economies and associated empires."[55] Second, the war represented a crisis of empire as imperial governments around the world faced unprecedented protests, strikes, and anti-colonial rebellions that created opportunities to imagine an alternative future.[56] The breakdown of a global economy that worked largely through imperial institutions prompted political leaders, investors, and intellectuals around the world to search for ways of disentangling their societies from a web of interdependence that centered around the imperial metropole. In short, they began to contemplate how to reorganize global capitalism after empire.

As British imperialism gradually ceased to provide an effective framework for accumulation on a global scale, some voices began to envisage alternative ways of managing economic life. In 1916, Vladimir Lenin, who would become a leader of the Russian Revolution, wrote that imperialism represented the "highest stage of capitalism" because it relied on the export of European financial and industrial capital into the colonies in order to continue generating profits.[57] As such, Lenin believed that the end of imperialism could create the conditions for the end of capitalism itself. Three years later, Austrian-born economist Joseph Schumpeter published *Imperialism and Social Classes*.[58] Unlike Lenin, he saw the origins of empire in a violent feudal past, rather than a modern capitalist era. Schumpeter believed that imperialism represented an alien body in a properly capitalist system. Though he did not predict the imminent fall of European empires, he did believe that imperialism's demise could in theory unleash a purer form of capitalism in which unfettered markets prevailed. In the United States, President Woodrow Wilson and his supporters criticized the acquisition of territory through secret diplomacy by European powers. After the war, he promoted principles of free trade, popular government, and self-determination, although the latter would only apply to those new nations in Central and Eastern Europe that emerged after the collapse of the Austro-Hungarian and Russian Empires. By this time, the idea of national self-determination had already circulated in different parts of the colonial world, and they were not uniquely Wilsonian or Leninist ideals.[59] But political movements in Africa, Asia, and the Middle East did seize the opportunity presented by a changing world order to either make or reinforce their demands to end foreign rule. The fate of the colonial world was on the agenda as the possibility of new political-economic forms that could replace empire suddenly became imaginable.

For more than a decade, Egyptian nationalists had already begun to reimagine the geographic parameters within which to organize economic life. A growing number of politicians, business moguls, and intellectuals had started to believe that political and economic independence were inseparable.[60] For them, genuine sovereignty required more than taking control of their country's formal institutions of government; it demanded a substantial transformation both in the everyday behaviors of Egyptians and in their material relationships with the world beyond their borders. Only in this way could they confront the interwoven forms of political and economic domination that had become characteristic of British rule in an imperial world economy.[61] After the war, the forms of wealth and power that prevailed in the Egyptian Nile Valley were shaken by unprecedented volatilities in the movement of goods, capital, and prices, which resulted in a veritable crisis of accumulation. Nationalist leaders searched for ways to protect Egyptian cultivators from the effects of these turbulent fluctuations. In 1919, a nationalist uprising swept the country, and Egypt was granted a conditional form of independence by the British three years later. The politics of the next two decades were largely shaped by a struggle between the Egyptian palace and its allies, the British embassy, and a nationalist movement that found its strongest expression in the Wafd Party. Under conditions of limited independence, nationalist leaders began to fashion a variety of mechanisms—like national banks, cotton buying campaigns, and cooperative societies—to reorganize the management of cotton within the protective boundaries of the nation. In the process, they created new agricultural institutions and practices, new forms of rural knowledge, and new understandings of economic sovereignty.

The Great Depression and the war that followed were a vital turning point in the history of Egyptian nationalism. The demise of large mortgage banks that financed the activities of wealthy growers, the wartime restrictions on cotton acreage, and the changing labor and cropping patterns on cotton farms combined to transform large landowners into an unproductive rentier class. As the structures of cash crop production that had long existed in the Egyptian Nile Valley were altered, a new cohort of anti-colonial voices started to fashion a program of national development—with land reform and industrialization as its twin pillars—in order to upend the agrarian foundations of their societies as they had existed under colonialism. This agenda became the prism through which independence, political legitimacy, and history would be widely understood under the reign of the Free Officers. Narrating the history of modern Egypt within this framework brought with it a distinct cast of characters. These included toiling peasants, corrupt politicians, heroic masses, and redemptive officers. Most importantly, it spotlighted those who became the main villains in Nasserist accounts of the Egyptian past: the large landholding class. After taking power, the officers immediately seized properties that belonged to the country's largest estate owners, eliminating one of the principal expressions of oligarchic power that existed in the colonial period. The concern with the feudal character of *'izba* owners became a ubiquitous fixture of post-1952 speeches, writings, and films about modern Egypt. But this preoccupation was the product of a particular historical moment, rather than a straightforward reflection of social relations as they had always existed in the countryside. Large landholders undoubtedly formed the nucleus of the ruling class before the revolution. Viewing them as antagonists who thwarted the country's development, however, reflected a particular form of historical consciousness that only acquired an appeal in a postwar world where nationally organized, industrial capitalism became widely embraced.

By the 1950s and 1960s, the Free Officers consolidated the visions and practices for agrarian relief, reform, and reconstruction over the previous two decades into a governmental regime of accumulation. They became more involved in the management of peasant labor to ensure the ever-increasing production of Egyptian cotton, and they relied heavily on international trade regimes to acquire the capital they needed to pursue their development program. The main argument of this book, therefore, is that Egypt witnessed a transformation from a regime of concessionary accumulation—based on monopolistic domains that were labor intensive, imperially scaled, less centralized, and rooted in islands of exceptional authority—to a regime of governmental accumulation—based on monopolistic domains that were capital intensive, nationally scaled, more centralized, and intrusive into everyday peasant life. In Nasserist speeches, writings, and films, however, this transformation was often misrecognized as a transition from feudalism to socialism, rather than from one kind of capitalist monopoly to another.

STRUCTURE OF THE WORK

The chapters that follow narrate the transformation in Egyptian understandings of economic sovereignty, independence, and history over half a century. Chapter 1 presents an overview of the basic mechanisms through which the production, processing, transportation, and exchange of cotton proceeded in the Egyptian Nile Valley on the eve of World War I. Following how cotton was grown on fields in the countryside, moved through railways stations, sold on markets in Alexandria, and shipped to Western Europe illuminates the specific mechanisms through which rural Egypt was constituted as a global plantation. Shortly after the war, an unprecedented level of volatility in international cotton prices destabilized the lives of millions of Egyptian cultivators across this space. What began as a phenomenon that arose from a set of wartime contingencies, however, became a regular experience in everyday life for nearly two decades. These instabilities coincided with a major political event: Britain's unilateral declaration of Egyptian independence in 1922. As a result, Egyptian leaders and intellectuals would spend the next twenty years or so scrutinizing the forms of market dependence that connected cultivators to other parts of the world and asking what these entanglements meant for their ability to achieve national liberation.

While ideas about development had been discursively a part of Egyptian nationalism since the early twentieth century, only in the 1920s did they become institutionally a part of it. Chapter 2 charts the intellectual history of economic nationalism in Egypt during the 1920s, when a cohort of thinkers, landowners, and investors began to rescale the mechanisms that underpinned economic life. With unpredictable buyers for their principal crop, difficulties importing finished goods, unregulated flows of capital across the country's borders, and volatile cotton prices, they began to call greater attention to the perilous dependence of Egyptian cultivators on foreign capital and markets.

In their view, the country's reliance on the export of primary goods was not a symptom of underdevelopment, nor did it require a stagist progression from agriculture to industry. Rather, it was a condition that called for the creation of national institutions that could insulate cultivators from the unpredictable shocks and swings of an imperial world economy in an age of crisis.

The Great Depression (1929–39) was a major event that further exposed the workings of power under a concessionary regime of accumulation and made it possible to change them. Chapter 3 follows the specific channels through which the depression was transmitted across the Egyptian Nile Valley and reveals the multifaceted ways in which the collapse of prices was experienced by those who cultivated, moved, and sold Egyptian cotton. During the depression, large estate owners, railway administrators, merchant families, and mortgage bankers witnessed a severe disruption in their dominant modes of accumulation. By the end of the decade, the depression had weakened or destroyed old centers of wealth, power, and monopoly; it paved the way for new practices for the rejuvenation of Egyptian agriculture through nationally scaled institutions and procedures.

Amidst the instabilities of the depression, national elites began to forge a new political-economic project in the 1930s—which is the subject of chapter 4—that took as its object the moral and material reform of the peasantry. They devised an assemblage of institutions and practices—including cooperative societies, agricultural banks, scientific agricultural manuals, hygiene and health instruction, model villages, and rural social centers—that aimed to furnish both the resources and knowledge required to produce a new Egyptian peasant. This project of agrarian reconstruction sought to instill a set of productivist rationalities in Egyptian cultivators who could then act as the basis of a rejuvenated social order. While the nascent regime of rural governmentality grew out of the depression, it would outlast the conditions that created it; by the 1950s and the 1960s, Egyptian leaders would integrate many of its ideas and practices into the apparatus of the postcolonial state.

The downswing in the 1930s and the war that followed had long-term consequences in the Egyptian Nile Valley, which will be explored in chapter 5. First, large landowners began to shift their accumulation strategies away from agricultural production towards leasing land. This trend was compounded by rising inflation, rural crime, urban migration, and landlord absenteeism that began to capture the attention of agrarian reformers. Second, the wartime presence of Allied troops in Egypt created a market for local industries that began to expand. In this context, a growing number of Egyptian intellectuals—many of whom had studied abroad and were exposed to new ideas in development economics—began to view industrialization as the end goal of a project that would subordinate the countryside to the needs of urban development. As these patterns persisted, critics began to condemn wealthy landowners for being estranged from the affairs of their own estates and for allowing their investments in agricultural properties to become idle capital. The growth of anti-landlordism, along with the material conditions that spawned it, shifted attention to the country's unequal land tenure system and encouraged a new generation of nationalists to demand agrarian reform. A project to gain freedom from the volatilities of an imperial world economy transformed into a mission to overcome economic backwardness.

While they claimed to make a decisive break with the colonial and monarchical governments that came before them, the officers in many ways represented an outgrowth of that past. The new forms of economic thought that emerged amidst depression and war created their discursive universe, a connection that is explored in chapter 6. After they seized power in 1952, the officers anchored their political legitimacy in a program of land reform and industrialization. To ensure the productivity of peasants on redistributed lands, they established a countrywide system of state-run cooperatives, agricultural banks, and collection depots through which to supervise their activities. This bureaucratic agrarian empire, and the mass engineering of peasant behaviors that it enabled, became crucial to the Nasserist state's ability to keep producing ever larger amounts of cotton. Although its export on preferential terms became one important means of acquiring the necessary goods for military defense and industrialization, Nasser's reliance on subsidies from foreign patrons also locked the country into relations of economic and technological dependence on global superpowers. The pursuit of national development thus turned out to be a straightjacket more than a path towards liberation. But these contradictions were masked by an enduringly appealing narrative in which the officers claimed to be revolutionizing the productive capacities of Egyptians in a way that would lift the country into a higher stage of history.

ONE

ANATOMY OF A GLOBAL PLANTATION

IN OCTOBER 1920, THE BRITISH acting high commissioner in Egypt received a report about rural unrest in the Nile Delta. An attempt by the owners of a royal estate (*daira*) to raise the rent on some of its cotton-growing lands in Munufiyya province resulted in "a considerable disturbance."[1] Tenants refused to rent the land belonging to a member of the Egyptian royal family. Those among them who worked as farm laborers on the estate went on strike and "opposed by force" any effort by estate authorities to bring in hired workers from elsewhere. The peasant agitation had been provoked by the sudden collapse of cotton prices that season, which left many cultivators unable to pay their expenses and averse to any attempts by landlords to maintain rents at or above their existing levels. In the face of unprecedented price volatility after World War I, many cotton farmers found themselves captive both to the vagaries of world markets and to the arbitrary actions of their landlords. Reacting to the events, the commissioner forecasted an inevitable reduction of rents from the "exorbitant heights" to which they had risen.[2] As landlords were unlikely to take any initiative to reduce rents on their own, the commissioner predicted that "the reductions would be accelerated during the coming winter by outbreaks of agrarian trouble." The actions of these peasants who refused to pay rent or perform labor on the *daira* was revealing: these were the two primary mechanisms on which landlords—whether private estate owners or government officials—depended to extract surpluses from rural producers. Any peasant mobilizations that threatened to withhold rent or labor could jeopardize those well-established accumulation strategies upon which Egypt's ruling class of financiers, landed oligarchs, and big export houses depended.

Although this episode of peasant resistance was short-lived, the conditions that precipitated it would last for many years. Understanding why the livelihoods of so many cultivators were threatened by the aftermath of the war requires an examination of the basic mechanisms through which the production and trade of Egyptian cotton functioned. For an entire century, from the 1860s to the 1960s, the majority of Egyptian cultivators depended in some measure on the production and export of cotton. Through a series of multisited interactions, millions of peasants who grew Egyptian cotton were connected to large manufacturers abroad. Recurring acts of cultivation, trade, transport, finance, violence, and knowledge production stitched Egypt into a transnational patchwork of sites whose interlinkages rendered cotton into a leading global commodity. What follows is a brief sketch of the ensemble of social, ecological, and managerial relations through which cotton was grown on fields in the Egyptian countryside; moved through railways stations, towns, and ginneries; sold on markets in the port city of Alexandria; and shipped overseas to Western Europe. These relations were forged out of repeated encounters between landowners, peasant laborers, financiers, state officials, and natural environments that ultimately constituted rural Egypt as a global plantation. The monopolistic domains that dominated the production and trade of cotton in the Egyptian Nile Valley—private estates, the Egyptian State Railways (ESR), the Alexandria General Produce Association (AGPA), and the mortgage banks—managed many of these interactions and, in doing so, acquired distinct powers that allowed them to accumulate disproportionate amounts of wealth. But World War I would mark the beginning of a protracted process, which lasted nearly half a century, by which these institutions would be transformed. As the circumstances that enabled the acquisition of these monopoly powers changed, so too did the ability to exercise them.

SOWING THE FIELDS

From the nineteenth century, Egypt was known for producing long- and extra-long-staple cotton—a crop with long individual threads that is only grown in a handful of countries and that is used for the production of high-quality, silky fabrics. Most cotton was historically produced in the Nile Delta, a fertile triangle located between the Mediterranean Sea and Cairo at its southern apex. As early as the 1820s, Egyptian modernizing reformers, led by Mehmed Ali Pasha, decided to promote the cultivation of long-staple cotton for commercial purposes. Initially, the government was heavily involved in producing and marketing the crop, but by the 1840s Egyptian rulers began to limit its role to building irrigation and transportation infrastructure to encourage cotton cultivation. The act of growing and trading cotton was left largely in the hands of new landowning classes, including the descendents of Mehmed Ali and their relatives, and a network of mostly French-, Italian-, and Greek-speaking traders that formed a powerful mercantile bourgeoisie. The remarkable expansion of Egyptian cotton production, however, only happened around the time of the U.S. Civil War. Until then, the American South had been by far the largest producer of cotton for British textile manufacturers who formed one of the dominant industries spawned by the Industrial Revolution. When the war broke out, the Northern blockade of Confederate ports (which lasted from 1861 to 1865) prevented the export of American cotton, thereby creating massive shortfalls of cotton supplies to European markets. This encouraged British manufacturers to search for alternative suppliers in existing or soon-to-be overseas colonies. As a result, cotton production and trade began to intensify across different geographical sites that became oriented towards the export of raw materials to Britain.[3]

Because the process of growing cotton was still largely unmechanized around the world, Egyptian laborers were able to compete with cultivators in the United States, India, and Brazil, among other places.[4] By the 1870s, cotton had become the most lucrative crop in Egypt. While gross returns from one feddan of cotton and wheat were almost the same in the late 1850s, 20 years later the former surpassed the latter by three or four times.[5] It was not until the British occupation, however, that Egyptian cotton began to solidify its special position on international markets, especially those that moved the crop to the heart of Britain's fine spinning industry. In the 1890s, the revival of old chemical treatment processes combined with improvements in spinning technologies that made possible the large-scale production of fine yarns and fabrics led to the emergence of a segment of the Lancashire trade that would be devoted to importing long-staple cotton.[6] At the same time, a flood of British investments in agricultural infrastructure enabled a significant expansion of cotton production, leading to what Roger Owen has described as a "green revolution."[7] By the end of the decade, the importation of chemical fertilizers had begun, and their widespread use helped to increase the productivity of the land.[8] Together, all these developments transformed the Egyptian Nile Valley into a monocrop plantation and engendered both regional and class disparities that shaped the contours of Egyptian politics until the Free Officers' Revolt.

Growing cotton was a labor-intensive enterprise that lasted from March to October every year and it involved plowing the soil, planting the seeds, irrigating the fields, picking any pests, and harvesting the crop. Those who actually performed the work of growing cotton included various combinations of smallholders, renters, sharecroppers, and regular and irregular wage laborers. The properties they labored on varied in size and type. According to Mahmoud Abdel-Fadil, the most striking feature of rural Egypt before 1952 was "the heavy concentration of landownership and the rapid increase in the number of smallholders in relation to the area of land possessed by them."[9] At the start of World War I, there were 12,000 large landholders who owned properties that were 50 feddans or more. Although they made up 1 percent of the landowning population they possessed 43 percent of landed property across the country. Those who owned the largest estates (200 feddans or more) constituted only a fraction of the population. At the same time, there existed one million and a half smallholders, by far the vast majority of landowners, who only possessed 27 percent of the land. Organizing land and human bodies for the cultivation of cotton on Egyptian farms involved a blend of different kinds of proprietorship, tenancy, and labor.[10] There were three major ways in which cotton-growing lands could be put to productive use: direct farming, leasing, or the *'izba* system. Notwithstanding the considerable problems in gathering and interpreting census data, Alan Richards estimates that for much of the interwar period 79 percent of cultivated land area was either exploited directly or under the *'izba* system, while the remaining 21 percent was leased for cash or crop shares.[11] Together, these three methods of land exploitation formed some of the fundamental dynamics of agrarian capitalism in interwar Egypt.

Most direct cultivation of land by its owners took place on small family farms. For both colonial and nationalist reformers, smallholdings had become an object of politics, particularly after the financial crisis of 1907. In the colonial era, smallholdings were often viewed as an invaluable asset for large-scale cash crop production. Under the British occupation, Egypt's leading botanist remarked that the prevalence of small farmer households provided a plentiful supply of manual labor that was necessary for hand-hoeing between closely planted crops, thus making Egypt "the most perfect cotton-country of the world."[12] After the war, nationalists continued to emphasize the need to strengthen smallholdings, and they proposed a variety of ways to do so. According to Yusuf Nahhas, who would become a leading spokesperson for large estate owners, the Egyptian government had a duty to "protect smallholdings that [were] threatened in Egypt more than any other country" because their disappearance would cause serious damage to the security of social and economic life.[13] Far from being viewed as a residue of pre-capitalist subsistence techniques, small family farms endured throughout the late nineteenth and twentieth century because the labor of women and children proved to be very suitable for the production of cheap raw cotton.

Smallholders grew cotton because the crop was readily convertible into cash through local markets that had been well established since the nineteenth century. Earnings from the sale of cotton were an essential source of income that allowed families to sustain themselves and to pay back debts and taxes that they had steadily accumulated. On small holdings, labor was typically performed by family members and their extended relatives, but the rise of large private estates in the second half of the nineteenth century began to transform the organization of labor on family farms. Males in peasant households left their family lands in greater numbers to perform labor on large estates, either as tenants or hired workers. According to Judith Tucker, this resulted in a deepening gendered division of labor whereby "men filled the ranks of day laborers, whether as service tenants or hired wage workers, while women tended the family plot."[14] As a result, women on family farms did much of the field labor, bought and sold crops, and performed other managerial tasks while their husbands and sons were away. Contrary to their masculinist conceptions of a timeless, male peasant who reigned over his individual plot of land, many of the small farms that nationalist reformers in the 1920s would so idealize had in some ways become increasingly female domains. The social division of labor that resulted from the consolidation of large estates in the second half of the nineteenth century reorganized gender relations on family farms.

As we can begin to see, the forms of proprietorship, tenancy, and labor that underpinned the production of cotton were not always mutually exclusive. Even though they owned property, it was common for smallholders to rent or work on land that did not belong to them. According to several accounts, many peasants owning three feddans or less did not possess enough land to support a family and therefore had to rent more land or work as hired laborers on somebody else's property.[15] Many farmed their own lands for subsistence while renting or working on additional lands to grow cash crops. The erosion of any neat distinctions between smallholders, tenants, and wage earners would lead Egyptian Marxist Ibrahim ʿAmir to conclude that "there exist[ed] no impermeable boundaries between these groups."[16]

Whether smallholders or not, many peasants entered into labor and tenancy arrangements with large landholders who compelled them to grow cotton. With the concentration of lands in the hands of big estate owners, the *ʿizba* system began to proliferate in the nineteenth century, and by the interwar period it appears to have become "the most common mode of exploitation for large estates."[17] *ʿIzbas* were labor settlements established by landowners on their private properties in which they would grant small plots of land to peasants, usually to grow subsistence crops and raise livestock, in return for their labor services on the owner's cotton fields. By the 1930s, there were more than 7,000 *ʿizbas* across the country, and the overwhelming majority of villages in the Nile Delta had them.[18] Every privately held estate had its own arrangements for managing agricultural labor, but in general workers on a *ʿizba* belonged to one of two groups: *tamaliyya* (resident workers) and *tarahil* (seasonal migrant workers).

The *tamaliyya* provided undercompensated labor services on a landowner's estate all year round, and in return they were granted a small parcel of land, occasionally with an obligation to pay a reduced rental fee. These parcels usually consisted of up to one feddan of fertile land for peasants to grow subsistence and rotational crops, like wheat and clover.[19] *Tamaliyya* workers were typically housed in small mud huts, and their labor was closely supervised by estate owners, their agents, and their family members. In many cases, these resident workers acquired their seeds and equipment from the landowner on loan. In this way, many *tamaliyya* became locked into a form of bondage in which whatever small wages they earned for their work would often be repaid to their landlord for outstanding debts. However, estate owners could also incur costs for the social reproduction of labor on their fields. In a detailed account of her own family's estate, Mona Abaza has contrasted the bifurcated lifestyles of wealthy, Europeanized landowners and resident workers living in labor camps. She describes how life for resident workers on her family's estate involved social bonds of provision and caretaking between estate owners and peasants. The estate owner would distribute fabrics twice a year for workers to make their own clothes, sell them food at reduced prices, and cover expenses for major life events, like weddings, illnesses, and burials.[20] As such, *tamaliyya* workers did not correspond in any simple way to the classical categories of production in European Marxism. Many of them were neither free wage workers, nor bonded laborers, nor simple commodity producers, nor subsistence farmers in any pure sense. In many cases, their productive activities combined elements of some or all of these forms.

By contrast, the *tarahil* were irregular laborers who worked for estate owners on a seasonal basis. *'Izba* holders would often rely on labor of this sort for work that was not required all year round, like the construction and maintenance of irrigation canals and drains as well as emergency labor for picking cotton worms in seasons where the crop was ravaged by pests. Many seasonal laborers who maintained irrigation works were either landless peasants or migrants from the Sa'id (Upper Egypt). The labor of picking cotton and fighting pests was often performed by young children. After a severe pest attack in 1904 devastated the country's cotton crop, British authorities passed a law allowing the government to recruit thousands of boys every season to pick damaging caterpillars from cotton plants. This revived form of forced labor, akin to the corvée that the British had abolished two decades earlier, expanded with the intensification of monocropping and the accelerated movement of imperial finance into Egypt's agrarian landscape, especially in the years before the 1907 financial crisis. According to one estimate, children between the ages of 5 and 10 provided nearly 60 percent of the labor input for cotton production and, unlike every other crop, more children than adult males were employed per acre of cultivation.[21] After the end of the occupation, the Egyptian nationalist movement fully embraced these cotton worm campaigns and the forms of coercive child labor upon which they depended even as they condemned the ravages of colonial exploitation.[22]

The final way to organize cotton production was by leasing property on both privately held and state-owned land.[23] The most important medium that connected tenants to their landlords were the rental payments that they made on a periodic basis. The value of the rent was determined by many factors, including soil quality, geographical location, and what crops would be grown. On many estates, however, rents were effectively determined in relation to what might have been the most ubiquitous variable in agrarian life, the price of cotton on the Alexandria Bourse. A former British inspector in the Land Tax Department, Francis M. Edwards, even argued that cotton prices "were the basis of land rents and borrowing."[24] At the end of every season, landlords fixed rents for the upcoming year on the basis of price rulings for October 15. If the previous season's cotton had been sold for a high price, lease contracts could stipulate extortionate rents, and vice versa. In other instances, large landlords would compel their tenants to sign blank leases that would be filled out later when they found it advantageous to do so.[25]

If the prevailing mechanism by which the value of rents was determined linked leases to volatile cotton prices, then the methods by which they were paid granted landlords almost full control over the crops that were grown on their lands. Tenants often paid between one quarter and one-third of their rent in May when their winter crops were harvested, and they paid the remaining portion the following October after they sold their cotton. Lease contracts could be either verbal or written. The agricultural leasing market was highly monetized as many landlords preferred their rents to be paid in cash, either upfront or over the course of a season. However, some tenants paid their rent in kind either as a fixed percentage of their crops at harvest or as a rate of crop volume per unit of cultivated area.[26] Regardless of which way the tenants paid their rent, landlords had the authority to distrain their crops until they were satisfied that the terms of the lease would be fulfilled. Edwards described in detail how this practice worked:

> Cotton is picked between mid-September and mid-October and the maize and the rice (water-conditions permitting) which are being simultaneously grown on the land not under cotton, are about ready for picking at the same time. Cotton is usually picked a few days before maize. The landlord or lessor holds both crops until he is satisfied that the cotton crop will cover the rent outstanding. If cotton prices are bad the lessor might compel the lessee to sell his maize. This leaves him almost destitute.[27]

The ability to finance both the purchase of land and the actual cultivation of cotton was crucial for peasants of all kinds. The earliest modern banks that were established in Egypt mainly lent to the khedives and their family members. The establishment of the Mixed Courts in 1876 introduced European-style mortgage laws into the country and allowed creditors to foreclose on their debtors.[28] As a result, three major mortgage banks began to operate in the country and dominated the market by the twentieth century, advancing credit mostly to large estate owners for the purchase of more properties.[29] The owners of medium-sized and moderately large properties relied on other banks to provide them with the funds for cultivation every season. Early in the year, these banks would make short-term advances either to cultivators or to merchant exporters who reloaned the money to the farmers from whom they would purchase the crop.[30] Banks would borrow sterling on the London money market and convert it into Egyptian pounds to make the loan. Eight months later, when the harvested cotton reached the port city of Alexandria to be sold to foreign buyers, the banks would discount the bills drawn by export houses on merchants and spinners abroad. In this way, banks found a profitable outlet for their capital by financing the movement of the cotton crop every season.

By the time the war began, smallholders and tenants who grew cotton could not obtain their funds from formal banking institutions. But this had not always been the case. In 1895, the Cromer administration began to extend loans to landowners in the Nile Delta who owned five feddans or less, and then it expanded the program under the auspices of the newly created National Bank of Egypt. Out of these efforts emerged the Agricultural Bank, an institution that was created in 1902 to channel foreign capital into loans to peasant smallholders until its directors abandoned the practice one decade later.[31] A couple of years before the war, Lord Kitchener passed the Five Feddan Law, which prohibited the foreclosure of properties that were five feddans or less. As a result, banks did not lend to the vast population of peasant smallholders in the country, nor did they lend to tenants who owned no land to pledge as collateral. For that reason, the vast majority of peasant cultivators borrowed seeds, fertilizers, and cash from local cotton merchants, moneylenders, and landlords.[32]

IN THE TRACKS OF EMPIRE

Although little foreign capital went directly into the cultivation of the crop, the world around cotton was a different story. European investors and financiers actively took part in funding, constructing, and/or maintaining the infrastructure that was necessary to produce and transport cotton, including a countrywide system of railways. Half a century before the British occupation of 1882, the export of British capital and industrial goods to Egypt had already begun, and over time, it rendered the country dependent on both metropolitan finance as well as on the export of raw materials to Western Europe.[33] The first railway lines that were constructed in Egypt connected Alexandria, Cairo, and Suez and dramatically reduced travel times along the Overland Route from Europe.[34] As larger amounts of acreage were devoted to cotton production, an ever increasing number of bales were carried by Egyptian trains. By the end of the 1880s, cotton had become the single most valuable commodity transported on the state railways, which moved the crop from the major towns in the Nile Delta to the port city of Alexandria.[35] As such, the Egyptian state railways, one of the first outside of Europe, were steeped in the dynamics of British imperialism.

Moving cotton from the fields to the port in Alexandria relied on three different scales of mobility. First, cotton had to be transported within the single plot of land where it was cultivated. Farmers typically did this by using their animals, or depending on where their properties were located and how large they were, they could rely on wooden sailboats. For those who worked on very large *'izbas*—made up of hundreds or thousands of feddans—moving cotton from one part of the estate to another could be a long journey. Some wealthier landowners therefore built and operated their own private lines that connected different plantations on their single estate. In her account, for example, Abaza writes that there was a light railway—known as the Decauville, which was the name of the French engineer who invented it—that connected different parts of the land together and linked the estate as a whole to its surrounding villages.[36] The initial phase of transporting cotton on the fields where it was grown could therefore rely on both motive and non-motive power depending on the size of the land that it came from and the affluence of its owner.

Second, cotton had to be transported from the property where it was grown—whether a family farm or a large estate—to the closest ginnery or train station that was usually in a nearby town. In the 1890s, the Egyptian government constructed thousands of kilometers of unpaved agricultural roads, mainly in the Nile Delta, to serve this purpose.[37] The success of this program encouraged the government to invest in the construction of narrow-gauge railways, many of which were installed on top of dirt roads, that could connect the fields where most of the cotton was grown to the main urban centers where it was gathered and processed—like Mansura, Zaqaziq, Tanta, and Zifta.[38] Until the end of the nineteenth century, animals and animal-drawn carts were used to transport most of the cotton from villages to larger towns that were served by the state railways. In 1896, the government granted two concessions for the construction of narrow-gauge railways. The first one went to an English firm, Messrs. John Birch and Co., to build train lines in the governorates of Buhayra and Gharbiyya, and the second went to a group of Egyptian firms owned by well-known capitalists—Suares, Minsha, Qattawi, and Plizaious—for construction in Sharqiyya, Daqahliyya, and Qalyubiyya. In 1900, an English firm, the Egyptian Delta Light Railways Company, acquired the shares of both companies as an unlimited concession and began to expand the network.[39] The company was administered by a board of directors in London but maintained offices in Alexandria with a staff of more than 2,000 managers and workers. Within two years, it was operating railways that connected many of the villages in the major cotton-producing regions in the Nile Delta. The principal commodities they carried were building materials and unginned cotton; in 1908, the Delta Light Railways carried more unginned cotton by tonnage than the ESR.[40] It had become the backbone of commercial transport in the Nile Delta, leading one British observer to remark that its network was "second only to irrigation as an agency for the advancement and prosperity of the Delta."[41]

Third, cotton had to be moved from the towns where it was processed, especially in the Nile Delta, to the port city of Alexandria. To do this, the light railways fed into a series of major train stations from which cotton could then be transported on standard-gauge tracks that were operated by the ESR. The expansion of the state railways was historically linked to two major events in the second half of the nineteenth century: the U.S. Civil War and the opening of the Suez Canal. The onset of the war in 1861 created shortfalls of U.S. cotton on the world market, after which Egypt became an increasingly important supplier to Lancashire.[42] In the following years, the state railways expanded along with the country's cotton acreage. When the canal opened in 1869, it gradually shifted railway traffic away from the Overland Route that had previously connected Britain and India through Egypt and caused the ESR to focus even more on the development of internal transport to maintain its revenues.[43] Between 1863 and 1869, there was a massive expansion in the state railway network—the length of existing tracks were tripled as they connected to cities in the Nile Delta that were surrounded by rich cotton-growing lands.[44] By the mid-1870s, the state railway network "had broadly reached its current extent."[45]

That railways and colonial expansion were almost inextricable was a fact long contemplated by observers of empire. Writing in 1913, Rosa Luxemburg noted that the vast expansion of international railway networks represented a "worldwide movement of capital" that intensified in the late nineteenth and early twentieth centuries.[46] The diffusion of European finance and investments around the globe produced an uneven geographical landscape, whereby some regions—like the United States and to a lesser extent Russia—were gradually transformed into capitalist economies, while others—for example, in Africa and Asia—were impoverished through war, military occupation, and colonial extraction and subordination.[47] Luxemburg reconsidered Marx's account of the dynamics of capitalist accumulation. She argued that capital's expansionary impulse required the ongoing incorporation of noncapitalist outsides in a way that fused together both economic and extra-economic forms of domination. While Marx had arguably suggested that the violent expropriation of resources around the world from the sixteenth to the eighteenth centuries—what he called "primitive accumulation"—was anterior to the history of capital, Luxemburg believed this dynamic to be a continuous feature of capitalism.[48] An "organic link" therefore existed between coercive forms of extraction (slavery, serfdom, corvée, colonial violence, etc.) that were prevalent in ostensibly noncapitalist societies and the market-based exploitation of labor in the capitalist production process.[49] Luxemburg turned to Egypt for a "classical answer" that illustrated how the global expansion of capital proceeded in this manner.[50] Two crucial mechanisms for this expansion were the expropriation of cheap labor and the international loan, both of which played an important role in the construction and management of the state railways.

The organic link to which Luxemburg alluded was on clear display in the way Egyptian administrators and their European financiers and suppliers managed the state railways. The corvée laborers who built many aspects of the railways were necessary for the construction of a transport system that ultimately moved cash crops to their destined markets. "In Egypt, the people have had to make the entire earth-works, and to assist in the skilled work, without being paid for their labor," wrote Consul George West in 1873. To charge them hefty passenger fares for riding the trains therefore meant that the state railways functioned as "an instrument for extorting revenue."[51] In West's opinion, it was fully justified that Egyptians would want to use the railways at an affordable cost because they had "so largely contributed by their forced and unremunerated labor to make them."[52] The other way in which the expansion of European capital was connected to the state railways was through international loans. More than simply locking the country into an endless cycle of debt, loans helped establish the conditions for ongoing accumulation in Egypt because they were used to purchase European capital goods that were necessary to build irrigation and transportation infrastructure in order to promote cash crop production for metropolitan industries. Roger Owen has estimated that a large part of the money transferred to Egypt in loans by the middle of the 1870s was either returned to Europe as payment for previous loans or spent on public works and economic enterprises, including sugar factories, railway construction, and port improvement.[53] The recycling of European loans into European goods created a peculiar set of monopoly powers, leading Luxemburg to observe that British capital that built railways in the colonies was "of English origin not only in its pure value-form, as money capital, but also in its material form, as iron, coal, and machinery."[54]

The monopoly powers that Luxemburg described, and the forms of unevenness they engendered, were not just derived abstractly from a set of material interests emanating from the metropolitan heart of the British Empire. They were built into the bureaucratic system of railway administration that was controlled largely beyond Egypt's borders. Nowhere was this clearer than in the way the procurement of railway inputs and equipment was organized. British firms had long been the dominant suppliers of coal, engines, rails, carriages, sleepers, and other goods to the state railways. In 1889, the president of the Egyptian railway board, W. F. Halton, estimated that in the final three years of that decade the percentage of British manufactures purchased by the ESR—as compared to French, Belgian, and German manufactures—fluctuated between 72 and 97 percent.[55] Until the end of the nineteenth century, the Egyptian government employed a private firm to inspect railway-related imports coming from Western Europe. After the creation of the Anglo-Egyptian Condominium in 1899, a government office was opened in Britain to serve both Egypt and Sudan.[56] The Inspection Office in London, which was staffed by former British railway officials who had worked in Egypt, was the main body that managed British-dominated railway procurements. It collected information on railway materials and machines that were needed and determined which suppliers would be included on a register of approved firms. It issued calls for tenders, submitted them to the Egyptian government, inspected orders while they were being prepared, and arranged shipping for European suppliers.[57] In short, the London Office set the product specifications and inspection standards for Egyptian railway materials—regulations that determined which firms could compete for government contracts—and in some cases it oversaw most of their sales and purchases through a controlled tender system that privileged British firms.[58] Though by the 1920s the London Office handled the provision of all kinds of British manufactures for the Egyptian government—including to the ministries of public works and education, among others—nearly 80 percent of the value of goods inspected were railway materials, so much that the office was "practically a branch of the Railway Administration."[59]

If the procurement of British supplies to the ESR was one way in which the state railways fed into circuits of European capital accumulation, then the servicing of outstanding government debts was another. Facing an effective bankruptcy in 1876, Khedive Isma'il accepted the creation of the Caisse de la Dette Publique, an international commission that brought together representatives of European governments and bondholders to manage the repayment of Egyptian loans. In the same year, however, another international commission composed of representatives from England, France, and Egypt was established by khedival decree to supervise the Egyptian state railways and the port of Alexandria. Its main purpose was to link the receipts of the state railways to the government's debt service obligations. The council members functioned as "trustees on behalf of the debt holders" and ensured that 55 percent of annual railway revenues were used to repay interest on Egypt's debts.[60] Until 1905, state railway accounts included a single figure for how much money was transferred to authorities overseeing the interest payments. For almost three decades, the state railways continued to be managed in this fashion, minimizing working expenses and diverting the majority of receipts towards the repayment of debts. In this way, the Egyptian government effectively purchased British raw materials and equipment through the London Inspection Office in order to generate revenues from the state railways that were used to repay loans to European banks.

In the first decade of the twentieth century, however, two pivotal events would begin to delink the state railways from these imperial arrangements that had governed them for the previous quarter century. The first event was Lord Cromer's decision to abolish the crossing fees that were charged to boats that passed under bridges and through locks along the Nile River. Until 1901, those tolls had helped to maintain the monopoly of the railways—which had become necessary to generate a consistent stream of revenue to fulfill Egypt's debt repayment obligations—by making river transportation costs prohibitively expensive. In place since the 1870s, Cromer believed that the policy represented an aspect of the Egyptian fiscal system that was "wholly incapable of justification."[61] According to him, the main reason it survived was to protect the revenues of the railways which, by virtue of the country's geography, "in many places [ran] nearly parallel to the river."[62] Had it not been for the peculiar arrangement that linked Egyptian railway revenues to debt repayment, competition between rivers and rails would have remained a "platonic affair."[63] Because of the unique significance of the ESR's revenues, however, the Egyptian government kept in place measures to deliberately impede other modes of transport. With pressure mounting from merchants in Alexandria, and with the consul-general himself dissatisfied with the existing system, these restrictions on inland navigation were abolished. The second event was the Entente Cordiale of 1904 in which France recognized British control over Egypt. As a result, the arrangement that placed the state railways under international supervision and tied its revenues to debt servicing was terminated. In 1905, the international commission was replaced with a Supreme Railway Board that was given powers "analogous to those of a Board of Directors."[64] Its formation completely transformed the logic of railways administration. The ESR would no longer be subordinated to the budgetary imperatives of the government and its creditors. Rather, it would operate as a public company that sought to maximize its profits. Nowhere was this transformation more visible than in the forms of calculation deployed in the annual finances of the railways. Whereas before 1905 the railways were governed by a fiscal logic—whereby the chief measure of financial soundness was the ESR's annual net revenue of which a fixed percentage was paid to foreign creditors—after 1905 railway accounting became oriented towards the goal of profitability as measured by return on capital.[65]

The transformation of the state railways into a public company had important consequences. First, it altered the internal labor dynamics of the organization. As the railway administration pursued maximum profits, its employees began to protest their low wages and working conditions. As a result, the first collective actions by railway workers began in 1906 and would continue for years.[66] Second, the new arrangements brought the railways into conflict with other modes of transportation as competition between rails and rivers intensified. In the interwar period, these pressures would manifest themselves in a struggle over which medium—trains or waterborne vessels—would capture a larger share of the profits from the transport of cotton. Because the Egyptian government's ability to levy taxes was still circumscribed by the capitulations—an extraterritorial legal system for foreigners in the country that was established in the nineteenth century—the railways remained an especially important source of state revenue, and moving cotton would continue to be the chief generator of its income. To safeguard its earnings, the railways administration would systematically try to sabotage other modes of transportation. As a result, the ESR would be accused by its critics of engaging in "the worst practices known to monopolists."[67]

OF SPOTS AND FUTURES

The cotton market in Alexandria historically consisted of two elements: an actual market (spot market) where bales of cotton were bought and sold and a contract market (futures market) where promises were exchanged to deliver cotton at a predetermined price and on a specified date. The former was located on the harbor where it could be reached by railway or canal, while the latter was housed inside the bourse building in the city.[68] Each of these markets was controlled by a different body. The spot market was presided over by the AGPA with little oversight by the government while the futures market was managed by a commission of brokers that operated under general regulations approved by the Egyptian government in collaboration with the Mixed Courts and internal regulations that were approved by the Ministry of Finance.[69] What follows is a brief examination of each market in turn.

The earliest spot markets in Alexandria were simple operations. Sacks of cotton were transported from Egyptian villages to the port city where they were stored on the banks of the Mahmudiyya canal.[70] Buyers who arrived in the city inspected each bag of cotton before offering the seller a price and making a purchase. Until the end of the 1850s, the market for Egyptian cotton remained relatively small—for example, only 60,000 bales of Egyptian cotton were purchased in 1859 and shipped across the Mediterranean Sea to Europe.[71] This meant that buyers had no trouble examining their cotton on a regular basis. After the sudden boom in the 1860s, the workings of the spot market in Alexandria started to become more complex. An actual marketplace was created in Mina al-Basal on the city's west harbor where buyers and sellers would meet regularly to conduct their business. By the 1880s, the market was moved into a building owned by the Société Egyptienne de la Bourse Commerciale de Mina al-Basal.[72] As buyers began to purchase cotton in larger quantities, it became difficult for them to physically inspect every bale that they sought to acquire. Although they still maintained the right to do so, it became conventional practice for cotton transactions to rely on a system of sampling.

Sampling was an innovation designed to assure buyers of the quality of their purchase. Whether those buying the cotton were small merchants or big exporting firms, sellers would provide them with a sample of their cotton, usually in a designated room in the building. Upon completing a successful inspection, the buyer would offer a price; if the seller accepted, the buyer would then send a professional sampler (usually an Arabic-speaking Egyptian) to collect a larger specimen from the seller's store. After inspecting the new sample for consistency, the buyer would either uphold his bid or make a new one, after which an agreement would be concluded. In this process, the buyer would probably never see more than 5 percent of the cotton being purchased and would accept on faith that the remaining 95 percent was of the same quality. But the whole procedure carried definite risks. Samplers could be paid off by sellers to provide false reports on the cotton that they inspected. The cotton could also be mixed with inferior varieties in the village of origin, or it could be falsely packaged after it was ginned, a practice which carried serious penalties under the law. If the buyer was not satisfied with the sample, he could travel to the seller's store after Mina al-Basal closed for the day to inspect each bale of cotton individually. Even if it was not always acted upon, maintaining a buyer's right to full inspection was crucial to the functioning of the system. In the words of Herbert Carver, one of the leading British exporters in Alexandria,

FIGURE 1. Inspecting cotton before pressing, 1909. Source: Wright, *Twentieth Century Impressions of Egypt*.

"bales of cotton are not like little bricks; they are composed of fiber which is most difficult to judge . . . if they [buyers] are going to pay the full value for a lot of cotton they must be able to satisfy themselves that the quality is just what they want."[73]

There were typically four ways that cultivators could dispose of their cotton.[74] First, they could sell it directly to merchants—usually small Greek or Egyptian merchants—who traveled around villages to buy cotton. By the 1860s, there were an estimated 90,000 migrants who had settled in Egypt, many of whom were affiliated with the cotton trade.[75] Large landowners who grew cotton could sell directly to the agents of major trading firms with whom they maintained ties. Before the war, the four biggest export houses in Alexandria were Choremi, Benachi & Co., Carver Brothers & Co, R & O. Lindemann, and Peel & Co. Ltd.[76] Second, producers could transport their crops to the dozens of ginning factories from which they had obtained advances. Third, they could deliver their cotton to stores (*zarbias*) that were managed by individual traders, banks, or owners of ginning factories with little or no government supervision. Although these stores existed all over the country, this method of sale was most common in the town of Mansura in the Nile Delta. Fourth, cultivators could sell their cotton in local markets, known as *halaqas*, which were introduced by the government in 1912 and were partly run by it.[77] These spaces were usually rented by cotton brokers who then supervised the weighing and selling of cotton. They were more common in the Nile Delta than in Upper Egypt, the most important *halaqas* being in Mahalla al-Kubra, Tanta, Damanhur, and Kafr al-Zayyat.

The spot market in Mina al-Basal was overseen by the AGPA. Its functions included the creation of regulations for all transactions on the market, the establishment of grades for different types of cotton and cotton seed, and the arbitration of disputes that arose between buyers and sellers, such as conflicts over cotton quality.[78] A committee of 16 members was elected to carry out arbitrations, though the association possessed no legal authority to punish those who failed to abide by its decisions.[79] Although these were the formal duties of the AGPA, its members also derived their powers from other activities. First, most of the major cotton exporters provided medium and large producers with funds at the start of every season. Whatever role they played as shippers was often eclipsed by their position as financiers in the cotton trade.[80] Second, they also possessed a near monopoly over the production and dissemination of information related to the cotton trade. Unlike estate owners, major export houses had agents all over the country, which created a difference in access to and control over information. They spent decades devising a system of unwritten rules that governed their business transactions with cultivators, transporters, and spinners. Having the ability to control information allowed brokers to exchange their cotton under conditions that were most favorable to them. For that reason, big cotton merchants insisted on keeping these powers within the institutional domain of the AGPA, rather than surrendering them to the hands of state officials. That said, the government did impinge on some of those areas where the AGPA's authority had long been uncontested. The creation of the Department of Agriculture in 1911 allowed state officials to compete with the AGPA over crop forecasting, and the formation of the Cotton Research Board in 1919 got them more involved in the production and dissemination of data about cotton markets for cultivators and traders around the country. These kinds of struggles over control of the cotton trade would only intensify during the interwar period.

The futures market (also known as the Alexandria Bourse) was one of the first of its kind in the world.[81] Unlike Mina al-Basal, where physical commodities were exchanged, the Alexandria Bourse was where contracts for the future delivery of those commodities were traded. It allowed buyers and sellers to hedge against fluctuating market conditions by exchanging claims to a given quantity of cotton at a predetermined time and price in the future.[82] When the delivery date for a futures contract arrived, the physical cotton underlying it was brought to the spot market in Mina al-Basal. In 1861, a group of brokers occupying a room in downtown Alexandria created a market for the exchange of contracts denominated in cotton and cereals. After splitting into two factions, they reunited in 1889 and formed an organization called the Association of Produce Brokers.[83] Over the next decade, they created an organized exchange that held a monopoly on futures transactions in cotton, seeds, and beans, and they moved into an imposing new building. Merchants dealing in physical cotton were originally not permitted to engage directly in futures trading; instead, orders had to be made through middlemen who were official members of the bourse.[84] This gave rise to a class of financial intermediaries that included brokers, jobbers, remisiers, and clerks.[85] These agents and their clients began to buy futures contracts not for the purpose of obtaining any actual bales of cotton, but rather in the hope that the price of cotton would go up in the future and they could sell their contract for a profit. As a result, the futures market became a major arena for financial speculation. According to L. G. Roussin, the financial secretary of the Egyptian Ministry of Finance, "the speculative element [was] in fact essential if the bourse [were] to carry out its proper commercial function."[86] But that very function of the futures market could also have a dangerous impact on the operations of the spot market. With the consolidation of the Alexandria Bourse in the late nineteenth century, critics could plausibly claim that the price of cotton was no longer determined exclusively by the quantity of bales exported but also, in large measure, by the volume of speculative activity on the bourse.[87]

As early as the 1910s, observers began to criticize the AGPA's monopoly over the cotton trade and, more importantly, its role in enabling financial speculation on the futures market. Every trading company in Alexandria developed its own "in-house" types of cotton that were tailored for manufacturers in Europe with whom the firm had a long-standing relationship. In 1912, Léon Polier warned that the power to determine cotton types, which was monopolized by the AGPA, was significant because "it ends up giving speculation a basis that is either real or unreal."[88] Establishing cotton types meant that speculators could then trade futures contracts for cotton they had not seen or inspected but whose quality was widely accepted. Moreover, the AGPA's regulations stipulated that any dispute over types would be decided by experts that were selected by each party from a list approved by the association, but those decisions could be appealed before the Association Committee which had the final word. This powerful committee was largely made up of cotton exporters who were "at the same time the speculators engaged in futures trading" and who had complete discretion to pass decisions that would benefit themselves. Polier believed that the only way to fix this system was for cotton exporters who belonged to the AGPA to renounce these privileges and to adopt an American model of bourse organization that was operated by salaried bureaucrats, not brokers. A few years later, former trader Hussein Teymur charged that the AGPA maintained a de facto monopoly that was sheltered from any interference by public authorities.[89] These kinds of complaints led to efforts by the Egyptian government to extend its supervision over speculative activities. As a result, the futures market was subjected to a series of state interventions. In 1909, the government amended the country's commercial code that had existed since 1883 and promulgated a decree for the general regulation of stock exchanges.[90] The bourse would be subjected to further regulations over the next half century. It is difficult to ascertain how the value generated by the production of cotton was divided between producers, traders, and processors—especially in light of the speculative activities that could yield hefty profits from year to year. Writing about the period before World War I, Owen maintains that there is not enough evidence to determine if merchant-moneylenders consistently underpaid cultivators or how those income streams flowing to cultivators, ginners, merchants, and exporters might have changed over time.[91] By the 1920s, however, this would become a major question for nationalist landowners who, in the face of unstable cotton prices, would to try to bring cotton merchants under the greater control of a semi-independent state.

"A SUCCESSION OF CIRCUMSTANCES"

The medium that bound together Alexandria-based cotton exporters with spinners in Western Europe, North America, and Japan in a nexus of commodity exchange was money. In 1913, John Maynard Keynes remarked that Egypt was the only country in the world whose monetary system was based largely on physical supplies of gold. He explained that gold was the basis of an international system that mediated exchanges between states—known as the gold standard—but nowhere except in Egypt was it also a local currency. Egypt therefore had a unique distinction in that it was "the only country in the world in which actual gold coins are the principal medium of exchange."[92] Keynes correctly observed that the movement of gold bore a strong relationship to the seasonality of Egyptian cotton. It traveled in a triangular pattern that reflected the imperial geography of the British Empire. From September to December, large banks in Alexandria imported gold coin (mostly in the form of British sovereigns) in order to finance the cotton crop for the upcoming season. Most of the gold would then leave the country again between January and September to pay for imports.[93] "Of the gold, therefore, which flows from London to Egypt every autumn," wrote Keynes, "very little finds its way back again to London; what is not kept by the cultivators in Egypt travels on in due course to India."[94] Because the cotton harvest in India was typically later than in Egypt, it attracted flows of gold into the country during a different time of year. The fact that India could import British sovereigns from Egypt or capture them in transit from Australia to Britain rather than acquire gold from London was important for its own currency system. The different rhythms of the cotton seasons in Egypt and India, along with their respective geographical locations, determined the way each country became stitched into the monetary web of the British Empire.

As Keynes remarked, the gold standard and gold currency were not the same thing. The former was the foundation of British monetary hegemony during the age of New Imperialism. From the 1870s to the 1920s, the gold standard maintained the stability of international prices in a British-centered world economy, it prevented long-term inflation, and it deterred governments from printing money excessively. Although it was the basis of long-distance imperial trade, most of the gold bullion did not physically travel around the world. Rather, it was held in the vaults of the Bank of England where countries with trade surpluses regularly transferred gold into the accounts of countries with trade deficits. Because the system kept London at the epicenter of world trade, Karl Polanyi wrote that the British Empire, which undoubtedly relied on the projection of its military force, more often exercised power "by the timely pull of a thread in the international monetary network."[95]

In Egypt, gold served an even more specific function because most of the large cotton transactions between European manufacturers and major exporting houses were settled using the precious metal. The circulation of British sovereigns was largely overseen by private banks in Alexandria, which were mostly branches of European financial institutions. Operating beyond the supervision of the government, these commercial banks controlled how much gold moved in and out of the country and at what times of the year. Every autumn, they imported millions of gold sovereigns into Egypt to finance the cotton crop. Major trading firms would borrow money from banks in their home country, which would then allow them to draw sovereigns from an Alexandria bank, and then loan out the money to cultivators.[96] Only after the National Bank of Egypt, a publicly traded company that was established with private capital, was incorporated in 1898 did the country begin to have a paper currency. Although it did not function as a typical central bank—it was not a formal state institution, nor did it influence the loans and deposits of commercial banks—the new institution did have the right to issue money.[97] Introduced the following year, these convertible banknotes were covered at 50 percent by a gold reserve held by the bank. For amounts exceeding L.E. 2, however, British sovereigns remained the only legal tender. Until the start of the war, the circulation of these banknotes remained limited in comparison to gold. However, Keynes's suggestion that Egypt was a strange place where people did all their business in gold was somewhat misleading. The large annual accounts of big banks and cotton trading houses may have been settled in gold, which is what mostly interested him, but on the level of smaller everyday transactions what presumably existed in this period were various arrangements of written and unwritten credit. In that sense, the reorganization in Egypt's monetary system that began during World War I did not simply involve a shift from gold to paper money; rather, it was also a transformation from multiple, overlapping systems of credit into a uniform system of national currency.

The outbreak of World War I was a pivotal event in global monetary history. It set in motion the gradual decline of Western imperialism and along with it a world economy that was organized around the British Empire and its imperial institutions. A key symptom of this demise was the collapse of the international gold standard, which broke down for several reasons. First, the British government lost its capacity to back the gold standard. By 1923, three quarters of the world's gold was in the hands of the United States, especially because Western European states that became indebted to American institutions during the war had to sell their gold reserves to continue paying for imports from the other side of the Atlantic.[98] Second, the hostile political atmosphere that developed in Europe after the war deterred individual countries from transferring gold to states whom they considered enemies, which meant the breakdown of cooperation between central banks—a key condition for the gold standard's success. According to Polanyi, the fall of the gold standard marked an epochal shift that signaled the end of international finance as it had existed since the nineteenth century. The gold standard had kept British financial hegemony afloat even after Britain started to lose its competitive industrial edge in the face of European and Japanese competitors. Its collapse exposed the temporal discontinuities in how global capitalism was structured. Giovanni Arrighi has argued that the suspension of the gold convertibility of the British pound in 1931 shattered the international web of commercial and financial transactions that provided the basis for London's wealth. In short, it marked what he called "the terminal crisis of British rule over the world's money" which signaled the veritable end of an era.[99]

The collapse of the gold standard after the war happened to coincide with the end of gold currency in the Egyptian Nile Valley. But the transition from gold to paper money was not a natural or intentional progression, it was a story filled with contingencies. "[T]he present monetary system of Egypt," wrote Roussin, "has been created and developed rather by the force of a succession of circumstances than as the conception of a deliberate policy."[100] The outbreak of the war sparked a wave of panic in Egyptian financial markets. In July 1914, creditors began to demand repayments on their loans, debtors needed advances to pay back their lenders, and depositors rushed to relocate their money out of the country. The threat of economic chaos loomed large as the whole financial structure "was on the brink of collapse."[101] Under ordinary circumstances, the banks could pay out gold to its customers and order more supplies from abroad as needed until the wartime crisis passed and economic stability was restored. But the military buildup during the war created outstanding obstacles. The positioning of German warships and submarines made it difficult, if not impossible, to transport large quantities of gold across the Mediterranean Sea. As a result, the ability of banks in Egypt to import more gold in order to mitigate the effects of the crisis was paralyzed. With a shortage of available funds to finance cultivators, the government began to panic about the prospects of the upcoming season's cotton crop. To avoid the twin threats of a bank run and an inability to finance cotton, the Egyptian government in cooperation with the National Bank decided to act by printing emergency currency. In August, it suspended the convertibility of banknotes into gold and declared them to be inconvertible legal tender.[102]

According to the National Bank of Egypt, the decree had "momentous effects on the Egyptian monetary system."[103] The volume of new banknotes had to be backed by some substance of value to give people the confidence to use them. In November, the Ministry of Finance agreed to a request by the bank's governor to use gold held in the Bank of England to maintain its statutory minimum of one-half gold cover (the other half would be covered by Egyptian bonds). Two years later, however, the Bank of England informed the National Bank that the financial strains caused by the war prevented it from being able to continue with those arrangements. The Egyptian government therefore decided to allow the National Bank to substitute its 50 percent gold cover with British treasury bills and war loans, which some considered "as good as gold."[104] Meanwhile, the Egyptian bonds that were used to cover the fiduciary issue were gradually replaced by British securities. When the National Bank wished to print more money, it would cable its agency in London to increase its holdings of British securities by an equivalent amount; when it sought to remove money from circulation it would withdraw British securities of an equal sum from its London deposits.[105] In backing Egyptian banknotes by British debt, the wartime currency system used the arrangements of the protectorate, which Britain had formally proclaimed in 1914, to make Egypt contribute payments to the British war effort.[106]

Delinking the Egyptian pound from gold would have profound consequences for the management of economic life in the country. After 1916, funds could be moved in and out of Egypt without any gold being shipped. An investor or consumer could pay in sterling at the London Office of the National Bank of Egypt and get an equivalent sum of Egyptian money in Cairo, and vice versa. These operations were conducted at roughly 97.5 piastres to the pound sterling. The value of the Egyptian pound was effectively linked to the pound sterling—what became known as the sterling-exchange standard—while the movement of gold in and out of the country declined to an insignificant level. Perhaps the most significant effect of this new monetary system was that the widespread use of paper currency that was printed by the National Bank allowed its officials to measure the amount of money that circulated within Egypt, not just across it borders. As one perceptive observer later remarked, any attempts to measure the volume of gold sovereigns in the country before the war "represented only the gold coming in or leaving the country, they threw no light on the volume of gold in actual circulation."[107] Without a local mint or a central gold reserve, it was impossible to ascertain how much money was actually being used inside Egypt. That would change with the proliferation of paper money. This transformation would prove crucial within a few decades. The ability to count money circulating inside the country became the basis for national income accounting, which provided the main metrics for measuring the growth of a national economy.

CONCLUSION

The monopolistic domains described above oversaw the production and trade of cotton in the Egyptian Nile Valley from the late nineteenth century. After the war, an unprecedented level of volatility in international markets for Egyptian cotton began to destabilize the prevailing modes of accumulation upon which these institutions depended. According to the National Bank of Egypt, the sudden collapse of cotton prices in the early 1920s was a "bitter disappointment" that pushed cultivators across the country to temporarily expand the production of other crops.[108] Such downturns would become a familiar recurrence over the next two decades as price volatility threatened the livelihoods of cultivators across the Egyptian Nile Valley, like those tenants on the royal estate with whom we opened this chapter. As a result, Egyptian leaders and intellectuals scrutinized the forms of market dependence that connected cultivators to other parts of the world. As we will see, they would largely conceal any questions about the equitable organization of rent and labor on cotton estates. But they would tirelessly investigate the reasons behind the wild fluctuations in the price of Egyptian cotton. They would continue to search for ways to insulate cultivators from the erratic behaviors of overseas markets and the dominance of foreign traders inside the country. Most importantly, they would seriously ponder what such entanglements with forces that appeared to be beyond their control meant for their ability to achieve genuine national sovereignty.

TWO

COTTON NATIONALISM AND THE CRISIS OF EMPIRE

IN 1921, LEADING textile manufacturers and financiers convened the second World Cotton Conference in Liverpool and Manchester. At the time, most of the world's cotton was exported from the American South, British India, and the Egyptian Nile Valley, but this imperial geography was not evenly represented among the participants of the conference.[1] Only a handful of delegates from these major cotton-growing regions were present. Among them were Yusuf Nahhas and Ahmad Hamdi Sayf al-Nasr, two leaders of an agricultural syndicate that had recently emerged as a powerful voice for wealthy landowners in Egypt. Standing before the assembly, a spokesperson read a speech they had prepared in front of hundreds of attendees who overwhelmingly represented major manufacturing interests in Western Europe and the United States. Nahhas and al-Nasr opened their address by describing the country in the following terms: "[E]gypt is essentially, we can even say uniquely, agricultural, and . . . the cultivation of cotton constitutes today the basis of her riches."[2] They went on to complain that a global cotton crisis after World War I had affected Egypt "more cruelly than all other cotton producing countries." The yields of Egyptian cotton had been ravaged by the spread of pests; the costs of imported coal, iron, wood, machinery, and clothing from

Europe had increased more than threefold from their prewar level; and, most importantly, the price of high-quality Sakelleridis—which constituted about 80 percent of cotton production in the Nile Delta—had collapsed. As a result, Egyptian cultivators were discouraged from growing fine cotton. To rejuvenate its cultivation, the Egyptian delegates argued, it was essential that cultivators obtain a higher income from the principal crop they produced.[3]

By describing Egypt as an agricultural country that fell victim to uncontrollable forces that originated beyond its borders, Nahhas and al-Nasr expressed a view that had almost become common sense in nationalist circles. The conception of sovereignty that they advanced—which posited that farming was the basis of the country's prosperity and that the circulation of a vast portion of that wealth should be kept within its borders—had become widely shared among Egyptian anti-colonial intellectuals and reformers over the previous decade. In their eyes, the main threat that imperial domination posed to Egyptians was its exposure of millions of peasants to the volatile movements of international capital, commodities, and prices through which much of the material wealth they produced was siphoned out of the country. The war and its aftermath were an unsettling affair. The fighting interrupted Egyptian imports from Western manufacturers and reduced British demand for Egyptian cotton. The end of the war initially brought about a renewed growth in trade—Egyptian imports more than doubled, while cotton exports nearly tripled—but the boom did not last long. Between 1919 and 1921, banknote circulation dropped by 50 percent, and cotton prices on the Alexandria Bourse fell by 60 percent.[4] What began as a phenomenon that arose from a set of wartime contingencies became a regular experience after the war. A combination of factors—pest attacks, bad weather, postwar deflationary recession, slumping British industries, labor and political mobilizations, and, of course, the collapse of the international gold standard—led to unprecedented levels of price volatility in the interwar years. Reflecting on the 1920s, the general secretary of the Crédit Foncier remarked that "during this ten-year period the cotton price curve was continually rising and falling, rather than following a general direction that would have allowed individuals to adapt, little by little, to its indications."[5] These instabilities coincided with a major political event: Britain's unilateral declaration of Egyptian independence in 1922. As the volatility of cotton prices persisted into the interwar period it became an object of concern for nationalist leaders. A cohort of voices who had protested these erratic dynamics for years continued to call attention to the perilous dependence of Egyptian cultivators on foreign capital, goods, and markets. With a greater degree of control over the country's political institutions, Egyptian nationalists spent the next two decades scrutinizing the forms of market dependence that connected cultivators to other parts of the world, asking what these entanglements meant for their ability to achieve genuine sovereignty.

This chapter explores the history of economic nationalism in Egypt amidst the turbulence of the 1920s. It examines different strands of thought that aimed to promote a variety of nationally scaled forms of economic regulation—from price support campaigns, to peasant uplift and reform, to agricultural cooperation, to balanced agricultural and industrial development. In following these political and intellectual currents, two major themes emerge. First, there was a plurality of visions and projects that came to constitute emerging discourses and practices of economic nationalism in Egypt after World War I. In existing scholarship, there has long been a tendency to assume that anticolonial economic nationalism primarily took the form of an unambiguous project of import-substitution industrialization. For example, Roger Owen describes the emergence of a cohort of politicians and businessmen after the 1919 revolution—including figures like Isma'il Sidqi, Tal'at Harb, Amin Yahya, and others—that shared "not just the belief that Egypt should industrialize,

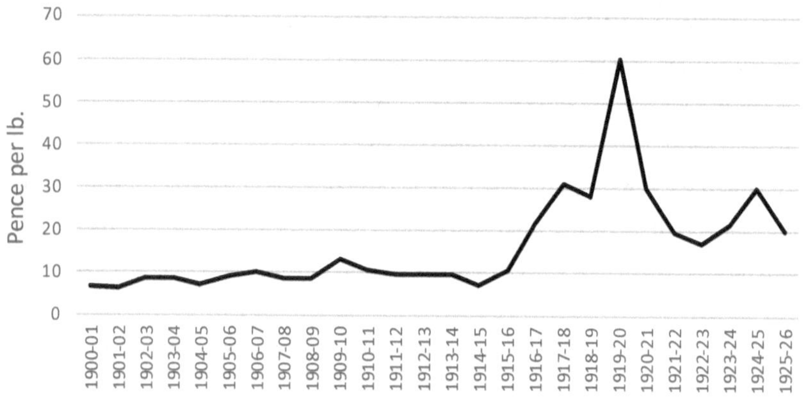

FIGURE 2. Egyptian cotton prices, 1900–1926. Source: Todd, *The Cotton World.*

but that this process should be the work of local capitalists using local funds."[6] A more recent iteration of this story can be found in Sven Beckert's celebrated monograph, *Empire of Cotton: A Global History*. Beckert describes how capitalists and state builders across the colonial world tried to assert their economic independence by embracing a model of European industrial capitalism, eventually giving way to "a world full of Manchesters."[7] His argument bears a striking resemblance to older left-wing nationalist accounts of colonial underdevelopment in which the predominance of foreign capital backed by colonial states and in cooperation with local compradors choked any possibility for indigenous industrialization. Beckert concludes that "stories like Egypt's indicated to capital owners throughout the global South that they needed to create a state supportive of their project of domestic industrialization, and that under conditions of colonialism such a state could not be forged."[8]

More than two decades ago, Robert Vitalis scrutinized these older narratives that treated Egypt's interwar economy as an arena in which an emerging national bourgeoisie oriented towards industrialization failed in its struggle against metropolitan capital and its local allies.[9] Instead, he argued, a budding class of commercial and industrial capitalists in interwar Egypt competed with each other and collaborated with foreign capitalists and members of Egypt's resident foreign bourgoisie in a variety of ways, often prioritizing the accumulation of rents and profits over any project of national industrial development. In advancing this persuasive critique, however, Vitalis all but dissolved any links between anti-colonial nationalism, on the one hand, and projects for capitalist restructuring, on the other.

The second theme that emerges from the writings of Egyptian nationalists in the 1920s is the peculiar way in which they began to imagine the relationship between the political and the economic. A growing cohort of interwar thinkers started to envision and develop institutions to refashion economic life in ways that they believed were inseparable from any project of political independence. Whereas before 1920 ideas and programs for economic development were discursively a part of Egyptian nationalism, afterwards they started to become institutionally a part of it. The major expressions of this institutionalization were Bank Misr (est. 1920), the General Egyptian Agricultural Syndicate (est. 1920), and, to a far lesser extent, the Federation of Egyptian Industries (est. 1922).[10] They would be joined by a variety of government ministries, departments, and initiatives in the 1920s and 1930s. To understand why the relationship between the political and the economic was imaginatively reconfigured, we might begin by taking seriously one of the central concerns of cultivators, intellectuals, and politicians in this period: the wild fluctuations in the movement of capital, commodities, and prices that had become a notable feature of life in the Egyptian Nile Valley after World War I. When the experience of unprecedented levels of volatility is placed at the center of the history of economic nationalism in the interwar period, we begin to come away with a different picture. Egypt's reliance on primary exports for overseas industries and the prevalence of non-national capital and finished goods within its borders were treated by nationalists in this period not so much as symptoms of underdevelopment that required a stagist progression from agriculture to industry. Rather, they were experienced as a series of unpredictable movements of capital, goods, and, most of all, prices that destabilized economic life in the country and that a rising cohort of elites believed national institutions should be created to regulate.[11]

Reorganizing the management of cotton and the profits that it yielded within national boundaries assumed paramount importance on the nationalist agenda. For planners, experts, and entrepreneurs, the destabilizing effects of the war spawned an extraordinary variety of efforts to restructure key aspects of economic life on a national scale. These anti-colonial engagements with the empire of cotton and the Egyptian Nile Valley's vexed position within it clustered around three major themes. First, politicians and businessmen increasingly supported a limited scope of industrial activities that would exist in complementarity with agriculture. Second, large landowners and their allies in government attempted to wrest control over the finance and trade of cotton from foreign-resident merchants based in Alexandria. Third, the most influential agrarian thinkers in the country began to institutionalize cooperative farming, especially among smallholders, as a way to ostensibly protect their wealth from escaping into in the hands of others. Together, these projects were viewed as mechanisms for refashioning economic life in the country that were inseparable from the struggle for independence. For those nationalists who championed these visions, sovereignty was not only a political question that required Egyptians to seize control over their country's formal institutions of government; it was a political-economic question that demanded a substantial transformation both in the mundane, everyday behaviors of Egyptians and in their material relationships with the world beyond them.

INDUSTRY WITHOUT INDUSTRIALIZATION

The idea of insulating Egypt from its hazardous reliance on international trade, capital, and prices had already existed during the war. In 1918, the publication of the *Report of the Commission on Commerce and Industry*, commonly named the Sidqi Commission after its chair, offered a lucid example. Isma'il Sidqi was a former minister of agriculture and an early Wafdist who was exiled with Sa'd Zaghlul after the 1919 revolution only to split with him months later at the Paris Peace Conference. He was a chief promoter of the balanced development of agriculture and industry that would be achieved through strategic cooperation between indigenous Egyptian business groups, resident foreigners, and foreign capital.[12] The final report was mainly authored by Sidqi and Sidney H. Wells, an official in the Ministry of Education. After visiting workshops, factories, and guilds in major Egyptian cities, they concluded that in order to overcome wartime interruptions in overseas trade the Egyptian government had to promote local commerce and industry as well as the diversification of Egyptian agriculture.[13] According to the report, the wartime trade imbalances indicated a deeper, structural problem in Egypt. The country's reliance on primary exports created a disequilibrium between what Egyptian cultivators supplied (raw cotton) and what they demanded (imported finished goods). Their dependence on foreign goods and markets exposed them to major price fluctuations and, as a result, considerable instability in their revenues and family budgets.[14] For that reason, the commission proposed a project of state-supported agricultural diversification and industrial production that could reconfigure Egypt's material relationships with the wider world and, in particular, with its main trading partners in Western Europe.

In conventional scholarship, the work of the commission is often treated as an early statement by Egyptian nationalists about the need to industrialize in order to achieve meaningful independence. Its members are understood to have embraced an incipient form of what would later become recognized as a state-led project of import-substitution industrialization.[15] These accounts therefore take a historically specific development ethos that only became regarded as normative in the postwar period—especially after the creation of the Bretton Woods system and the consolidation of modern development economics into a field of study—and project it into the past. When situated in their appropriate context, however, the concerns of the commission appear to take on a different hue. The authors of the report did not seek to create a heavy industrial base that would transform the country into Manchester; in fact, they insisted that such a vision was far from their purpose.

> The Commission has envisaged industry as a mean to come to the aid of agriculture and not to supplant it. It is not about Egypt becoming an industrial country . . . that is to say a country of factories that billow smoke and furnaces that transform and subjugate ore for the needs of humanity. It is simply about Egypt producing all that she can in order to meet her own needs . . . and to remedy the crisis that threatens it; it is about getting it as close as possible to economic autonomy without which political autonomy has only a very relative value.[16]

In other words, genuine independence did not demand a linear progression from agriculture to industry. It required a reconfiguration of the material relationships and institutions that underpinned economic life through a program of economic diversification and what we might call industry without industrialization. Achieving this kind of economic autonomy required that Egyptian state officials and investors devise mechanisms to address a continuous tension between the production of what they considered to be "national wealth" and its circulation beyond Egypt's national borders.

After the war, Egyptian nationalists began to institutionalize these ideas in new organizations. By then, business tycoon Talʿat Harb had earned a reputation as a seasoned critic of the British occupation. After the 1907 financial crisis, Harb focused his attention on the relationship between political and economic independence, and he emerged as a leading proponent of economic nationalism. In *ʿIlaj Misr al-Iqtisadi* (Egypt's Economic Cure), he attacked foreign banks that pursued the interests of their shareholders at the expense of Egyptian cultivators. In their place, he championed the creation of a national bank that would unite the interests of lenders and borrowers, avert the tendencies that led to the financial crisis, and guide peasants towards a more prosperous future.[17] A few years later, Harb coauthored a study of nineteenth-century German industrialization for the Sidqi commission in which he concluded that the model was not fully suitable for Egypt.[18] Within less than a decade, he founded an institution that went on to become a powerful business conglomerate in the interwar period. At its inaugural meeting in 1920, Harb spoke candidly about the program of Bank Misr. "In [Egypt], there is a lot of capital that is stored away and idle," he warned. "[T]here are many deposits and savings that are mostly invested in other countries . . . [if] Egyptian commerce, industry, and agriculture were aided by them, Egyptian wealth would increase exponentially."[19]

Actively investing in commerce, industry, and agriculture necessarily meant becoming involved in the cotton trade. In 1925, Harb called on the Egyptian public to purchase shares in one of his newest enterprises, Misr Cotton Ginning and Trading Company. Established one year earlier, the company was among the bank's first forays into new commercial and manufacturing enterprises that would eventually form the holding company known as Misr Group.[20] His choice of a ginning company attested to the importance that Harb accorded to the cotton industry and the need to seize it from the hands of foreigners. The significance of Egypt's most lucrative fiber extended well beyond the fields where it was grown. "Since cotton is the hub of national wealth and the axis around which livelihoods rotate every year between individuals of every class," Harb said in a speech, "it is reasonable that Egyptians would not be confined to its cultivation, the improvement of its varieties, and caring for its reputation, leaving its commercial and industrial exploitation in the hands of others."[21] The cotton season was composed of various stages—cultivation, ginning, transportation, trade, and manufacturing—that offered business opportunities at every point. Harb believed that extending his activities into each of these moments in the life of cotton was essential to the success of his project. Establishing Egyptian control over the cotton cycle was a national responsibility that Bank Misr could help to fulfill. For that reason, he announced, the board of Bank Misr would try to acquire vessels in order to move cotton upstream, especially from Minya province where the bank had recently established a ginning factory. In the same year, he announced the establishment of the Misr Transport and Navigation Company.[22] As Bank Misr went on to establish its largest industrial enterprise—the Misr Spinning and Weaving Company—Harb continued to view the production of cotton as the basis of the country's riches.[23]

The program of industry without industrialization was complemented by the efforts of nationalist activists who launched a boycott campaign of British goods from 1922 to 1924.[24] Spearheaded by the Wafdist Women's Central Committee and its elite spokeswomen (like Esther Fahmy Wissa and Huda Sha'rawi), the campaign was then taken up by university students, charitable organizations, and local boycott groups across the country. It aimed to discourage Egyptian consumers from buying British goods in order to reverse the effects of their detrimental reliance on their former occupier. The boycotts contributed to broader interwar efforts by Egyptian nationalists to create a more autonomous national economic space that they believed was indispensable to the achievement of complete independence. The aim of these nationalists was to Egyptianize economic life in the country rather than to fully industrialize it. What they endorsed was a territorial consolidation of agricultural, commercial, and industrial activities within a unified national space. The purpose of this consolidation would be to insulate the inhabitants of the Egyptian Nile Valley from the volatilities of goods, capital, and prices that tied the country to other parts of the world, especially England. It was not to supplant agrarian life with a more developed industrial future. In fact, many industrial ventures that did exist in these years were often imagined to serve the agricultural sector, not the other way around. In his study of interwar business coalitions in Egypt, Vitalis has shown that one of the most ambitious and costly industrial development schemes of this period was a project in Aswan to generate hydropower and build a nitrate fertilizer industry.[25] To construct an autonomous and nationally scaled economic space, as many nationalists aspired to do, industry was a vehicle more than an endpoint.

Another institution that promoted industrial development was the Federation of Egyptian Industries. Established in 1922, this business association was pioneered by commercial and industrial entrepreneurs from around the Mediterranean who had been living in Egypt for decades—what Tignor has called a "resident foreign bourgeoisie"—but it also included Egyptian entrepreneurs like Harb and Ahmad 'Abbud.[26] In May 1927, Isaac G. Levi, the secretary general of the federation, delivered a lecture on industry and the future of Egypt at the Royal Society for Political Economy, Statistics, and Legislation.[27] Levi challenged what he described as a widespread belief that Egypt could not become an industrialized country. He insisted that one of the goals of the federation was to uproot this prejudice and encourage the government to carry out industrial reforms. He went on to argue that affirming Egypt's status as an agricultural country demonstrated a remarkable ignorance of modern economic conditions because "only exploitation colonies that are subject to the directives of their mother country as well as states that nourish no ambition have an exclusively agricultural economy."[28] In a similar vein, other observers even described the widespread dependence on cotton production in the Egyptian Nile Valley as a contemporary paradox. In 1928, H. Clayton Hartley, a British textile expert, wrote that "cotton grown on the banks of the Nile is dispatched thousands of miles away to be manufactured and then returned a like distance until it reaches the hands of those who grew it as a woven fabric."[29] His commentary underscored the geography of power and accumulation to which the Egyptian Nile Valley belonged yet he argued that with a steady supply of capital, machinery, and skilled labor Egypt could assume its "rightful position as a manufacturing country."[30] While Levi and Hartley promoted the complete industrial transformation of the country as a way to overcome what they perceived to be its retrograde condition, their voices had little influence on the nationalist movement in Egypt.

By the end of the decade, government officials aimed to carve out a greater degree of fiscal autonomy. The expiration of Egypt's "capitulation" agreement with Italy in 1930 presented an opportunity to do so. That year, the government introduced a three-tiered tariff system that resulted in higher duties on imported cotton textiles and led to a considerable decline in imports from struggling British spinners over the next decade (the government would reform the tariff system again in 1936 and 1939). The nationalist press celebrated the decision as "tangible proof that Egypt enjoyed full tariff autonomy."[31] While some architects of the law—like Levi and Sidqi—hoped to create a "cotton and textiles alliance" between export-oriented landowners and local industrialists, that plan never materialized.[32] Apart from the Union of Agriculturalists, which represented European land companies and expatriate landowners, none of the major agricultural organizations or interests got behind the reforms. And groups for whom the tariff reform was not primarily intended were even less enthused. Wealthy merchants, like Sam'an Sidnawi, warned that higher tariffs could unintendedly raise the cost of living for the country's rural majority.[33] Meanwhile, European spinners hesitated to purchase Egyptian cotton so long as their access to the country's markets for finished goods was impeded by high tariffs.[34]

In existing scholarship, the 1930 tariff is often considered to be an important milestone—like the Sidqi commission—in Egyptian nationalists' steady embrace of import-substitution industrialization.[35] Yet the origins of the law and the motivations behind it might suggest otherwise. The architects of the tariff reforms never intended for them to function as a harbinger of industrialization. Rather, they admitted to being preoccupied with budgetary concerns above anything else, and they even confessed that the "protectionist function of the new tariff with regard to national production was therefore incidental."[36] To understand what motivated the tariff reform then we must go back to a pivotal transformation in the country's fiscal history that began in the late nineteenth century. In the second decade of the British occupation, colonial authorities expanded the cultivation of cotton across the Nile Delta. To obtain the support of large landowners, they refrained from seizing an excessive share of the increased agricultural wealth.[37] At the end of the century, they made a semi-permanent settlement, backed by the force of the law, that fixed land taxes for a period of 30 years. Between 1895 and 1913, the amount of tax that cultivators paid as a percentage of cotton value per feddan declined

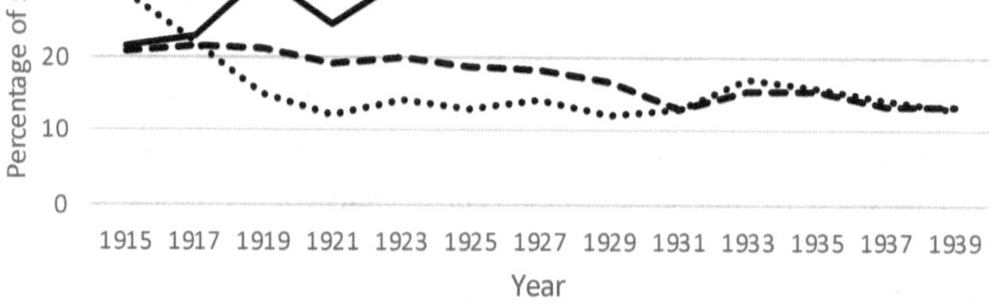

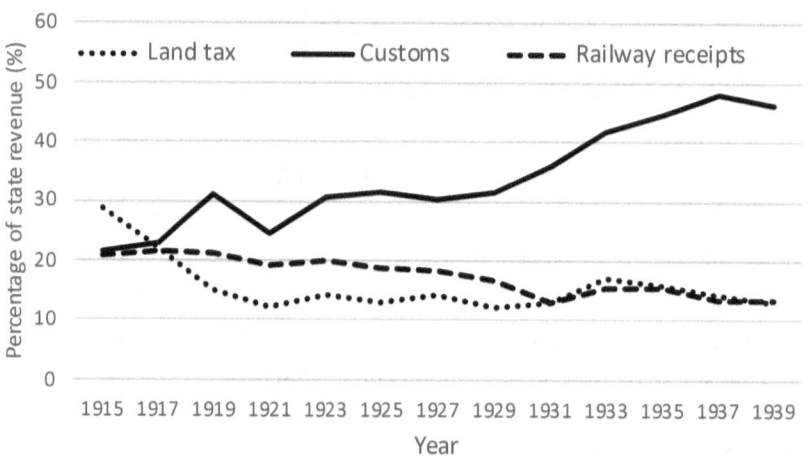

FIGURE 3. Sources of Egyptian state revenue, 1915–1939. Source: Wizārat al-Māliyya, *Mizāniyyat al-Dawla al-Miṣriyya* from 1919–1920 to 1938–1939.

by an estimated 2 percent, which proved to be an effective way to satisfy the large landowners who dominated much of the countryside.[38] By 1928, as the settlement was about to expire, land taxes made up less than 15 percent of the state's annual income, even though agriculture accounted for roughly half of the country's national revenue.[39]

"In a period of almost forty years," wrote British Ambassador Miles Lampson in the 1930s, ". . . the real rental value of the whole country had almost doubled while the amounts taken in land tax had remained practically the same."[40] Unwilling to collect more revenue from the direct taxation of agricultural land, the government turned to other sources of revenue, namely customs and railway receipts (see figure 3). A state that had relied primarily on land-based forms of revenue before the twentieth century now depended in large measure on forms of revenue that derived from the circulation of people and commodities. As tariffs were the chief source of income for the government, the reforms were intended primarily to fill the state's coffers and only secondarily to promote domestic industries.

OUSTING THE MIDDLEMEN

Making capital circulate within Egyptian borders meant, to some extent, displacing those commercial agents who profited from moving cotton from Egyptian villages to Western manufacturing centers. In May 1916, Muhammad Abu al-Futuh, a large landowner, put forward a plan for a decisive overhaul of cotton trading in Egypt. He presented his proposal in the form of a memorandum on the "reform of the system for selling cotton" to the Council of Agricultural Trade (Lajnat al-Tijara al-Zira'iyya), which had been established during the war to study the creation of new markets for Egyptian agricultural products.[41] At its core was the idea that agricultural producers in Egypt and textile manufacturers in Europe were capable of doing business without any intermediaries. Rather than relying on networks of cotton merchants and brokerage firms to move Egyptian cotton from the countryside to the factories of Lancashire, as the existing system did, spinners in Britain would be called upon to send their own representatives to Egypt to purchase cotton directly on their behalf. The memorandum was met with skepticism by powerful policymakers and businessmen—like Gerald Dudgeon, the head of the Department of Agriculture, and Henry Naus, the director of the Egyptian

Sugar Company—who expressed misgivings about both its feasibility and presumed equitability. In the end, Abu al-Futuh's proposal was referred to a subcommittee for closer study, only to be forgotten. Over the next half century, however, his ideas would be taken up by nationalist reformers, politicians, and landowners who eventually ended the dominion that merchants and brokers had held over the cotton trade since the nineteenth century.

Yusuf Nahhas was one such reformer who wanted to control the workings of markets for Egyptian cotton. He was born in 1876 in the town of Zaqaziq in the Nile Delta. His parents were nineteenth-century Levantine émigrés who arrived to Egypt from one of the Syrian provinces of the Ottoman Empire. After graduating from the French law school in Cairo, he traveled to Paris where he became the first Egyptian to earn a doctorate in economics.[42] Nahhas was no stranger to ruling circles in Egypt. He belonged to a large landowning family, he knew many landed and political elites, and he maintained good relations with the nationalist movement, including a close friendship with the leader of the Wafd party, Sa'd Zaghlul. In the 1900s and 1910s, he became a vigorous critic of the British occupation, which he argued had drained Egypt's wealth through interest payments on both private mortgages and public debt, and he championed the creation of national institutions to ensure the value that Egyptians produced remained inside the country.[43] After the war, Nahhas joined other nationalists in turning his attention towards what he believed to be a chief threat to the prosperity of Egyptian rural producers: the volatile price of cotton.

When the price of Egyptian cotton fell in 1920, Nahhas and his associates decided to "join together through the bond of a union in order to better defend their interests."[44] They created the General Egyptian Agricultural Syndicate, a lobby group for large landowners, and Nahhas became its secretary general from 1921 until the 1940s. In one of the earliest reports to its board of directors, Nahhas forecast that the syndicate could become "among the greatest national economic forces."[45] It promoted the cultivation of Sakelleridis—a low-yielding strand of high-quality, extra-long-staple cotton grown mainly in the Nile Delta—with the aim of segmenting international cotton markets and securing high premiums from overseas buyers. Nahhas and his allies persuaded government officials that because Egyptian cotton possessed unique qualities its market was "influenced by economic factors of its own" that were unaffected by price trends for other varieties around the world.[46] Boosting the price of Egyptian cotton simply required investing in the reputation of the crop and regulating how much of it was supplied to foreign manufacturers. Producing quality, therefore, formed part of a conscious strategy on the part of Egyptian landed and political elites to fashion a reputation for Egyptian cotton as "the world's best" in exchange for a quality premium.[47] Doing so required that the state create a whole set of practices and institutions—establishing research institutions, standardizing seeds, controlling pests, regularizing the distribution of water, and constructing proper drainage systems to protect against overwatering—to produce a uniform set of attributes in Egyptian cotton. In the early twentieth century, the country's rulers promoted the selection and dissemination of good seeds through parastatal organizations, like the Khedival Agricultural Society (est. 1898), and the Department of Agriculture (est. 1911).[48] After the war, the most important institution they created to continue this mission was the Cotton Research Board (est. 1919) in which a staff of both local and foreign experts worked to streamline all research related to the botanical, entomological, chemical, and physical sides of Egyptian cotton in order to enhance its reputation.[49] While some British advisors warned that Egypt's seasonal crop was not big enough to affect global prices, the syndicate operated on the premise that the distinctive qualities of Egyptian cotton allowed it to possess its own market.[50] Among the principal functions laid out in its charter was the "defense of crop prices during periods of crisis."[51] When the price of Egyptian cotton collapsed in 1920, the syndicate sought to protect the revenues of large landowners. It advocated for the abolition of an existing cotton tax on cultivators, it conducted research to improve cotton strains, and it helped reduce the costs of ginning raw cotton and transporting it by rail and steamships. As prices remained unstable over the course of the decade, the syndicate devised three enduring strategies: it encouraged the government to restrict the acreage of cotton, it urged officials to purchase a portion of every season's crop, and it sought to subordinate or bypass major cotton merchants in Alexandria.

Building on its wartime experience, the Egyptian state turned to acreage restrictions as a first resort. Following the recommendations of the syndicate, the palace issued a decree in December 1920 that limited the permissible acreage of cotton to one-third of an individual's property and banned cotton cultivation in those parts of Upper Egypt that relied on basin irrigation.[52] These attempts to impose geographical restrictions on the cultivation of cotton threated to exacerbate regional and class disparities that already existed in rural Egypt. The decree might have been supported by wealthy landowners in the Nile Delta who grew low-yielding, high-quality cotton that earned premiums on international markets, but it was swiftly contested by landowners in the Sa'id who did not cultivate Sakelleridis. In the *Manchester Guardian*, a group of landowners from Minya, Asyut, and Girga publicly petitioned British officials to intervene and reverse the decree in order to "safeguard the interests of landowners of the three provinces in Upper Egypt and those of Lancashire spinners."[53] The petition provoked a flurry of hostile reactions in the nationalist press from writers who believed the decree was intended to protect the wealth of the country and who attacked the petitioners for appealing to foreign authorities. After consulting with the syndicate, the Egyptian government decided to keep the acreage restrictions in place for two more years.[54]

Because the acreage restrictions were insufficiently effective, the syndicate's focus shifted towards another strategy: encouraging the government to purchase cotton directly from cultivators. To achieve this objective, syndicate leaders lobbied state officials through a combination of private appeals, media campaigns, and petition drives. In February 1921, cultivators from the province of Munufiyya in the Nile Delta warned the palace that prices "had deteriorated to an unbearable degree and the wealth of the country had become in great danger."[55] Others complained about the looming threat of famine. They demanded that state officials support cotton producers by temporarily closing the futures market in Alexandria, by legalizing seed exports so that they could dispose of their inventories stacked in warehouses, and by directly purchasing two million *qintars* of cotton. At the syndicate's behest, the government entrusted the National Bank of Egypt to buy cotton directly from cultivators on its behalf and then sell it to local buyers or cooperate with Alexandria-based firms to export it.[56] The bank would continue to do so almost every season for the rest of the decade.[57]

The cotton buying campaigns aligned well with the goals of ascendant nationalist politicians in a semi-independent country. In the 1920s, political life in Egypt was shaped by a four-cornered struggle between the liberal Wafd Party, the palace, the British, and a host of minority parties. The Wafd was the largest political organization in the country with broad support among landowners and urban professionals. Even though the architects of Egypt's constitution intended to limit the party's strength, the Wafd still received the highest number of votes in four consecutive parliamentary elections between 1923 and 1929 (the first three under the leadership of Zaghlul). For most of the decade, it formed short-lived governments that were usually thwarted by the British or the palace. Under the Wafd, price support campaigns become a fixture of policy. From 1921 to 1925, the government purchased cotton either directly from cultivators in the interior or from the spot market in Mina al-Basal. Amidst a massive price slump in 1925 and 1926, the government bought the largest portion of the crop up to that point, leaving it with nearly half a million *qintars* under its command. Having accumulated so much cotton, it declined to purchase additional amounts on the market from 1926 to 1928; instead it offered advances to cultivators, enforced production quotas, regulated cotton quality, imposed mild restrictions on the Alexandria Bourse, and offered subsidies to agricultural cooperatives. As the depression began in 1929, the government made its largest purchase yet in the futures market, requiring it to accept the delivery of nearly three million *qintars* of cotton.[58] Most of these cotton buying campaigns were undertaken by Wafdist governments to keep prices high and therefore strengthen their alliance with large landowners. According to Ellis Goldberg, price supports and direct payments to landowners in the 1920s were "an important method by which the Wafd created a political base for itself in the countryside."[59]

As the 1920s came to an end, large landowners who had relied on state officials to bolster the price of cotton began to face obstacles. First, the Egyptian government had all but depleted its reserve funds, leaving it with little money to continue financing its cotton buying programs.[60] Second, the government's cotton buying campaigns began to irk manufacturers in Britain. Amidst falling demand for British textiles, cotton brokers and spinners in England began to grow weary of the high costs of Egyptian cotton to the point where long-standing trading relationships between them were threatened with disruption. In 1927, the Egyptian consulate in Liverpool collected opinion surveys from leading traders and factory owners in Lancashire, and almost all of them complained about the Egyptian government's price support programs.[61] A representative from Reynolds and Gibson, a cotton brokerage firm in Liverpool, warned that spinners and manufacturers were finding alternatives to high-quality Egyptian Sakelleridis. Many had begun reducing their purchases of cotton from Egypt, or mixing Egyptian cotton with cheaper varieties from Peru, Brazil, and East Africa. He predicted that if the situation persisted resentful brokers would continue to purchase alternative varieties in ever larger quantities. Three years later, a representative from the same firm urged Egyptian officials to consider Lancashire's perspective more seriously as it remained "the largest single user of Egyptian cotton," while others complained that the cotton buying campaigns had "cost every spinner of Egyptian cotton a great deal of money."[62] Egyptian officials who were influenced by the syndicate and the accumulation strategies it promoted became reluctant or unable to continue purchasing cotton from producers. As a result, the cotton buying campaigns would be swiftly abandoned at the turn of the decade and the government would adopt a radically new approach during the Great Depression.

The most concerted efforts of the syndicate aimed to curtail the power of major export houses in Alexandria. In one of its earliest reports, the syndicate emphasized the importance of "diminishing, to the extent possible, the number of intermediaries between the producer of Egyptian cotton and the European spinner."[63] Its members believed that traders collected a larger share than they deserved from the rural surplus that cultivators produced. In a letter to the head of the syndicate, Nahhas estimated that cotton cultivators only received 50 percent of the price that manufacturers in Europe paid for Egyptian cotton, and therefore the purpose of ousting the middlemen would be to "save a large part of the difference between what the industrialist pays and what the producer receives."[64] A few months after the country was granted a conditional form of independence, Nahhas began to directly condemn the Alexandria General Produce Association (AGPA) for being an organization run by resident foreigners who self-servingly aimed to "monopolize the trade in cotton and cotton seed."[65] It set regulations in Mina al-Basal that operated in the interests of its members at the expense of Egyptian producers and brokers. It established itself as an appellate court for any disputes that arose at the time of delivery, with no possibility of appealing its decisions. And it oversaw the settlement of futures contracts. Many of the AGPA's members sat on the board of directors of the Alexandria Bourse and acted on behalf of foreign-owned export houses in Alexandria. These exceptional arrangements ultimately "enabled 60 brokers to control the futures market and gave a few commercial enterprises control over spot goods."[66] Over the following years, Nahhas insisted that such privileges threatened the country's national wealth because "the owners of cotton lose a lot of money that leaves their hands to go into the pockets of the foreigner."[67] To diminish the power of these large export and brokerage houses, Nahhas demanded that the AGPA be subjected to greater regulation by the government.

At the heart of the conflict between large landowners and merchants were the divergent methods through which they sought to secure their profits. Unlike the large landowners who wanted to guarantee a high price for their cotton, merchants and brokers were more interested in the volatility of price. For that reason, the syndicate tried to contain the activities of those who they believed affected the price of cotton in Mina al-Basal by trading excessively on the futures market. Since the late 1900s, the bourse had become an arena for speculation that drew criticism from observers and, as a result, was subjected to some government regulation. By the early 1920s, Nahhas started agitating more forcefully against major export houses whom he accused of saturating the bourse with contracts (*filyarat*) "for the purpose of speculation and exhausting the market."[68] Through such activities, traders managed to drive down the price of cotton in Mina al-Basal at harvest time and then inflate it once again when the crop passed into their hands for export. The chief mechanism they used to do this was known as "on-call" contracts, a common practice whereby cultivators, merchants, and spinners exchanged claims for physical cotton at a price to be determined later based on the value of futures contracts in the Alexandria Bourse.[69] Exporters who made on-call sales to spinners abroad would then aim to protect themselves against any losses by making on-call purchases from rural producers in Egypt.[70] This arrangement offered landowners a way to acquire immediate cash to finance their crop because merchant-financiers would offer them advances on the condition that they deliver the cotton after it was picked.[71] Although cultivators had the right to choose when to complete the sale, they could still fall victim to merchants and brokers who affected the price of spot cotton by engaging in a high volume of trade on the futures market. "Verily, prices are in the hands of God," Nahhas complained, "yet we are the ones who work to bring them down."[72] He concluded that the spot and futures markets had become analogous to a pair of traps that allowed merchants "to capture the money of the cultivator."[73] Just as large landowners sought to guarantee a high price for their crop by lobbying for government purchases, merchants aimed to maximize their profits by using futures contracts to manipulate the spot prices of cotton.

Facing repeated complaints by landowners about the dangers of financial speculation and market manipulation, the Egyptian government tried to forbid on-call contracts. In 1923, it proposed a law that would require all contracts for the exchange of cotton to include a fixed price at the time of the sale.[74] Preventing large landowners, merchants, and spinners from trading substantial amounts of unpriced cotton would effectively frustrate their ability to hedge their position on different markets. Although syndicate members often presented their demands as serving the interests of all cultivators, in reality fixed contracts would largely affect transactions between large landowners and big export houses in Alexandria. Many smaller cultivators and rural tenants relinquished their cotton as soon as it was harvested in order to pay off their outstanding debts to their creditors or their landlords, and so they did not enter into written contracts. For that reason, a manager at Lloyds Bank observed that the projected law was "framed to protect the large grower only."[75] Fearing an imminent threat, the big export houses in Alexandria immediately appealed to the British government. The president of the AGPA, A. W. Jessop, believed the law to be "undoubtedly aimed against the association."[76] The director of Carver Brothers, one of the largest trading houses in Alexandria, went so far as to ask English officials to shield him from the "prejudice that will arise in [his] business if this action is allowed to become binding on European companies."[77] They insisted that all matters related to the buying and selling of Egyptian cotton remain in the hands of the AGPA. Facing a flood of opposition from powerful merchants, the British high commissioner ultimately intervened with the Egyptian government and secured an assurance from the Prime Minister Yahya Ibrahim to postpone the adoption of the law indefinitely.[78]

Although large landowners and their political allies failed to abolish unfixed contracts, the syndicate continued its campaign against big cotton merchants. In 1926, Nahhas delivered a lecture at the Agricultural Club (Al-Nadi al-Zira'i) in which he remarked that the exchange of stocks and financial instruments was an enterprise that was almost as old as trade itself, akin to a "living organ in the body of commercial life."[79] Any deviations from this natural balance, however, turned cultivators into "the victims of price manipulators" because unregulated trading on the futures market led to massive fluctuations in the price of an actual bale of cotton. To restore a sense of equilibrium, Nahhas proposed a series of reforms that included limiting the number of brokers and agents on the bourse; raising the bar of entry into the market to L.E. 20,000; forbidding traders and speculators from creating brokerage firms under any pseudonyms; reducing the outsized representation that traders from the AGPA enjoyed on the bourse commission; and forming an oversight body half of whose members would come from the agricultural syndicate because it "represent[ed] the Egyptian producer who is the mainstay of wealth in the country." His appeals did not go unheeded. The following year, the government passed a code that aimed at "ensuring the regularity of operations conducted, preventing fictitious maneuvers, and protecting the market from practices which endanger its stability."[80] Among the 431 people registered on the Alexandria Bourse that year, only 60 individuals (known as adherent members) actually traded physical cotton while the rest were brokers, stockjobbers, and head clerks (formerly known as remisiers).[81] The new regulations established stricter rules for membership in the bourse, it imposed new restrictions (including a minimum tax) on the activities of financial intermediaries, and it created a guarantee fund composed of obligatory contributions from brokers as well as a percentage commission on all transactions on the exchange. But the struggle by large landowners against the AGPA would be a prolonged affair that only made serious headway during the Great Depression.

While the new regulations represented a victory for the syndicate, Nahhas continued to protest against merchants, brokers, and speculators for the rest of the decade. "[T]he rapacious middleman," he told an audience at the 1927 International Cotton Congress in Cairo, "placed himself between the grower and the consumer and adds so enormously to the difference between the price the former gets and the price the latter pays."[82] He was joined by other prominent landowners and politicians. The following year, for example, the undersecretary of the Egyptian Senate Amin Yusuf Bey traveled to Lancashire to promote a scheme for Manchester spinners, who he claimed were paying double what they should to buy Egyptian cotton, to deal directly with an Egyptian Cooperative Association. "The *fellaheen* of Egypt as well as the merchants of Manchester are discontented with the prices of cotton," he said in an interview in London. "The intermediaries take most of the money now, but if there were direct relations between producer and manufacturer much money would be saved."[83] Their description of these middlemen often portrayed their behaviors as a series of excesses, rather than a central feature of the cotton trade. In naturalizing their financial activities, Nahhas suggested that any disturbances in the spot market that were caused by arbitrage and speculation represented a deviation from a normative balance, rather than a systemic impulse towards the endless accumulation of profit for its own sake. Moreover, he pointed to a recent census which revealed that among the 86 brokers who were active in the bourse there were only 32 Egyptians, while the rest were largely Greek, Italian, English, French, and Austrian. This created a fundamental disharmony between the activities of the brokers and the concerns of other producers, traders, and consumers in the Egyptian Nile Valley who shared a single, national identity. "When the broker is patriotic," Nahhas proclaimed, "he proceeds, of course, to consider the interests of his country and give it priority of all other interests."[84] By attaching such importance to the nationality of the broker, Nahhas turned the question of market manipulation into a problem of disruptive foreign capital, rather than capital itself.

FARMS OF THE FUTURE

In 1918, a young Egyptian named Ibrahim Rashad embarked on a journey that would have profound consequences for the Egyptian Nile Valley. Born into a wealthy landowning family, Rashad had traveled to Europe in his mid-twenties to study political economy at Cambridge. On the advice of his professor he relocated to Ireland at the end of World War I to pursue his doctorate. Rashad would spend the next two years traveling around the country during a tumultuous period of nationalist upsurge and peasant-led resistance against the British Empire. He became closely acquainted with leading Irish agrarian reformers, and according to his biographer, he would return to his country in 1920 as "the first Egyptian scientifically qualified in agricultural economics."[85] While it may seem odd that Rashad was instructed to search for a development model in Ireland, rather than in an industrialized country like England, his choice had much to do with the similarities that he perceived between the two places. Rashad understood Ireland and Egypt to be predominantly agrarian societies that specialized in the production of raw materials for distant markets and that were subjected to British imperial control. And both countries were sites of vigorous anti-colonial mobilizations that would soon result in incomplete forms of independence from the British Empire.[86]

Rashad was born in 1886 into a wealthy family from the Turco-Circassian aristocracy. At the age of 23, he traveled to London to complete his studies in medicine, but four years later he decided to interrupt his education to join a British medical aid mission to Istanbul during the Second Balkan War. After contracting an intestinal disease, he returned to England and moved from one medical facility to another looking for treatment. During his recovery, he had a serendipitous encounter with the dean of the Royal Agricultural College in Cirencester—the first agricultural college in the English-speaking world—who invited him to enroll in the institution where Rashad would soon obtain a diploma. In 1916, he moved to the University of Bristol where he completed a baccalaureate in natural science, and then relocated to St. Catherine's College in Cambridge to study political economy.[87] There, he developed a sustained interest in the study of cooperative economics.

Rashad was familiar with the cooperative movement long before pursuing his graduate degree. As a medical student in Egypt, he had joined the Nationalist Party (al-Hizb al-Watani)—the main party opposing the British occupation of Egypt—and like many young Watanists he would frequent the Higher Schools' Club (Nadi al-Madaris al-'Ulya) to listen to speeches by leading nationalist figures. One day he heard 'Umar Lutfi, a lawyer and landowner who founded Egypt's first agricultural syndicate in 1909, speaking about agricultural cooperatives, after which Rashad became aware that a cooperative movement was gaining popularity outside of Egypt.[88] At Cambridge, Rashad embraced the study of cooperatives as an academic endeavor. He coauthored his first book with his professor, which inspired him years later to produce a two-volume work in Arabic that became the first textbook on cooperatives to be taught at Egyptian universities.[89] Towards the end of his studies, Rashad decided to pursue a doctorate in Ireland.

Rashad's two-year stay in Ireland proved to be a formative intellectual experience. He lived there during the Irish War of Independence (1919–21) and became acquainted with leading cultural and reform figures in the Irish nationalist movement. But nobody had a greater influence on Rashad's thinking than the Anglo-Irish agrarian reformer Horace Plunkett—so much that Irish playwright and activist George Bernard Shaw, Rashad's friend, would later call him the "Plunkett of Egypt."[90] The two men became friends, and Rashad would spend time at the Plunkett House, where Plunkett's Irish Agricultural Organization Society was headquartered. There he described joining reformers from Europe, the United States, and the colonial world in a transnational circulation of ideas about agricultural reform and revitalization. He described the Plunkett House as "a Mecca of agricultural cooperation to which pilgrimages are made from all parts of the world."[91] It was in such spaces that the global appeal of the cooperative movement in the early twentieth century was being forged.[92]

In the first half of the twentieth century, these kinds of discussions about cooperative farming were often concerned with the management of rural laborers who were neither divorced from their means of subsistence, nor did they become a reserve army of labor for urban industries. Many rural societies around the world, including cultivators in the Egyptian Nile Valley, did not undergo a process of mass dispossession from the countryside in order to create a proletarianized workforce. In this context, cooperative advocates on both sides of the Atlantic were preoccupied with strengthening smallholder farms in the face of the social transformations of the modern world.[93] Plunkett maintained close ties with American progressive-era leaders who did not see the future of their societies in a replication of English-style industrial capitalism; rather, they envisioned an alternative capitalist future based on an idealized agrarianism. In this view, smallholders would remain the basic unit of economic life, but they would engage in the production of agricultural commodities on terms that were favorable to them. Development would be achieved not by displacing peasants from their villages, but rather by unifying isolated small producers into collective institutions that could underpin a productive agrarian order.[94]

Within more radical traditions, there were also those who reconsidered the relationship between peasants and capitalist production. In 1881, Karl Marx wrote a letter to Vera Zasulich, who would later become a Menshevik, about the emancipatory potential of the Russian peasantry. He clarified that the development of capitalism through the complete separation of producers from their means of production was only a historical inevitability in Western Europe. He then suggested that the Russian peasant commune, which was based on common ownership of land rather than private holdings, could spearhead an alternative path towards communism if it shed its primitive trappings and became the basis of collective production on a national scale. "Precisely because it is contemporaneous with capitalist production," Marx wrote, "the rural commune may appropriate all its positive achievements without undergoing its frightful vicissitudes."[95] Almost 40 years later, members of the Second Congress of the Communist International debated the colonial question and concluded that not all countries had to pass through the capitalist stage of development.[96] Before arriving in Moscow, the Indian delegate Manabendra Nath Roy published a manifesto in which he proclaimed that the "masses of the East" could transition directly to communism without having to "go through the hell fires of capitalistic exploitation."[97] He presented his thesis before the Comintern, and it was adopted with some amendments in the congress's final resolution (along with Lenin's theses on national and colonial questions). A few years later, Soviet agricultural economist Alexander V. Chayanov advocated peasant cooperatives as a way to organize production on small farms, and he became a strong critic of Stalin's collectivization program. Chayanov argued that most peasant households sought to balance their subsistence needs with the hardships they endured in the labor process, rather than pursue capitalist profit as an overriding imperative.[98] Instead of collectivization, he believed the future of the peasantry lay in cooperative organization that could allow small farmers to scale up their production.

Rashad articulated a set of convictions that were aligned in different ways with these traditions. He associated industrial capitalism (rather than agrarian capitalism) with an inherent form of unfreedom that could imperil Egypt's future as an independent nation.

> It is possible for a nation to be politically free and economically enslaved . . . Capitalism, that is, autocratic government in industry, whether native or foreign, is detrimental to the interests of the people . . . The god of all capitalists is Capital. I would like to warn my fellow-countrymen of the danger inherent in any policy advocating Egyptian capitalism. Egyptian capitalism is almost as dangerous to our national interests as foreign capitalism. . . . We have a warning in Western civilization. It is stricken with the disease of capitalism; the masses are slaves industrially, even when politically free.[99]

Since a mass industrial society was not his desired endpoint, Rashad questioned the presumption that Egypt had to pass through a set of necessary historical stages to become modern. He rejected the belief that in its struggle against colonialism the Egyptian working class had to support the rise of national capitalists who could act as agents of a historical transition, first to industrial capitalism, then to socialism. In his view, Egypt did not have to "taste the fire that Europe has tasted."[100] Instead, Rashad preached an alternative to capital-intensive, Western-style industrialization: the takeover of what he believed to be a small number of mostly foreign-owned capitalist enterprises in the country by cooperative institutions that could ensure "our banks, our shops, and our factories [would] be the property of the people." His vision for a harmonious cooperative utopia, while still oriented towards the endless pursuit of profit, represented a different kind of capitalist modernity that avoided the massive social dislocation caused by the Industrial Revolution. As such, the small farmer would not only be protected from dispossession but would remain the cornerstone of economic life. What Rashad proposed was both a project of peasant subject formation and a developmental program. He envisioned bonds of solidarity between Egyptian cultivators that could only be achieved through cooperative association and that would ensure they reaped the greatest benefit from the fruits of their labor. Cooperatives would also develop their national consciousness and turn them into unalienated "worker-citizens" rather than simply "wage-earners" who were subordinated to their employers.[101] For Rashad, independence required more than a transfer of control over political institutions from colonial to national authorities; it also needed mechanisms for building a strong national collective that could bring about a broader social and economic transformation.

In the spring of 1920, Rashad set off on a journey home to Egypt after spending 11 years abroad. He arrived one year after an anti-colonial revolt had swept the country. During his two-week trip by sea, he met Arthur T. McKillop, the former chief inspector of finance in Egypt's Department of Agriculture and chairman of the newly established Cotton Research Board, and the two men discussed Rashad's experiences studying in London as well as his intentions to encourage the spread of agricultural cooperatives in Egypt. Towards the end of the trip, McKillop invited Rashad to take a job in the Ministry of Agriculture where he could fulfill his ambitions. With an undisguised paternalism, McKillop told him that state custodianship was necessary in backward societies "until the people attain reason and reach maturity and can therefore be entrusted with the matter themselves."[102] Like other parts of the world, the cooperative movement in Egypt underwent a process of institutionalization during the interwar period. In 1923, the Egyptian government granted legal recognition to cooperative societies, allowed them to take loans, and mandated the creation of a Cooperatives Section in the Agricultural Ministry. Rashad became its first director, thereby inaugurating his project to transform the Egyptian countryside. He helped draft a more important piece of legislation in 1927 that granted cooperative societies exemptions from the payment of certain taxes and dues and established the Higher Council for Cooperatives, which brought together state officials and cooperative representatives.[103] Although the law governed the formation of various kinds of cooperatives, the main type that would develop in these years and that received the most attention from state officials were those that specialized in the provision of agricultural credit. The government selected Bank Misr to offer advances to cooperatives that did not exceed 4 percent interest, and in the four years that followed, the bank extended hundreds of such loans.[104] Many of the Wafd's political opponents helped finance cooperatives in order to build their own bases of political support in the countryside when the Wafd was out of power.[105]

In the decade after the war, Rashad actively publicized his vision for reorganizing economic life in Egypt. In 1924, he published a series of articles for the Ministry of Agriculture's monthly magazine in which Rashad argued the country had recently gained its political freedom, represented by Britain's Unilateral Declaration of Egyptian Independence in 1922, but it had to be complemented by another victory over two internal enemies: economic weakness and social retardation.[106] For Rashad, the ultimate reason for such an inferior condition was the domination of Egyptians by foreign capital. Like other economic nationalists, Rashad argued that Egypt suffered from a continuous tension between the production of "national wealth" and its circulation beyond Egypt's national borders. "If the wealth of the country increases and then seeps into the hands of foreigners," he wrote, ". . . it remains lost wealth of which our only share is the toil it took to produce it."[107] His prime example was cotton, which peasants labored to cultivate "only for the foreign merchant to arrive and to gain most of the profit." Rashad recognized that cotton was the foundation of the country's wealth. He advocated a three-stage process to reorganize cotton production and trade along cooperative lines.[108] The first step was for cotton cultivators to organize into voluntary associations that could negotiate with banks and merchants for better loan and sales conditions, citing an example of village notables in Bani Mazar (Minya Province in Upper Egypt) who had begun undertaking this kind of organization. The second step would be to establish cooperative ginning factories across the country that could gin Egyptian cotton and manufacture secondary products, like cottonseed oil.[109] The third step would be to create cooperatively run textile factories and sell the manufactured fabrics through a wholesale marketing society. If genuine independence required a reconfiguration of those relationships and institutions that underpinned socioeconomic life, then only through a harmonious and well-balanced cooperative order could it be achieved.

Rashad's writings were marked by an unresolved tension. His diagnosis of the condition of Egypt's peasantry attributed their immiseration to commercial or psychological factors. In addition to condemning foreign merchants, he attacked what he saw as a stubborn traditionalism of peasant smallholders that prevailed across the Egyptian countryside. "[Farmers] are slow to exchange old methods for new. They believe in hereditary knowledge rather than in knowledge acquired by experiments and research. They are suspicious of new things," he wrote. "They are essentially individualists, and are averse to letting their neighbors know anything about their affairs."[110] Like nationalists in the previous two decades, Rashad believed that under colonial rule Egyptian peasants had become self-interested individuals whose inclinations towards the pursuit of personal gain could only be overcome by nationalist mobilization.[111] Portraying the individualistic smallholder as an authentic representation of the Egyptian peasant, however, required a certain degree of abstraction from the complexity of social relations that shaped everyday life in the countryside. Rarely in his writings did Rashad mention the specific social relations of class or gender in which peasants existed. His peasants were not renters, or sharecroppers, or wage earners, or female laborers in peasant households; they were simply peasants that possessed a little bit of land and distinct cultural features. It was those features that provoked Rashad's ire, rather than the unequal arrangements of land tenure, or tenancy, or gendered labor in actual villages. Even while Rashad took aim at historical teleologies and the class divisions upon which their realization depended, he neglected to account for social hierarchies that actually existed in rural Egypt. Only by abstracting the peasant into an archetype of irrational individualism could Rashad then make arguments about the necessities of collective endeavor and rural solidarity that would be achieved through a strong cooperative movement.

While the figure of the Egyptian peasant in Rashad's writings was removed from any social context in the countryside, Rashad also pointed to the ways that Egyptian agricultural producers were embedded in a wider set of power relations with foreign capital. He argued that even though Egypt had achieved formal political independence the country still suffered from a drain of wealth due to the predominance of foreign capital, mainly in the form of real estate, land mortgage, transport, and trading companies. The solution to this basic tension—between the production of what he considered to be "national wealth" and its circulation beyond national borders—lay in efforts to fix commercial and other profits within the spatial boundaries of the Egyptian nation-state. Like other economic nationalists, Rashad believed that national capital formation could insulate Egypt's population from the unpredictable movements of money and wealth in and out of the country, and national subject formation could turn Egyptian smallholding peasants into rational agents united by bonds of collective solidarity. To the extent that he provided any structural explanation for the condition of the peasantry, then, Rashad focused almost exclusively on the realm of exchange, rather than production. By ascribing the problems of the countryside to the behaviors of foreign merchant capital, rather than capital in general, he could only explain how asymmetric international trade in an imperial world economy compromised the prosperity of Egyptian peasants. But he could not do the same for the country's unequal land tenure system.

Rashad's description of the predicament of the Egyptian countryside therefore relied on a set of visibilities and erasures. He effaced any power relations that existed on the level of the village while foregrounding Egyptian cultivators' uneven insertion into the global economy. This kind of discursive maneuver, which was not uncommon, was necessary to portray foreign capital as the ultimate impediment to the realization of freedom for Egyptians. After World War I, agrarian reformers who promoted new projects for rural reconstruction did not, for the most part, challenge the power of large landholders who still dominated Egyptian politics and social life. They typically framed the predicament of Egypt's peasantry in terms of commercial factors, like powerful foreign merchants and volatile prices, or cultural factors, like peasant traditionalism, while avoiding questions about the unequal distribution of landed property. By invoking the overbearing forces of international trade and culture to explain the hardships of rural life in the 1920s, these reformists ultimately effaced politics from the landscape of the Egyptian countryside.

As we saw in chapter 1, the realities of social and economic life in the Egyptian Nile Valley involved layers of entanglements between peasants, landlords, the state, and world markets. Though the arrangements of rent and labor on cotton estates were hardly the focus of interwar nationalists, they are visibly apparent in records from the period. A petition submitted by peasants who rented land from a wealthy landowning family provides a window into how tenant labor and rent on large *'izbas* were managed through an untidy mix of economic exploitation and extra-economic coercion.[112] Around the same time that Rashad published those articles, some 65 peasants who rented and worked on land belonging to Muhammad Badrawi 'Ashur, a large landowner and major funder of the Wafd, addressed a series of complaints to the Prime Minister Zaghlul. Like most *'izba* owners, 'Ashur relied on their undercompensated labor to grow cotton. Each peasant family on the estate had to offer family members as *tamaliyya* to perform obligatory daily work on the owner's fields. They received a paltry wage of two piasters per day, which 'Ashur often paid in wheat every three or four months. If they showed up late to work or if they disobeyed 'Ashur's sons, the peasants were charged hefty fines. If any of the peasants farmed cotton on their plots they were prevented from ginning it before they ginned 'Ashur's cotton. On top of these restrictive and disciplinary arrangements that governed their daily life and work, the peasants complained about relentless "beatings, punches, and insults" by 'Ashur's sons who "treated them like slaves in an age of freedom." Apart from the direct exploitation and/or expropriation of labor, another common way in which landowners or the state appropriated cotton surpluses on their lands was through the manipulation of tenancy contracts. When the tenants on 'Ashur's estate complained about the arbitrary powers of their landlords, their grievances were not limited to how 'Ashur's sons enforced labor discipline. They also complained that their landlords arbitrarily set their rents. 'Ashur's tenants were required to pay a reduced rent in exchange for their plot of land, a practice that was neither uncommon nor universal. He would often compel them to sign blank rental contracts and then "at his own whim" he would later fill them out. "[The owner] sets the rent at one *qintar* of cotton, if he wishes, or higher," they protested. Some tenants called on the government to pass legislation, as it had begun to do in 1920, to limit agricultural rents in order to guarantee that landowners "share the increase of cotton and its prices."[113]

The difference between Rashad's idealized agrarian society and the farmers' conception of what justice would entail in their particular rural setting was clear. The perceived injustices that the tenants complained about on 'Ashur's land derived largely from an unequal tenure system that allowed landlords unchecked powers over the internal management of their estates. Though the peasants did not talk directly about land reform, their primary concern was to curb the powers of big landlords who exploited labor on private agricultural estates. By contrast, Rashad did not even see the abusive powers of landlords as a problem to be addressed. That peasants working on *'izbas* were disciplined on a regular basis through coercion and violence is well known.[114] The account of 'Ashur and the peasants working on his estate also suggests that *'izbas* functioned as an institution through which large landowners could extract undercompensated or uncompensated human labor. They were sites where agrarian capitalists (i.e., big estate owners) could deploy a variety of political and legal mechanisms to maintain a cheap workforce in order to reduce their production costs. At the same time, whatever costs those estate owners might have incurred in order to supply housing and other basic provisions for their agricultural workforce were almost certainly cheaper than paying those workers a full wage. We might therefore think of the *'izba* as an institutional domain in which capitalist landowners viewed pure wage labor as being costlier than other modes of compensating the social reproduction of labor. For these tenants, freedom did not only mean being shielded from domination by foreign capital and markets; it also meant the ability to be unconstrained by the abusive powers of their landlord that ensured the extraction of their undercompensated labor.

WEALTH OF THE NATION

The conception of sovereignty that underpinned economic nationalist discourse in the 1920s was one in which cultivators would be insulated from the unruly forces that imperial domination had introduced into the Egyptian Nile Valley. To be free meant being liberated from the inequities and instabilities that the preponderance of foreign capital and entanglements with distant markets had imposed on the countryside. When Nahhas affirmed Egypt's status as an agrarian country and complained that it was threatened by international price volatility, or when Rashad extolled the virtues of rural cooperation and solidarity, they imagined a future in which cultivators who were emancipated from the intractable dynamics of an imperial world economy would become the basis of a truly independent society. According to them, rural producers would continue to grow large quantities of cotton, but most of the wealth they produced would return back into their own hands. To elucidate this vision, some of these nationalists began to distinguish between those forms of labor that generated agrarian wealth and those activities that simply redirected it out of the country. It was on such grounds that landowners, policymakers, and agrarian reformers launched a trenchant critique of the merchants, brokers, and speculators who dominated the cotton trade from Alexandria.[115] Their activities deprived Egyptian cultivators of the fruits of their own effort and stood in contrast to labor in the countryside that created wealth, rather than drain it. The dichotomy between allegedly productive cultivators and unproductive foreign merchant-financiers was often presented by interwar nationalists as a timeless feature of the Egyptian Nile Valley. But their critique emerged at a moment when the vicissitudes of interwar capitalism had prompted nationalists to imagine new ways of generating agrarian wealth and territorializing it within Egyptian borders.

Only by grasping the historical specificity of their critique can we appreciate its growing appeal after the war. Whereas in the 1910s, the primary target of Nahhas's criticisms were foreign creditors who charged exorbitant rates of interest on loans to both the Egyptian government and large cotton producers, by the 1920s and 1930s his attention turned to the merchants, brokers, and speculators in the Alexandria Bourse.[116] What changed was not the activities of merchant-financiers themselves so much as the context in which they operated. During the interwar period, opportunities to make profits from the production and sale of cotton could expand or shrink unpredictably from one year to another because of the recurrence of price volatility that resulted from recent transformations in the organization of global capitalism. Before then, merchants and landowners could both engage in the steady accumulation of capital without significantly impeding each other's ability to do so. That changed after the war. As large landowners and their allies began finding their way into positions of authority in a nominally independent government, they increasingly used the instruments of the state to sideline the cotton traders of the AGPA. From 1924 to 1942, large landowners constituted between 39 percent and 50 percent of elected representatives in the Chamber of Deputies (Majlis al-Nuwwab); their representation in the Senate (Majlis al-Shuyukh) was even higher, and they tended to hold an overwhelming majority in parliamentary committees that handled matters related to cotton.[117] In this context, the relatively symbiotic relationship between large landowners and merchant-financiers that had underpinned their dominant accumulation strategies when cotton prices were more stable began to fracture as landowners wanted a consistently higher price for their cotton while traders preferred fluctuating prices so long as they could manipulate them to their own advantage. As a result, many large landowners began to turn against merchant-financiers and portray them as villains that diverted wealth away from its rightful producers.

The critical stance taken by large landowners and their allies towards the middlemen of the cotton trade was rooted in a fetishization of agrarian labor. As early as the 1890s, nationalist *'afandiyya* (urban, middle-class intellectuals and professionals) began to represent the peasantry in newspapers, literature, and popular entertainment as an authentic repository of Egyptian culture that formed an indissoluble part of a national people and its history.[118] As a short-lived financial boom began to falter in the mid-1900s, early nationalist critics of British rule who confronted the proliferation of agrarian credit and the inflation of land prices started to take aim at imperial finance for encouraging speculative activities that did not substantively improve the lives of rural producers.[119] What began as an attack on foreign banks in the late 1900s and early 1910s expanded into a larger critique of the entire structure of the cotton trade by the interwar period. In the 1920s and 1930s, Egyptian economic nationalists began to regularly distinguish between cultivators who created tangible material wealth that could bring prosperity to the whole nation and cotton traders, brokers, and speculators who dealt largely in fictitious wealth that moved seamlessly across the country's borders in a way that did not serve the interests of the majority of Egyptians.[120] But this portrayal depended on a profound simplification. To fetishize agrarian labor was to isolate one part of a social process and misrecognize it as the entire process itself.[121] Cultivators were detached from their surroundings and assigned a set of mystical powers that made it appear as though outcomes emanated solely from their own actions, rather than from their embeddedness in a wider set of social relations through which they were constituted. In the eyes of Egyptian nationalists, for example, the expenditure of labor by a cotton grower was a singular source of prosperity—Nahhas suggested as much when he described cultivators as the mainstay of wealth in the country. In other words, wealth emanated from the activities of fetishized individuals rather than from their location in a system that compelled them to produce value at or above an average rate of efficiency determined by their interactions with other producers, financiers, manufacturers, consumers, machines, and natural environments.

What these nationalists did then was glorify the concrete (i.e., tangible material wealth) in the face of the abstract (i.e., fictitious money wealth).[122] The problem with this formulation was that land, laborers, and crops that were celebrated for their ostensibly material properties were only tangible insofar as their particular usages were concerned. But the overriding objective behind the cultivation of cotton was not the production of what classical political economists referred to as qualitatively specific use-values. It was the acquisition of exchange-value, a purely quantitative form of wealth. Physical resources, goods, and people could embody this kind of value in a capitalist world, but they were not themselves value. Just as mercantile and financial capital possessed an excessively mobile and immaterial quality, capital that was invested in producing cotton for the purpose of exchange was never fixed as such for it could easily be moved elsewhere. This would happen in the 1940s after the experience of depression and war prompted many large landowners to shift their accumulation strategy from agricultural production to leasing land. By personifying the tyranny of capitalist abstraction in the figure of the merchant-financier who did not belong to the national community, these nationalists presented an essential feature of the capitalist value form (i.e., its abstract dimension) as an exclusive problem of foreign merchant capital.

FIGURE 4. Cartoon by artist Zuhdī al-ʿAdawī. Source: al-ʿAdawī, *Bidāyat al-Maʿraka*.

The fetishization of agrarian labor and the institutions that it inspired nationalists to create rested on a belief that the country's colonial condition resulted from its lopsided insertion into chronically uneven structures of imperial finance and trade that were beyond the control of rural producers. For that reason, nationalists who sought to overcome inequalities between those who profited from producing cotton and those who profited from trading it did so by reorganizing the prevailing methods through which the value attached to this prized crop circulated. The promotion of national banks, government cotton purchases, and rural cooperatives aimed to address one dimension of the Egyptian Nile Valley's incorporation into an imperial world economy, namely the volatile and wealth-draining movements of finance and trade that it imposed on the countryside. But it served to mask another dimension: the conflicts that existed between landlords, peasants, and state officials over the appropriation of rural surpluses that were largely rooted in an unequal land tenure system oriented towards commercial agriculture. In the end, these nationalists championed a project that largely aimed to restructure the dynamics of circulation rather than production, and in doing so, they advanced a vision for independence that aspired towards equality between nations, but not necessarily within them.

CONCLUSION

The main intellectual accomplishment of Egyptian economic thinkers in the 1920s was to reconfigure the relationship between the political and the economic in the nationalist imagination. The range of ideas and projects that they advanced—limited industry, direct relations between local cultivators and foreign spinners, and agricultural cooperation—rested on two beliefs that were acquiring a widespread appeal among Egyptian nationalists. First, politicians and intellectuals were convinced that agriculture remained the basis of prosperity in Egypt, and they insisted on the primacy of farming as an ideal form of wealth-creating activity. Second, Egyptian landowners, industrialists, state officials, and experts continued to search for ways to rescale the circulation of capital, goods, and profits within the boundaries of the nation-state. This included efforts to create new banks that could finance local industrial and agricultural activities, to sideline export houses owned by foreign residents, to reform the tariff system, and to eliminate the privileges that foreigners had enjoyed since the nineteenth century. These interwar tendencies towards agrarian idealism and the territorialization of capital established a repertoire of ideas, policies, and practices that nationalist reformers and state builders would continue to develop in the next three decades. As we will see, some of these ideas would become vital to the functioning of political and economic power in the Egyptian Nile Valley, but some of them would be profoundly transformed, especially after the Great Depression, as the country continued its struggle for independence.

THREE

GLOBAL DEPRESSION IN THE NILE VALLEY

EXTRAORDINARY EVENTS often reveal a system of power's ordinary workings and create the conditions that make it possible to transform them.[1] The global depression that began in 1929 represented such a historical moment. It destabilized the lives of millions of producers, traders, and consumers and underscored the kind of turmoil that could come with living in an interconnected capitalist world. That Egypt was inextricably located in a transnational web of relations forged for the purpose of growing cotton and moving it overseas was a widely discussed feature of life in the country since the late nineteenth century. Living in an imperial space where the wealth and welfare of so many depended on the export of a single crop meant being vulnerable to the uncontrollable behaviors of people, processes, and institutions in distant parts of the world. After World War I, those imperial arrangements that had long facilitated the Egyptian Nile Valley's incorporation into the empire of cotton began to erode. The regular experience of price volatility in the interwar period brought into clearer view the inequities and instabilities that could unsettle the lives of cultivators, traders, transporters, and buyers in this tangled geography. The arrival of the depression in the 1930s marked a watershed that hastened the disintegration of the imperial world economy that was inherited from the late nineteenth century. The breakdown of practices and routines to which the livelihoods of millions of people who produced, processed, and moved Egyptian cotton were bound laid bare a set of underlying tensions and contradictions that threatened to transform the Egyptian Nile Valley more than ever before.

Describing what happened in the 1930s was as fraught with contradictions as the event itself. In 1931, the governor of the National Bank of Egypt, Edward Cook, presented a dilemma that he believed lay at the heart of agrarian life in the Egyptian Nile Valley. "[T]he prosperity of the Egyptian peasant, working on his field many thousands of miles from the market where his product is bought and sold," he wrote, "can be sensibly affected by civil war in China, by political events in India, by labor disputes in England, by a stock exchange collapse in New York."[2] In this brief statement, Cook offered an incisive commentary on the geography of power and accumulation to which people in the Egyptian Nile Valley belonged. From the nineteenth century, the valley had been integrated into a patchwork of sites—including cotton fields in the American South, British India, and Brazil; exchanges in Alexandria, Liverpool, and New Orleans; textile factories in Manchester; and retail stores around the world—that together fueled the industrial engine of the British Empire. By the twentieth century, dependence on distant markets had become a regular feature of life in the Egyptian countryside. Although they were constituted by the quotidian actions of ordinary people, markets had assumed powers of their own in the eyes of many cultivators. In their petitions to the palace, for example, peasants often complained that abstract forces—like "the general decline of prices" and "the movement of supply and demand"—had wielded a certain mastery over their lives. Formidable as they were, however, international markets did not exist separately from local people, actions, and events, nor did they precede them in a sequence of causation. Any processes or institutions that appeared to be global were actually located in concrete sites and institutions around the world. Rather than treat the global market as a singular force that stood apart from the people and things that it impacted, we might instead conceptualize markets as complex machines that do not exist independently from any of their moving parts—including agricultural estates, railway stations, banks and export houses, cotton exchanges, and government offices and research centers. Zooming in on those parts and considering their relationship to each other offers a series of vantage points from which we can observe the peculiar conjunctures that destabilized global capitalism in the 1930s and their uneven consequences in the Egyptian Nile Valley.

The account that follows begins with an investigation of the particular imperial geography of power and accumulation to which the main agents who profited from Egyptian cotton were attached and how it transformed in the interwar period. It then narrows its aperture around the Egyptian Nile Valley, focusing on the social history of cotton in every major stage of its lifecycle—including its cultivation in the fields, its transportation along railways and riverways, its exchange in the Alexandria markets, and its export to manufacturers overseas. The monopolistic domains that managed the most lucrative aspects of the production and trade of Egyptian cotton in each of these stages—the private estates, the European-owned mortgage banks, the state railways, and the big cotton trading houses—began to face challenges that would ultimately reshape them and, in some cases, set the stage for their demise. During the depression, large estate owners, railway administrators, merchant families, and mortgage bankers witnessed a severe disruption in their dominant modes of accumulation. As cotton prices fell, *'izba* owners who were unable to repay their loans became threatened by a growing tide of foreclosures, and they successfully lobbied government officials to support them. The state railways saw its revenues drop precipitously, and its managers responded by systematically sabotaging other modes of transport on roads and rivers. Big trading houses in Alexandria faced stiffer challenges from nationalists who sought to fashion new powers to regulate cotton, workers who demanded fairer compensation for their labor, and rival Egyptian merchants who wanted to capture a larger share of the cotton trade. Mortgage banks were all but crippled by insolvent debtors and unfavorable settlements imposed on them by the Egyptian government. And a growing cohort of monetary nationalists became painfully aware of the hazards of Egypt's continued linkage to an imperial monetary system that ensured a relatively cheap supply of Egyptian cotton to British mills, and they sought to establish national control over the management of money in the country. By the end of the decade, the depression had weakened or destroyed old centers of wealth and power and paved the way for national elites to refashion some of the basic mechanisms that underpinned the workings of cotton production and trade in the Egyptian Nile Valley.

UNTANGLING THE EMPIRE OF COTTON

The Great Depression (1929–39) was a global event that reshaped agrarian life for cultivators across the colonial world, especially those whose livelihoods depended on growing cash crops. The experience was particularly devastating for cotton producers. In 1929, cotton was still the most valuable agricultural commodity in world trade, its estimated global acreage had reached a record of 85.5 million acres, and it made up more than 11 percent of raw materials exports worldwide.[3] Roughly half of the world's cotton was produced for export (China and the Soviet Union produced large amounts of cotton, but much of it was for domestic consumption), and its cultivation largely occurred in four regions: the American South, British India, the Egyptian Nile Valley, and Northeast Brazil. The arrival of the depression in the Egyptian Nile Valley revealed the ways in which that space had become stitched into an interconnected capitalist world. "The Egyptian crisis is a function of the global crisis," a professor at the French School of Law in Cairo proclaimed in 1931, "which has caused the value of raw materials to drop throughout the world."[4] At the start of the 1930s, cotton constituted roughly four-fifths of Egyptian exports and accounted for almost 12 percent of world exports.[5] Three years before the Wall Street Crash of 1929, the price of Egyptian cotton had already fallen, and although it recovered partially for the next two seasons, it would collapse with the onset of the depression.[6] In 1930, the average price of one *qintar* of Egyptian cotton in Mina al-Basal dropped nearly 40 percent from what it was the previous year, and by 1933 the value of the cotton harvest fell to the lowest it had been since World War I.[7] Though it began to recover slowly in the middle of the decade, the price of Egyptian cotton fell again in 1937 and 1938, and agricultural production in the country would not be fully restored until after World War II.[8]

The behavior of international prices and their impact on cultivators in the Egyptian Nile Valley fascinated many observers. In 1931, Edwards noted that Egyptian peasants considered their prosperity or poverty "to depend on the price of cotton and *nothing* else."[9] He warned that if prices remained so low a substantial readjustment in the economic life of the country would become necessary. But Edwards declined to offer any specific explanation for what exactly constituted prices, who had the authority to determine them, and how they shaped peasant life so profoundly. Prices might have been experienced

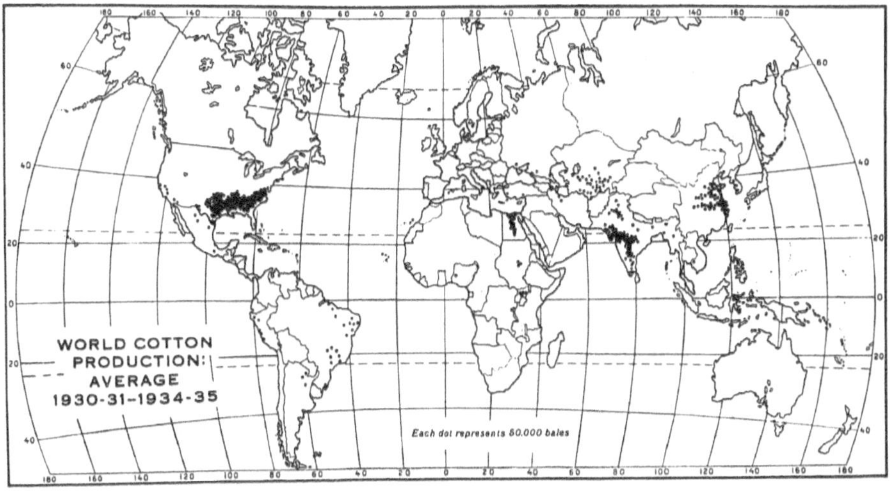

FIGURE 5. World cotton production, 1930–1935. Source: Howell, *Cotton Prices in Spot and Futures Markets.*

as a self-propelling force that pulsed through the landscape of the Egyptian Nile Valley. However, the abstract powers that Edwards ascribed to them were forged in particular sites by the concrete actions of people and institutions. These included the speculative activities of traders on the Alexandria Bourse; the declining productive capacities of Lancashire spinners; the expansion of both cotton cultivation and textile manufacturing in East Asia, Africa, and Latin America; the relief efforts of U.S. agricultural policymakers and their unintended consequences; and the decision of Egyptian officials to abandon their cotton buying campaigns along with their strategy of trying to segment the market for high-quality Egyptian cotton.

The most immediate source of price instability that sparked public outrage was speculation, particularly in the Alexandria Bourse. "Most of the cultivators sell their cotton in advance according to the price of the futures contract," wrote landowner 'Abd al-'Aziz Maqlad in a letter to *al-Ahram*.[10] In an effort to diagnose the reasons behind the intensification of the slump, he complained that such a practice ultimately left cotton producers "at the mercy of the merchant." Another farmer from Giza called for the creation of an "impermeable system to control the conditions of the bourse and to set the prices of cotton."[11] But other observers believed that such a sustained decline in prices could not be explained solely in terms of the operation of the futures market because speculators did not have the power affect long-term price trends that were ultimately "determined by deeper causes."[12]

The most important deeper cause was the recent fall in demand from the major industrial manufacturers who imported Egyptian cotton. When the depression began there were about 27.5 million spindles around the world that spun Egyptian cotton, of which 65 percent were located in England.[13] In 1930, England imported 300,000 bales of Egyptian cotton, twice as much as the next largest importer, the United States. But this figure had dropped more than one-third from what it was six years earlier. Among the major importers of Egyptian cotton only English consumption had so severely fallen. The reasons for this precipitous decline were manifold. First, spinners in Lancashire saw some of their key export markets shrink in the 1920s because states around the world started to impose tariffs to protect their domestic industries.[14] Second, the decline of Lancashire was a symptom of what the International Institute of Agriculture described as a shifting center of gravity in the global cotton industry from West to East. Between 1927 and 1935, the percentage share of European consumption of the world's cotton diminished from 44.3 percent to 38.6 percent while consumption in Asia rose from 25 percent to 35.23 percent.[15] This deterioration was particularly acute in England where employment in the cotton textile industry between 1929 and 1939 dropped by almost one-third, and in roughly the same period its mule spindles (the spindle most commonly used in fine spinning) fell by 41 percent.[16] The main reason behind this geographical relocation of textile manufacturing capacity was the relatively lower labor costs of spinners in Asia. In 1933, the average cost of labor per bale of cotton in England was about 2.5 times higher than it was in Japan.[17] A peculiar convergence of factors created this difference. These included the success of state-guided "late development" in Japan that kept labor costs and unrest low since the Meiji restoration; the formation of a reserve army of Chinese labor that suffered disruptions from warfare and rural displacement since the 1840s; the strength of the British trade union movement in the interwar period; and more than a century and a half of British capital accumulation through imperial expansion and conquest that raised English standards of living relative to other parts of the world.[18]

The sharp drop in demand for Egyptian cotton in Lancashire—still the heart of Britain's fine spinning industry—prompted some Egyptian landowners to call upon their government to take regulatory measures. In September 1931, the country's flagship newspaper, *al-Ahram*, began to publish letters from readers offering suggestions for ways out of the depression. "We grow cotton . . . not to consume it in our country but to sell it to our customers abroad who are destitute, and the most important of whom are our customers in Lancashire," wrote Hashim Yahya.[19] He went on to propose that the Egyptian government restrict cultivation to whatever quantity was demanded by spinners in Lancashire that year because growing any additional cotton would drive down its price. Other contributors, like the *al-Ahram* correspondent in Belqas, reported that many cultivators backed a proposal to limit the acreage of cotton in most of the Nile Delta and require producers to devote one-third of their cultivated area to low-yielding Sakelleridis. Others went so far as to suggest burning raw cotton that was held in storage in order to bolster the price of the crop.[20]

Another reason for the prolonged slump in cotton prices during the 1930s had to do with the actions of agricultural policymakers in the largest cotton producing country in the world, the United States. Observers in Egypt had long suspected a strong connection between the prices of Egyptian and American cotton. As early as 1873, a report in an Alexandrian newspaper, *Le Nil*, lamented that Egyptian cottons were influenced by variations in the price of its American counterparts that "occur here by ricochet, striking though England."[21] More than 40 years later, two experts working in the Statistical Department of the Ministry of Finance—Isaac G. Levi and James I. Craig—compiled data on weekly prices in Liverpool and published a note in the department's monthly bulletin with similar conclusions.[22] While none of them elaborated on the reasons for this close relationship, scholars later surmised that cultivators in the United States produced an overwhelming portion of global cotton supplies, and if the price of Egyptian cotton got too high spinners in Lancashire could easily substitute longer-staple American varieties for it.[23] The events of 1929–30 sparked a renewed interest in the movement of Egyptian cotton prices in international markets and prompted a series of in-depth investigations by experts that were largely based in Cairo.[24] In 1929, two Egyptian researchers—M. A. Zahra and Mahmoud El-Darwish—began a yearlong statistical study of the factors affecting Egyptian cotton prices, and their findings were published the following year by the Ministry of Finance's Cotton Bureau in the first of a series of technical bulletins. Another important figure who presented his own research in the same year was Italian statistician and economist Constantino Bresciani-Turroni. Having acted as an advisor on German war reparations after the signing of the Dawes Plan, he arrived to Cairo in 1927 where he taught briefly and became a contributor to *L'Égypte Contemporaine*, the influential journal of the Société Khédiviale d'Économie Politique de Statistique et de Legislation.[25] In their seminal work, Zahra, El-Darwish, and Bresciani-Turroni relied on the use of correlation coefficients, a relatively novel tool in econometrics, to demonstrate that the price of Egyptian cotton closely followed the price of American cotton. In a direct rebuttal to Yusuf Nahhas, these researchers argued that the size and quality of the Egyptian crop, especially during the volatile interwar period, did not determine its own price—an axiom that Craig believed should be "inscribed at the door of every government office that has anything to do with cotton."[26]

While arguments about Egypt's inability to substantially affect international cotton prices had been made since the nineteenth century, only during the depression did the political context allow for their widespread embrace at the highest echelons of government. As cotton prices began their downward spiral in 1930, Egyptian politics were dramatically shaken up. The palace forced the Wafd out of government (the third palace coup in seven years) and appointed Isma'il Sidqi, the former finance minister and author of the 1916 report, to the premiership. After taking power, Sidqi dissolved the parliament, postponed the elections, abolished the 1923 constitution, and ruled by decree until his resignation in 1933.[27] Sidqi appointed a new undersecretary of finance, Ahmad Abdel Wahab, and entrusted him to develop a cotton policy, which he elaborated in an influential memorandum.[28] The impetus for the new cotton policy was more specific than a general decline in world cotton prices. In a 1930 report to the finance minister, Abdel Wahab warned that English spinners had stopped making long-term orders for Egyptian cotton due to the government's cotton buying campaigns.[29] As a result, he sought to halt the state purchase of cotton directly from cultivators, a practice for which the General Egyptian Agricultural Syndicate had lobbied for almost a decade. Relying on the research of Zahra, El-Darwish, and Bresciani-Turroni, Abdel Wahab's cotton policy aimed to achieve two objectives. First, it abandoned the existing strategy of segmenting the market based on the superior reputation of Egyptian cotton and instead promoted a shift away from lower-yielding to higher-yielding varieties of cotton.[30] Over the course of the 1930s, long-staple Sakelleridis was almost entirely replaced by short-staple Ashmouni and medium-staple Giza cotton.[31] Second, it sought to reduce the costs of growing cotton by regulating rents, reorganizing the provision of rural credit, and reducing other expenses that weighed heavily on farmers as the prices they received for their cotton diminished. The Abdel Wahab memorandum established a new foundation for cotton policymaking that would be pursued by Egyptian leaders in the 1930s.

The reorientation of Egyptian cotton policy under Sidqi immediately drew censure from those who had benefited from the government's cotton buying campaigns in the 1920s. The syndicate had recently approved a proposition to restore the law that would restrict the acreage of cotton and require producers to devote one third of their cultivated area to low-yielding Sakelleridis.[32] The following year a string of criticisms of Sidqi appeared on the pages of the journal *al-Dia'*. Nahhas mocked the Sidqi government's embrace of "mass production" on grounds that representatives of nearly two dozen countries who had recently attended the fifteenth International Cotton Congress in Paris agreed that both the collapse of prices and the decline of industry resulted from the overproduction of cotton.[33] The cotton program implemented by the Sidqi government in the 1930s eroded much of the rural support base that the Wafd had built over the previous decade. When it came to its relationship with the syndicate, however, the government sought a compromise. In order to win the support of its members, Abdel Wahab allowed the cultivation of Sakelleridis to continue in some parts of the northern Delta, and he acceded to their long-held demand to constrain the powers of the Alexandria General Produce Association (AGPA), which government officials pursued intently in the following years.[34]

While these policies helped maintain a high volume of cotton exports during the depression, they did not fully insulate cultivators in the Egyptian Nile Valley from the erratic instabilities of international cotton markets. As the decade wore on, the disproportionate influence of the American crop induced another round of price volatility, even if American policymakers did not intend it. After taking office in 1933, U.S. President Franklin D. Roosevelt began to enact a series of federal programs known as the New Deal. To bring about an agricultural recovery, the Roosevelt administration put in place what it called a domestic allotment plan: a program to pay cotton farmers to voluntarily reduce their crop output.[35] By 1934–35, the efforts of the New Dealers to induce artificial scarcity had managed to reduce the area harvested in cotton by more than 30 percent. The rise in prices that resulted from these policies, however, encouraged cultivators in other parts of the world to expand their cultivation—particularly with high-yield strains—to such an extent that by 1936–37 world cotton production exceeded what it had been seven years earlier.[36] As a result, international prices for cotton suffered another major decline, worse than any other leading raw commodity in the world. But the resumption of low prices no longer had anything to do with conditions in the global textile industry. One year into the depression, mills around the world—especially in Japan and the United States where textile manufacture underwent a considerable expansion—began to increase their purchases of cotton again. By 1936–37, consumption by the world's mills had grown by no less than 19 percent from what it was at the start of the depression, and their rising demand for cotton was fed largely by producers outside of the United States.[37] Since the start of the depression, the acreage restrictions on American cotton had reduced its portion of world production from 60 percent to 42 percent while all other exporting countries increased their share.[38] "The current surfeit of cotton," a journalist for *The Economist* concluded, "is due partly to the American Government's price-raising measures, which stimulated the extension of cultivation in other countries, and partly to a succession of high-yields per acre in all countries."[39] The low prices of Indian, Egyptian, and Brazilian cotton in the late 1930s were therefore partly a function of U.S. acreage policies that helped encourage an expansion of cotton production around the world.

The recurring collapse of cotton prices during the depression provided an opportunity for new forms of economic management. Some planners wanted to revive a proposal for an international agreement to stabilize cotton prices that was first put forward in 1933 at the London Monetary and Economic Conference. However, the largest cotton exporters—namely the United States and British India—had little interest in cooperating with smaller producers, like Egypt, while English spinners feared that a global accord would inflate the price of cotton. Rather than enhance intergovernmental cooperation, the cotton crisis of the 1930s pushed states in the opposite direction as they increasingly turned towards the creation of institutions that were managerially scaled at the level of the nation. The director of the Economic Relations Section in the League of Nations, Pietro Stoppani, concluded that cotton producers around the world preferred "various kinds of direct and indirect government subsidies and indemnities . . . to the advantages of an international agreement."[40] This is exactly what would happen in the Egyptian Nile Valley. The political-economic conjunctures described above resulted in a multifaceted crisis of accumulation that was differentially experienced by people whose power, wealth, and/or livelihoods were attached to Egyptian cotton. As price turbulence became a signature feature in the lives of people in the Egyptian Nile Valley, political leaders in the 1930s would seek to address its various manifestations through nationally scaled procedures and institutions.

TURMOIL IN THE FIELDS

The collapse of the price of cotton, and the incomes that derived from its export, meant that many cultivators were suddenly unable to repay their loans. By the 1930s, the accumulation of outstanding debts by medium and large landowners had turned into a veritable mortgage crisis. An estimated one million feddans—nearly 18 percent of the county's cultivated area—had been collateralized by their owners, many of whom suddenly found themselves threatened with foreclosure by major banks.[41] According to official estimates, the mortgages held by landowners represented between 5 and 7 percent of the total value of land in the country.[42] Although this was a relatively low figure, the matter was taken very seriously by government officials and financiers because the debtors comprised some of the largest landowners in the country, including members of the royal family. The amount of wealth commanded by landholders did little to mitigate their financial hardships because, as one report succinctly put it, "the bigger the estate, the worse off its owner."[43] Furthermore, the mortgaged properties included some of the best quality land in the country from which more than one and a half million cultivators obtained their livelihoods either directly or indirectly.[44] If tenants on mortgaged land could not pay their rents to landlords who had mistakenly anticipated high revenues when they purchased those lands in the 1920s then the ability of those landlords to repay their loans to mortgage banks would be further compromised.[45]

The majority of the debts were owed to three financial institutions: the Crédit Foncier Égyptien, the Land Bank of Egypt, and the Land and Mortgage Company of Egypt. Because these companies were largely owned by British and French shareholders, most cases of landowner insolvency were presented before the Mixed Courts, which adjudicated disputes between Egyptians and foreigners and still functioned as one of the most powerful judicial authorities in the country. Between 1929 and 1933, the Mixed Courts in Cairo, Alexandria, and Mansura heard more than 4,750 cases involving medium and large properties that resulted in the compulsory resale of 136,266 feddans of land.[46] "Our case [has] reached the most embarrassing of situations," a group of landowners from Mansura complained, "with regard to the confiscation of our properties by the courts and the signing off on administrative seizures [to collect] taxes and outstanding debts."[47] Not only did the forced sales remove properties from the hands of some of the wealthiest owners, they also reduced the value of arable land thereby further increasing the debt burden on many landholders. Between 1930 and 1932, the value of lands that were auctioned in the courts declined by nearly 20 percent, which brought down real estate prices across the country.[48] Regardless of whether or not they lost their properties, most landowners were therefore affected by the mortgage crisis.

Abandoning the price support programs that large landowners had promoted in the 1920s had strained the relationship between the Sidqi government and the General Egyptian Agricultural Syndicate.[49] But the cabinet did adopt a couple of measures to try to prevent the total collapse of the value of land. First, it allocated funds through the newly created Société Foncière d'Égypte (est. 1931) to purchase foreclosed properties and either keep them for five years or resell them to their original owners.[50] Second, it transferred funds directly into the hands of cultivators by remitting a portion of the land tax to them and by becoming less diligent about its enforcement of rural tax collection.[51] A few months before Sidqi's resignation, however, the government began to appease the large landholders more assertively by trying to stem the tide of foreclosures. In March 1933, King Fu'ad decreed Law 7 that aimed to restructure certain mortgage debts that were already within the Mixed Courts system. It placed an eighteen-month moratorium on the pursuit of any legal proceedings against debts that had already been initiated before the courts. Based on agreements with the banks, it then consolidated many arrears held after 1929 with installments that had not yet come due and converted them into new loans that were payable in 30 to 35 annuities at reduced interest.[52] The banks would also forgo some overdue interest and, in return, the government would transfer to them the proceeds from treasury bonds in order to provide them with liquidity.[53] Of the total amount of liquidated claims that were covered by the accord, nearly 60 percent were owed to the Crédit Foncier and the rest were owed to the Land Bank of Egypt, the Land and Mortgage Company of Egypt, and the government.[54] The accord ultimately prevented the foreclosure of nearly 150,000 feddans of agricultural land.[55]

There was a widespread consensus among observers—whether bankers, landowners, politicians, or nationalist intellectuals—that the global depression only hastened the arrival of a mortgage crisis whose seeds had already been sown in the previous decades. But they did not agree on where the source of the crisis lay. The representatives of major banks, trading houses, and the British residency often blamed the profligacy of medium and large landowners for precipitating the mortgage crisis. In their reports to the high commissioner, British merchants and bankers complained that in the early 1920s landowners had engaged in a series of recklessly wasteful expenditures because the price of cotton was relatively high. "The Egyptian is a ready borrower," they reported, "and his optimism leads him to undertake unjustifiable obligations."[56] Navigating the volatilities of the interwar period was therefore a responsibility to which the defective psychology of the Egyptian cultivator was ill suited. Since landowners were responsible for overleveraging themselves, the most vocal representatives and publicists of the mortgage companies—including Samuel Avigdor, Emile Minost, and Elie Politi—repeatedly praised the leniency of the banks towards their debtors, predicted the impending recovery of cotton prices, and argued that landowners were more than capable of repayment.[57] By ascribing the mortgage crisis to the improvidence of Egyptian cultivators, these reports turned a set of contingent behaviors and reactions by large landowners into proof of timeless features that were ingrained in their minds and attitudes.

For their part, the owners of large agricultural properties placed less blame on their own reckless behaviors and more on foreign banks. In August 1931, a former parliamentarian from al-Fayyum charged that the desire for "quick enrichment" through speculative activities only arrived to Egypt with Western financial expansion.[58] Although many Europeans claimed that "the Egyptian cultivator loves to borrow money," he wrote, cultivators had only taken on debts because they believed that "[their] possession of new property was final." In reality, however, the "real owners" were the banks to whom the land was collateralized and whose rights "multiplied abundantly like tiny creatures." Two years later, Nahhas published a series of articles in which he argued that the relatively high price of cotton since 1900 had artificially bolstered the value of land for years and arranged its related transactions—from sales, to mortgages and interest rates, to rents, to rural taxes—on the basis of a fictitious price. "We cannot absolve the banks and the government of responsibility," he wrote. "Rather, the greatest blame falls on them and only the least of it falls on the Egyptian for his passion for acquiring the land."[59] What might have been a reasonable debt burden a few years earlier now represented a liability that exposed landowners to the risk of losing their land.

His diagnosis was echoed by many large landowners who began to organize themselves. More than one hundred notables (*a'yan*) from Munufiyya convened a meeting that year in Kafr Rabi' where they complained that "the mortgage banks [were] on their case, wanting to collect their dues during this difficult time without cutting them any slack."[60] One of the notables, Mustafa Bey Radi, elucidated the mechanisms by which the collapse of land values had compromised the ability of debtors to repay their loans. "The *feddan* that a bank used to accept as security on a loan in exchange for its great estimated value no longer finds anyone who will lend such a sum," he explained. Because the terms of the loans, including repayment schedules and installment sizes, that were agreed upon in the 1920s when the value of land was inflated were no longer suitable, he wondered rhetorically whether it was "fair to ask for installments to be paid as if we were in the days of prosperity?"[61] For that reason, large landowners began to agitate for a more generous restructuring of their rural mortgages. In December 1933, the General Egyptian Agricultural Syndicate held an assembly in which they protested that the settlement concluded with the major banks that year was insufficient given the continued deterioration of the global economic situation. The syndicate put forward a bolder proposal that would require banks to forgive one quarter of the principal on every loan, lower the interest on the remaining portion to 4 percent, make it payable over 60 years, and observe an indefinite moratorium on foreclosures.[62] Those landowners who still failed to pay their installments on time would then have their debts taken over by the government.

Notwithstanding the initial measures taken by the government, the anger of large landholders over the foreclosure and forced sales of their agricultural properties continued to grow in the second half of the decade. In April 1935, hundreds of petitioners identifying themselves as the "notables and property owners of Gharbiyya" protested against what they believed to be government inefficacy in confronting a mortgage crisis that swept through the biggest cotton-producing governorate in the country.[63] The petitioners from Tanta, Kafr al-Shaikh, Talkha, and other districts worried that five years into the depression there was still no end in sight. They complained that the banks refused to compromise on any of the principals or interest they were owed. As a result, foreclosure cases continued to surge in the Mixed Courts. The landowners even accused the banks of forcing the sale of properties whose value greatly exceeded the unpaid debts against which those lands were used as collateral. They complained that previous governments had only acted in the interests of the mortgage banks and, like the General Egyptian Agricultural Syndicate, they recommended that the current government either buy part of their unpaid debts or agree with the banks to restructure the borrowers' mortgages.

As the foreclosures continued, some cultivators began to mount various forms of resistance to the confiscation of their goods and properties. The landowners in Gharbiyya expressed a deep sense of humiliation about having to petition the state or to make any mention of the creditors' ongoing seizures of their seeds and household goods. For fear of a public scandal, many of them even felt embarrassed to file legal claims to try to recover goods confiscated from their families. Instead, some of these debtors tried to physically prevent the confiscation of their goods, preferring "prison and its hardships over the starvation of their women and children."[64] Although large landholders were the main target of these expropriations, they also affected tenant farmers who worked on private estates. In many cases, tenants who had already paid their dues to estate owners still had their share of the land expropriated by banks and put up for auction. For example, a village rebellion broke out in Kafr al-Zayyat after a major bank foreclosed the *'izba* of a notable who had been renting his land to resident workers for more than 20 years.[65] When a bank official arrived in April 1936 to process the foreclosure, the residents of the *'izba* protested and the police intervened. Efforts to intimidate the villagers did not work as they began to cut telephone wires, to burn the official's automobile, and to hurl stones at police officers. Only after multiple security reinforcements arrived were they able to contain the rebellion.

By the mid-1930s, Abdel Wahab acknowledged that the settlement reached between indebted landowners and mortgage banks was insufficient because it did not anticipate the persistence of low cotton prices into the latter half of the decade. The prices of Ashmouni and Sakelleridis cotton had improved only slightly by 1935, but they had not returned anywhere close to their pre-depression levels. Moreover, a boll-weevil attack had ravaged certain areas in the Delta, thereby diminishing the capacity of landowners to repay their annuities. Abdel Wahab concluded there was no way that landowners could earn enough from the sale of cotton in one season to repay their current annuities and their outstanding arrears. Meanwhile, he accused the mortgage banks of "lavishing their boons upon their shareholders, distributing to them dividends unequaled by those distributed by other institutions."[66] Between 1919 and 1933, for example, the Crédit Foncier paid dividends to its shareholders that exceeded 14 percent of the paid-up value of its stocks, and by the end of that period it had accumulated an enormous reserve fund that almost reached 140 percent of its equity capital. As a remedy, Abdel Wahab proposed a combination of urgent relief measures, like extending repayment periods and conducting new value estimates under the supervision of the government, and long-term measures, like demanding that banks draw on their inflated reserve funds to cancel some of the debts owed to them. Doing so would require the banks to "make a small sacrifice in favor of the country's debtors from whom they derive their prosperity and draw their profits."[67] His proposal to alleviate the mortgage crisis began to shift the balance of power in favor of indebted landowners. According to one British official, the banks found themselves in a very difficult position as Abdel Wahab could count on "indiscriminate popular support in attacking them."[68] His offensive against the mortgage companies was bolstered by public appeals to create a national loan that would protect interest-paying Egyptians from the loss of millions of pounds that were "milked annually from the cultivator's sweat into the coffers of the banks and the pockets of the moneylenders."[69] Two more settlements were reached in 1935 and 1936 that resulted in the reduction of mortgage interest rates as well as the government purchase of the vast majority of loans owed to the Mortgage Company of Egypt, an effective buyout that transferred a considerable portion of mortgage activity from the banks into the hands of the state.[70]

By the end of the 1930s, the mortgage crisis had transformed the political economy of Egyptian cotton. The settlement laws undoubtedly benefited the large landholders who constituted the majority of debtors to the three most important banks, rather than smaller cultivators who borrowed from cotton merchants, moneylenders, and landlords.[71] Between 1925 and 1939, more than 70 percent of the foreclosed land that was auctioned came from large holdings of 50 feddans or more.[72] To leverage the powers of the state in the face this crisis, the widespread presence of large landowners in the legislature proved to be boon. The settlement accords were approved by overwhelming majorities in parliament, with one Egyptian senator even remarking that "the problem of mortgage debts [was] more important than the problem of national defense."[73] But the impact of the accords went beyond shoring up the position of the country's landed ruling class. First, they also served to protect medium landowners who were indebted to large mortgage banks against the possibility of foreclosure.[74] Second, they began to transform the structures of agrarian finance that had been firmly established across the country for decades. Between 1931 and 1939, mortgage banks seized 3 to 4 percent of Egypt's cultivated surface area, but the expropriations, forced sales, and settlements failed to uphold the patterns of accumulation that had been pursued for decades by the most powerful financial capitalists in the country.[75] Instead, the crisis helped pave the way for the ultimate demise of land mortgage banks and the forms of agrarian wealth and power that they helped sustain. The case of the Crédit Foncier offered a lucid example. In 1939, its board of directors complained that the settlements, which only imposed a minor penalty for missed payments, allowed many debtors to get away with paying no more than a handful of the installments they owed that typically amounted to 3 or 4 percent of the value of their mortgaged land. Though it had bought a portion of the unpaid loans owed the mortgage banks, the government was unable to collect installments in a timely manner because debtors tried to avoid repayment in whole or in part. "Neglect on the part of borrowers," they wrote, "and growing distrust on the part of creditors are two phenomena that will quickly hit lending at its core if they are not resisted."[76] The directors of the bank realized that no return was possible to the prosperous state of affairs it had enjoyed a quarter century earlier. The total value of the loans owed to the Crédit Foncier had decreased 52 percent from what they were in 1914, and the annual installments due on these loans had fallen by 60 percent. Meanwhile, the Land Bank of Egypt was unable to pay dividends for much of the decade because of its inability to collect sufficient annuities, and in 1936, the Mortgage Bank of Egypt was liquidated and taken over by the government (which effectively became the third-largest lender in the country).[77]

Others, too, realized that the golden age of the mortgage banks was coming to an end. "The banks are no longer looking to develop the network of their debt," wrote one observer at the end of the decade. "It is the fate of their old loans that they care about the most."[78] While these enterprises remained lucrative in the 1930s, the total amount of profits they earned fell sharply because the mortgage settlements imposed on them a heavy financial burden. By 1939, the net profits of the two largest mortgage companies in the country—the Crédit Foncier Égyptien and the Land Bank of Egypt—had fallen more than 40 percent from what they were at the start of the decade.[79] More importantly, the central place they occupied in circuits of capital accumulation in rural Egypt began to wane. At the start of the depression, these banks accounted for 41 percent of the capital of all joint-stock companies in the country, but by 1939 they had reduced their capital by more than half in order to continue making profits.[80] The demise of these mortgage companies represented a major blow to the central institutions that had financed the purchase of land for the production of Egyptian cotton since the turn of the century.

NEW PASSAGES TO OLD PLACES

In January 1933, the managers of the world's railways gathered in Cairo to discuss an emerging crisis. Around 500 delegates traveled from Europe, Asia, and North and South America to attend the twelfth session of the International Railway Congress Association.[81] Standing before the assembly, the president of the association, M. E. Foulon, opened the meeting by underscoring the gravity of the situation. "Transport by rail is traversing a critical period," he warned. The crash that began four years earlier had "calamitous consequences" for the movement of people and goods by trains, leading to an alarming drop in railway revenues around the world. "Railways are the first to suffer from such depressions," he confessed. "They are therefore anxious to overcome them and all their efforts are centered on that purpose."[82] To elaborate on the particular manifestations of the crisis in Egypt, Abdel Wahab published a study for the occasion of the conference.[83] He acknowledged that the depression had brought about a significant reduction in the revenues of the world's railways. But he also emphasized that they were suffering from a more lasting challenge: the invention of the internal combustion engine. By the 1930s, trains that were powered by steam were facing growing competition from motor vehicles that burned fuel.

The history of the railways, Abdel Wahab recounted, was one of indiscriminate expansion. Motivated by technological zeal and easy profits, railway owners and promoters in the nineteenth and early twentieth centuries eagerly built tracks anywhere they could, regardless of whether or not they did it in areas that were "compatible with the nature of the railways." He estimated that one-third of the railway lines in Egypt were built where they were not needed. But this state of affairs changed the day fuel burning became a widely used source of motive power. The competition that ensued between vying modes of transportation was, in Abdel Wahab's view, a doubled-edged sword. On the one hand, it helped to expose the historical excesses of the railways and it could possibly correct them. On the other hand, it could create a wasteful and uncoordinated transportation system. This landscape of rivalrous machines in motion threatened to throw local, regional, and international systems of trade into disorder. Only through greater planning could Egypt enjoy what Abdel Wahab called a "perfect system of transport"—an optimizing technological order in which people and things only moved on those means of mobility best suited to them.

In the 1920s and 1930s, moving cotton along railways, riverways, and roadways in the Egyptian Nile Valley became the focus of an intensifying feud. The development of the internal combustion engine after World War I along with the decision of the state railways to maintain wartime increases in freight charges invited competition from inland navigation companies and road haulers who were able to capture a greater portion of local trade.[84] Most of the navigation companies were affiliated with the Federation of Egyptian Industries, and by the end of the decade they formed an active business lobby. In 1928, they created the Chamber of Inland Navigation of Egypt to advocate for policies favorable to river transport. The network brought various strands of Egypt's interwar bourgeoisie into the business of moving cotton. It included companies like Central Navigation, Egyptian Star Navigation, United Egyptian Nile Transport, and La Fluviale that were mostly owned by foreign residents as well as the Société Misr Pour le Transport et la Navigation that was largely owned by Tal'at Harb and 'Abdullah Fikri Abaza.[85]

Most of these inland navigation companies used barges drawn by power-driven tugs or self-propelled boats to transport cotton along the river, usually from the Sa'id to Alexandria. Their numbers were dwarfed by thousands of smaller wooden sailboats (*dahabias* and *feluccas*) that employed tens of thousands of laborers who moved cotton regularly from fields to local markets and railway stations.[86] After picking their cotton, many cultivators would package it into hessian bags and transport them on camels—usually two sacks per animal—to the nearest point along the river. Once it arrived, boatmen would load the cotton bags onto *dahabias* and *feluccas* and take them to a wharf near the market where the crop was sold. Transporting cotton by sailboat from the villages where it was grown to Alexandria was a time-consuming endeavor. First, a single sailboat could only transport between 100 and 350 sacks of cotton; if two boats were lashed together as a pontoon it could carry up to 700 sacks. Moving any larger amount of cotton required a fleet of sailboats. Second, *dahabias* and *feluccas* were not propelled by mechanical engines, and so they moved slower than power-driven vessels. A sailboat could travel a distance of 250 miles in ten days, while a mechanically propelled vessel could travel 300 miles—for example, from Minya to Alexandria—in as little as seven days.[87] Within a decade and a half, the inland navigation companies were operating nearly 350 power-driven vessels with a carrying capacity of 40,000 tons that could rival these sailboats.[88]

The struggle between mechanized vessels and trains that ensued happened along the axes of what scholars have called relational space. For those seeking to profit from moving cotton, the ideal route between two points was not measured by its distance, but rather by the time it took to complete a trip and the money that it generated.[89] More than entrepreneurial acumen or ingenuity, moving cotton lucratively depended on auspicious political management. The railway administrators employed a couple of strategies to configure the dimensions of relational space in a way that ensured the profitable shipment of cotton by trains. First, the natural and built environment of the Nile River imposed geographical limits on mobility that Egyptian State Railways (ESR) officials could harness to their advantage. The valley had long been an integrated space where the physical makeup of the river determined where people and goods could move. In a 1928 report, which the chamber endorsed, British engineer Henry Ashman Reed argued that the construction of irrigation works since the nineteenth century, especially in the Nile Delta, had disfavored river navigation.[90] Building new dams, barrages, and canals brought great benefits to agriculture and created new navigable routes, but they also introduced a network of locks and bridges that hampered the movement of waterborne traffic. As the decade wore on, the inland navigation firms protested that this lopsided transportation system led to uneven geographical development. "Of a total of 3571 residential centers—cities, villages, and localities—no more than 496 are served by the railways of the state," one representative of the navigation firms complained. "We find ourselves in an age where, more than ever, 'time is money,' and where the sluggishness of trains, especially freight trains, are no longer in harmony with the exigencies of commerce and industry."[91] Reaching many of those areas required that vessels move through a vast network of canals that furrowed the Nile Valley. Only three of those canals—Baguriyya, Mahmudiyya, and Isma'iliyya—were used for fluvial transport while the majority of vessels moved along the main waters of the Nile River that were less encumbered by irrigation infrastructure. Those vessels that did travel along canals in Lower Egypt suffered from endless waits at bridges and locks, poorly timed interruptions during periods of cleaning, and frequent traffic jams that resulted in considerable losses of both time and money for river transporters.[92] Though power-driven vessels moved faster than sailboats, they did not necessarily navigate the river waters as easily. The ability of vessel owners to move cotton profitably depended on the infrastructural landscape through which it traveled, not just the technological capacities of the vessels themselves. In 1840, the journey from Alexandria to 'Atf, the closest point to Cairo on the Mahmudiyya canal, took between 12 and 14 hours. By the middle of the twentieth century, the same trip took two days because of "numerous locks and bridges, uncoordinated and inadequate openings, and other obstacles."[93] In the end, the creation of a rational system of transport was not a straightforward matter of assigning technologies to those routes best suited to them. The refusal to lift restrictions on waterborne traffic, to dredge existing waterways, and to build adequate tow paths and navigable channels signaled that the government was ultimately invested in harnessing the river to grow crops, rather than to move people and goods.[94] The obstacles that confronted inland navigation ultimately worked to maintain the relative monopoly of the state railways over freight transport.

Second, the managers of the state railways could pull away traffic from their competitors by either manipulating the costs of moving cotton or by regulating the quantities of cotton that navigation companies were permitted to transport. When the depression began, the ESR—the country's biggest shipper of cotton to Alexandria—was already locked in a decade-long rivalry with navigation companies over freight charges. The purpose of these rate wars, as the firms called them, was for each side to attract customers by lowering the cost of carrying cargo by river and rail. They became particularly acute at the turn of the decade because of the renewed restrictions on cotton acreage by the government and the reduction of cheap imported goods that resulted from the tariff reforms.[95] As cotton prices sank in the early 1930s, the competition between the state railways and the navigation companies became less tenable. Although the state railways had charged preferential rates for years—usually through multiyear contracts with individuals or companies for the transport of vital commodities, including cotton—the general trend was for freight rates to increase on the long run, especially for cotton transported at the risk of the ESR.[96] Abdel Wahab complained that freight costs were too high at a time when cotton prices had fallen so low. Between 1913 and 1930, the cost of shipping cotton by rail to Alexandria had increased across major train stations, in some cases by as much as 300 percent. "If the railways could reduce the freight charges on cotton," he wrote, "the charges for water transport would come down at the same time from the high and unjustifiable level at which they now stand."[97] Because the world was passing through a difficult crisis, one Egyptian senator wrote in 1931, it was imperative to adjust the costs of transport by rail and river relative to the depressed prices of cotton.[98] That year, the administration of the railways was placed in the hands of a reconstituted Supreme Railway Board—in part to keep railway matters outside of parliamentary control—and it immediately decided to reduce freight costs for cotton.[99]

After lowering their rates, the managers of the ESR became dissatisfied with the share of revenue that the system of competitive pricing had earned them. In a memorandum to the board, the general director of the state railways, Muhammad Shafiq, complained that the reduction in freight charges after 1930—namely at train stations near ginning factories or on lines running parallel to riverways—did not boost the volume of ginned cotton transported by rails, while the amount of cotton shipped by river was increasing steadily.[100] Two years later, he candidly observed that many of the shareholders of the navigation companies were themselves cotton merchants who preferred to use rivers over rails.[101] The majority of their activities involved moving cotton along the main waters of the Nile, from the Saʿid to Alexandria, which were not encumbered by bridges and locks in the way that existed in the Nile Delta. To stymie this competition, ESR officials reached an accord with the navigation companies to regulate the quantities of cotton that each side was allowed to move and the prices at which they shipped them. In 1933, they agreed to reserve the transport of cotton and grain from the Saʿid for the navigation

FIGURE 6. A barge loaded with bales of cotton on the Nile River. Source: Getty Images.

companies. The companies would be allowed to set river transportation rates with the consent of the ESR and they could only increase them in tandem with railway fares. As a result, the ESR reversed the fare reductions it had introduced in previous years, and in return, the navigation companies promised not to transport any grain, cotton, or cottonseed from the Nile Delta to Alexandria.[102] As rail receipts from the Saʿid declined, the head of the ESR amended the agreement in 1934 to allow the five largest navigation companies to transport 2,400,000 *qintars* of cotton and anything above that would be subjected to a 30 percent indemnity to the ESR.[103]

The accords between the ESR and the navigation companies appeared to work briefly. In June 1934, E. W. Slaughter, the deputy chief mechanical engineer for the state railways, delivered one of the first radio addresses on the government's newly established broadcasting station. "When taking the air on the new Khedive Ismaʿil Bridge," he boasted, "[many of us] will have realized the recent development of river transport when seeing the efficient power-driven boats hauling cargoes of cotton and produce to Alexandria."[104] But the arrangement did not last long. As the threat of war once again loomed, cotton exporters felt pressure to get rid of the 1936 crop while shipping across the Mediterranean was still easily accessible. They urged ginners and commercial agents in the interior to move large amounts of cotton to Alexandria as soon as possible. Premiums for cotton that was immediately deliverable skyrocketed so quickly that traders raced to gin and ship everything they had physically available to them. The government reacted by prohibiting the transport of cotton from the Saʿid by power-driven vessels that competed with trains. What ensued was heavy congestion along the railways as ginning factories and railroad loading docks found themselves overstocked with bales of cotton.[105] Despite the high premiums, ginneries were compelled to rent storage facilities for unused cotton, hire watchmen to look after the stored crops, and pay haulage fees to move cotton to the warehouses. The navigation companies complained that they were left with a "pitiful amount" of cotton and cottonseed for which they had to pay hefty royalties to transport. According to them, the situation laid bare the consequences of government attempts to systematically sabotage river transport in order to safeguard the earnings of the state railways. By 1937, the system of regulated cotton transport collapsed, the rate wars resumed, and freight charges were cut by more than half.[106] But the return to competitive pricing would be short-lived. The arrival of World War II prompted state officials to regulate navigation once again by requiring vessel owners to obtain government authorization and approval for their rates. More importantly it would reorder the country's domestic transportation system in a way that ultimately favored petroleum, and especially road transport, over steam power.[107]

SYMBOLS AND STANDARDS IN MINA AL-BASAL

The Great Depression was a profoundly transformative experience for major export houses in Alexandria. According to a prominent financial journalist, big traders in the early 1930s still "formed a privileged class . . . [that] was the ruling dynasty over the economy of the country."[108] However, the composition of these trading firms, the authority they wielded, and the role they played in the cotton trade began to change. Major European export houses such as those operated by the Carver, Moss, and Lindemann families started to lose the monopoly powers they had built since the nineteenth century as newcomers began to enter the Alexandria cotton trade.[109] As we saw in the previous chapter, Tal'at Harb was the biggest Egyptian tycoon who entered the business of moving and processing cotton. In the 1920s, he established a number of subsidiary firms under Bank Misr that specialized in transport, ginning, and spinning and weaving. In 1929, the bank absorbed what remained of the holdings of the Lindemann family, who exported cotton primarily to manufacturers in Germany, and it created the Société Misr pour L'Exportation du Coton.[110] Another emerging cotton trader was Muhammad Farghali who joined an alliance of businessmen and politicians that formed around the Sidqi government. When he traveled on a trade mission to England in the middle of the decade, an Alexandria-based lawyer affiliated with the AGPA complained to the British Residency that Sidqi had allowed Farghali to ship cotton, especially to Germany, on behalf of the government. "Having sat on Sidqi's side," he wrote, "[Farghali] became his protégé and his exports nearly doubled."[111] As a result, Farghali was disliked by members of the AGPA who went so far as to reject his candidacy in elections for the bourse commission in Alexandria. The emergence of these new traders who championed an Egyptian national identity and who dealt mainly with continental European manufacturers that rivaled Manchester was one of many indications that the AGPA was slowly losing its monopoly over the cotton trade. The biggest signs of the association's gradual demise, however, could be discerned in a variety of disputes over mundane commercial practices.

To operate as a site of regularized transactions, market information in Mina al-Basal circulated through symbols that cultivators, traders, spinners, and state officials mobilized to create a standard set of norms and expectations among themselves. Determining who had the authority to mobilize these symbols and under what conditions was a matter of political struggle. The experience of the depression helped to incubate a set of conflicts over three particular symbols that were widely used to stabilize a variety of potential uncertainties: crop forecasts, cotton types, and weights. In the 1930s, the AGPA faced challenges from rival merchants who wanted to redefine the rules for who could profit from trading cotton, state officials who sought to fashion new powers to predict forecasts and to regulate cotton quality, and workers in the spot market who demanded fairer compensation for their labor. Conflicts between these actors were not reducible to simple dualities, like the state versus the market. Instead, they were articulated through techniques, practices, and concepts that helped constitute those domains rather than being sited within them from the start, and they yielded a variety of evolving alliances.

After the war, the ability to predict every season's crop became a domain of contestation. A precipitous fall in the price of cotton stirred anxieties among newly empowered national elites, leading members of an economic council that Sidqi had assembled in 1921 to observe that "the great mass of Egyptian producers . . . are very ill informed about the general workings of things and find themselves at the mercy of a small interested minority."[112] They complained that only a handful of brokerage houses possessed comprehensive information about prices, competition, and overseas markets that was not available to the majority of Egyptian cotton farmers. Estimating the size of the cotton crop from one season to another had long been an operation monopolized by the AGPA, and according to its vice-president, it constituted "one of the most delicate tasks of the association."[113] The AGPA published monthly reports on the cotton crop from April to November (with the October issue containing forecasts for the next season) based on information it had received from its correspondents around the country.[114] Making an estimate was a process more than a single act. It began with qualitative observations about land, water, crops, weather, disease, and people from the moment cotton was sowed until it was picked. Turning these observations by correspondents into a quantitative prediction was no straightforward matter. The correspondents' reports were compiled by a cotton subcommittee that was elected at the AGPA's general meeting, and it would use this information to set maximum and minimum projections. Each committee member would then make their own estimate that ranged anywhere between those two figures, and the mean of all the individual estimates would become the association's crop forecast for the upcoming season. From its creation in 1911, the Department of Agriculture (which became a ministry two years later) began to publish regular "condition reports" that also included crop estimates for the upcoming season.[115] Provincial inspectors closely monitored cotton, and they estimated the size of the crop at every stage from sowing until picking. In the first week of November, they would obtain data about actual yields from cotton producers, including large estate owners and smallholders. Every inspector would then give a forecast for his province, and they would be compared and aggregated into a final estimate for the entire country. Beginning in 1924, the Cotton Research Board began to direct the work of agricultural statistics, including crop forecasting, and its technical secretary obtained data from a wider range of sources, including cultivators, provincial agents, ginning managers, bank representatives, and traders. As the decade wore on, the estimates produced by the board and published by the ministry competed with those of the AGPA.

Predicting the size of a season's crop in the Egyptian Nile Valley was supposed to be relatively simple since most of the crop left the country through one port in Alexandria where figures could be verified.[116] Regardless of who made them, however, crop estimates encountered serious difficulties because the qualitative properties of the landscape in which raw cotton was produced and traded were not stable. Provincial inspectors and AGPA correspondents had to contend with many irregularities including bad weather, pest attacks, poor acreage statistics collected by *sarrafs* (tax collectors), misreports by cultivators, and variable levels of consumption in the interior. This made it hard to predict the size of an upcoming season's crop with any precision.[117] To get around these problems, forecasters turned qualitative irregularities into quantitative averages. Crop forecasts represented an approximation derived from smaller individual estimates that the AGPA received from traders and that the ministry received from provincial inspectors. Both of them distrusted the information they obtained from local officials and cultivators; as a result, they took considerable liberties in calculating their figures. Many traders, for example, routinely inflated their estimates by at least 10 percent because they did not trust the numbers provided by government officials.[118] Meanwhile, provincial inspectors only gathered information about actual yields from cultivators that were "known to keep proper records of their crop."[119] The results were highly inconsistent estimates that were rarely accurate.[120] By the 1930s, the statistics produced by the government were increasingly regarded as "the basis of a more reliable calculation of the crop actually grown in each agricultural year."[121]

The battle over standardizing cotton types was more protracted. The collapse of prices in 1930 meant that many of the costs associated with moving cotton from the fields where it was grown to the market in Mina al-Basal suddenly become more burdensome. Transforming raw cotton into an exportable commodity required several stages of processing—from ginning, to pressing, to baling—most of which were paid for by cultivators.[122] A central plank of Abdel Wahab's new cotton program was to reduce those outlays. Although it did not form the largest portion of cultivators' expenses, the cost of storage could be easily reduced. Most of the raw cotton that reached Mina al-Basal was kept in warehouses (*shunas*) that were owned either by banks, pressing companies, or export houses. Many cultivators, traders, and state officials preferred to store their cotton in Alexandria because its facilities were more spacious and better equipped than those in the rest of the country. For that reason, the cost of renting space there for large volumes of cotton could become quite prohibitive.

But storage costs were as much a function of the technologies used to prepare cotton for export as the people handling it. To ship the largest amount possible in a single overseas trip, raw cotton that arrived to Mina al-Basal in bulky sacks had to be compressed into densely packed bales before being loaded onto steamers that moved it across the Mediterranean. Pressing was done by machines that could be powered either by a hydraulic cylinder or by a steam compress. Most of the cotton that was shipped to Mina al-Basal by rail or river was already pressed hydraulically before it got there. It would then be stored in *shunas*, and exporters would unbale the cotton before shipping it so that they could prepare their consignment according to the specifications of a spinner's order. This meant that raw cotton was effectively pressed twice: once by hydraulic press in the interior and once by steam after being prepared for export in the port city.[123] The choice of pressing method largely determined how the bales of cotton were stored. Because they were heavier, steam-pressed bales could be stacked one on top of another. Three bales of steam-pressed cotton could be stored in the space taken up by one bale of hydraulically pressed cotton. A lot of money could be saved—about L.E. 1.5 million annually in Abdel Wahab's estimation—if double-pressing was eliminated. "If all cotton coming into Alexandria was steam-pressed immediately on its arrival," he wrote, "those figures might be reduced to about one third of the present charges for storage and to about one half for the cost of insurance."[124] The only reason that prevented it from happening was that exporters insisted on adhering to a well-established system of types that they had fashioned long ago for selling Egyptian cotton. Making a simple adjustment to existing storage practices during the depression therefore required something of an overhaul of long-standing trading practices in Mina al-Basal.

Before the 1920s, the power to guarantee cotton quality was held almost exclusively by the AGPA. Every trading company in Alexandria had developed its own "in-house" types of cotton that were tailored specifically for manufacturers in Europe with whom the firm had a long-standing relationship.[125] Brokers were responsible for guaranteeing that each bale of cotton they sold contained a uniform variety that was agreed upon with their buyers. The authority to determine types was not simply a matter of satisfying spinners in England who expected their purchased cotton to meet certain quality standards. It also affected the extent to which speculators in the futures market could make a profit. Confronting the AGPA's de facto monopoly over the regulation of quality was simultaneously an effort to rein in speculators on the Alexandria bourse, many of whom were members of the association. In the mid-1920s, state officials who had access to greater legislative powers after the country gained its nominal independence began a 12-year endeavor to re-standardize Egyptian cotton.

The price slump in 1926 had already prompted the government to pass legislation that aimed to prohibit the mixing of cotton types (which it modified in subsequent years) and to regulate speculative activity on the bourse.[126] But spinners in England were not entirely satisfied. The following year, delegates from the International Federation of Master Cotton Spinners' and Manufacturers' Association warned traders in Alexandria about the dangers of mixing different types of cotton in the same bale and implored them to take energetic measures against it. "Among those who cultivate cotton," said W. Heaps of the Manchester Cotton Association, "there is no country except for Egypt that deliberately makes every effort to depreciate its cottons by mixing together different varieties."[127] Three years later, Nahhas submitted a report to Finance Minister Makram 'Ubayd calling for the government to exercise greater control over the spot market in Mina al-Basal and over the standardization of cotton types to improve the situation of cultivators.[128] As the depression gathered pace, the government attempted to pass new legislation, but some of the most powerful cotton traders in the country stood against it. In June 1930, it proposed a law that would both require any exporter who purchased cotton in rural Egypt to secure a government-issued permit and allow state officials to seize cotton for inspection after the bales had been pressed in Alexandria. Major exporters, like Herbert B. Carver and Constantin J. Chorémi, objected vehemently on grounds that the proposed law would not only threaten them with financial losses; more importantly, it would empower state officials, who they claimed lacked practical knowledge of the cotton trade that merchants had accumulated over decades, to prevent exporters from doing business freely with their buyers. As one reporter observed, "Their objections relate less to the provisions of the law than to its very principle."[129] Meanwhile, the big exporters in the AGPA tried to blunt any criticisms directed at them by Western manufacturers by undertaking their own internal reforms, rather than by submitting to the dictates of the government. For example, English spinners had repeatedly complained that the level of humidity in Egyptian cotton was too high.[130] Optimizing the moisture content of the crop was crucial to ensuring that it did not become too dry, which could make the fibers brittle, or too damp, which could cause it to mold.[131] Of course, individual bales of cotton could be tested for moisture, but cotton was priced by type, not by the bale. In 1931, Alexandria-based exporters signed a provisional accord with English spinners to regulate the level of humidity in Egyptian cotton, and they would renew it annually.[132]

Abdel Wahab's cotton memorandum included a proposal to completely restandardize Egyptian cotton varieties. Rather than allowing every export house to determine their own special types, as the old system did, he proposed to create a standardized list of cottons that ginners and traders would prepare under government supervision before it reached Alexandria. In the early 1930s, Abdel Wahab presided over a contentious meeting with exporters in which his allegation that they were all thieves prompted those in attendance to get up and leave the room.[133] He was joined by others in distinguishing between smaller traders in the countryside and big exporters in Alexandria where much of the merchant capital invested in the cotton trade was concentrated. "For the exporter who buys in the interior," wrote Hugo Lindemann, the managing director of the Société Misr pour L'Exportation du Coton, "the difference [between paying fees for double pressing or not] is not that big, but it is for the trader who sends his cotton to Mina al-Basal to be sold."[134] To exert more abiding control over the AGPA, Abdel Wahab also proposed to change the composition of the bourse commission and its various committees that administered Mina al-Basal to include fewer representatives of Alexandria-based export houses who dominated the body and more cultivators and traders from the interior.[135] His efforts drew opposition from merchants and bankers who claimed to possess authoritative knowledge and experience that made them uniquely qualified to determine what kinds of cotton to supply to their buyers. "[P]rogress in the distribution of our cotton," wrote A. W. Jessop, a representative of Barclays Bank and the president of the AGPA, "depends more on the individual ability of our exporters to give the mills exactly what they want."[136] While the standardization of cotton types would not happen until the end of the decade, the AGPA would soon be governed by new regulations, it would be brought under the oversight of government officials, and its activities would be opened up to a greater diversity of people.

The distinction these big exporters drew between the regulatory abilities of the state and the inherited competencies of private enterprise was something of a misnomer. The commercial activities of the AGPA could not function without a state that built railways and roads to transport crops, constructed irrigation works to expand cultivation, promoted new cotton strains to increase yields, enacted laws and regulations to manage trading activities, and organized policing and security around the country. Its members were more than willing to appeal directly to the government when they needed the support of bureaucrats, courts, and police. One of the more decisive appeals to state authority by the AGPA happened in 1931 in response to a series of labor strikes led by an inconspicuous group that worked largely on a seasonal basis in Mina al-Basal.

The daily trading activities that took place in the Alexandria market could not function without the work of thousands of porters, wagon drivers, and weighers who were employed either directly or indirectly by the AGPA. The vast majority of them were peasants who worked in Alexandria for four or five months during the cotton season and returned to their villages for the rest of the year.[137] An estimated 10,000 porters who handled cotton in the warehouses where it was stored or on the docks where it was loaded formed the largest group of laborers. A separate group of around 1,000 porters carried cotton in the stations where it was weighed. No matter where they worked in the market, porters were the lowest paid laborers in Mina al-Basal, earning between five and ten piasters per day. Another group of workers consisted of 2,000 drivers that were hired by ten wagon companies to move raw cotton around the market. A wagoner typically earned more than double the daily earnings of a porter. The smallest group of laborers in Mina al-Basal specialized in weighing cotton. They formed a minor segment of the 5,000 or so weighers around the country who made their living largely in the cotton and jewelry trades and who were required by law to obtain an official license from the government even if they were employed by private entities.[138] Weighers could perform their jobs at different points in the lifecycle of cotton. Some of them traveled around villages with their steelyards and weighed cotton in the fields where it was harvested. Others weighed the crop in *halaqas* where larger amounts of cotton were collected. By the late 1920s, however, provincial authorities had closed down many *halaqas* due to their high maintenance costs.[139] The most organized group worked in Alexandria where the AGPA hired about 300 individuals to weigh all the cotton that arrived there.

Most of the workers in Mina al-Basal were hired on a seasonal basis by labor contractors (*muta'ahidun*). These intermediaries collected lump sums from the AGPA from which they deducted a commission for themselves and distributed whatever remained to the porters and wagoners on a piece-rate basis. Because they mediated interactions between most workers in Mina al-Basal and the AGPA, many contractors "look[ed] upon themselves as quasi-employers," and in labor disputes they would often become the target of complaints by seasonal workers.[140] By contrast, cotton weighers worked directly for the AGPA and had to be certified by the government. One observer described them as "a strong organized body" that could exercise leverage over their employers and government officials.[141] When the government adopted new countrywide standards for oscillating steelyards in 1916, for example, the weighers in Mina al-Basal rejected them and continued to use their older steelyards whose readings, officials warned, could be altered by slight pressure from the fingers of the weigher. Only after the government threatened to take over the weighing of cotton entirely did the weighers capitulate. Since weighers had to be licensed by the government they usually worked on a permanent basis for the AGPA because they were harder to replace than porters and wagoners. Due to the small size of their workforce, its experience in collective action, and the relative stability of their jobs, the weighers managed to organize themselves into a trade union, the Mina al-Basal Weighers' Syndicate.

The work stoppage in Mina al-Basal happened against a backdrop of heightened labor activism and its repression by the state.[142] The Wafd returned to power in 1930 amidst widespread layoffs and wage reductions induced by the depression. Their short tenure witnessed a revival of labor activism, especially by workers employed by the state railways and the Suez Canal Company. When the Sidqi government was installed six months later it responded by creating a permanent labor office headed by R. M. Graves inside the British-run

FIGURE 7. Weighing cotton in Alexandria, Egypt in 1930. Source: Getty Images.

interior ministry in order to monitor the labor movement. By early 1931, worker protests had spread against Sidqi's new electoral law that imposed suffrage restrictions, and a newly established trade union federation led by a rebellious member of the royal family, ʿAbbas Halim, grew to include tens of thousands of members. As the government deployed police agents to infiltrate meetings, to shut down trade union offices, and to intimidate unionized workers, there was little space left for labor activism by the middle of the year. In this repressive context, nearly 15,000 workers in Mina al-Basal took collective action.

The strikes in Mina al-Basal grew out of a sequence of events that began during World War I. The sharp fluctuations in Egyptian cotton prices between 1919 and 1924 were accompanied by a sudden increase followed by a reduction of wages in Mina al-Basal. As cotton prices fell further in the 1920s, the AGPA refused to pay wages that were previously owed to its workers. In March 1931, cotton porters and wagoners in Mina al-Basal went on strike to demand a raise. Their leaders were invited to the provincial headquarters where the subgovernor of Alexandria reached an agreement with them for a new piece-rate system.[143] Four months later, the leaders of the AGPA decided to reduce wages in Mina al-Basal by 25 percent, and some contractors assented to its decision. Rather than split the pay cut between themselves and the workers, contractors asked wagoners and porters to bear the entirety of the reduction. As a result, the announcement by the AGPA was met with widespread opposition in Mina al-Basal. When a delegate from the interior ministry failed to reach a compromise in late August, the possibility of another strike suddenly became imminent. Anticipating a large-scale workers' action, an Irish member of the Alexandria police, Colonel Fitzpatrick Bey, began to meet with labor leaders and high-ranking security officials. More importantly, he turned to the president of the AGPA, A. W. Jessop, for counsel on how to move forward. To prevent the spread of the strike throughout the city, they believed that a combination of "great force and pressure on the one hand with a conciliatory attitude on the other" had become necessary.[144]

On September 2, 1931, thousands of workers in Mina al-Basal began their strike—what one member of the British Consular Service described as "the biggest industrial movement that has ever taken place [in Alexandria]."[145] With the threat of paralysis looming over the cotton trade, police forces along with a unit of sentinel soldiers moved in during the early hours of the morning to guard those laborers who were still willing to do their jobs and to arrest strikers who attempted to sabotage equipment or to prevent others from going to work. Only after the police crackdown did strikers and the AGPA begin to negotiate a settlement. Wagoners and porters only interacted with the AGPA through the contractors who had hired them and who the workers accused of betrayal. Ahmad Sadiq al-Ajhuri, a lawyer who represented a group of transport workers in Mina al-Basal, submitted a petition on their behalf to Prime Minister Sidqi that was published on the front page of the country's flagship newspaper. "The transport workers of Mina al-Basal, who number more than 1,600 persons, seek your majesty's intervention," they protested, ". . . to champion them in the face of the contractors who have broken their previous pledges."[146] Representatives of all the workers in Mina al-Basal were eventually summoned to meet directly with their employers in the headquarters of the Alexandria governorate, but the negotiations between seasonal workers, the weighers' syndicate, contractors, and AGPA executives were inconclusive. To reach a settlement, the governor himself presided over a session at the Labor Conciliation Board in which he "practically dictated Mr. Jessop's terms to the strike leaders."[147] While the second strike in Mina al-Basal only lasted briefly, it indicated that the AGPA's ability to control its own workforce, either directly or through contractors, could not exist without the coercive and arbitrational capacities of the state.[148] Relying on these kinds of overt political intervention, however, did not completely stifle labor activism. Over the following years, workers in Mina al-Basal would continue to threaten collective action over their wages and working conditions.[149]

By the end of the decade, the AGPA had lost its monopoly control over the spot market in Alexandria and, in the process, it was profoundly transformed. First, the constitution of the AGPA was reorganized to allow government officials more control over its operations. As we saw, the composition of the administrators that oversaw its activities changed to include fewer representatives of Alexandria-based export houses and more cultivators and traders from the interior. In December 1931, the name of the association was changed to "Bourse des Cotons et Graines de Coton Disponibles" or Bourse de Mina al-Basal for short.[150] Control over the production of commercial statistics about cotton—forecasts, arrivals, exports, stocks, and prices—was no longer in the exclusive hands of the big export houses that dominated the association. Whereas in the

1920s the Ministry of Finance simply recorded the weekly prices of different varieties of cotton in Mina al-Basal as quoted by the AGPA in its bulletins, now government officials maintained a statistical service in Mina al-Basal and actively worked with traders to produce this data.[151] As the ability to produce market data—in the form of estimates, price quotations, and shipping statistics—began to move from the hands of Alexandria-based export houses to government officials in Cairo, so too did efforts to gather, examine, and interpret this information.

Second, the AGPA lost the battle over the standardization of cotton types. The Minister of Agriculture Ali al-Manzalawi spoke candidly in 1934 about the impact of standardization on exporters in Alexandria. "Some traders might be inconvenienced by no longer being able to continue a profitable trade," he said in an interview. "As respectable as their interests may be, they will themselves agree that we cannot allow the general interest of Egypt to be sacrificed any longer."[152] Four years later the system of special types that had long been essential to the AGPA's operations was permanently eliminated. In July 1938, the palace issued Law 59 by royal decree to regulate the varieties of Egyptian cotton.[153] It contained an appendix that specified nine varieties of cotton that cultivators were allowed to grow and prohibited the cultivation of any other varieties. Any types of cotton that were not on this official list were not allowed to be grown. The list was amended several times in the next few years. The decision marked a victory for the alliance of large landowners and nationalist politicians that had spent years trying to constrain the powers of the AGPA. Nahhas himself remarked that the extension of government control over Mina al-Basal and the standardizing of cotton types was the high point of his friendship with Abdel Wahab.[154] At stake in their conflict with Alexandria-based merchants was not whether the state or the market should regulate quality. Rather, it was the kinds of monopoly powers that were necessary to wield control over the reputation of Egyptian cotton and in whose hands those powers belonged. Reorganizing the accumulation of capital from an imperial scale to a national scale in the Egyptian Nile Valley simultaneously involved a relocation of various regulatory and epistemic powers—especially the power to produce market data and to regulate cotton quality—from banks and export houses in Alexandria to offices and research centers in Cairo.

GOLD, COTTON, AND NATIONAL CURRENCY

In the interwar period, the relationship between currency, empire, and international trade underwent a profound transformation. Prior to World War I, the gold standard served as the foundation of stable commercial exchanges that facilitated "free trade" on an imperial scale. The British government ended this arrangement during the war. It briefly tried to restore the pound's convertibility to gold in 1925, but it abandoned this effort six years later as its budget and balance of payments deficits grew, and large sums of gold held in London began to be withdrawn. The definitive collapse of the gold standard in 1931 amounted to what Giovanni Arrighi has called "the terminal crisis of British rule over the world's money."[155] For the next few decades, Britain's imperial monetary system came to rely on the sterling area—a monetary bloc made up of countries and colonies that conducted much of their trade with Britain, that linked their currencies to the pound, and that held some or all of their foreign exchange reserves in sterling.[156]

Alongside these readjustments that emanated from London, the management of money underwent its own changes in the Egyptian Nile Valley. As we saw in chapter 1, the war prompted a shift from a monetary system based on flows of gold coins that were managed largely by the local branches of private European banks to a system of paper money issued by the National Bank of Egypt. The value of the Egyptian pound became linked to the pound sterling—what became known as the sterling exchange standard. This shift in the workings of the country's monetary system had three major implications. First, the National Bank of Egypt acquired a monopoly over issuing paper money, which had become legal tender, and it emerged as one of the most important financial institutions in the country. According to one observer in the mid-thirties, it had become analogous to one of two suns (the other being Bank Misr) that lay at the "centre of the Egyptian firmament."[157] Second, the volume of notes issued by the bank became the principal vector that facilitated the export of raw cotton and that moved in relation to it. Every year, the money it put into circulation would begin to increase in September, reach its peak during the cotton harvest in October, and then steadily return to the bank after the settlement of imports, debts, and merchandise purchases.[158] "An excess of exports over imports will result in an increase of the note issue in Egypt," wrote Bresciani-Turroni in 1934, "while before the war it resulted in a net inflow of gold."[159] Third, the new arrangement tied the fortunes of Egyptians, and particularly its capitalist classes, more closely to the fate of the British monetary system. The monetary wealth that Egyptians possessed could be subject to inflationary pressures that emanated from the relationship of Britain, rather than Egypt, to the rest of the world.[160]

The management of money in interwar Egypt was a highly contentious matter. In conventional accounts, the collapse of the gold standard is often associated with the demise of economic liberalism that accompanied the weakening of the British empire. According to Barry Eichengreen and Peter Temin, the gold standard fostered a set of attitudes and convictions among bankers, financiers, and politicians in Western Europe and the United States that persisted into the 1930s, even after the system's formal demise.[161] These included a firm belief that the unhindered movement of gold (and the trade imbalances it reflected) were self-regulating; that international monetary stability stimulated foreign investment; and that the gold standard encouraged deflation and balanced budgets. The persistence of what they call a "gold standard mentality" delayed the embrace of Keynesian policies among Western countries even though deficit-financed expansion was necessary to deal with unemployment and low economic growth during the Great Depression. But the actors in Egypt who debated whether the country should have kept its currency pegged to the pound sterling or returned to some version of the gold standard did not fall neatly on either side of this ideological divide. In the minds of Western politicians and financiers, the gold standard mentality might have represented a fanciful conviction that a bygone era of free trade could be easily restored. Outside of the Euro-American world, however, the contours of this debate took on a variety of other forms.

On one side, there were British exporters, advisors, and officials in Egypt who strongly backed the sterling exchange standard. Their justifications largely revolved around protecting the interests of British manufacturers who imported Egyptian cotton. After the British decision to abandon gold convertibility in 1931, the Egyptian government decided to keep the two currencies linked.[162] At the time, Egypt had no bilateral trade agreements or exchange controls, meaning that the movement of money and goods across the country's borders was not subjected to heavy government regulation.[163] Tying the two currencies together would therefore maintain the stability of Egyptian cotton prices in pounds sterling, even as the latter fluctuated. In a letter to the British residency, Cook invoked the specter of widespread rural misery in the absence of the sterling exchange standard. "Had [Egypt] followed gold instead of sterling," he wrote, "the Lancashire spinner's pound would have bought in Alexandria about 78 piasters. How many bales of cotton could Egypt have sold on this basis?"[164]

On the other side, there were nationalists, bankers, and currency traders and speculators who wanted to maintain the convertibility of Egyptian pounds into gold. Rather than mount a defense of economic liberalism, these bullion believers represented an untidy blend of interests. Egyptian nationalists were the loudest voice in this chorus. In other parts of the British Empire, a distinctively monetary nationalism had begun to take shape in the interwar period. In India, for example, nationalists challenged the sterling exchange standard on grounds that it only benefited those engaged in foreign trade while preventing the country from exercising sovereign control over its domestic prices, from maintaining the purchasing power of its people, and from ensuring its own access to gold.[165] In Egypt, monetary nationalists opposed the pound's continued linkage to sterling, demanded a return to parity with gold, and supported financial institutions that championed an Egyptian national identity. They did not advocate a gold standard out of an unyielding confidence in the magic of free markets, but rather as an assertion of the powers of the nation-state to manage its own money supply. In the words of one author writing for *al-Ahram*, their demand was to "liberate the Egyptian pound from the hegemony of English sterling."[166]

Egyptian monetary nationalism found an exemplary expression in the writings of Muhammad ʿAli Rifʿat. He studied economics in the United Kingdom, and in 1935, he published his research on the reasons behind Egypt's insertion into the sterling exchange standard.[167] He acknowledged that printing emergency money during the 1914 banking crisis was a necessary measure on the part of the National Bank of Egypt to avoid financial collapse in the early days of the war. But there was no need to continue such emergency measures once shippers resumed their ability to transport gold across the Mediterranean Sea. That they did so led Rifʿat to believe there was another rationale behind the adoption of the sterling exchange standard in Egypt: to stabilize the rate of exchange between the two currencies in order to safeguard the cotton trade.

This became especially imperative as the value of the British pound depreciated after the war. "It was the recognition of these facts," he wrote, "that convinced the 'Englishmen' who 'controlled the machinery of Government' that the interests of Great Britain required the abandonment of the gold standard in Egypt, and its replacement by a sterling-exchange system."[168] As the depression proceeded, monetary nationalists continued to attack the National Bank for keeping the country's currency regime firmly tied to Britain's imperial monetary system. They began to agitate for the creation of a central bank so that monetary policy could be made in Cairo, not in London.[169]

The demise of the gold standard signaled the end of imperial globalization. Over half a century, the pound sterling went from being the dominant currency in the capitalist world economy before World War I, to a system of money imposed by the British imperial state on its dependent territories in the interwar period, to a national currency that lost much of its status as world money in the postwar era.[170] In Egypt, these changes unleashed a variety of conflicts over the country's monetary system. Those who wanted to see the Egyptian pound return to parity with gold stood against powerful interests in London that refused to concede, and as a result, Egypt would remain a member of the sterling area until 1947. In the process, the nature of money underwent a transformation that would not be reversed. As commercial transactions between actors in different states became increasingly mediated by nationally managed money supplies, the question of exchange rates, international reserves, and monetary sovereignty became a major arena of contention that would shape Egyptian politics in the age of national independence.

CONCLUSION

The experience of the Great Depression in the Egyptian Nile Valley transformed many of the institutions that constituted the four monopolistic domains through which Egyptian cotton had been financed, produced, and traded since the nineteenth century. The state railways, the mortgage banks, and the Alexandria merchants' association were considerably weakened. Meanwhile, the large landowners survived the depression, partly because of the support they received from the government, but their predominant accumulation strategies would fundamentally change over the next decade. More importantly, the depression began to lay the material foundations for an ideological shift that would happen in the late 1940s and 1950s as Egyptian nationalists grappled intellectually with the significance of the transformations that were brought upon the political economy of cotton.

The depression represented something of an ending to a longer chapter in the history of economic thought in Egypt. The statement by Cook, the governor of the National Bank of Egypt, with which we opened this chapter represented a view that had become common sense among many nationalists over the previous two decades. In the 1910s and 1920s, they had consistently warned that the exposure of Egyptians to the perilous volatilities of foreign markets and capital was the main threat that colonial rule had introduced into the country. After the Great Depression, however, a younger cohort of intellectuals and political activists turned their attention to a new villain whom they blamed for inflicting misery on the countryside: the large landholding class. Of course, the impact of interwar nationalists continued to shape the country's trajectory as its moved closer to complete independence. If Nahhas's chief achievement was to help bring about the subordination of the AGPA to an emerging national government, then Ibrahim Rashad's contribution was to institutionalize new mechanisms for rural credit and cooperation that would eventually become integrated into the agrarian bureaucracy under Nasser. But the emergence of a new generation of middle-class thinkers in the 1940s—many of whom did not come from large landowning families—and their embrace of a new conception of development in the postwar period would profoundly shape the worldview of the Free Officers when they seized power, and the character of the Nasserist project in the 1950s and 1960s.

FOUR

RURAL RECONSTRUCTION AND THE NEW PEASANT

IN 1944, AHMAD HUSAYN, the head of the Fallah Department in the newly created Ministry of Social Affairs, praised the recent accomplishments of Egyptian agrarian reformers. "In the last few years," he wrote, ". . . public opinion, parliament, and government have given proper attention to the problems of the fellah: Feeling more responsible towards the fellow of whom the majority of the population consists, the producer of the wealth of the country."[1] Over the previous few years, Husayn had come to oversee the ministry's most important division. After obtaining a doctorate in agricultural economics in Berlin, he returned to Egypt in 1927 and began to work as a government inspector for agricultural cooperatives. More than a decade later, he would be placed in charge of the department whose purpose was to "awaken" the rural population so that it would "participate morally and materially having once been convinced of the need for reform."[2] Through this institution, Husayn would pursue his vision for the establishment of rural social centers that mobilized government employees to supervise and instruct peasants in their everyday lives. "[T]he fellahin are to be taught and convinced of the importance of improving their conditions," he wrote, "and made aware of the share they have to carry out in this work."

Husayn's assertion that the state should be responsible for fashioning political subjects who embodied the ideals of strength, rationality, and education was grounded in a set of convictions that were becoming widely accepted by reformist writers and thinkers. As the depression persisted, many of them began to embrace an agenda of peasant uplift and rehabilitation that required the construction of an institutional apparatus to supervise, regulate, and discipline the behaviors of peasants across the country. His insistence on changing their conduct was slowly acquiring the status of common sense in nationalist circles. In the late 1920s and 1930s, Egyptian nationalists began to believe that the reinvigoration of rural life in the face of the depression was an endeavor that required a state-guided transformation in the mundane practices of agricultural producers. They began to intensify a relatively new political-economic program that sought to transform Egyptian peasants into healthy, rational, productive subjects who could act as the basis of a robust and remunerative agrarian order.

The harsh realities that afflicted the mass of laborers in the countryside prompted a growing number of national elites to adopt an array of visions for rural reconstruction. To understand why this agrarian consciousness appeared when it did, it is necessary to begin with the experience of the depression from the vantage point of the millions of peasants who produced Egyptian cotton. As the prices of cotton collapsed, many who suffered under the weight of various financial obligations began to complain that they were victims of a set of phenomena that they did not cause. Among urban politicians, intellectuals, and reformers, there was a widespread perception that the countryside faced an agrarian crisis which underscored the need to reform peasant life. They were not alone. Around the world, reformers and revolutionaries alike had embraced similar programs for rural reconstruction to mitigate the impact of the depression on agrarian societies. The ideas, policies, and institutions that they embraced—from peasant cooperatives, to agricultural banks, to rural education—began to reconfigure the relationship between colonial and nationalist governments, on the one hand, and their rural populations, on the other hand. They would profoundly shape the character of postcolonial states, like Egypt, as they entered an era of national independence.

PEASANT LABORERS GET SQUEEZED

The collapse of international cotton prices was widely felt across rural society, especially in the Nile Delta. The majority of cultivators saw their earnings from the sale of cotton plummet. Between 1929 and 1937, real income per capita dropped by as much as 9 percent around the country.[3] But the decline was not evenly felt across all rural classes. The largest landowners could protect themselves to an extent by selling some of their less productive properties. The situation for rural laborers who were directly involved in growing cotton was considerably worse. Those who worked on a regular or irregular basis for *'izba* owners saw their earnings diminish over the course of the depression as agricultural wages fell by nearly 40 percent.[4] The masses of peasants who owned little or no land but were not primarily dependent on wage labor faced an equally dire situation. Bearing the heavy burdens of taxes, rents, and debts meant that smallholders and tenants maintained very little control over the fruits of their own labor because after they picked their cotton it was immediately transferred into the hands of tax collectors, landlords, and creditors. In that respect, the working lives of smallholders and tenants closely resembled those of wage laborers who produced mainly for other people rather than for themselves. As receipts from cotton plunged, the consequences for these different kinds of cultivators varied depending on the particular arrangements of land tenure, labor, and credit to which they were bound. Their diverse experiences can be illustrated by a brief examination of the three major vectors—taxes, rents, and debts—through which peasants encountered the hardships of the depression.

Smallholders felt mounting pressures to pay their taxes with whatever earnings they had. At the start of the depression, the capitulations that had established an extraterritorial legal system for foreigners in the nineteenth century were still in place; they would not be eliminated until the adoption of the Montreux Convention (which was signed in 1937 and went into effect 12 years later). This meant the government had very few sources of direct levies—apart from land taxes—that it could draw upon to expand its revenue base.[5] Between 1919 and 1939, the amount it collected in land taxes remained relatively unchanged while peasant earnings from the export of cotton diminished. As a result, the tax burden for smallholders increased significantly as a percentage of the value of cotton that they sold. Whereas in the 1920s it had constituted

14 percent on average, by the 1930s that figure had more than doubled.[6] An account of the earnings and expenses of Muhammad Ahmad—a smallholder who owned two feddans of land in the governorate of Buhayra—illustrates some of the hardships they faced. Ahmad devoted one feddan to cotton cultivation, which generated his only source of income, and he used the other feddan to grow wheat and rice for his family's subsistence.[7] One third of his income in 1933 went towards paying the land tax and other smaller levies and fees, and the remainder was not enough to cover the costs of seeds, irrigation, hoeing, and picking. Unlike most small cultivators, Ahmad held no older debts and yet he was still unable to cover his expenses.

Just as the incongruity between taxes and prices compromised the ability of smallholders to meet their financial obligations, the divergent relationship between rents and prices did the same to tenants. The collapse of cotton prices was most palpably experienced in the preparation of their rental contracts. On private estates and lands owned by the Ministry of Religious Endowments, rental rates were long tied to the price of cotton. Landlords had the authority to hold cotton, maize, and rice that cultivators grew until they were satisfied that it would cover any outstanding rent. In the 1930s, these powers would start to impinge on peasant livelihoods. As the depression began, the gap between falling cotton prices and agricultural rents widened rapidly. Because many tenants had agreed to multiyear leases in the mid-1920s when cotton prices were higher, they suddenly found themselves with rental agreements that they could no longer afford. On private estates, rents had increased up to 80 percent from their prewar levels, while on lands administered by the Ministry of Religious Endowments (Wizarat al-Awqaf) and the Administration of State Domain (Maslahat al-Amlak al-Amiriyya), the average rental rate at the end of the 1920s exceeded what it was 15 years earlier by 20–30 percent.[8] The situation amounted to what one group of tenants in Sharqiyya vividly described as a "cotton calamity." The disparity between the rents that tenants paid and their earnings from the sale of cotton meant that they were left with burdensome leases that "had become iron chains on their legs."[9]

In their petitions, tenants offered a diagnosis of the crisis that pointed the blame at different culprits. Thousands of tenants from across the country gathered in Cairo to submit a petition to Prime Minister Isma'il Sidqi pleading for rent reductions that were commensurate with existing prices. "Among the most wretched and miserable communities," they wrote, "are the renters who constitute a majority of the people and are a mainstay of the life of the country."[10] They demanded that the value of agricultural rents be brought down in accordance with the difference between what tenants earned from the sale of cotton when they signed their leases and what they earned at present. Such requests were fairly common among petitioners. Those who signed multiyear leases in the 1920s when the cotton buying campaigns were at their peak suffered when the government decided to abandon its crop purchases at the start of the depression.[11] The result was that tenants who earned less from the sale of their cotton in the 1930s were still stuck with expensive leases. In October 1930, hundreds of cotton producers from Daqahliyya who rented lands from the Ministry of Religious Endowments complained about "hardships that [were] unprecedented since the days of [their] earliest ancestors."[12] The low price of cotton had combined with a pink bollworm attack to reduce their incomes such that they could no longer afford to cover their own expenses. As a result, the ministry began to confiscate their cotton in order to recover the value of their rent and other costs of using the land. Like many tenants, these cotton producers believed the underlying problem was that rents were inadequately adjusted in relation to erratic cotton prices. They petitioned the royal *diwan* to postpone the collection of a portion of their rent and to renew their lease at the same ratio of rent to cotton prices that existed in 1924 when they began renting from the ministry. Otherwise, the tenants warned, they would be forced to abandon the land. By protesting the forcible seizure of their raw cotton by state agents, the tenants drew attention to the impact that very personalized forms of domination had on their lives. But they also exhibited an awareness of the ways in which their own means of subsistence were bound up with dynamics beyond the control of any discrete individuals.[13] They blamed their predicament on the fact that "the movement of supply and demand had become paralyzed." These kinds of market idioms acquired a conceptual plausibility among tenants who became accustomed to encountering the variability of cotton prices in the way their leases were prepared. By ascribing their domination to the workings of abstract forces, the tenants signaled their own embeddedness in a broader set of relations that came with their dependence on the production of commodities for international markets. The experience of being acted upon by a seemingly external force, albeit one that the peasants themselves constituted through their daily activities, was a distinctive feature of life under capitalism.[14]

To offer some measure of protection against what they experienced as heteronomous market forces, the government responded to requests by tenants for financial relief. In the first three years of the depression, the Ministry of Finance enforced a partial moratorium on the collection of agricultural rents. In the 1929/1930 season, it postponed the collection of 20 percent of the rent owed by any a lessor or sublessor for one year while many landlords amicably agreed to forgo up to one quarter of the rent. Because most tenants did not possess the financial capacity to pay most of their rents these arrangements simply "consecrated an existing state of affairs."[15] In the 1930/1931 season, the ministry postponed the collection of 30 percent of agricultural rents, and over the next few years, politicians considered the implementation of similar relief measures.[16] As some observers noted, large landlords were more than willing to accommodate the needs of their tenants because they were motivated, above all else, to uphold the reproduction of peasant labor power on their estates.[17] In the end, however, these efforts to mitigate the financial burdens of tenant farmers were largely ineffective because the rent reductions were not proportional to the fall in cotton prices, they were not enforced on land owned by foreigners, and they did nothing to slow down the continued decline of prices for the rest of the decade.

The majority of cotton producers in the Egyptian Nile Valley faced a mounting burden of rural debts that resulted in what commentators described as an epidemic of usury in the countryside. Unlike large landowners, small cultivators did not typically take out loans from large mortgage banks because they had been legally debarred from doing so in 1912; instead, they borrowed from local cotton merchants, moneylenders, and landlords. At the start of every season, many smallholders and tenants acquired seeds and fertilizers on loan for higher rates than they would have otherwise paid in cash. The loans they received generally fell into three types—advances against land, or crops, or gold and jewelry—with interest that could reach as high as 60 percent.[18] Those who found it difficult to borrow could acquire these inputs by selling their crops in advance at 50 or 60 percent of the previous year's closing price.[19] Lenders could also rely on an informal version of futures trading to hedge against volatile prices. In February 1931, the assistant prosecutor of the Tanta

Native Court, Mahmoud Allam, described cases before his court in which local moneylenders in this important center for cotton ginning and trading were taking advantage of their clients. At the time of making a loan, the moneylenders forced their debtors into signing sales contracts for their cotton crops. When the time for repayment arrived, the moneylenders would either collect the value of the loan with a high interest rate, or they would redeem the crop if its market value at the time was higher.[20]

Even if they did not borrow from formal banks, smallholders and tenants could still lose their land to uncompromising lenders. While the Five Feddan Law had effectively prohibited the foreclosure of smallholder properties, rural creditors found ways to circumvent these restrictions. At the time of making a loan, some of them would purchase three or four feddans from their debtors on the understanding that the land would be returned to its original proprietor at the end of the season in exchange for its sale price and additional interest. Because many smallholders did not earn an income that was sufficient to repurchase their land, the sale to the merchant or moneylender would become final, an effective foreclosure.[21] These kinds of extortive credit relations that rural debtors could not escape led many to call for the expansion of alternative financial institutions, like agricultural banks and cooperatives, in order to protect peasants from the "lawsuits of banks and seed and fertilizer merchants" and the "claws of cruel usurers."[22]

THE CRÉDIT AGRICOLE D'EGYPTE

The Great Depression marked a turning point for the institutionalization of agrarian development in the nationalist project. As we saw in the last chapter, the price of cotton fell so sharply at the start of the depression that the Egyptian government had to reconsider its mechanisms for managing a spasmodic crisis that continued to unsettle the countryside. The Sidqi government understood that confronting the interrelated problems of low cotton prices, declining land values, and rural indebtedness required a lasting institutional fix. Moreover, Abdel Wahab's reevaluation of his country's position in U.S.-dominated international cotton markets deepened the government's conviction that nationally scaled institutions were necessary to protect the interests of Egyptian cultivators. To reduce their debt burden and boost their incomes, Abdel Wahab stressed the need for agricultural credit to be provisioned under national government auspices. If government policy could not keep the price of cotton high, as it aimed to do with its cotton buying campaigns in the 1920s, then it could attempt to reduce the costs borne by the cultivator.[23] To achieve these goals, the Sidqi government created a new institution in 1931 that he described as "an integral part" of his cotton policy: the Banque du Crédit Agricole d'Egypte (or the Crédit Agricole).[24]

The establishment of the Crédit Agricole represented one of the most significant efforts to restructure agrarian finance during the depression. The new bank embodied a partnership between state officials, industrialists, and private bankers. The Egyptian government provided half of the initial capital for the bank while the rest of the funds came from the National Bank of Egypt, Bank Misr, the Crédit Foncier, and others private banks.[25] Shareholders were guaranteed a rate of return of 5 percent, and the bank's activities were exempted from the provisions of the Five Feddan Law.[26] The committee that proposed the creation of the bank included leading members of Egypt's interwar commercial and industrial bourgeoisie, like Tal'at Harb and Henry Naus, as well as powerful state elites, like Isma'il Sidqi and Ahmad Abdel Wahab. The Crédit Agricole therefore embodied a confluence of political and financial power that blurred any putative distinction between state and capital.

The founders of the Crédit Agricole believed that Egypt's system of rural credit was heavily skewed towards large landowners who had access to the private mortgage banks that existed across the country. Because of the provisions of the Five Feddan Law, those institutions did not offer loans to smallholders whose properties they were barred from foreclosing in the event of a default. As a result, smallholders and landless farmers could only obtain credit from "outside proper banks"—including from local merchants, landlords, and moneylenders.[27] Peasants who got entangled in these informal debt relations had little control over the fate of their crops. According to the committee, usurers and cotton merchants who extended loans to smallholders would later "acquire the peasant's crop on unfair terms." Landless tenants were in an even worse position because their crop was usually allocated in advance towards rent payments, and therefore very few lenders would agree to provide them with credit.

In creating the new bank, the Sidqi government built on a longer history of attempts to provide rural credit to small and landless peasants with limited access to the banking system. For the previous 35 years, Egyptian officials had gained experience in making advances to small cultivators. In 1895, the Cromer government began to extend loans to landowners in the Nile Delta who owned five feddans or less, and then it expanded the program under the auspices of the newly created National Bank of Egypt. Out of these efforts emerged the Agricultural Bank, an institution that was created in 1902 to channel foreign capital into loans to peasant smallholders until its directors abandoned the practice one decade later.[28] In the 1920s, the National Bank continued to make advances to cultivators against their crops, and it opened dozens of new depots around the country for cultivators to deliver their cotton.[29] Alongside these activities, it also maintained a reserve fund that officials drew on to provide loans to cultivators, to undertake cotton purchases, and to buy government securities.[30] In similar fashion, the purpose of the Crédit Agricole would be to offer relatively low-interest loans to peasants with little or no land who put up their crops as collateral in return for either cash advances or loaned farming inputs (seeds, fertilizers, etc.). Within a short period of time, the bank completed preparations to open branches in every governorate capital and field offices in every provincial district (*markaz*). Its primary focus would be to make loans against cotton. Towards that end, peasants could obtain an application for a loan from local tax collectors in their subdistricts (*nahiya*) and then submit it to the nearest village-level committee that belonged to the bank.[31] Those peasants who belonged to an agricultural cooperative could rely on it to provide the necessary documentation for a loan; those who did not could turn to their village mayors, local tax collectors, or landlords to support their loan requests and to guarantee their loans.

The first obstacle that confronted the founders of the Crédit Agricole was the opposition of other powerful bankers. Although the new institution enjoyed fairly wide support from major financiers in the country, not all of them were enthusiastic about it. A few representatives of institutions that played a major role the country's formal credit markets feared that the new bank's activities might extend to their primary customers, the large landowners. To cast doubt on the bank's mission, they invoked images of an irrational, profligate class of smallholders whose wasteful spending habits made them undeserving of modern credit institutions. "[T]he early experience of the Agricultural Bank showed that the small owner did not use his credit for agricultural purposes," wrote A. W. Jessop on behalf of Barclays Bank in 1930, "but for very different purposes such as purchase of crass bedsteads, marrying wives, etc."[32] To assuage their concerns, Sidqi assured these bankers that the Crédit Agricole would not impinge on the markets of other financial institutions.[33] But those promises would soon ring hollow.

The Crédit Agricole devoted a substantial amount of its resources towards attenuating the costs of the depression that were borne by large landholders. First, the law that established the bank allowed it to sell seeds and fertilizer to all cultivators regardless of how much property they owned. Whereas individuals borrowed from the bank at an annual interest rate of 7 percent, cooperative societies were only charged 5 percent.[34] This proved especially beneficial for those large landowners who created agricultural cooperatives as a means of acquiring cheaper farming inputs. Second, the bank's administrators were entrusted with the task of preventing the decline of agricultural real estate values that resulted from the mortgage crisis.[35] At the start of the 1930s, reports in the Egyptian press began calling upon the government to stem the expropriation of mortgaged land.[36] Because the statutes of the bank precluded it from engaging directly with individual large landowners, Sidqi created a special fund of L.E. 2 million and invited the directors of the Credit Agricole to form a consortium that would oversee its disbursement. According to him, the main objective of this program was to slow down the pace of foreclosures in order to uphold the price of agricultural land.[37] Under this scheme, the bank would pay arrears of interest on existing mortgages, and if necessary, it would do the same for arrears on installments of capital—whatever sum would persuade creditors to abstain from any foreclosure proceedings for at least one year. Although the bank was intended to support small and medium landholders, one fifth of its funds were devoted to large landowners. Because the bank continually redefined small and medium ownership in very broad terms—for example, the limit for small proprietorship reached as high as 200 feddans in 1937—larger landowners could capture an even greater portion of funds that were not intended for them.[38] For that reason, the British acting financial advisor remarked there was "little or no distinction made between the various classes" and that at its worst the program would amount to a futile "attempt to bolster up the price of land."[39] Within a few weeks, Mahmud Shukri, the head of the bank, boasted that it had successfully canceled or postponed the forced sale of hundreds of properties, some of which would have incurred expenses on the debtor that were more than seven times the value of the original debt.[40] At the same time, domestic critics began to complain that the program was insufficiently ambitious. In a report on land debt, Muhammad Shafiq Jabr, an engineer in the Ministry of Public Works, warned that the funds allocated to the Crédit Agricole for the purchase of foreclosed properties were not enough to acquire more than one-third of the properties that were in danger of confiscation.[41] Another critic questioned the very premise that the Crédit Agricole was suitable for this task because it relied on "friendly mediation" with foreign banks, its authority was not always recognized by the Mixed Courts, and it was partially owned by foreigners.[42] Instead, he called for the establishment of independent adjudication committees that could pave the way for the creation of a national real estate bank under full Egyptian control.

Although the Crédit Agricole helped large landowners, especially during the first few years of the mortgage crisis, its raison d'être was still to extend loans to smallholders. A shortage of credit from merchants and landlords in the 1930s made this mission all the more imperative. During the depression, it was nearly impossible for small cultivators to acquire loans for any crop other than cotton.[43] As existing credit arrangements began to freeze up, local officials started to arouse public concern about the need for more liquidity. In 1931, for example, a representative from Damanhur submitted a petition calling upon the Crédit Agricole to rescue peasants in his district from an ongoing credit crunch.[44] In 1932, the Sidqi government created the Crédit Hypothécaire d'Egypte to provide mortgage credit to smallholders under the supervision of the directors of Crédit Agricole.[45] Although it only made a modest amount of loans, the new bank did serve other important functions—for example, it confronted the heavy decline in the import of Chilean nitrate fertilizers in the early 1930s by executing a barter transaction with German bankers that saw the exchange of Egyptian cotton for German nitro-limestone.[46] Over the following years, observers continued to insist that the mission of the Crédit Agricole was still to combat the prevalence of unregulated, high-interest moneylending to which peasants in the countryside continuously fell victim. "Usury raged across the Egyptian countryside in the most appalling way and the Crédit Agricole was established to fight it," wrote Joseph Zannis, an associate in the Litigation Department of the Crédit Foncier. He insisted that the Crédit

Agricole offered loans to individual smallholders, tenants, and cooperative societies on significantly better terms than informal lenders did. "It lends to farmers at a reduced rate," he wrote, "[unlike] the money they borrowed at 30 or 40 percent."[47] With paltry incomes, however, many peasants still struggled to repay their loans. To address this situation, the Crédit Agricole resorted to both punitive and rehabilitative measures. It took coercive action against those who failed to pay their outstanding debts in a timely manner, yet it also helped promote new ways for peasants to adopt modern habits of profitable farming, physical well-being, and financial discipline. These two modes of power, one repressive and the other generative, worked in tandem to reinforce the authority of the new bank and the wider agrarian regime overseen by nationalist reformers during the depression.

COERCION IN THE COUNTRYSIDE

Ensuring the uninterrupted payment of taxes, rents, and debts during the depression required powers of coercion that extended deep into village life. To punish those peasants who failed to settle what they owed, officials could physically confine land, crops, and cultivators from state lands through measures such as administrative seizures and imprisonment. Many cultivators complained about what they believed to be the unjust confiscation of goods and properties that they owned. One tenant from Asyut, ʿUthman Hirdan, objected to the sequestration of his crops. In 1925, he had begun renting more than two dozen feddans of land from the Ministry of Religious Endowments. After signing a three-year lease, he complained, the "general decline" of cotton prices prevented him from paying the rent he owed, which prompted the ministry to forcibly seize his crops every year. When Hirdan renewed his lease, he did so on the security of his deceased brother's land so that he could use his own assets to pay what remained of his outstanding rents. As the depression intensified, his family was compelled to sell their own property in order to amortize their remaining debt. These recurring hardships impelled Hirdan to implore the King not to accept "that young children from [his] family be displaced with no breadwinner."[48] Other cultivators complained about facing punitive measures, like prison sentences, because they could not afford to meet the terms of their leases. In 1935, a group of tenants from Giza were similarly unable to pay their rents due to low cotton prices and to damage wrought upon their crops by leafworms.[49] They were swiftly arrested. A local court then ruled that the tenants had to pay the full value of their rent, and it gave some of them suspended prison sentences, which prompted them to appeal to the King for a one-quarter reduction in their rents.

The coercive methods that were employed to collect rent on state-owned lands were also used to exact taxes and debt repayments from small and landless peasants. Just as bank officials tapped into existing networks of local administrative power to determine if peasants qualified for a loan, they did the same to punish those who did not meet their seasonal repayments. They could authorize local *'umdas* (village mayors) and *sarrafs* (tax collectors) to confiscate farmers' crops in order to ensure that their outstanding liabilities were settled. In October 1933, the British Residency in Cairo asked major cotton traders around the country to submit brief reports on the economic conditions of the peasantry. Many merchants were displeased that the government's crop seizures hampered their ability to buy cotton. They described a countryside in which the movement of the crop was nearly paralyzed while peasants suffered under the weight of taxes, debts, and rents. An agent from Carver Brothers & Co.—one of the biggest cotton export firms in the country—complained that the requisitions were slowing down the seasonal trade. In Bani Swayf, he reported that "the movement of the crop has been more interfered with this year than ever before, owing chiefly to the *saisies* made by the government."[50] In Minya and Abu Qurqas, he estimated that three quarters of small cultivators owed tax arrears or outstanding debts to the Crédit Agricole. The movement of cotton was further hampered because the bank had offered loans on generous terms to peasants who agreed to deliver their cotton to government warehouses (*shunas*).

Another merchant who toured the governorates of the Nile Delta in 1933 gave a vivid description of the punishing effects that crop seizures had on peasant life. They struggled to pay taxes to the finance ministry and debts to the Crédit Agricole that were scheduled for the end of the cotton season. After smallholders picked their cotton, he recounted, local officials would put it under the supervision of armed guards who ensured that it was not sold until the owners paid their outstanding dues. Even if temporary, these administrative seizures prevented cultivators from obtaining a satisfactory price for their cotton that could cover their expenses because the only way to release their impounded crops was to accept whatever a merchant offered to pay. "In some cases," he reported, "[the grower] gets a 50 percent lower price than the actual daily price quoted."[51] To be able to fulfill their financial obligations, many cultivators felt compelled to sell their livestock, gold, and jewelry at whatever price they could get. As a result, the Crédit Agricole was "hated by the *fellaheen* who claim that instead of being the farmers' help it has been converted into a means of screwing every possible piaster out of its unfortunate clients."[52]

Though these traders might have had an incentive to embellish their depiction of rural misery, the existence of many peasants who complained in petitions about the policies of the Crédit Agricole suggests that these reports were not entirely fabricated. As a result, many small cultivators preferred to continue obtaining their farming supplies from local merchants and moneylenders rather than become debtors to the bank. Over the course of the decade, no more than 13 percent of peasant smallholders borrowed from the Crédit Agricole in any given year.[53] To mitigate the effects of the compulsory sale of foreclosed land, the bank willingly channeled funds to help large landholders while appropriating surpluses from its smaller clients through crop seizures. In this way, the Crédit Agricole functioned, at least in part, as a mechanism for large landholders to displace the costs of the crisis onto borrowers who owned little or no land. However, the bank's coercive methods alone could not achieve all of the objectives of its founders. From the start, the Crédit Agricole was envisioned as being part of a constellation of institutions that were intended to format the behaviors of peasants in ways that conformed to the visions that interwar reformers had for an independent agrarian society.

THE NEW EGYPTIAN PEASANT

The devastation wrought upon societies that were oriented towards the production of agricultural raw materials in the 1930s meant that projects for rural reconstruction began to proliferate around the world. These efforts chiefly aimed to regenerate agricultural production, to improve standards of living in the countryside, and to promote the social uplift of the peasantry. In United States, New Deal reformers launched a program of supervised government loans to poor farmers as well as expert assistance to help them manage their homes and farmlands, while in Mexico intellectuals promoted a new notion of the "revolutionary peasant" around which the modernizing ideology of the postrevolutionary regime and its attempts at state formation were consolidated. Although both countries followed different paths in the 1930s—the United States pursued agricultural protectionism while Mexico implemented land reform—they still exchanged ideas about rural rehabilitation that ultimately had differential effects on tenants, smallholders, and migrant farmworkers.[54] In China, local and international experts promoted the use of new social scientific methods in the 1930s to address what they perceived to be an agrarian crisis that manifested itself in declining yields, peasant indebtedness, liquidity shortages, and rural outmigration.[55] In India, promoters of rural welfare and improvement (especially in Bengal) sought to overcome peasant backwardness by holistically addressing the social, economic, hygienic, and educational dimensions of village life.[56] Across the agrarian hinterlands of the world, the peasant became an object of both inquiry and intervention by social reformers and revolutionaries who devised a variety of projects to revamp rural society.

Amidst the agricultural recession of the 1930s, Egyptian nationalists began to forge a new political project—which we might describe as a form of rural governmentality—that took as its object the moral and material reform of the peasantry.[57] Its aim was not simply to increase the products of the land through bureaucratic regulation (property titles, surveys, etc.), infrastructure (irrigation, transportation, etc.), and technology (seeds, fertilizers, etc.). More importantly, the politicians, writers, experts, and civil servants who were behind this project sought to exercise control over the bodies and behaviors of peasants by maintaining a continuous, regulatory presence in their lives. As the decade wore on, they fashioned a robust apparatus through which they could take on the responsibility to educate, rehabilitate, and revitalize their rural subjects. To achieve these goals, they either devised or expanded an assemblage of mechanisms that included cooperative societies, agricultural banks, scientific farming manuals, health and sanitation facilities, model villages, and rural social centers. As Omnia El Shakry has shown, these methods of discipline relied on new social scientific discourses of positivist criminology, social hygiene, architectural modernism, and neo-Malthusianism that were introduced in the 1930s to regulate peasant modes of life.[58] At the same time, as Jennifer Derr has argued, new prevention methods and treatment centers began to spread across the countryside to protect peasants against the effects of endemic diseases, like schistosomiasis and hookworm, that proliferated with their greater exposure to perennial irrigation.[59] All of these discourses, practices, and institutions aimed to furnish both the resources and the technical knowledge required to produce a new Egyptian peasant.

The harsh conditions of the depression prompted many reformers, officials, writers, and capitalists in Egypt to revise their conventional wisdom about the workings of economic life. By the middle of the decade, a cohort of urban writers began to sound the alarm about what they often described as a triad of "poverty, ignorance, and disease" that afflicted the countryside.[60] For many of them, the category of population emerged as a central object of reform. In the late nineteenth century, there were almost no concerns among British administrators and experts that Egypt was overpopulated. In his *Modern Egypt*, Lord Cromer noted that the rulers of Egypt "never had to refer to the pages of Malthus" because, unlike other parts of the colonial world, the country they governed did not have "a congested population, of whom a large percentage were in normal times living on the edge of starvation."[61] This began to change in the final years of the British occupation. In the late 1910s, colonial statisticians and irrigation engineers began to exhibit an interest in the quantitative relationship between population growth and the supply of land, and by the 1920s many of them worried that Egypt would become overpopulated.[62] The arrival of the depression intensified the urban intelligentsia's demographic anxieties, and as El Shakry argues, they began to produce a "veritable onslaught of publications, conferences, and debates on population."[63] The growth of this new literature did not simply represent an intensification of demographic concerns; it also marked an important shift in the way populations were measured. The category itself no longer simply referred to the number of people in relation to an area of land. By the 1930s, the study of population was increasingly apprehended through a different set of metrics, like birth rates, mortality rates, health, etc.[64] At the time, a handful of American and European experts had begun to formulate the question of overpopulation as a global problem. Their efforts represented a shift from the late imperial mobilization of population statistics that reinscribed notions of colonial difference to mid-century demographic transition theory—which would develop more fully during the Cold War—that understood history in terms of a stagist movement from high fertility/mortality to low fertility/mortality that any country could undergo.[65] By the late 1930s and early 1940s, elite Egyptian reformers began to insist that demographic patterns were a central question that should guide thinking about social and economic improvement.[66]

Amidst a growing concern with the condition of rural populations, several texts appeared that treated the peasant as an object of paternalistic inquiry and intervention. Many began to promote new ideas about social reform that emphasized the inclusion of health, education, housing, and other services into a vision of comprehensive rural development. The earlier texts were literary accounts that produced elaborate descriptions of the ravaging afflictions of village life. Some of them depicted a primitive rural society that was irredeemably mired in a state of backwardness. In 1937, novelist Tawfiq al-Hakim published his semi-autobiographical work, *Yawmiyyat Na'ib fi al-Aryaf* (Diaries of a Country Prosecutor), in which a public prosecutor assigned to a village in the Nile Delta encounters a rural landscape overrun by degeneracy, corruption, and ignorance that perpetually evade the moral and rational authority of the law.[67] Others lambasted urban elites for their habitual neglect of the masses of rural producers who formed the bedrock of Egyptian society. If Hakim apprehended the countryside as a terrain of intractable chaos, then 'A'isha 'Abd al-Rahman portrayed its inhabitants as unremunerated toilers whose labor underpinned the mirage of natural riches that many commentators had associated with the Egyptian Nile Valley. Known by her pen name Bint al-Shati', she fashioned herself as a voice for smallholders, tenants, and landless peasants in the 1930s whom she called the "mud bearers" of society.[68] She contributed to discussions within the Wafd over the party's 1935 national program that featured a social reform agenda—including the promotion of rural health and education facilities along with a fairer tax burden for peasants—which was more explicit than anything it had articulated in the past.[69] Having migrated from the countryside herself, Bint al-Shati' became the first woman to publish extensively on social reform in the countryside, and she compiled her journalistic columns into two books, *Al-Rif al-Misri* (The Egyptian Countryside) and *Qadiyyat al-Fallah* (The Peasant Question).[70] She faulted state officials for levying onerous taxes on peasants in order to build a luxurious life for city dwellers without providing adequate rural schools, hospitals, housing, and potable water to the generators of much of that wealth. While previous governments had glorified the wonders of the Nile River, she contended, they neglected the peasant bodies who lay behind the "inexplicable magic that the river breathes into the heart of the blazing desert, turning it into a lush paradise."[71]

Towards the end of the decade, several treatises appeared on the future of Egyptian politics, society, and culture amidst the struggle for independence, including Taha Husayn's *Mustaqbal al-Thaqafa fi Misr* (The Future of Culture in Egypt), Mirit Butrus Ghali's *Siyasat al-Ghad* (The Policy of Tomorrow), and Hafiz 'Afifi's *'Ala Hamish al-Siyasa* (On the Margin of Politics).[72] All of them emphasized the need for social reform as a patriotic duty, and they included various levels of discussion about the expansion of education, health, and housing. Perhaps Ghali best exemplified the liberal reformist perspective upon which these studies were founded. Some of the leading foreign capitalists in the country had already begun to reassess the fundamental principles of economic liberalism. In the early 1930s, the secretary general of the Crédit Foncier Égyptien, Emile Minost, publicly questioned those who still subscribed to what he called a form of economic determinism that assumed "crises would somehow carry their own remedies."[73] In his opinion, it was a mistake to apprehend the rhythms of economic life in terms of self-correcting cycles whereby an excess of prosperity would generate a crisis and a prolonged depression, in turn, would bring about a recovery. Ghali would display a similar understanding in his short book that became the basis of the program for the Society of National Renaissance, one of the foremost liberal advocacy groups in the 1930s and 1940s.[74] In *Siyasat al-Ghad*, Ghali argued that previous reformers had mistakenly treated social progress (living standards, education, etc.) and economic improvement (infrastructure, technology, etc.) as independent objectives while in reality they were tightly bound. Though he opposed any unnecessary state intervention in the workings of ostensibly free markets, Ghali went on to prescribe a set of initiatives that belied the laissez-faire principles he appeared to espouse. He preached that the overarching goal of any reform program should be to "raise the material and mental level of the classes of the nation."[75] Doing so would involve a vast effort by state officials to improve disease prevention, nutritional intake, housing conditions, and educational facilities, especially in the countryside. In other words, Ghali implored the government to regulate the behaviors of millions of Egyptians who constituted markets through their daily activities. Although elite reformers, like Ghali, sought to maintain the structure of class relations in the countryside, their vision for markets that would be embedded in a broader program of social engineering was becoming widely shared by an array of writers and thinkers.

Meanwhile, an emergent generation of trained social scientists began to enter the realm of government where they would have a lasting impact on its institutions. Some of them were associated with the Egyptian Association for Social Studies (EASS), an organization established in 1936 to investigate and promote social reform and rural reconstruction.[76] At the same time, the government established a Higher Council for Social Reform, and three years later it would become a full-fledged ministry. Underscoring the urgency of its mission, the royal advisor to the ministry, Muhammad al-ʿAshmawi, warned that the poverty, disease, crime, and idleness that had come to characterize village life lay at the root of the country's ailments.[77] In addition to Ahmad Husayn, the ministry's principal organ, the Fallah Department, would also attract other specialists, like Mohamed Riad Ghonemy and Abbas Mustafa Ammar, who went on to publish key studies on Egyptian agriculture and peasant life over the next decade and a half. The ideas that were developed by this cohort of writers and reformers during the depression—and who promoted comprehensive rural development without challenging the underlying land tenure system—began to slowly find their way into the apparatus of the state.

The growing awareness of the plight of the peasantry in the nationalist imagination inspired some writers to focus their attention on a new target of critique: the large landholders. Some of them began to condemn *ʿizba* owners as an extractive class of absentee landlords who posed an incessant threat to the well-being of the countryside. In a series of articles, Muhammad ʿAbd al-Latif Saʿudi, a former parliamentarian from al-Fayyum, excoriated them for "building palaces and furnishing them, acquiring servants, and rushing into the flaws of the new city."[78] According to one estimate, the majority of large landholders—at least 70 percent—lived in Cairo or Alexandria and left the management of their estates to agents (sing. *wakil*) and stewards (sing. *nazir*) who lived on site.[79] As the crisis persisted, portrayals of a wealthy landholding class that was estranged from the affairs of their own estates grew more common. One of the more devastating criticisms appeared in 1938 with the publication of Henri Ayrout's study of the Egyptian peasantry. He described estate owners as a westernized elite who lived in Cairo or Alexandria during the year and who spent their summers in Lebanon or Europe where they acquired a reputation for wasteful and extravagant spending. "[I]n one evening," Ayrout charged, "he would fling away money enough to have kept his fellahin alive for a year."[80] He denounced their uncaring detachment from the villages they owned and their disregard for the human life and social needs of the peasants who worked on their estates. "Like the old absentee abbots with their benefices," Ayrout wrote, "he went as seldom and stayed as short a time as possible."[81] Because large landowners had no interest in their *'izbas* except as a source of revenue, the only tangible link that bound them to the laborers on their estates were the cash payments that they collected through local stewards. For these reasons, Ayrout concluded that "there is no landed aristocracy in Egypt, only an aristocracy of wealth."[82] The same qualities of fictitiousness and intangibility that were associated with the wealth of cotton brokers in the 1920s now characterized the activities of large landlords.

The project of rural governmentality was vividly on display in the realm of cotton cultivation. It was premised on three major institutions and practices through which national elites would attempt to transform the minds and habits of small cultivators. First, peasants who obtained their loans from national banks and agricultural cooperatives were acquainted with new methods of financial and farming discipline. While the number of smallholding and landless peasants who borrowed from the Crédit Agricole was still relatively small, it had emerged as a novel vehicle for the distribution of money, crops, and farm inputs. By 1933, one observer even remarked that the bank had "considerably changed the conditions of the fertilizer trade in the country."[83] Moreover, it provided a substantial amount of credit to agricultural cooperatives. According to a major financier who helped establish it, the bank could not extend serious services to the peasantry unless it offered loans to cooperative societies that were "more qualified than any private or governmental organ" to determine the needs of more than two million smallholders.[84] As the decade wore on, opportunities to do so presented themselves with increasing regularity. In the 1930s, the agricultural cooperatives movement expanded moderately. As we saw, large landowners found it advantageous to form cooperatives in order to acquire fertilizers at the discounted interest rates offered by the Crédit Agricole.[85] Their desire to benefit from the advantages afforded by these societies ultimately helped to "stimulate the extension of the cooperative movement across the country."[86]

More important than their widespread prevalence or lack thereof was the function that cooperatives began to play in peasant life. By the end of the decade, there were 750 agricultural cooperative societies that provided loans, inputs, and equipment to tens of thousands of members and helped them sell their crops.[87] Nearly three quarters of the money handled by these societies was loan capital advanced by the Crédit Agricole to finance agricultural expenses, like the purchase of cattle, machinery, and cotton seeds.[88] These loans were guaranteed either by members of the cooperative management committee who acted as sureties or on the security of the debtors' crops to which the bank held the right of administrative foreclosure in the event of a default. All cooperatives were required to allocate a percentage of their net profits—usually 10 percent—to establish rural schools, to build libraries, and to maintain infrastructure and sanitary conditions in their districts.[89] While Ibrahim Rashad warned about the need to "reduce the burden of bureaucracy" so as to maintain the popular-democratic character of the cooperatives movement, he also insisted that its expansion was "the surest means of spreading the spirit of concern for the public interest."[90] By the end of the decade, he noted that peasants' agricultural knowledge and business methods had improved because cooperatives acted as vehicles for "circulating results of scientific research and . . . introducing modern ideas."[91] During World War II, membership in cooperatives that provided rural credit increased rapidly to more than half a million.[92] According to one government publication, cooperative societies that had multiplied by the end of the war were "serving as economic units by means of which schemes for reconstruction, amelioration, or welfare for them could be introduced."[93]

Second, the production and popular dissemination of instructional knowledge about the cultivation and sale of cotton expanded greatly. In the same year the Crédit Agricole was established, one of the first documentary films in Egypt to engage in nationalist propaganda was produced. Famed director Muhammad Karim's *Al-Ta'awun* (Cooperation) promoted the cooperative organization of agriculture and encouraged its expansion.[94] Between 1929 and 1933, several new agricultural journals and instructional manuals were launched, including *Sahifat al-Ta'awun* (The Cooperation Journal), *Zimil al-*

FIGURE 8. Distribution of advances for cotton cultivation to cooperative members in Kafr Sālim, Buḥayra province. Source: Rashād, *Kitāb al-Taʿāwun*.

Fallah (The Peasant's Companion), and *Al-Fallah al-Iqtisadi* (The Economic Peasant). These publications featured discussions about how to confront the cotton crisis, and they advised peasants about rational methods of farming. They aimed to educate small cultivators in the most gainful techniques for sowing, maintaining, picking, and selling their cotton in order to help them increase their incomes and improve their health and living conditions.

In one of its earliest efforts to disseminate advice across the countryside, the Ministry of Agriculture launched a monthly instruction manual. The authors who produced *Zamil al-Fallah* were clear about its objectives. The publication would "act as the Ministry of Agriculture's tongue that speaks to the farmer in simple, easy terms."[95] The contents of the publication were mostly organized around simple questions addressed to farmers such as "why don't you sell your cotton at the best prices in town?" or "why is your cotton crop less than that of your neighbor?" In response, farmers were advised to look after their land and maintain the quality of their soil by properly draining, leveling, fallowing, and solarizing it. They were taught how to purchase good quality seeds, uproot weeds from their plots, and pick cotton at the most suitable time. Through photographs and pithy guidelines, they were taught how to clean their harvested raw cotton in order to rid it of dirt, leaves, sticks or anything else mixed into it. They were also encouraged to form cooperative societies in order to be able to collectively negotiate with merchants from a stronger position. And they were counseled against seeking monetary gain though trickery or deception. "Beware of the devil whispering to you about soaking your cotton with water," it cautioned, "because that does not fool the merchant and it degrades your cotton and drives down its price."[96] Cultivators who engaged in such a practice to artificially increase the weight of their cotton sacks in the hope of receiving a higher price were warned that doing so could in fact compromise the sale because the excess moisture would adversely affect the length and fineness of their cotton fibers. Alongside these government efforts at popular rural education, there also existed private publications like *Al-Fallah al-Iqtisadi*, a monthly journal published in Cairo by businessman Thabit Thabit and distributed at no charge to readers across the countryside. Its stated purpose was to offer guidance to farmers in "modern methods that lead to improving his soil . . . and increasing his production by the means that other peoples and countries have adopted."[97] It carried a special section in every issue that offered tips and advice for cotton farmers on topics such as the frugal management of farm expenses, the protection of cotton from boll weevil attacks, and the proper selection of seeds and fertilizers. It also featured articles and discussions about peasant indebtedness, agricultural cooperation, industrial expansion, and other topics of concern to urban reformers and intellectuals during the depression.

Third, the creation of a rural social centers program under the auspices of the Ministry of Social Affairs gave rise to new techniques for the regulation of peasant life. If the Crédit Agricole slowly became an instrument for urban elites to supervise the distribution of money, crops, and inputs, and if new publications became an outlet for them to disseminate agricultural knowledge into the countryside, then the establishment of rural social centers became a crucial mechanism for them to monitor and rehabilitate everyday peasant behaviors. As a board member of the EASS, Husayn had overseen a pilot project that consisted of two experimental villages in al-Manayil and Shatanuf.[98] After the creation of the ministry, he brought the program under its purview, and the centers became the focal point of its efforts at village reconstruction.[99] Although their establishment was delayed by the start of the war, they began to appear in greater numbers in the late 1940s, and by the end of the decade, they were serving 1,500,000 peasants across the country.[100] In villages that lacked sufficient funds for a center, the ministry could establish rural reconstruction societies that did not have any paid staff members.[101] The results of these reconstruction efforts were soon on display. In 1949–50, cotton yields in areas with rural social centers were 50 percent higher than those on other lands.[102]

The rural social centers provided an avenue for regularized supervision by urban civil servants over the lives of peasants in the countryside. All centers were staffed by paid employees from the Fallah Department who typically had a college degree and were not from the village itself.[103] Each center had an agricultural and social welfare specialist who helped villagers to obtain seeds from the Ministry of Agriculture or the Crédit Agricole, taught them how to market their crops, organized night classes to reduce illiteracy, established a village library, supervised the cleanliness and hygiene of the village and its residents, and more. It also included a doctor who studied the health problems of the village, physically examined each inhabitant, treated those peasants with fevers or endemic diseases, performed minor surgeries, distributed medications, inspected food supplies in local markets, and instructed villagers in food storage and safety. The department organized regular trips to the village by health visitors, typically female graduates of Qasr al-ʿAini hospital in Cairo, to look after pregnant women, mothers, and children as well as to instruct village women in proper methods of housekeeping, health and hygiene, and home industries. "We are glad to notice a progress in the change of the attitude of the fellahin in these centers," Husayn reported at a 1944 conference on agricultural development in the Middle East. "They feel more responsible towards their villages, they respond better, their whole morale is better." However, he insisted that the project was still very far from completion. At the same gathering, Husayn ʿAnan, an undersecretary of state for agriculture, elaborated on the work that he believed still needed to be done. "Our research has produced valuable results," he wrote, "that we have to communicate to every farmer in terms that he can understand in order to bring about their wide application."[104] The further extension of such programs into daily peasant life would continue over the next two decades, especially after the Free Officers' Revolt.

NATIONALISM AND RURAL GOVERNMENTALITY

The agrarian regime that started coming into being in the late 1920s and that took on a more institutionalized form in the 1930s was different from any of its predecessors. In existing studies of modern Egypt, particularly those that were written in the last two decades, there is a tendency to treat the forms of discipline, regulation, and subject formation that began to appear in the nineteenth century as a generic expression of colonial power. In making this argument, historians of Egypt have often taken their cue from scholars of South Asia.[105] In his seminal article, for example, David Scott has argued that "in the colonial world the problem of modern power turned on the politico-ethical project of producing subjects and governing their conduct."[106] Doing so required a transformation of the everyday habits, attitudes, and desires of Indian colonial subjects. The problem with this formulation, however, was that Scott relied almost entirely on evidence from a brief period in the history of colonial South Asia—which lasted from the 1830s to the 1850s—when British rule was largely guided by the principles of liberal political theory. In other words, he took the liberal experience in India and applied it as a model for understanding the workings of modern colonialism everywhere.

Under the British occupation, colonial administrators in Egypt consistently decided not to engage in any sustained project of transforming Egyptians into liberal political subjects because they relied on a theory of distinct racial types that suggested Egyptians could not be reformed in this way. While they might have lacked the political rationality that was needed to justify self-rule, Egyptian subjects still possessed an economic rationality that could provide the basis of their consent to foreign occupation.[107] As Aaron Jakes argues, British authorities operated on the assumption that Egyptian peasants were utility-maximizing actors who were capable of pursuing their bare material interests when given the proper incentives. But they did not involve themselves too much in the creation of mechanisms that could shape peasant behavior in ways that conformed to their view of the world. Achieving agricultural growth that was regular, predictable, and remunerative had long been an objective for Egypt's colonial rulers. To do so, however, they relied far more on the development of land, infrastructure, and fiscal and security administration than they did on the active production of political subjects and the regulation of their conduct. Their investments in agricultural infrastructure, canals, roads, and seed and fertilizer technologies—particularly in the 1890s—far exceeded their commitment to any institutions that could underpin a project of peasant subject formation.[108] The criminalization of farmers who neglected to inform authorities about cotton-eating caterpillars or who refused to offer up their children to pick infested cotton leaves was a preferred way for colonial authorities to confront pest attacks that threatened the size of each season's crop.[109] The extension of British control over the legal system, including the expansion of police and courts into the countryside, was a crucial method of state building under the occupation.[110]

The repertoire of British imperial rule in the countryside was not vastly different from those that existed elsewhere in the Middle East. For example, Sara Pursley has argued that British officials in mandatory Iraq relied heavily on punitive violence rather than biopolitical discipline as a primary means to exercise imperial control.[111] Through such actions, like aerial bombardment, they sought to impose their sovereign prerogative to govern Iraqis by penalizing any disobedience or resistance to their authority. Though colonial officials did not always rely on overwhelming military force in Egypt, their efforts to wield control over the countryside often revolved around the exercise of sovereign power through public works and infrastructure, law and policing, and taxation and fiscal prudence. In the eyes of British administrators, the occupation's success was chiefly measured in terms of high crop yields, low crime rates, and sound public finances—not transformations brought about in peasant character and conduct. Unlike the English Utilitarians who informed colonial policy in British India during the first half of the nineteenth century, the overseers of the occupation were hardly determined to transform improvident Egyptian cultivators into productive English-style proprietors.[112]

Of course, the modern state in Egypt, as it existed from the 1830s to the 1910s, did exhibit some features of discipline and governmentality. As Timothy Mitchell has argued, Mehmed Ali's government relied on the exercise of generative forms of power that sought to produce new subjectivities rather than simply impose restrictions on the actions of individuals.[113] This effort to "colonize Egypt" began with the introduction of new methods of military conscription and organization. It continued with the transposition of these techniques from the army barracks to other sites, including schools, model houses, and planned urban spaces. Under the British occupation, efforts to cultivate modern subjectivities would persist. In response to colonial representations that feminized Egyptian men, for example, urban bourgeois writers constructed a notion of the self that emphasized physical fitness and bodily strength—what Wilson Chacko Jacob has called "effendi masculinity"—which contributed to the formation of an Egyptian national subject.[114] These exercises of power that began to appear in nineteenth-century Egypt undoubtedly transformed the way political authority was experienced by many Egyptians, but their impact on the laboring activities of cotton cultivators or their capacity for social reproduction was probably limited.[115] To the extent that they were applied to the countryside, the main objective of these techniques was often to supervise the actions of agricultural producers in order to punish infractions or to ensure that output targets were being met.

By contrast, the regime that arose in the 1930s did not simply rely on a form of sovereign power that sought to generate revenue and penalize transgressions, or a supervisorial mode of power that aimed to monitor peasant bodies. It increasingly deployed an instructional mode of power that sought to rehabilitate and reform peasant behaviors. Whereas colonial authorities were convinced that the application of self-governing principles to everyday rural life would protect cultivators from the vagaries of arbitrary rule, interwar nationalists believed that actively molding peasant behaviors was necessary to shield them from economic forces beyond their control. From the late 1920s, Egyptian nationalists began to understand that the regeneration of agriculture required the maintenance of a regularized assemblage of practices, procedures, and institutions through which reformers could instill a set of rationalities in the minds and habits of peasants. What began as a government effort to provide relief to cultivators through national banks and cooperatives, which resembled earlier attempts to do so after the 1890s, morphed into an interventionist project of peasant rehabilitation by the end of the depression. More than a principle that swiftly reordered politics across the country, the entry of meticulous forms of regulation and instruction into the minute aspects of daily life was a lumpy and inconsistent process. The ideas and practices that reordered the political management of Egyptian agriculture in the interwar and early postwar period grew out of dispersed sites—including private estates, independent cooperatives, lobby groups, and parastatal organizations—and then slowly crept into the realm of formal government. The emergence of the postcolonial state in Egypt was therefore less about an existing government extending its control over society than about scattered ideas and practices gradually taking over what it meant to exercise political power.[116]

When they did appear, these techniques of discipline and governmentality were configured in relation to the historical circumstances that surrounded them. The prolonged turbulence of the depression and the dislocation that it created in agricultural societies around the world prompted nationalists who had some measure of control over their state institutions to embrace forms of discipline and reconstruction that were scaled at the level of the nation. Rather than treat it as a generic feature of modern power, then, we might think of the regime of rural governmentality that began to appear in 1930s Egypt as a situated response to the disruptive conjunctures of interwar capitalism. As postcolonial scholars have argued, nationalist leaders and movements justified their rule by internalizing a variety of derivative discourses concerned with the overarching themes of development, progress, and modernization.[117] In doing so, they reproduced the logics and epistemes of colonialism in ways that fundamentally determined the character of nationalism and nation-states. But the significance of this process did not simply lie in the fact that it involved a replication of colonial forms of knowledge. That Egyptian reformers only began to fully embrace instructional forms of power over the countryside in the interwar period said as much about the historically specific circumstances in which these techniques became appealing as it did about their Western provenance.

CONCLUSION

The expansion of rural governmentality in the Egyptian Nile Valley helped to institutionalize nationalist ideas about development and to establish the conditions for their further transformation. Although these projects for village-level reconstruction would take on a different character during World War II, their adoption by national elites would continue to have a lasting impact on Egyptian politics. They became part of a repertoire of ideas, practices, and institutions that state builders would draw upon in the 1950s and 1960s and that would become integrated into the apparatus of the postcolonial state.[118] Most importantly, they would become central to the pursuit of national development, a new objective that firmly took hold over the Free Officers' republic in the postwar era.

FIVE

REIMAGINING DEVELOPMENT

IN 1945, MARXIST WRITER Ahmad Sadiq Sa'd offered a scathing indictment of the landed oligarchy that owned some of the biggest estates in the Egyptian Nile Valley. "[T]he system of agricultural production contains clear proof of the accusations directed at the 'real estate class,'" he wrote, "namely its lack of interest in production and its complete separation from it."[1] These allegations appeared alongside many critical accounts after the war that began to focus their sights on the harmful role that large estate owners played in agrarian life. As we saw in the previous chapter, the nascent regime of rural governmentality in the late 1920s and 1930s—which aimed to fashion a new kind of peasant subject—did not present a serious challenge to the large landholders who still formed the core of the country's ruling class. If anything, those discourses and institutions, which sought to ameliorate the living conditions of the rural population, served to silence any public discussion of inequality by avoiding questions of land distribution altogether. But the tide began to turn after World War II. In the mid to late 1940s, Egyptian reformers, activists, and intellectuals started to devise a political project that was unprecedented in previous decades: the redistribution of landed property. For the first time, a cohort of nationalist politicians, activists, and intellectuals began to recognize that glaring inequalities in landholding were hampering their priorities for development, and as a result, they began to systematically articulate proposals for land reform.

Until then, very few politicians, capitalists, or intellectuals in Egypt had considered land reform to be a viable or desirable project. In the early 1920s, for example, the short-lived Egyptian Socialist Party (renamed the Egyptian Communist Party in 1922) adopted a program that called for the abolition of private *'izba* ownership and the cancellation of rural debts for peasants who owned less than 30 feddans.[2] Almost a decade later, in 1931, Emile Minost timidly broached the subject. As the depression prompted a wave of rural foreclosures, the general secretary of the largest mortgage bank in the country voiced his frustration with estate owners who had become "hypnotized" by the acquisition of land in a manner that was detrimental to the development of the country. Their ceaseless accumulation of agricultural properties led Minost to publicly question the basis of the land tenure system itself. "We should be concerned about the distribution of land ownership," he wrote, ". . . 1,500,000 owners only possess an average area of 41 percent."[3] Realizing that he was touching on sensitive matters Minost quickly backpedaled. Yet he insisted that if large landowners wanted to get through the turbulent swings that characterized economic life during the Great Depression they had to find outlets for their abundant capital apart from the exclusive purchase of land. "The industrialization of the country," he wrote, "[would be] justified from the point of view of 'combating the crisis.'" Although it had not previously appeared on the nationalist agenda, the marriage between land reform and industrialization that Minost proposed would quickly gain traction among politicians, reformers, and activists after the war.

This marked a reversal of the conventional wisdom that long defined the nationalist movement. In the 1910s and 1920s, there was no shortage of serious diagnoses of the social problems that Western imperialism had introduced into the Egyptian Nile Valley. In their rigorous critiques of the status quo, nationalists insisted on maintaining the country's agricultural character; they ascribed any signs of rural immiseration to the intractable movements of international prices, goods, and money; and they sought to territorialize the circulation of capital in order to insulate local cultivators from the vagaries of the imperial world economy. But they never challenged the tenure arrangements upon which the power of large landowners rested, nor did they want to industrialize the country. By the 1940s that was no longer the case. This was not simply because nationalists grasped something after the war that an earlier generation had failed to realize. More importantly, their changing perception of the *ʿizba* owners was born out of the circumstances of the depression and war and the transformations that they brought about in the activities of large landholders themselves. As the landed oligarchy became a primary object of critique in the 1940s, a variety of new terms to describe the *ʿizba* owners—like real estate class (*tabaqa ʿaqariyya*), feudal system (*nizam al-iqtaʿ*), and princes of land (*ʾumaraʾ al-ard*)—began to circulate widely. Large landholders who were celebrated by economic nationalists two decades earlier for their productive capacities were now being described as a class that was disinvested from the creation of real wealth. Their transformation into villains was rooted in a particular set of historical experiences. The wartime growth of industrial activities, the changing patterns of accumulation by large landowners, and the transmission of ideas from the nascent field of development economics combined to produce an entirely new conception of postwar development that would profoundly shape the character of the postcolonial state in Egypt.

WARTIME COTTON

The outbreak of World War II created another shipping crisis, yet it called forth a different resolution than the one that British and Egyptian authorities implemented more than two decades earlier. Whereas the previous war had compelled the government to revamp its monetary system after banks in Alexandria could no longer obtain shipments of gold from Europe, the renewal of combat more than 20 years later threatened to halt the movement of consumer goods, not precious metals, into the country. Shortly before the "phony war" began, King Farouk appointed Ali Mahir, a royal advisor who had recently split from the Wafd party, to the premiership. In September 1939, the government declared a state of siege, Mahir became a military governor, and British forces effectively began to reoccupy the country.[4] Because of the Anglo-French blockade and the government's decision to sever diplomatic relations with the Nazis, Egyptian cotton producers lost access to markets in Germany whose buyers had typically purchased up to one-sixth of the crop. Though the sudden loss was largely compensated by increased French purchases, the disposal of the next season's crop was a much bigger challenge. In

June 1940, the fall of France to Nazi forces and the decision by Italy to join the war exacerbated anxieties about wartime shipping. The continuation (and eventual extension) of the blockade, along with the closure of the Mediterranean Sea due to fighting between the Italian and British navies, impeded maritime transport between Europe and North Africa as well as through the Suez Canal to Asia. The result was a glut of raw materials that could not leave the global commodity frontiers where they were produced and that the British and American governments would confront with joint planning that set the stage for international economic governance in the postwar period.[5] The Italian, German, Polish, and French markets for Egyptian cotton that were lost by that summer had accounted for 40 percent of exports at the start of the war.[6] That month, Mahir was removed from office at the behest of the British due to what they perceived to be his pro-Axis sympathies. Because the new government projected a budget deficit, it was unable to buy the unmarketable cotton itself, and so it asked British officials to offset the shortfall in demand by purchasing the entire crop. The big export houses, who had protested the encroachment of state officials on their ability to dominate the cotton trade in the 1930s, were already irked by the willingness of the previous government to rely heavily on British assistance.[7] However, their opposition was ultimately eclipsed by the trepidation of British and Egyptian officials who worried that millions of cultivators would not be able to acquire their financial requirements for the next season. The rapid sequence of events could not have happened at a worse time as cotton producers needed loans in the summer to prepare their lands for cultivation in October. Fearing widespread instability, the British government established a board to buy Egyptian cotton and cotton seed at prices that would "ensure to the peasant his expenses on the crop plus a reasonable standard of subsistence."[8]

The British Government Cotton Buying Commission—which brought together state officials, bankers, and major traders—purchased any cotton that was offered to it for the entire season. Rather than completely sideline members of an already weakened mercantile bourgeoisie, the commission conducted its purchases in Alexandria through a panel of cotton brokers from a list of delegated firms. Under the wartime regime, the commission continued to rely on existing methods for moving cotton from villages across the country to Mina al-Basal, and it only stepped in once the crop had reached Egypt's main port city. What did change was the extent to which big merchants—like Carver, Choremi, Peel, and others—had to navigate the state bureaucracy to dispose of the cotton they purchased from the interior. For each bale of cotton sold to the commission, merchants had to disclose the date and location where it was ginned, the warehouses where it was stored, and the variety, weight, and price of the cotton.[9] Still, the commission became the most important purchaser of Egyptian cotton that season, buying an estimated three quarters of the crop.[10] The following season, 1941–42, the British and Egyptian governments joined together to purchase any cotton that could not find a foreign buyer. To fund these purchases, the national bank issued short-term treasury bills and a new cotton loan that absorbed some of the surplus funds that wartime inflation had left in the pockets of landowners, professionals, and businessmen.

By this time, tens of thousands of Allied troops had arrived in Egypt as tensions with the Axis powers escalated in North Africa. Their presence drove up the overall demand for food while the sharp reduction in nitrate imports that resulted from the closure of the Mediterranean diminished local grain output.[11] Provisioning these soldiers, meanwhile, required a reallocation of cargo space on vessels that had previously transported civilian goods to the Middle East. As a result, the British authorities created a regional program in 1941 that aimed to make available the ships that were needed for the import of military supplies. Over the next few years, the Middle East Supply Center expanded its activities to include the local management of agriculture, manufacturing, and trade in order to offset the reduction in imported civilian goods from overseas.[12] The kinds of measures that made up the program—like import licenses, food rations, trade quotas, and price controls—provided a repertoire of policies for newly independent states that would pursue economic planning over the next two decades. To boost the production of cereals, the military authorities organized a large-scale compulsory delivery system for grain. They also implemented an extensive series of acreage restrictions in 1942 that dramatically curtailed the cultivation of Egyptian cotton for the remainder of the war. With the annual size of the crop shrinking to less than half of what it was before the war, the Egyptian government could now offer to purchase the entire harvest through a newly created Egyptian Cotton Commission, although it only ended up buying a small portion of it every year.[13] Relying on acreage restrictions, government purchases, and other forms of intervention to regulate the cotton market was not a novel response from government officials. Many of these strategies had been tried and tested in the 1910s and 1920s. However, the adoption of these policies in the 1940s, and the war that prompted them, had far greater consequences for the Egyptian countryside.

First, the shipping crisis led to a significant growth of large-scale industry in Egypt. According to Anouar Abdel-Malek, the war was "like a whip to the development of Egyptian capitalism" because it stimulated greater investments in manufacturing and commercial enterprises.[14] By the middle of the war, the sectoral distribution of capital in Egypt—which previously favored real estate and banking activities in the countryside—had significantly changed. Between 1914 and 1942, the mortgage sector dropped from 43 percent to 19 percent of total capital investments in the country while industry grew from 9 percent to 22 percent.[15] The main reasons behind this shift were the achievement of tariff autonomy in 1930 that helped incubate some domestic industries; the decline of mortgage banks and industrial imports during the depression; the gradual abolition of the extraterritorial privileges (known as capitulations) that foreign capitalists enjoyed until the late 1930s; and, most of all, the wartime disruption of overseas trade and the increased demand for manufactured goods by Allied troops stationed in the country. The industrial expansion that resulted was driven, in large measure, by some wealthy landowners' decision to buy shares in local companies, like Bank Misr, or in foreign and *mutamassir* enterprises.[16] By the late 1940s, Egyptian capitalists played a larger role in the industrial sector than ever before, especially after a 1947 law mandated an increase of Egyptian capital, directors, and workers in joint-stock companies across the country.[17] But heavy industry remained concentrated in the hands of a small number of investors, many of whom were affiliated with Bank Misr, which led one observer to conclude that "large-scale mechanized industry is highly monopolistic and all forms of monopoly organization known to the capitalist world are represented [in Egypt]."[18]

Second, the wartime shift from cotton to food production reduced the demand for agricultural workers, while the growing need for labor in urban industries prompted hundreds of thousands of peasants to leave the countryside. Between 1939 and 1950, the agricultural labor force declined by more than half a million workers, largely because of rural outmigration and a malaria epidemic that claimed tens of thousands of lives, mostly in the Sa'id.[19] Many of these migrants abandoned the lands that they farmed in order to find urban employment in military and industrial enterprises that were created amidst the British war effort. Between 1937 and 1947, the proportion of Egyptians living in cities jumped from 28 to 33 percent, and the population of Cairo alone grew by an estimated three quarters of a million people, more than half of whom were rural migrants.[20] As the war drew to a close, the country had undergone a visible change in the geographic distribution of its working population as urban observers began to complain about villagers who "filled the streets of the capital and crowded its neighborhoods."[21] After the war, the reduced agricultural workforce posed a dilemma for those large landowners who sought to resume the production of cotton directly on their own lands. To their consternation, the shortage of peasant labor resulted in a considerable rise in the cost of hiring daily workers. Over the course of the war, remuneration for agricultural work soared—more than tripling for men while increasing only moderately for women and young boys—and, by 1951, real wages had grown more than 60 percent from their prewar level.[22]

Third, the wartime regulations, labor shortages, and financial insecurities in the early 1940s combined to bring about a transformation in the tenure system itself. The acreage restrictions hampered the ability of landowners to produce their most lucrative cash crop and reduced their need for permanent agricultural workers (*tamaliyya*) on their estates.[23] The increase in rural wages that resulted from peasant outmigration further disincentivized them from hiring more laborers. Meanwhile, the continued fear of foreclosure by mortgage banks prompted indebted landowners to search for other ways to use their properties that were not as costly as directly farming it. All of these barriers to the accumulation of capital started to undermine the *ʿizba* system. As a result, estate owners began to lease their land on a greater scale rather than directly produce on it. According to a former researcher in the Fallah Department, Mohamed Riad Ghonemy, the lease market for agricultural properties "overshadowed every other form of use—or ownership transfer—in Egypt."[24] In 1939, an estimated 17 percent of all cultivated land was rented out to tenants; by 1949, that ratio had increased to 60 percent; and by 1952 it had become 75 percent.[25] In his field research, Ghonemy visited four large estates across the country and found that their owners leased the majority of their lands.[26] In contrast to the prewar period, most of the rents that landlords collected in the

1940s were paid in cash, and they yielded incomes that often exceeded whatever could be earned from direct farming.[27] According to the Ministry of Social Affairs, the average rate of agricultural rent nearly tripled over the course of the war.[28] By the end of the decade, renting out a feddan of land could return more than double the revenue that would have been generated from cultivating it; soon thereafter, the Fallah Department estimated that landowners earned one-third less from cultivation than they did from leasing their properties.[29]

Part of the reason that landlords could extract such large revenues from their tenants was that they had the power to impose lease agreements that were heavily skewed towards protecting the interests of the lessor. On large estates, the duration of a rental contract was short—typically for one year—and tenants were often expected to pay for their agricultural inputs. In 1949, an American visitor from the National Cotton Council, Read Dunn Jr., remarked that the terms of a lease in Egypt required that "the tenant furnishes everything."[30] In their petitions, tenants often complained that their landlords "neglected the costs of agriculture" and charged rental prices that they could not afford after paying for their own water, fertilizers, seeds, and food.[31] And there was little that tenants could do to change these realities through collective action because the legalization of trade unions, which happened for the first time in 1942, deliberately excluded agricultural workers, personal servants, or government employees.[32] Meanwhile, no laws existed to regulate work hours/wages or to enforce prohibitions on child labor in the agricultural sector, nor were there serious efforts to control rents.[33] The ability to set the provisions of a lease did not reside exclusively in the hands of private estate owners. It could also be wielded by officials who rented out plots from the Administration of State Domain, intermediaries who managed the estates of big landlords, and large tenants who dominated the bidding market and subleased their rented lands.[34] For example, a one-year lease agreement drawn up by the steward of a waqf in Qalyubiyya contained provisions that shielded her from any responsibility to help the tenant use the land; granted her the right to impound the tenant's crops, livestock, and other belongings to guarantee payment of the rent or any portion of it; and required the tenant to cover her legal fees should a dispute arise between them that was to be settled in court.[35] With such power to determine the conditions of a lease, landlords often charged rental prices that could greatly exceed the production capacity of the land itself.

The rapid metamorphosis of *'izba* owners into rentiers resulted in a massive upwards transfer of wealth. During the war, the real estate and rental values of agricultural land began to climb due to a combination of rising food prices, population density, and its profitability to landowners, and they continued to skyrocket after the war. The acreage restrictions remained in place until the end of the decade in order to allow the government to sell the stocks of cotton it had accumulated during the war. Afterwards, the Korean War (1950–1953) stimulated a cotton boom, which led to a significant increase in both the output and price of the Egyptian crop. By the end of the decade, Dunn remarked that the rising prices of food and cotton had driven up land values in Egypt to the point where they were "probably the highest in the world."[36] Meanwhile, the productivity of cotton estates fell because mortgage banks had scaled back their provision of liquid funds to finance the expansion of agricultural production, and the restrictions on cultivation that were put in place during the war reduced overall yields. Between 1939 and 1950, the real output from agriculture declined between 7 and 20 percent while the real estate and rental values of agricultural land increased between 50 and 60 percent in real terms.[37] Most of the value from inflated land rents and prices accrued to large landlords while decreased production meant that cultivators earned a net income that was lower than the cost of their lease.[38] During the depression and war, the accumulation of capital by large landowners depended so heavily on collecting agricultural rents that it came to constitute nearly half of total agricultural income in Egypt.[39] Even though there was a growing detachment between those who owned the land and those who tilled it, landlords still collected a large portion of the value that their leaseholders produced. As one evicted tenant complained, cultivators like himself had "fall[en] prey between the claws of the unjust owner who cares about nothing other than filling his coffers from the sweat of the small peasant's brow."[40] Because tenants and farm laborers—who constituted 81 percent of the agricultural workforce—did not have the ability to own or operate the majority of the farms on which they worked, those who wished to expand their production could only do so by leasing more land. As a result, they could not escape what Ghonemy called "the tenancy rung of the agricultural ladder."[41]

These far-reaching transformations in the political economy of Egyptian cotton were accompanied by intellectual shifts that began to converge around a new conception of development. Whereas economic nationalists in the 1910s and 1920s had faithfully celebrated the country's agrarian status, a new generation of thinkers in the 1940s sought to confront what they perceived to be a paralyzing condition of agrarian backwardness that could only be overcome by encouraging the growth of industrial production. In their writings, they relied on new terms and concepts to describe economic life in Egypt against a normative model of Western industrial development that was presumed to be universal. More than an accurate representation of the countryside, however, these new notions of backwardness reflected the circumstances in which they emerged. Even though the production of cotton had returned to its prewar levels by the early 1950s, the arrangements of labor and land through which it was grown had thoroughly transformed and with them arose new understandings of what it meant to build an independent national economy.

"THE HIGHEST MANIFESTATION OF THE HUMAN MIND"

In 1943, Muhammad 'Abd al-Karim visited the most immense industrial complex in the country. Founded in 1927, the Misr Spinning and Weaving Company quickly became Bank Misr's most profitable enterprise, and within a decade it had grown to become the largest textile firm in the Middle East.[42] Inside the gates, 'Abd al-Karim described a sense of amazement as he stood amidst "a large army, marching in their blue uniforms to that edifice whose ends are barely perceptible."[43] The growth of the company's manufacturing capacity meant that the site he visited eleven years earlier had become completely unrecognizable. According to its director, the capitalization of the company had increased more than threefold since its establishment and its labor force had grown to more than 30,000 workers. So impressive was the conglomeration of human and mechanical power that 'Abd al-Karim described it as a "vast domain filled with many thousands of machines, replete with tens of thousands of men and women."[44] Though he admired what he saw, 'Abd al-Karim identified some challenges that could only be overcome by greater state intervention, namely by housing those migrant workers who came from the countryside and ensuring the well-being of Mahallawi handweavers who struggled to survive in the face of competition from mechanical looms.[45] If these problems were addressed, he prognosticated, there would be an even greater renaissance in what had become rightfully considered the largest industrial country in the region.

The lived realities of industrial growth, which ʿAbd al-Karim and others described, had a lasting intellectual impact on many nationalists after the war. A new generation of Egyptian reformers began to reject the premise—long held by both colonial officials and earlier nationalists—that Egypt was fundamentally an agricultural country. From the 1910s to the 1930s, there existed only a handful of voices that advocated for the expansion of urban industries as a principal way to achieve development. These included resident foreigners and *mutamassir* industrialists who invested in various manufacturing enterprises along with an even smaller number of Egyptian intellectuals who expressed an unambiguous admiration for Western civilization. For example, Fabian socialist Salama Musa unreservedly championed a future in which "all [the country's] production can be done by machines and not by hands."[46] When Mohandas Karamchand Gandhi visited Egypt in the early 1930s, Musa publicly spurned the Indian anti-colonial leader for his endorsement of homespun cloth and instead praised Fordist industrial production as a better path towards genuine sovereignty.[47] As the war drew to a close, these kinds of convictions began to spread among Egyptian capitalists, intellectuals, and politicians. In 1944, Egyptian senator Zakariyya Mahran lambasted those who still held the "corrupt doctrine" that glorified the country's agrarian status. Instead, he vowed that as the nationalist movement acquired a greater degree of independence it would necessarily stimulate new kinds of manufacturing activity. The Minister of Agriculture himself wrote about the "the misconception among almost all people that the acquisition of agricultural land is the best thing in which to invest capital."[48] To others, like writer Muhammad Subhi al-Daghashi, the idea that "Egypt [would] remain a purely agricultural country" had already been disproven by the rapid expansion of industrial activities during the war.[49] By 1948, Muhammad Rushdi, one of the directors of Bank Misr, catechized those who believed only a quarter century earlier that Egypt could not industrialize and "lodged this feeling into the souls and minds of the people until it became a general delusion that Egyptians, whether individuals or groups, were incapable of working jointly towards a major industrial endeavor."[50] The interlocking transformations of the 1940s led many intellectuals and political leaders to begin viewing state-led industrialization as the end goal of national development.

There were many reasons that prompted a growing cohort of nationalists to make such a pivot in their thinking. Some continued to argue, as their predecessors did in the 1910s and 1920s, that the general reliance of Egyptians on monocrop agriculture made them vulnerable to the erratic movements of international capital, goods, and prices. The exposure of Egyptian cultivators to such external shocks would only increase after the invention of nylon and polyester between the mid-1930s and early 1940s led factories in Lancashire to substitute artificial silk fibers for high-quality Egyptian cotton.[51] "[T]he future of cotton is gloomy and unreliable," wrote Mahran who had previously worked with Bank Misr. "It is best for us to think seriously about not linking our prosperity to this crop that is threatened by the dangers of competition."[52] More than anything, however, proponents of industrialization claimed that it was a necessary remedy for unrelenting population growth. As we saw in the previous chapter, the concerns of bourgeois reformers—like Ghali and 'Afifi—with rural welfare in the late 1930s led them to advocate for greater state investments in public health, education, and housing for the peasantry. At the time, Ghali argued that the declining ratio of cultivated land to people, which he estimated had fallen by one quarter over the previous 40 years, threatened the per capita share of agricultural wealth.[53] According to one estimate, agricultural workers in Egypt were seven times less productive than those in the United States—which one author attributed to a difference in land-to-labor ratio and rural mechanization.[54] Towards the end of the war, nationalists increasingly sought to improve the quality of rural life by regulating the numerical relationship between natural resources and those who worked on them. This growing demographic consciousness combined with widespread admiration for the wartime industrial boom prompted a growing number of politicians, intellectuals, and opposition groups to believe that population growth could be resolved by creating new outlets for the absorption of excess rural labor. In his treatise on textile industrialization in Egypt, André Eman, a lecturer at the French School of Law in Cairo, declared that "of all the economic problems that concern this country, overpopulation is undoubtedly the most important."[55] For his part, Mahran argued that the development of industry had become a necessity in Egypt because the exponential growth of its population—which had increased almost threefold since 1882—outpaced the government's ability to reclaim new agricultural land. "It is impossible," he concluded, "for Egypt to depend on agriculture alone as a source of livelihood."[56] Others insisted that Egypt had reached a demographic watershed after World War I because its agricultural income, which suffered from low cotton prices during the interwar period, was no longer enough to satisfy the needs of a growing population. As a result, Egyptians had to nurture more advanced forms of production that did not depend solely on the use of agricultural land. In the words of Isma'il Sidqi, the experience of war offered a bitter lesson that "growing population, dependence on future imports, and the misery of the peasant all required a shift towards industrial production."[57]

By the late 1940s, the new industrialization ethos started to be transformed into a policy program by a generation of Egyptian students who earned their graduate degrees in the United States and Western Europe. As such, they joined the circuits of intellectual transmission through which postwar development ideology was disseminated. One of the most lucid expositions appeared in the work of economist Ali El-Gritly who had recently returned to Egypt. El-Gritly graduated from Cairo University in 1933 and traveled to England in the 1940s where he completed his doctorate at the London School of Economics (LSE) under the supervision of a principal founder of postwar development economics, W. Arthur Lewis. Like many early development economists, Lewis was shaped by the world of ideas and concepts that demographic transition theorists had recently created. After being hired as the first Black professor at LSE, Lewis went on to publish many reports and memorandums for the British Colonial Office in which he diagnosed the reasons behind ongoing turmoil in the colonies and prescribed a template for their development in the future. In the late 1930s and 1940s, Lewis was still working out what would become known as his "dual sector model" that he believed offered a pathway towards development for countries in the high-fertility/high-mortality stage of their demographic evolution.[58] According to him, colonial societies with large surpluses of cheap, unskilled labor that were concentrated in agriculture possessed a valuable factor of production—workers—whose carefully induced migration into the industrial sector could catapult those societies towards unprecedented economic growth. His ideas would become central to the new field of development economics that came into being during the decade and a half after the war.

In 1947, El-Gritly published his doctoral thesis in Cairo's leading journal of political economy. After providing a detailed survey of the history, structure, and scale of industrial production in Egypt, El-Gritly went on to provide prescriptions for the future, and in doing so, he foreshadowed the main arguments that Lewis would soon publish. "[T]he only way out of the present morass of poverty," he wrote, "is the transfer of a substantial part of the agricultural population to secondary and tertiary occupations."[59] Doing so would increase the ratio of land and capital per active worker in agriculture, bolster industrial output, and raise the overall level of national income in the country. Relying heavily on data published by Paul Rosenstein-Rodan—an early advocate of state-led industrialization in Central and Eastern Europe and an important precursor to Lewis—El-Gritly went on to estimate that reducing agrarian overpopulation in a manner that was consistent with the goals of industrialization would require the creation of 150,000 manufacturing jobs every year.[60] To promote this model of development, he argued, the Egyptian government would need to rely on the erection of tariffs to incubate domestic industries, the training of industrial managers and workers, and the provision of subsidies and credit for manufacturing enterprises. Such a program would be financed by a combination of domestic savings, foreign borrowing, and the Egyptian government's sterling balances held in London. Only in this fashion could the country undergo a genuinely progressive economic transformation. In the years that followed, other Egyptian graduate students continued to investigate the link between demographic patterns and developmental trajectories. In 1951, Aziz Sidky, who would later oversee the first five-year industrialization plan under Nasser, completed his doctorate in economic planning at Harvard University. In his dissertation, he provided a stagist theory of development that hinged, more than anything, on population management. "[I]n an absolute primary economy," he wrote, "it is very seldom possible to expand the land production at a greater rate than that of the population growth."[61] Attaining a higher stage of development required "a new source of income" that would only come about through industrialization. The recent electrification of the Aswan Dam, he argued, provided just the kind of novel power supply that could stimulate iron and steel production in Egypt.[62] Relying on recently calculated figures for national income, Sidky claimed that present standards of living in Egypt fell far behind those of advanced countries, but that they could be raised by the implementation of an industrial program.[63]

While appeals for industrialization by young economists and social scientists often reflected the newly emerging paradigms and conventions of their disciplines, the enthusiasm about wartime industrial expansion also encouraged Egyptian nationalists more broadly to imagine what it could portend for the future. In addition to solving underlying demographic problems, many of them believed that the growth of mechanized industry could also transform modern Egyptian subjectivities and, therefore, offer a blueprint for more genuine forms of independence. "[I]ndustry is the highest manifestation of the human mind," wrote al-Daghashi in 1945, "and the most accurate measure of the development of a people's civilization."[64] Five years later, the secretary general of the Egyptian Federation of Industries, Subhi Wahida, offered a "philosophic interpretation of the whole Egyptian history" in which the country's postwar industrial bourgeoisie would play a central role.[65] In *Fi 'Usul al-Mas'ala al-Misriyya* (On the Principles of the Egyptian Question), he reminded his readers that exploitation always occurred upon contact between a "backwards agricultural economy" and a "modern industrial economy."[66] According to Wahida, Egyptian society retained its traditional agricultural character until the wartime growth of domestic industries, especially spinning and weaving, began to transform the mindsets and habits of the country's inhabitants. Whereas the industries built in the nineteenth century by Mehmed Ali and his descendants were driven by fiscal and military imperatives, those that were established during the war represented the "fruits of individual economic thinking."[67] In such accounts, the twin associations between labor-intensive agriculture and backwardness, on the one hand, and machine-driven industrialization and modernity, on the other hand, became pervasive as the wartime transformations of economic life in Egypt rendered them more compelling. As such, these Manichean binaries began to solidify their place in postwar Egyptian discourses of national development.

The historical claims of postwar Egyptian intellectuals, reformers, and policymakers were remarkably different from those of an earlier generation of economic nationalists. Yusuf Nahhas, Ibrahim Rashad, and other agrarian reformers were profoundly shaped by events, like the 1907 financial crisis and the wartime disruption of trade in the 1910s, that revealed the perils of Egypt's dependence on foreign markets. Their grievance against the British occupation was not that it permanently resigned Egypt to the status of a raw materials producer. Rather, their primary concern was to shield Egyptians from the international volatilities of capital, goods, and prices that characterized the imperial world economy in the interwar period. They sought to do this by ensuring that agricultural labor remained productive and that a larger portion of the wealth it created was kept inside the country. Promoting industrial growth was only necessary to the extent that it protected Egyptians from an excessive dependence on imported finished goods. The devastation of cash crop production during the depression, the wartime divergence between the interests of large landowners and those of industrialists, and the transmission of new ideas from the emerging field of postwar development economics laid the conditions for a major intellectual shift. The idea that development entailed a stagist transition from an agricultural to an industrial economy gradually became a central tenet of nationalist discourse, institutions, and practices. Many of them sought to dissolve the bonds between hundreds of thousands of cultivators and the land they tilled by inducing the migration of a substantial part of the working population from agriculture to industry. They argued that the reserve armies of rural labor that existed in Egypt should be separated from their means of production, rather than fastened to them, in order to stimulate growth. The leading voices in the nationalist movement no longer shared the principal aim of protecting agrarian populations from their exposure to global volatilities, as their predecessors did two or three decades earlier. Instead, they sought to absorb surplus peasant laborers into new urban enterprises and transform them into sedulous industrial workers.

"LAND IS THE PROPERTY OF THOSE WHO CULTIVATE IT"

In the 1940s, calls to limit the ownership of landed property became the central tenet in a discourse of social reform that acquired a widespread appeal among Egyptian opposition parties, groups, and intellectuals. The unequal landholding system that became the target of critics across the political spectrum—from liberals, to communists, to ultra-nationalists, to Islamists—was not a new feature of rural Egypt, nor was there any noticeable increase in tenure inequality that prompted these concerns.[68] Rather, the sudden appearance of land reform proposals in the 1940s was brought about by the transformative impact that depression and war had on social relations in the countryside. The wartime regulations, labor shortages, and changes in financial markets and cropping patterns that occurred from the late 1930s to the mid-1940s encouraged large landowners to shift their accumulation strategies. Their transformation into rural rentiers caused reformers and activists to exhibit what would become an abiding skepticism of the role that large landowners played in the development of the country. Their suspicions led them to endorse programs for the redistribution of landed property.

By the middle of the decade, several efforts to introduce land reform were underway.[69] In 1944, Egyptian senator Muhammad Khattab presented an unsuccessful bill before the senate that aimed to prohibit owners of 50 feddans or more from acquiring new properties. The following year, two important treatises on land reform were published by thinkers who represented radically different ideological positions: liberal Mirit Ghali's *Al-Islah al-Zira'i* (Agrarian Reform) and Marxist Ahmad Sadiq Sa'd's *Mushkilat al-Fallah* (The Problem of the Peasant).[70] Both of them began their treatises by highlighting the importance of industrialization, and they agreed that any land reform program had to be comprised of laws that regulated three areas of rural activity: ownership, tenancy, and wages. But they disagreed on the scope of the reforms and the political rationale behind them. Ghali belonged to a wealthy Coptic family that had long been involved in national politics. After serving as a parliamentarian, he became an active member in the Society for National Renaissance—an elite liberal group in the 1940s made up of estate owners, intellectuals, and politicians—which published his booklet. In the late 1930s, Ghali had opposed land redistribution on grounds that it would not steer the country away from an inevitable Malthusian trap. While he endorsed new forms of social welfare—especially in the realms of housing, education, and public health—he distanced himself from those he described as communists, anarchists, social democrats, and fascists who championed a complete overhaul of the landholding system.[71] The changing circumstances of the 1940s caused Ghali to modify his position. Although he continued to reject the outright expropriation of land by the government, he did embrace a gradualist program that would prohibit landowners who possessed more than 100 feddans from buying additional properties on the assumption that their estates would eventually fragment into smaller holdings through inheritance. Since the possession of large properties was unsuitable for a resource-scarce country like Egypt in which "peasant hands were in search of land," some plots that belonged to government bodies or liquated companies would be redistributed to nearly 350,000 small peasant families over a quarter of a century.[72] Meanwhile, a combination of progressive taxation, minimum wages, and rent controls would encourage absentee landowners to sell their rural properties and redirect their capital into industry. In this way, Ghali candidly asserted, the existing landholding system could undergo "reform and modification, not revolution and replacement."[73]

By contrast, Sadiq Sa'd (born Isidor Salvador) was a communist who belonged to a Jewish family that settled in Egypt in the late nineteenth century. In the mid-1940s, he cofounded a Marxist group, al-Fajr al-Jadid (New Dawn), that would become an important political and intellectual force within the Egyptian communist movement.[74] A critical evaluation of Ghali's booklet appeared in the group's newspaper almost immediately. A major flaw in his analysis, the reviewer noted, was that Ghali sought to improve the distribution of land "by giving morsels of charity to poor peasants" rather than seriously confronting the "monopoly over one of the means of production" from which the class power of large landowners derived.[75] Rejecting this premise that was shared by bourgeois intellectuals, Sadiq Sa'd proposed a more radical plan. Whereas urban social reformers wanted to improve the quality and availability of agricultural land or to ameliorate the condition of the peasant—as though these were separate phenomena—Sadiq Sa'd insisted the "heart of the problem [was] the peasant and the land."[76] The only way to lift millions of cultivators out of their miserable state was through a wholesale redistribution of wealth. In addition to rent and wage controls, he therefore called for an immediate restriction of all individual holdings to 50 feddans or less and a reallocation of lands in excess of that amount to small and landless peasants.

Despite the major differences in their proposals, Ghali and Sadiq Sa'd offered strikingly similar portrayals of the activities of large landowners. Ghali opened his treatise by accusing *'izba* owners of treating their properties "merely as a means of making money."[77] Many of them had migrated from the countryside a generation or two earlier, settled in the city, and abandoned their duty to "remain present among [the] people." For this absentee class, land had become an instrument for the extraction of exchange value rather than a resource that could enrich the lives of those who tilled it. Whereas an earlier generation of agrarian reformers had faithfully valorized land as real wealth, Ghali questioned what seemed until then to be a durable presupposition. Because the owners of agrarian property could simply generate revenue without improving the productivity of their farms, those who possessed a lot of land had, in a sense, begun to act like those who dealt in large amounts of money. They could grow their personal wealth without enhancing the material prosperity of the country. Placing restrictions on the possession of large properties would therefore dissuade the "owners of capital" among the landed oligarchy from hoarding agricultural land and instead encourage them to divert their funds towards industry and commerce. Only then could the economic culture that prevailed in the country transcend the "obsolete mentality that real wealth is land alone."[78] Yet Ghali understood that transforming attitudes towards rural property in this way could never happen so long as big landlords found it seductively profitable to lease their land. "Among the clear indications that rents have risen beyond a reasonable limit," he wrote, "is that they return to the owner almost the same profit as direct farming."[79] Overseeing many of these channels of rent extraction were hundreds of rural sublessors who profited from brokerage activities, usually at the expense of smaller tenants, even though they "did not perform an economic or social service."[80] Just as the greatest beneficiaries of the land were detached from it so too were the millions of precarious tenants on short-term leases who did not "feel a bond between themselves and the land they cultivate."[81]

Sadiq Sa'd offered an even more scornful indictment of the country's landed magnates. He recounted how the development of capitalism in Egypt had proceeded in asymmetrical fashion because the dramatic expansion of cotton cultivation under the British occupation acted as a double-edged sword. For rural laborers, it represented a heavy burden on their shoulders because they were drawn into a field of exchange in which their lives could be unexpectedly disrupted by price fluctuations in foreign markets. However, large landowners who saw an opportunity to make enormous revenues by exporting the world's most valuable raw material aligned themselves with the policies of the colonial authorities.[82] Among the main consequences of this alliance was that large landowners preferred to accumulate their wealth through the pursuit of rents rather than through innovation and expansion. Invoking Ricardian theory, Sadiq Sa'd maintained that rents represented a form of unearned income that accrued to landlords regardless of the productivity of labor on their lands. The amount of rent that could be extracted from one farm to another was determined by natural factors—like the fertility of the soil or the scarcity of land—rather than the intensity of human effort applied to it.[83] Relying on these insights, Sadiq Sa'd argued that *'izba* owners who engaged in these rentier activities functioned as a parasitic class because they only extracted value without increasing it. This method of accumulation prevailed in societies that were subjected to colonial rule because landlords could appropriate surpluses from cultivators even if they did not produce innovatively or efficiently enough for their goods to compete on international markets.[84] "They receive an absolute rent from their tenants," Sadiq Sa'd wrote, "for no reason other than their control over them because [the landlords] are the owners of the land."[85] Because the accumulation of rents mainly benefited one class at the expense of others it could not enhance the collective well-being of an entire society. The reason for the prevalence of these rentier activities was that large landowners could not obtain sufficient capital to hire and supervise agricultural workers that would cultivate their lands on a regular basis. Sadiq Sa'd correctly recognized that these rent-seeking behaviors stemmed from an inability to acquire the funds needed for productive investment. But he mistook a historically specific pattern of accumulation that had only intensified during the war as an enduring feature of the Egyptian countryside that originated with the colonial encounter in the nineteenth century. Only in the 1940s, however, did large landowners fully acquire the parasitic attributes that contemporary reformers had come to believe hampered nationalist priorities for development.

The fidelity to productivism that characterized these thinkers did not only color their perception of *'izba* owners; it also aroused their misgivings about the mass of smallholding and landless peasants. According to Sadiq Sa'd, the redistribution of landed property had to be followed by the widespread formation of cooperative associations and collectivized farms in order to enhance the productivity of peasant smallholders. He charged that those who sought to "continuously link small properties with small-scale production" made a grave error that would lead to wasted time, energy, and resources.[86] A very similar set of observations led Rashid al-Barrawi to conclude that "a large farm is more economical than a small field."[87] A few years later, Rashad submitted a proposal to King Faruq for the development of collective farms in the final days of the monarchy.[88] In addition to criticizing the glaring disparities in landownership, he advocated large-scale farming based on agricultural mechanization, efficient inputs and cultivation techniques, improved productivity, and profit sharing. He attacked family farms as an uneconomical hindrance to agricultural modernization and proposed a pilot project that would begin with the development of collective farming on reclaimed land, but the project failed to obtain the approval of the palace. These emergent concerns about small farmers and their inability to achieve economies of scale that were widely shared by agrarian reformers in the 1940s would grow into an abiding suspicion under the Free Officers in the 1950s and 1960s.

The critique of *'izba* owners quickly spread beyond the writings of intellectuals and became widely embraced by political leaders and organizations across the spectrum. By the middle of the decade, there was a campaign in the nationalist press that began to challenge large landowners for their careless detachment from their estates and to call upon them to return to the land.[89] A circular that was likely published by the Muslim Brotherhood in the 1940s attacked the monopoly powers held by the landed oligarchy, which caused the mufti of Egypt to affirm the religious sanctification of private property. His response, in turn, prompted some members of the Islamist group to insist on the antagonism between Islam and monopoly capitalism.[90] For its part, the ultra-nationalist *Misr al-Fatat* (Young Egypt) published its own proposal for sweeping land reform and adopted the slogan "land is the property of those who cultivate it by themselves."[91] In 1950, two more bills for the restriction of landownership were presented before parliament—one by Ghali and another by a former member of *Misr al-Fatat*—but with no success.

Towards the end of the decade, the situation approached a tipping point as the high rents charged by landlords around the country had begun to generate sustained rural unrest. From the late 1940s, peasant revolts broke out against land companies, mortgage banks, and, most of all, absentee landlords.[92] During the Korean War, the sudden increase in cotton prices prompted landlords in different parts of the country to charge higher rents. In 1951, a string of peasant revolts erupted on *'izbas* that were located in some of the largest cotton producing governorates, like Gharbiyya, Sharqiyya, and Daqahliyya.[93] Big estate owners responded by calling upon police and hired security to quell the unrest. In the villages of Buhut and Kafur Nijm, tenants attacked private guards, confronted police with weapons, destroyed crops and agricultural machinery, and set fire to buildings. The estates of prominent *'izba* owners and members of the royal family—like Badrawi 'Ashur, Yusuf Kamal, Fu'ad Siraj al-Din, and others—became "battlefields of insurrection" which may have further discouraged large proprietors from farming their land directly.[94] "The situation became extremely critical," reported *al-Ahram* about one of the properties of Badrawi 'Ashur. "[T]he people left their homes and began to quickly gather in large numbers, waving sticks and throwing stones with their hands, and many of them were carrying rifles and firing them into the air."[95] In the eyes of most opposition leaders and groups, the abuses of landlords had become a rallying cry around which they would attempt to mobilize the peasantry.

The growth of anti-landlordism after the war represented a significant departure from conventional wisdom adopted by economic nationalists over the previous three decades. From the 1910s to the 1930s, as we saw, nationalist leaders and reformers typically distinguished between what they considered to be real wealth—embodied in land, crops, and farming—and fictitious wealth—embodied in money, finance, and the nonproductive activities of foreign traders. It was on this basis that Nahhas, Rashad, and others argued that the problem with the colonial order was that mercantile and financial wealth could easily leave the country, expose cultivators to ensuing shocks, and divert capital away from activities that could make the country richer by insulating it from volatility. Those earlier nationalists offered a critical appraisal of the forms of economic life that existed under colonialism, but they never directed any of their allegations towards the large landholding class to which they belonged and whom they continued to view as engines of the country's material prosperity. By the 1940s, a new generation of thinkers began to view large landowners—much like the foreign merchants and financiers of the 1910s and 1920s—as a class that shunned productive investment and instead preferred to earn their wealth through fruitless activities that did not ultimately make the nation more affluent or independent. "Land to the eyes of the Egyptian investor possesses in a permanent way the same charm, which money does to the eyes of investors generally during other slumps," wrote economist Ahmad Nazmi 'Abd al-Hamid.[96] Like many of his contemporaries, 'Abd al-Hamid regarded the growing concentration of landed wealth as an encumbrance to accumulation because land in the countryside acted as "a bottomless sink where Egyptian capital disappears." The distinction between real landed wealth and fictitious money wealth began to collapse as it turned out that many large landowners could themselves engage in patterns of accumulation that did not proceed through production. The immateriality of value that foreign merchants and financiers appeared to embody in the eyes of earlier agrarian reformers was now perceived to be a characteristic of large landowners.

TEMPORALITIES OF "EGYPTIAN CAPITALISM"

The embrace of postwar development by Egyptian nationalists—with land reform and industrialization as its major pillars—brought with it a new way of writing history. If the Egyptian Association for Social Studies (EASS) and the Fallah Department became incubators for a new generation of social scientists in the 1940s, then the Faculty of Commerce at Fu'ad I University (later renamed Cairo University) brought together a cohort of professional academics who started to become vocal about the need for economic reform. These included some of the first Egyptians who secured faculty positions, like Muhammad Fahmi Luhayta, Ahmad Nazmi 'Abd al-Hamid, Muhammad Hamza 'Ulaysh, and, most importantly, Rashid al-Barrawi.[97] During the war, some of these trained economists began to construct a framework that could explain Egypt's present condition in developmentalist terms. In 1944, al-Barrawi and 'Ulaysh became two of the first Egyptians to publish a comprehensive economic history of their country since the Napoleonic invasion. In *Al-Tatawwur al-Iqtisadi fi Misr fi al-'Asr al-Hadith* (Economic Development in Egypt in the Modern Era), they offered a reinterpretation of the previous century and a half with three major elements that became widely reproduced by contemporary authors. First, they celebrated Egypt's nineteenth century governor, Mehmed Ali, as a determined reformer who "introduced modern industry into Egypt."[98] Second, they condemned the expansion of imperial power—in the form of financial penetration under Khedive Isma'il (1863–1879) or military occupation under the British "veiled protectorate" (1882–1914)—for granting undeserved privileges to foreign people and capital, for saddling the government with unwieldy debts, and for turning the country into a producer of raw materials.[99] As a result, Egypt had failed to undertake an "industrial coup" that had succeeded in more advanced nations. Third, they portrayed the policies of successive nationalist governments from the 1910s to the 1930s—including the Sidqi Commission, Bank Misr, and the 1930 tariff law—as being chiefly concerned with restoring the country's path towards industrialization, a task that was necessary for genuine self-determination.[100] "Industry is one of the great factors," they concluded, "that bring us closer to realizing political independence in its true sense and that eliminates political and economic imperialism."[101] Modern Egyptian history was a protracted and unsteady march towards industrial modernity. Al-Barrawi and ʿUlaysh therefore heralded a new generation of reformers who began to reconceptualize the relationship between sovereignty, economic life, and history.

Apprehending history as a sequence of ascending stages had already existed in European thought since the eighteenth century. Scottish philosopher Adam Smith inaugurated this way of thinking when he postulated that all human societies moved through four stages that corresponded to different modes of subsistence: hunting, pasturage, agriculture, and commerce.[102] This historical progression ended with the generalized opulence that resulted from a commercial society founded upon the division of labor. The terms "vassalage," "fief," and "feudalism"—as they became widely understood by classical political economists—played a central role in their historical consciousness. These concepts had been invented between the sixteenth and eighteenth centuries to describe earlier forms of government and society in Western Europe. But they only acquired their modern pejorative meanings during the French Revolution, and they began to dominate the study of the European medieval past by the middle of the nineteenth century.[103] Rather than offering a well-founded empirical description of medieval Europe, however, these concepts reflected a contemporary valorization of capitalist growth in Western societies. Of course, Smith wrote on the eve of the Industrial Revolution, and he was mostly interested in forms of productivity that were small-scale and labor intensive; there was no reason for him to anticipate that industrial capitalism represented the future of human societies. Unlike the Smithian interpretation of history, the postwar writings of Egyptian nationalists did identify capital-intensive, mechanized industry as the objective of development, and any society that had not yet reached this endpoint was not fully mature.

By the 1940s, the Arabic word for feudalism—*iqtaʿiyya* or *nizam al-iqtaʿ*—had undergone an etymological transformation in Egypt that was only a few decades old. For centuries, the term *iqtaʿ* had existed as an administrative category to describe various systems of imperial land grants under Muslim empires in the premodern era. In *Al-Ahkam al-Sultaniyya* (The Ordinances of Government), the eleventh-century Shaf'i jurist Abu al-Hasan al-Mawardi described the Abbasid and Fatimid systems in detail and traced their origins back to the companions of the Prophet Muhammad.[104] In the modern period, the term *iqta'* began to acquire a new meaning that could be largely attributed to the influence that works of Western theory and history had on Arab intellectuals. In his translations of Western books, Rifa' al-Tahtawi does not appear to have used the term to refer to the Middle East or to other parts of the non-European world. In the context of Tsarist Russia, for example, he translated the word serfdom as "a kind of slavery" (*naw' min al-riqq*).[105] In the twentieth century, however, the term *iqta'* (along with *iqta'iyya* and *nizam al-iqta'*) began to appear in literary and scientific publications to describe a variety of legal, military, and political customs and arrangements that existed in the premodern world.[106] As early as the 1900s, Nahhas used these terms to describe Mamluk tributary arrangements in Egypt prior to the nineteenth century, which he believed resembled the system of duties and obligations in medieval Europe.[107] For him, the term "feudalism" began to denote a distinct historical phase—characterized by hereditary privileges and overt forms of inequality—that belonged mainly to European history and to which Egypt's past could be usefully analogized. But it hardly functioned as a descriptor for the country's present, nor did it point to any kind of fetter on Egypt's ability to develop its productive capacities in the future.

During the interwar period, the term "feudalism" became deployed with increased frequency to describe the contemporary situation in rural Egypt. In the 1920s, Lebanese-Palestinian writer Mai Ziada published a series of articles about the concept of equality in which she claimed that Egypt was ruled by a "double aristocracy" of large landowners and financiers in relation to whom the condition of Egyptian wage-earners was "almost like the position of the slave [*raqiq*] towards the noble in the feudal system [*al-nizam al-iqta'i*]."[108] In one of her gloomy exposés about peasant life in the 1930s, Bint al-Shati' compared the European feudal system of the "dark middle ages" to the rural power structure that existed in the Egyptian Nile Valley. She complained that even in the modern era when the authority of rulers was derived from the people rather than from customary rights, the village headmen "often [played] the role of representing the lord in the village."[109] In his book, which al-Barrawi and ʿUlaysh cited, Russian-Jewish historian Abraham Nahum Poliak concisely surveyed a variety of imperial land grant systems that existed in Egypt and the Levant since the fall of the Abbasid caliphate. He designated various fiscal-administrative practices—like the Mamluk *iqtaʿ* system (1250–1517) or the Ottoman *iltizam* system (1517–1856)—as feudal, and he contentiously described peasants in many parts of the region as serfs.[110] He concluded that the cessation of Egyptian tributary payments to the Ottoman Empire in 1914 "put an end to the last lawful vestiges of the feudal system in Egypt."[111] Even if they were no longer codified in law, he suggested, remnants of these feudal arrangements continued to exist informally in the twentieth century. In its modern usage, then, *iqtaʿ* was no longer just an administrative designation that referred to imperial land grants; it was a temporal category that denoted a system of government or a mode of production that belonged to a distinct stage in history and that represented surviving forms of premodern oppression that were no longer justified by modern legal and political norms.

Only in the 1940s did the term of "feudalism" enter into the mainstream political grammar of the Egyptian nationalist movement. Over time, it began to serve as a concept that could explain why the county's ability to industrialize was constrained by conditions of colonialism. Like these writers, al-Barrawi employed the term *iqtaʿ* in some of his earliest writings. In his doctoral thesis, for example, he used it to refer to the premodern land grant and tax farming systems that existed in Egypt from the Fatimid to the Mamluk era. He believed that the nineteenth-century project of defensive development that was inaugurated by Mehmed Ali and continued by his heirs had largely eliminated feudalism in Egypt. However, he hinted that the term could be anachronistically applied to those areas in rural Egypt where the Ministry of Endowments and large landowners "still offer[ed] the land for auction among farmers every year or for a limited period to be announced."[112] In their wide-ranging economic survey, al-Barrawi and ʿUlaysh included a more substantial discussion of feudalism and the problems with the concept. They began by discussing how the intellectuals who came to Egypt with the Napoleonic invasion misread the Mamluks and *multazims* in Egypt as a French feudal aristocracy.[113] However, al-Barrawi and ʿUlaysh maintained that the stagnation of premodern agriculture under the Fatimid, Ayyubid, and Ottoman empires resembled feudalism in that it necessitated an "agricultural revolution" akin to the one in England.[114] The institution of private landed property by Mehmed Ali in the nineteenth century, they argued, largely represented a transition from the feudal age to the modern age, but one that would eventually be slowed down by the British occupation.[115] A few years later, al-Barrawi began to formulate a general theory of backwardness.[116] In contrast to histories that portrayed individual protagonists as "the driving force in the development of nations," al-Barrawi argued that singular events and people were located in "a more general chain" that cumulatively represented the growth of human society. "Political, social, or economic history are manifestations or aspects of the same thing," he wrote, "the history of human development."[117] What propelled the progress of any society was the organization of production. Al-Barrawi faulted many writers before him who failed to recognize material life as "the driving force in the functioning of society and the foundation upon which all other developments are based."[118] He utilized this approach in his study of Soviet central planning that attempted to place the country's development within a schema of universal history. Relying on the work of American political scientists Frederic Austin Ogg and Walter Rice Sharp, he divided the economic history of Russia into five phases. Within this framework, he described serfdom in Russia—which he translated as *al-riqq al-iqta'i*—as an obsolete social formation in which economic progress was hampered by the "dominance of outdated feudal systems" until their abolition in the late nineteenth century.[119] Applying the same paradigm to Egypt, he concluded that the country had not fully rid itself of archaic forms of social life. "Its agricultural economy is characterized by a semi-feudal nature," he wrote, "and its agricultural and mineral wealth has not been exploited in a sound scientific manner."[120]

As al-Barrawi underwent this intellectual shift, a new generation of Egyptian Marxists began to present a similar account of colonial underdevelopment. Whether they believed that it designated a vanished chapter from the past or a surviving relic in the present, many of them embraced the concept of feudalism to apprehend the country's historical trajectory. In the late 1940s, the so-called second wave of Egyptian communism included three major tendencies.[121] The largest was the Democratic Movement for National Liberation (DMNL) or HADITU, which formed in 1947 out of a merger of two smaller groups. The strongest faction within the organization, which was loyal to its leader Henry Curiel, adopted the category of feudalism to describe rural Egypt and believed that the country needed to undergo a national-democratic revolution before reaching socialism.[122] The second tendency was al-Fajr al-Jadid (also known as Workers Vanguard). In the early 1940s, Ahmad Rushdi Salih, the future editor of the group's newspaper, published *Krumar fi Misr* (Cromer in Egypt) in which he argued that Egyptian history followed a universal path that was "no different in essence from the history of any other people."[123] Offering the first Marxist history of modern Egypt, he argued that British imperialism had both transformed the country's feudal character by integrating it into global capitalism and impeded its industrial development. Like most of his contemporaries, however, Salih believed that the war had given an impetus to the development of industrial capitalism. It spawned an Egyptian bourgeoisie and proletariat that began to take a country that was ruled by "the princes of the land and the princes of money" to a higher stage in which popular forces could guide the national movement.[124] The third tendency was represented by a smaller group known as al-Raya (The Banner, also known as the Communist Party of Egypt). In the year it was established, its founder, Fu'ad Mursi, published *Tatawwur al-Ra'smaliyya wa-Kifah al-Tabaqat fi Misr* (The Development of Capitalism and Class Struggle in Egypt) in which he rigidly applied Lenin's thesis in *The Development of Capitalism in Russia* to Egypt. He argued that Mehmed Ali's introduction of private landownership had rid the country of any feudal vestiges by the end of the nineteenth century. As a result, Egypt was sufficiently capitalist that it could plausibly undergo a socialist revolution.[125]

Sadiq Sa'd exhibited a similar mode of historical consciousness by applying the categories of universal history to the contemporary Egyptian countryside. He argued that the development of capitalism in Egypt represented a deviation from the normative path followed by more advanced nations. In Europe and America, the intensification of mechanized production had preceded the subordination of industrial capital to the imperatives of financial accumulation in the second half of the nineteenth century. This sequence was reversed in Egypt where the bulk of the funds that were allocated, by institutions like Bank Misr, towards manufacturing enterprises remained "under the influence of finance capital since its birth."[126] This abnormality was a sign that the development of economic life in the country had gone awry. Another one was the land tenure system itself. "In Egypt, we find traces of the feudal system . . . ," he wrote, "that still exist in our agricultural economy."[127] Sadiq Sa'd considered feudalism to be an economic system that had disappeared in most countries except for those that had not yet undergone a modern revolution in their means of production. He complained that *'izba* owners were the undeserving beneficiaries of "feudal privileges" because they accumulated unearned wealth from extractive landlordism rather than productive investment—which represented "one of the most important obstacles to [Egypt's] agricultural renaissance." At the same time, he maintained that capitalist social relations had extended far into the countryside. While he believed that industrial societies represented mature capitalism, he still acknowledged that the massive expansion of cotton cultivation under the British occupation had encouraged the growth of agricultural wage labor and the migration of peasants into the cities. Ironically, Western colonialism was both "the biggest reason for creating the capitalist system in Egyptian agriculture" and the primary obstacle that constrained its further development.[128] To capture this ambiguous position, Sadiq Sa'd designated Egypt as a semi-feudal society that had not yet made a complete transition into capitalism.[129]

Though he sought to apprehend Egyptian history through universal categories, Sadiq Sa'd's analysis also revealed ambiguities that unsettled them. For example, he remarked that peasant smallholders were "forced to rent [their] hands to large landowners" as their primary means of survival.[130] This could take the form of their "employment as agricultural worker[s] or as tenant[s]," both of which led to their gradual proletarianization. By blurring the distinctions between ownership, tenancy, and wage labor, his observation highlighted why the analogy to feudalism was deeply flawed. In feudal Europe, serfs did not produce principally for markets under a system where the accumulation of profit for its own sake was an overriding imperative. In twentieth-century Egypt, however, peasants did. The lands on which they grew cotton were closer to modern plantations than medieval fiefs. A vast army of socially differentiated cultivators with limited access to their own means of subsistence engaged in the mass production of a raw commodity for which they were poorly remunerated. Whether they were smallholders, rural tenants, or wage earners, those who belonged to this class of disenfranchised cultivators experienced remarkably similar rhythms of economic life. Although it was the principal means of production, the possession of land in rural Egypt did not mean that peasant smallholders were independent, self-sufficient cultivators. As Sadiq Saʿd pointed out, many of them had come to depend almost entirely on agricultural tenancy or wage labor to earn a living. The patterns of work that characterized both of these arrangements were hard to tell apart. In a 1945 report, the Fallah Department observed that rental values were almost equivalent to the whole yield of plots that were cultivated largely on the tenant's account. "[T]he tenant does not usually get a profit," the report noted, "what he gets is the wages due to him for his work."[131] A few years later, Dunn found it to be "questionable whether a renter under this system can earn much more than he could working at the rate of 35 cents a day."[132] For these reasons, Ghali astutely remarked that the condition of the tenant farmer in the Egyptian Nile Valley was "almost indistinguishable from the condition of the agricultural worker."[133] Whatever differences existed between these categories were often rendered irrelevant by the lived experiences of rural laborers who could belong to all of them at once. Regardless of their status—as owners, tenants, or wage earners—most of these cultivators spent an overwhelming portion of their working lives performing undercompensated labor for other people, rather than producing for themselves.

That exorbitant rents had transformed tenancy into a life of incessant work for landlords was a continuous theme in records left by peasants from this period. The kind of productivist language deployed by nationalist intellectuals after the war barely registered in countless petitions submitted by rural tenants to the palace. What concerned them was not the developmental trajectory of the nation so much as the cruelties of an unremitting labor process they had to endure in order to satisfy their rental obligations. In 1942, a group of tenants from Daqahliyya pleaded to the king to protect them from the unjust treatment they received at the hands of their landlord. They complained about the "pain and misery of life in constant work" for an owner who charged them a rental rate that was eight times greater than what he paid in land taxes. "[T]he cultivator who toils, along with his wife and children, and suffers hardship and humiliation," they wrote, "does not find enough food or clothing and, in the end, [the landlords] want to take everything that is produced from his land."[134] Although many of these tenants also owned small properties, the distresses they faced on a daily basis resembled those of dispossessed laborers who were compelled to produce for other people, rather than those of smallholders who sustained themselves by cultivating their own family farms. One such group from Luxor complained about the labor they had to endure to afford the excessively high rents they owed to a larger landowner. "Look at the condition of the tenants who are required to work," they wrote in 1947, ". . . and who have become poor and unable to make a living."[135] When pest attacks that year prevented them from being able to fulfill their rental obligations, the landlords began to seize their small properties. To protest this situation, they submitted multiple complaints to parliament that ultimately fell on deaf ears because, as the tenants pointed out, "its members [were] themselves the owners of leased properties." By describing a life of perpetual work for the sake of those landlords who provisioned them with their means of production these tenants painted a picture of their own labor routine that was almost indistinguishable from that of wage earners.

The nomenclatural choices of Egyptian thinkers in the 1940s were an expression of a particular historical context. More than an attempt at descriptive accuracy, they reflected anxieties about what it meant to be free, independent, and modern in a postwar world where nationally organized growth and industrialization were being widely embraced. Writing about similar debates among Chinese, Soviet, and Japanese Marxists in the 1930s, Rebecca Karl has argued that the concept of an "Asiatic mode of production" yielded exceptionalist interpretations of Chinese history—in which its peculiarities elided any meaningful comparisons with the West—that operated as a "form of world history born of the global capitalist era and not as a descriptor of real-existing societies or geographies."[136] Similarly, those Egyptian critics who lambasted the feudal privileges of large landowners advanced claims that only acquired their plausibility within the context of postwar capitalism. While they did not yet create exceptional categories, like the Asiatic mode of production, to explain Egyptian history, these thinkers did begin to understand the prevailing regimes of land and labor that existed in the Egyptian Nile Valley through universal categories that had become widely used to interpret the history of the West.[137] In doing so, however, they took features that distinguished landownership in the Egyptian Nile Valley from an ostensibly normative model in Western Europe and presented them as expressions of a distinct stage of historical development. This temporalization of difference—a process by which coeval phenomena that unfold across space are assigned to different stages in linear time—mistakenly treated the dissimilarities between two contemporaneous landholding systems as evidence that Egyptian landowners had failed to complete a historical mission. In reality, however, what separated Egyptian landowners from their counterparts in Western Europe was their access to geographically scaled forms of power and wealth, not their location in a historical teleology.

Of course, these thinkers were not wrong in recognizing that a transition had begun in Egypt, but it was not from feudalism to capitalism; rather, it was from one kind of capitalism to another. What they described as feudalism in fact referred to relatively new forms of rentier accumulation in the countryside that had only taken hold in the 1940s. More than a factual diagnosis of the country's condition, their analysis reflected the circumstances of its own creation. In a world where depression and war had constrained the productive capacities of export-led agriculture, stimulated local forms of industrial production, transformed the predominant modes of surplus extraction on large estates, and spawned a new generation of international development experts, the concept of feudalism emerged as an indictment of Egypt's present condition that took the form of sustained references to its past.

These Egyptian thinkers in the 1940s helped inaugurate an important shift in the nationalist movement's understanding of imperialism, sovereignty, and history. Their ideas would soon make their way into the program of the Free Officers. When the movement formed after the 1948 Palestine War, members of the DMNL played a key role in formulating its agenda. In his memoirs, Khalid Muhi al-Din, a member of the Free Officers, remarked that the DMNL's relationship with the movement "left a noticeable impact on our slogans and the goals and objectives declared in our publications."[138] A group of officers and DMNL members—which included Nasser, Muhi al-Din, and others—collaborated to draft leaflets for the movement as well as its program.[139] It began with a call to eliminate colonialism from the country because it was chiefly responsible for Egypt's economic backwardness, and it went on to elaborate an unambiguously stagist conception of historical development. "[Colonialism] has prevented our industrial progress and destroyed our existing industry so that it would not compete with its industries," the program declared. "It has turned Egypt into a purely agricultural country that still uses backwards techniques that were employed by the Pharaohs."[140] The faction of the DMNL that was loyal to Curiel would become the only communist group to support the July Revolution.[141] According to Ahmad Hamrush, the Free Officers' program to abolish feudalism in the 1950s originated in early meetings that al-Barrawi had with the Revolutionary Command Council, the body that ruled Egypt for two years after the coup.[142] The category soon became enshrined in the six principles of the revolution—widely believed to have been formulated by Hamrush and Muhi al-Din—that were adopted by the new revolutionary leadership.

CONCLUSION

The mode of historical consciousness exhibited by both nationalist and Marxist intellectuals in the 1940s profoundly shaped the public rhetoric and self-understandings of the officers after they rose to power. One of the foundational claims of the Nasserist state in the 1950s and 1960s was that it had enabled Egyptians to triumph over the inequities of an archaic feudal order. This assertion became a centerpiece of Nasserist propaganda. The regime's unequivocal embrace of the concept, however, all but erased the generative ambiguities that had surrounded it one decade earlier. The priorities of the Free Officers and their supporters were heavily shaped by an imperative towards industrial growth that had assumed paramount importance for nationalist planners in the postwar period. As postcolonial rulers deepened their commitment to pursuing national development, it continued to color their perception of parasitic landlords as an impediment to historical progress. But it also helped foster an abiding suspicion of smallholders and their productive capacities that would animate the Free Officers' approach to agricultural modernization. In the process, the category of feudalism went from being a seriously debated concept in the 1940s to a principal term of denunciation whose deployment became a national duty for thinkers, writers, and policymakers who wished to legitimize the Nasserist state.

SIX

GROWTH POLITICS AND THE OFFICERS' REPUBLIC

IN 1953, THE MINISTER of agriculture appointed by the Free Officers, 'Abd al-Razzaq Sidky, outlined an agenda for rural development. "The new policy should evidence the spirit of the new era," he wrote, "namely, perpetuating revolution against slowness and against hinderance of any effort to achieve a speedy and perfect development of efficiency."[1] Embracing this ethos, he believed, was imperative in Egypt where agriculture constituted a major portion of the country's wealth and employed most of its labor force. The Free Officers had seized power one year earlier, deposed the royal family, and anchored their legitimacy in principles of social justice, national independence, and development. Having the ability to boast about the realization of such a revolutionary program would profoundly shape the ways in which they wielded state power. Sidky claimed that while two-thirds of Egypt's national income was invested in agriculture it still lagged behind other countries in the efficient production of its most important crops. After the war, for example, the average yield of cotton per feddan had steadily fallen from what it was two decades earlier.[2] Many studies that were produced during the Nasser era arrived at similar conclusions. Even in years where a given amount of land produced more crops than normal, the same could not be said about labor.

Despite the growing use of synthetic fertilizers, selected seeds, machinery, and modern crop rotations, the average output per agricultural worker had continuously declined in the twentieth century.[3] The underlying reason, Sidky contended, was that population growth continually outstripped any advances in agricultural productivity per unit of land.[4] This historical trend could only be reversed by adopting a program of state-led agricultural modernization and industrialization. "Progress in agriculture," he affirmed, "creates conditions favorable to progress in industry through the supply of raw materials needed for industrial expansion."[5] Nearly a decade and a half later, the effects of this project were discernable. After declining for more than 40 years, real income per capita rose steadily from 1956 to 1966, mainly because of industrial expansion and partly because of growing agricultural output. By the mid-1960s Egyptian agriculture had achieved one of the highest yields per acre in the world.[6]

Sidky's words captured something important about the mood of the age. As decolonization gathered pace, the valorization of industrial growth became widely embraced by superpowers, international organizations, nationalist leaders, and development experts around the world. The Nasserist project firmly embodied this attitude. More than anything, it prioritized the pursuit of self-sustained, nationally scaled growth through a program of industrial development that would both enlarge the country's national wealth and socialize many of the costs of reproducing Egyptian labor. The officers would find ways to raise capital and channel it into large-scale industrial enterprises while simultaneously promoting social redistribution through public services and employment, price controls and subsidies, and, most importantly, land reform. Their faithful devotion to this project was the result of more than a decade of theorizing about economic development in the face of the changing historical circumstances of the 1930s and 1940s. The fruits of those efforts would be realized with the elevation of Rashid al-Barrawi to the status of an economic mastermind for the new regime.

What follows is an examination of the material and ideological underpinnings of Nasserism that explores some of its fundamental tensions and contradictions. Though the officers significantly transformed the countryside, their commitment to national growth did not bring Egyptian peasants closer to genuine independence as it was idealized in Nasserist discourse. Rather, it involved the imposition of new kinds of discipline and control over the rural population. It also locked the country into inescapable relations of dependence on global superpowers because, as John Waterbury has observed, the Free Officers were regularly constrained by "the search for great power patronage, arms supplies, external aid, and investment capital."[7] While they sought to establish their legitimacy by portraying themselves as deliverers of development and modernization, whatever hegemony the officers were able to build—through welfare policies, upward class mobility, and ideological control—ultimately rested on the support of foreign powers. But these arrangements were obscured by a historical account, promoted by the officers and their allies, that praised the July Revolution for having successfully reversed the condition of backwardness that colonial powers imposed on Egypt and that celebrated the officers for being the only force capable of doing so. The enduring structures that continued to subordinate the country within an international hierarchy were therefore obfuscated by an officially sanctioned narrative that identified historical time, rather than global space, as the primary vector through which the Free Officers' mission was to be apprehended.

THE POSTWAR INTERNATIONAL ORDER

The ideas that came to form the central tenets of Nasserism emerged in a postwar world that had fundamentally changed. The destruction of Western Europe propelled the United States to the status of a global superpower. After the war, it spearheaded the reconstruction of the international economic order through the Marshall Plan, which provided aid for the recovery of Western Europe, and the Bretton Woods system, which promoted the development of the so-called Third World within a set of global arrangements that maintained American monetary hegemony. Together, they established the foundation for a U.S.-led international strategy to allocate funds for individual states—especially those that were devastated by war and colonialism—to pursue nationally scaled economic growth. In January 1949, U.S. President Harry Truman introduced an agenda for the postwar era in which his country would "embark on a bold new program for making the benefits of our scientific advances and industrial progress available for the improvement and growth of underdeveloped areas."[8] His invocation of this particular geographical descriptor signaled a new zeitgeist that would define the postwar era. In his assessment of Truman's Point Four program, al-Barrawi observed that the term "underdeveloped countries" began to fill the publications of international organizations and experts who regularly produced data about national income, living standards, and growth rates.[9]

None of the postcolonial states that adopted development programs in the 1950s and 1960s did so outside of the strictures of the postwar global order; for that reason, their efforts to achieve economic independence cannot be understood simply in national terms. The Bretton Woods system, which was the main vehicle to realize this vision in the formerly colonized world, stood on two major pillars. First, it championed a new conception of development—based on growth through Western-style industrialization—as a universally realizable goal that any state could achieve. To serve this purpose, the World Bank was created to provide large-scale funding for national infrastructure projects in the Global South while the International Monetary Fund (IMF) would provide short-term loans to countries whose national currencies were destabilized by balance-of-payments difficulties. Second, it established the rules that organized monetary relations between formally independent countries in a way that maintained the central position of the United States in world trade. Governments and central banks that participated in the system could convert the dollars that they owned into a fixed amount of gold bullion while their own currencies were pegged to the value of the dollar. The system brought a degree of stability to international exchanges, thereby reducing the price volatilities that had existed during the interwar period. But it also solidified the position of the U.S. dollar as a dominant reserve currency, and it amplified many of the problems that arose from a world in which trade was conducted with national currencies that did not stand on an equal footing vis-à-vis each other.

The multiplicity of bilateral monetary relations that Egyptian leaders had to manage with individual countries was a major departure from the way money functioned during the age of imperialism, and it signaled the consolidation of a world of nation-states by the middle of the twentieth century. The adoption of national currencies allowed postcolonial governments to measure their economic growth, and to make political claims about their ability to achieve it, in ways that they could not have previously done. It rendered national economies legible in a manner that was necessary to achieve the major goals of the Bretton Woods system. Before World War I, for example, it was almost impossible for the Egyptian government to measure the money in circulation within its national borders; it could only count money that private banks moved through its major ports in accordance with the rhythms of the cotton trade. That changed in the postwar period as the growing prevalence of national money—which would be managed by the National Bank of Egypt until the creation of a central bank in 1961—enabled new forms of national accounting that became the primary metric for measuring growth.[10] However, the adoption of national currencies also exposed postcolonial states to a fundamental paradox. Because they aimed to foster domestic industries that could only operate, at least initially, with imports of technology, capital, and intermediate goods, the scope of industrialization was "always determined by the availability of foreign exchange."[11] But massive inflows of hard currency into many developing states could only happen after they had erected industries that could competitively produce finished goods for Western markets. In a postwar world where exchanges between actors in different states were increasingly mediated by nationally managed money supplies, then, the main ingredient that postcolonial states needed to industrialize—i.e., hard currency—could only exist in abundance after they had successfully industrialized.

In the early 1950s, a new generation of experts outside of the United States and Western Europe became increasingly aware that national development was constrained by the uneven structures of world trade that continued to exist after the war. Some of the first Egyptians who engaged with postwar international forums and institutions began to ascribe Egypt's underdevelopment to its subordinate position in an international division of labor that was fundamentally unequal. Alluding to reports by the United Nations and the International Bank for Reconstruction and Development, international lawyer Zaki Hashim observed that a new understanding of development—based on indicators like low income per capita, low productivity, and meager capital formation—had begun to circulate widely. Those countries that performed poorly by these standards tended to have a lopsided structure characterized by a "backward state of primary production" that discouraged the formation of capital for domestic industries.[12] Because they had long been incorporated into a system of "colonial trade," the development of these countries was inhibited by imperial powers that sought "to preserve them as sources of raw materials and, to a lesser extent, markets for manufactures."[13] By presenting things in this way, Hashim joined those voices in Egypt who increasingly viewed monocrop agriculture as a retrograde condition that could only be overcome by a project of state-led industrialization. More importantly, by postulating that the pursuit of national development was historically constrained by uneven exchange on a world scale he echoed the views of Argentinian, Brazilian, and Chilean economists at the helm of the newly founded United Nations Economic Commission for Latin America and the Caribbean (CEPAL). In 1949, Raúl Prebisch, who soon became the executive director of the commission, argued that economic development was impeded in peripheral nations that mainly produced raw materials in exchange for manufactured goods from the world's industrial centers. "The enormous benefits that derive from increased productivity," he wrote, "have not reached the periphery in a measure comparable to that obtained by the peoples of the great industrial countries."[14] According to historian Margarita Fajardo, the conception of a world divided between center and periphery became "the foundation of the *cepalino* world-making project for decades to come."[15]

Writing against the theory of comparative advantage—a staple of nineteenth-century classical liberalism—Prebisch argued that, in the long run, the prices of raw materials from the periphery tended to fall in relation to the prices of manufactured goods from the center. This meant that even as primary exporters tried to industrialize, they could not obtain the hard currency that was necessary to do so. To address the development paradox, the *cepalinos* advocated for greater international cooperation between the center and periphery—through commodity agreements, price stabilization, and aid—in order to guarantee better terms of trade for the developing world. By treating national development and world trade as fundamentally inseparable, Prebisch helped inaugurate the concept of what North American economists would eventually call the "foreign exchange gap."[16] Over the next two decades, many commentators around the world would go on to regard it as an unmistakable feature of the postwar world. In 1965, for example, American journalist Walter Lippman—who had popularized the term "Cold War" almost 20 years earlier—warned that developing countries "cannot earn enough by their exports to provide the capital they must have for their own development."[17]

After their renouncement of the Cuban Revolution and their embrace of U.S. President John F. Kennedy's Alliance for Progress, *cepalinos* began to face criticism from more radical intellectual trends in Latin America that would eventually converge into the *dependentistas* movement.[18] Feeling threatened by emergent strands of revolutionary Third Worldism, Prebisch sought to foster an alternative forum in which developing states around the world could work together. In 1962, he attended a conference in Cairo, which was opened by Nasser, that brought together leaders from developing nations in Africa, Asia, and Latin America.[19] The participants doubled down on the strategy of international aid and cooperation between center and periphery. The Cairo Declaration of Developing Countries, which resulted from the proceedings of the conference, protested that "the terms of trade continue[ed] to operate to the disadvantage of the developing countries."[20] The signatories recognized that developing countries had made some progress—in spite of unfavorable factors that were "mainly inherited from a colonial past"—but affirmed that external assistance from wealthy nations needed to be substantially increased. Only in this manner could peripheral states hope to achieve a rapid expansion in their export earnings that was so vital to their economic development. Based on the recommendations of the Cairo meeting, the United Nations Conference on Trade and Development (UNCTAD) was created two years later to promote the interests of developing countries in world trade, and Prebisch became its founding secretary general. With these efforts underway, the institutionalization of Third Worldism—albeit a less radical variant than what Cuban leaders would try to cultivate later in the decade—gradually began to confront the unequal realities of the postwar global order, but on terms that did not fundamentally threaten them.[21]

Notwithstanding these various forms of international cooperation, newly independent states were often left to themselves to confront the development paradox in more immediate ways. To obtain hard currency, many of them depended on political transfers of value—funds that were acquired through overtly state-mediated mechanisms such as aid, debt, rents, and expropriation. Otherwise, their limited ability to competitively export finished goods would prevent them from acquiring enough foreign exchange to pay for the import of foodstuffs, raw materials, and capital goods that were necessary for continued industrialization. By relying on the right combination of these methods, some countries were able to creatively navigate the development paradox. In Egypt, the terms of trade were heavily determined by the value of cotton on international markets, and they suffered an overall decline in the decade or so after the revolution.[22] To obtain additional funds, the Free Officers nationalized foreign assets inside the country and made preferential trade agreements with global superpowers. By the 1960s, Egypt had become one of the world's largest importers of food aid from the United States and capital goods from the Soviet Union, in both cases using politically mediated forms of exchange that did not operate through conventional markets. In this postwar landscape, the country's prized crop assumed a peculiar kind of importance. While it had been a major source of public revenue since the nineteenth century, by the middle of the twentieth century it became a chief means of either acquiring hard currency or circumventing the need to do so. This led one contemporary observer to conclude that the officers' pursuit of national development meant that the country's "need for foreign exchange and her dependence on cotton exports [became] more rather than less acute."[23] Although it declined as a proportion of Egypt's export receipts, the sale of cotton abroad still allowed the Nasserist state to obtain the weapons, machinery, and foreign exchange that were necessary to undertake its development project. For that reason, the careful management of the production and trade of cotton remained a major priority for the Free Officers.

The growth imperative was on display in every major stage of the crop's lifecycle. The officers sought to make cotton farmers more productive by subjecting their activities to new modes of supervision, and they appropriated rural surpluses that peasants produced through a compulsory delivery system. The export of cotton then allowed them to acquire the cash needed to import capital goods or to bypass the need for foreign exchange altogether by engaging in barter trade with the Warsaw Pact countries. Through international aid and assistance, they reorganized transportation networks, they fed a growing population of industrial textile workers, and they financed their ability to build both a military and an industrial base. For these reasons, the ability to efficiently produce the country's most important raw commodity and to convert it into essential funds and supplies for development became an overriding concern for the leaders of the new republic. But this strategy was not sustainable. From the mid to late 1960s, a combination of trade deficits, debt, war and military occupation, and weaponized aid undermined the foundations upon which the Nasserist project was based. Like other postcolonial states, the program of import-substitution industrialization (ISI) adopted by the Free Officers remained vulnerable to a particular kind of crisis tendency that ultimately stemmed from its reliance on global powers to circumvent the development paradox.

COOPERATIVES CO-OPTED

The new regime anchored its legitimacy in a promise to transform Egyptian society that began with land reform. For years, there had been a growing awareness among civilian political leaders that glaring disparities in landownership were threatening any prospects for development and, hence, the country's economic independence. As we saw in the previous chapter, there were numerous agrarian reform proposals that circulated in the 1940s, even if the palace and its allies in government had refused to implement any of them. Two months after seizing power, the officers passed a law—which al-Barrawi helped to draft—that established an ownership ceiling of 200 feddans (or 300 feddans for families with more than two children) along with rent controls and a minimum wage for agricultural workers. Anything above that limit was redistributed to small farmers in plots of two to five feddans and large landowners who lost their properties would be compensated with government bonds worth ten times the rental value of the land.[24] The officers showcased the reforms as evidence that they had decisively broken with the past by combining the imperatives of national liberation and national development. "The day we marched along the path of political revolution and dethroned [King] Faruq," wrote Nasser, "we took a similar step along the path of social revolution and decided to limit the ownership [of agricultural land]."[25] Although the officers claimed that their rule represented the dawn of a new era, their policies and programs largely grew out of an existing repertoire of reformist thought that had become widely embraced by groups across the political spectrum. In the end, the reforms pursued by the officers were less radical than those proposed by Egyptian Marxists in the 1940s or even those carried out in parts of East Asia, like Japan and Taiwan, and they were fully endorsed by the U.S. State Department as an effective tool to combat the spread of communism.[26]

For the officers and their allies, land reform represented a victory over their powerful opponents, the large landholding class. But it also posed a problem that captured the attention of reformers. When large sequestered properties were divided into smaller plots, officials wanted new owners to use their lands in ways that aligned with the state's overall goals for agricultural productivity. Ensuring that small cultivators achieved economies of scale and that officials captured a significant portion of the rural wealth they produced became a major concern for the administrators of the reform program. There were two ways in which state bureaucrats could extend their control over the productive activities of Egyptian peasants. Either they could embrace a system of cooperative farming under which officials would supervise the production and marketing of crops by peasant landholders, or they could promote collectivization under which farmers would be required to give up their individual properties and join large collective farms. While the officers initially experimented with both approaches, by the mid-1950s the former had decisively won out.

While some reformers had promoted the benefits of collectivization in the 1940s, the only serious attempt to experiment with it happened shortly after the Free Officers' Revolt. In 1953, Nasser appointed Magdi Hasanayn, a young leftist reformer, to build a socialist peasant commune on reclaimed land, known as the Tahrir Province (Mudiriyyat al-Tahrir).[27] Hasanayn was a competitor, however, to another figure who was emerging as the most powerful administrator overseeing the reform program: Sayyid Mar'i.[28] As an activist with the Sa'dist Party (an offshoot of the Wafd) who came from a family of landed elites, Mar'i's political track record was anything but revolutionary. After those parties were dissolved, however, the officers found his training in agronomy to be a useful asset. Six months after taking power, they selected Mar'i to head the newly created Higher Committee for Agrarian Reform (HCAR), a body that soon emerged as a bureaucratic empire that oversaw most aspects of the reform program. Two years later, he was chosen to head the Agricultural Credit and Cooperative Bank (the new name for the Crédit Agricole), and Nasser eventually appointed him as the Minister of Agriculture. By the late 1950s, Mar'i had leveraged his authority over these institutions to control the distribution of seeds, fertilizers, and supervised credit to peasants who farmed redistributed lands, thus making him the "undisputed lord of the entire agricultural sector."[29] Under his influence, the officers turned away from any further attempts to collectivize agriculture and instead embraced cooperative farming to realize their vision of agrarian development. There were a couple of reasons behind this decision. First, Nasser himself strongly preferred smallholdings over any kind of collectivism, a position that was consistent with his reported antipathy toward communism which he believed to be little more than a sanctimonious cover-up for political intrigues.[30] Second, the appeal of collectivization would become obviated by Egypt's heavy dependence on food imports. Unlike the Soviet Union and China, Egypt had not yet adopted an industrialization plan in the 1950s. When it did so in the 1960s, the question of how to feed a working population that was moving away from agriculture into industry was approached differently by the officers, especially since their country had become one of the world's largest recipients of American food aid. For these reasons, the officers preferred to extend their control over agriculture through state-run cooperatives, and Mar'i, whose name become synonymous with agrarian reform, became the chief architect behind their policy to scale up the management of Egyptian farms.

While the officers presented their land reform program as a revolutionary triumph over a colonial-era tenure system that favored large landowners, in reality they felt equally if not more threatened by peasant smallholders. Indeed, the staunch opposition of large landholders to the reforms, including occasional acts of armed resistance, did present an initial impediment to their execution.[31] But Mar'i believed that the biggest obstacle to a successful reform program was the predominance of smallholdings. In an ironic admission, he wrote that "the direct enemy threatening the success of any land reform is a drop in agricultural production—it is far more dangerous than the opposition of feudal landlords."[32] In the summer of 1955, Mar'i visited cooperatives in Italy and Holland and presented his findings before the U.N. Food and Agriculture Organization. He found that those societies allowed farmers to obtain inputs and machinery as well as to market their bulk crops at better prices.[33] Mar'i came to believe that the absence of state-appointed experts who were capable of supervising Egyptian peasants had prevented agricultural cooperatives from flourishing in his country before 1952.[34] "[C]ooperatives are considered the driving force of Agrarian Reform," he wrote two years later, "the purpose of which is to increase the return from the small holding assigned to the peasant in order to increase his income."[35] For Mar'i, land reform did not end with the breaking up of large estates. He created a vast a network of state-run agricultural cooperatives that would empower bureaucrats with the capacity for "supervision of the village farms."[36] The ministry would appoint trained managers to oversee the finances of cooperative societies, to identify the needs of peasant communities, and to advise them accordingly. According to Wolf Ladejinsky, an American land reform advisor in Asia, the experience of Egypt and other countries in the Global South provided "ample evidence that agrarian reform and productivity go hand in hand."[37]

By linking land redistribution to cooperative membership, the small cultivators who were supposed to be empowered by the land reforms were instead enmeshed in a web of power relations with the state. Though instances of peasant resistance to these arrangements were uncommon, they did not escape criticism from other rural activists and thinkers. In the 1950s, for example, Ibrahim Rashad would remain a firm critic of the new regime's agrarian policy. In the months before the Free Officers' Revolt, he had already turned against the Crédit Agricole which he believed had been taken over by a reactionary leadership with little interest in financing an autonomous cooperative movement.[38] After the officers took power, Rashad retired from public life. He returned to his village in Daqahliyya where he began to establish his own cooperatives and to publish a monthly magazine called *Al-Risala al- Ta'awuniyya* (The Cooperative Message). He protested that the movement for which he laid the foundations had fallen victim to state bureaucratization. Using language that he never would have employed in the 1920s, Rashad described a struggle against the "dregs of feudal society" who sought to maintain unchallenged state hegemony over peasant cooperatives.[39] While farmers could elect representatives onto a board, most observers understood early on that authority over cooperatives was "effectively in the hands of their appointed directors responsible to ministries in Cairo."[40] When it came to boosting peasant productivity, the cooperatives achieved mixed results. After 1955, agricultural output per capita began to increase for the first time since the start of the war, yet throughout the 1960s and 1970s Egyptian peasants did not increase their productivity relative to other parts of the developing world.[41] In her ethnography of an agrarian reform village, Reem Saad observed that after the 1961 reform law—which further reduced the maximum holding size to 100 feddans—farmers on redistributed lands had little or no interest in growing cotton except in return for other benefits of the reform. Because the repayment of their annual debts was collected from whatever cotton revenue they earned, the farmers regarded the compulsory delivery system as imposing a kind of tax burden they were obligated to shoulder in return for gaining access to more land. The reduction of their independence in managing their own properties ultimately led many of them to "prefer [being] wage laborers rather than agrarian reform beneficiaries."[42] According to Richard Adams, who conducted extensive field work in two rural areas, the Egyptian state relied heavily on local institutions—like agricultural cooperatives, village banks, rural councils, etc.—to enhance its extractive powers over rural producers.[43] What began as a campaign to protect Egyptian peasants from the interwar vagaries of an imperial world economy had, by the 1960s, transformed into an immense agrarian bureaucracy through which the postcolonial state could improve the welfare and productivity of farmers while deepening its capacity to supervise, control, and tax them.

In the end, the land reforms that the Free Officers undertook between 1952 and 1969 had three major achievements. They gradually limited individual ownership to 50 feddans and redistributed almost 13 percent of the country's cultivated area; they established protections for farmworkers and rural tenants, like minimum wages and rent controls; and, most importantly, they subjected new owners (and eventually all peasants) to compulsory supervision by a countrywide system of cooperatives.[44] The reforms undoubtedly helped transform the class structure of the Egyptian countryside. According to Alan Richards, they consolidated the position of a new class of rich peasants who owned what would have been medium-sized holdings before the officers' revolt.[45] At the same time, the vast population of smallholders also saw their fortunes grow; between 1950 and 1965, their share of total agricultural income nearly doubled.[46] In later years, however, these gains were largely offset by rising prices and cultivation/cooperative costs, including those imposed by newly rich peasants who found ways to evade rent controls.[47] While the proportion of peasant families who were landless declined under the Free Officers, they still represented nearly one-third of the rural population.[48] A substantial portion of these landless peasants began to find seasonal jobs in the construction and maintenance of public works. Because landless migrant workers (*tarahil*) were still vital for the production of cotton, especially the manual removal of pests, their absorption into other sectors created labor shortages that contributed to an economic crisis in 1961.[49] However, the most important effect of the reforms was the power that it gave to a new agrarian bureaucracy over the supervised production and pricing of cotton. By the end of Nasser's rule, the number of cooperatives had almost tripled, and cooperative membership increased sixfold. The proportion of rural loans that were owed to the Agricultural Credit and Cooperative Bank grew from 21 percent to 100 percent.[50] And nearly one-sixth of the rural population had joined agricultural cooperatives. According to Mahmoud Abdel-Fadil, they became integrated into a compulsory delivery system that "transfer[ed] to the state the functions of the old landlord."[51] As we will see below, the disciplining of peasant labor helped the Nasserist state maintain its political viability by allowing it to produce and sell cotton in return for foreign exchange and bartered goods amidst the global superpower rivalries that prevailed during the Cold War.

FROM RAILS TO ROADS

The postwar period saw an accelerated transformation from an imperial world of steam-powered trains to a new order based on petroleum-fueled railway and automotive transport. The main developments that hastened this shift in the late 1930s and 1940s were the expansion of paved roads in Egypt and the greater use of diesel-fueled trains. Until the mid-1930s, Egypt had no more than 400 kilometers of paved roads.[52] The signing of the 1936 Anglo-Egyptian Treaty marked an important turning point that committed Egypt to the construction of agricultural and desert highways, like the Cairo-Alexandria road, mainly to serve British military needs.[53] By 1954, the country had almost 4,000 kilometers of paved roads connecting governorate capitals and most of the major towns.[54] After a decade of restrictions on commercial automobile transport, cargo trucks were permitted to operate in 1940 under a new licensing regime, but it was only after the war that their numbers increased rapidly.[55] At the same time, the state railways were devoted to the wartime transport of military personnel, weapons, and supplies for Allied troops. But acquiring railway supplies, from coal to rolling stock, during the war proved difficult because many European factories had shifted to the production of military hardware, and the German and Italian military presence in the Mediterranean posed a threat to the overseas transport of goods. Between 1940 and 1944, the Egyptian State Railways (ESR) completed a scheme to convert almost three quarters of its more than 600 locomotives from coal to diesel fuel that arrived from the Persian Gulf.[56] In 1948, 'Abd al-Salam 'Uthman, an assistant manager for Royal Dutch Shell and Anglo-Egyptian Oilfields Ltd., estimated that oil consumption in Egypt had more than tripled over the previous decade in large part because of the conversion of the state railways to diesel fuel.[57] He concluded that the country's growing oil consumption would depend fundamentally on the railways' continued reliance on petroleum.

At the same time, the built environment that had facilitated the local transport of cotton in the first half of the twentieth century fell into obsolescence. A few days before the officers seized power, the Delta Light Railways suspended its operations due to alleged financial difficulties that made it impossible to pay back wages to its 3,000 or so employees. Its services were temporarily resumed the following month under the supervision of the ESR and the Ministry of Communications.[58] One year later, the Egyptian cabinet cancelled the concession of the Delta Light Railways that had allowed it to operate narrow-gauge lines in the Nile Delta.[59] Owing to competition from motor trucks, the light railways system had become unprofitable. An official from the U.S. State Department even remarked that the company's equipment and rolling stock were "hopelessly antiquated," and he warned that it could "never be re-organized, re-equipped, and operated at a profit."[60] Within two years of coming to power, the Free Officers issued a decree to close the London Office.[61] The demise of the light railways was therefore accompanied by the termination of a principal institution through which the state railways had long been managed.

The expansion of a countrywide network of paved roads and the transformation of the railway system meant that the transport of cotton largely shifted from trains to trucks. Between 1952 and 1956, motor vehicles moved between 60 and 80 percent of Egypt's ginned cotton shipments to Alexandria.[62] As receipts from the transport of cotton dwindled, the state railways turned to the shipment of petroleum as its chief source of revenue. One month after the Free Officers' Revolt, the head of the ESR complained to its council of directors about competition from motor vehicles. "Last year trucks transported 100,000 bales of cotton in Lower Egypt," he wrote, "in comparison to 4200 bales transported by rail."[63] By reducing their fares, truck companies had made it more difficult for the state railways to compete with them. They also had an added advantage of being able to provide services, like moving cotton from ginning factories to *shunas*, that were not possible on railways lines. He proposed to reduce freight rates in important cotton gathering centers—like Mansura and Zifta—as well as eight other Delta towns to three quarters the rate of trucks in order to attract more traffic. Unlike the 1930s and 1940s, however, such attempts to combat the prevalence of automotive transport would not succeed. The countrywide network of paved roads and the accessibility of motor vehicles that traveled on them had become far too great a competitor that brought the monopoly of the state railways to an end.

After the Free Officers' Revolt, Egypt's internal transportation system became a target of American efforts to counter expanding Soviet influence. Within months of taking power, the officers requested American technical and financial support under Truman's Point Four program that aimed to provide aid and assistance to underdeveloped countries.[64] The U.S. Technical Cooperation Administration—which was created under the auspices of the State Department in 1950 to manage Truman's program—made an agreement with the Egyptian government to assess the country's industrial potential.[65] As part of the accord, the consulting firm Arthur D. Little was contracted by the U.S. government's Foreign Operations Administration (FAO) to produce a survey of inland transportation in Egypt.[66] As a necessary step towards industrialization, the authors of the report argued, the Egyptian government needed to ensure the provision of cheap transport in order to improve access to raw materials and to markets for finished goods. They estimated that of the 13,000 privately owned motor trucks circulating in Egypt nearly 2,000 operated as public carriers over long distances, competing with trains and barges, while many more operated privately in long- and short-haul service.[67] Motor trucks generally used whatever routes were available to them, whether it was the growing network of paved roads and highways that were built in the previous two decades or the thousands of kilometers of dirt roads that reached most Egyptian villages. Unlike trains and barges, trucks could drive directly to fields across the country to pick up crops "wherever the existence of some sort of road permits."[68] The report concluded that the provision of cheap and efficient transportation remained necessary in Egypt in order for industry to "make [its] largest possible contribution to the growth of the total national output."[69]

By the late 1950s and 1960s, American assistance played a larger role in reshaping Egypt's domestic transportation infrastructure. Guided by the Eisenhower Doctrine, the United States offered economic and military support to states in the Middle East that faced "overt armed aggression from any nation controlled by international communism." Some of the largest U.S. loans to Egypt that did not take the form of food aid were allocated for communications and transportation equipment for Egypt's railway system.[70] For example, the American government extended a loan to Nasser in 1959 that would help the Egyptian government complete a program for the replacement of its steam locomotives with diesel ones.[71] In cooperation with the U.S. Department of State and the Export-Import Bank, American companies, like General Motors, found new business opportunities in Egypt (which by then was officially called the United Arab Republic) by providing the country with dozens of diesel locomotives.[72] With a new set of relationships forged between the ESR, American multinational corporations, and successive U.S administrations, the dieselization of Egypt's railway fleet was nearly completed by 1963.

In the postwar period, the physical and administrative landscape of cotton transportation was completely reorganized. Agricultural railways fell into disuse, road networks expanded, and the bureaucratic arrangements that maintained a British monopoly over railway procurements were eliminated. The material relationships that had underpinned British imperial interests in Egypt were replaced with a new set of connections. If the ability of steam-powered trains to move cotton had depended on arrangements that linked the state railways to centers of power in London, then the development of diesel engines, motor vehicles, and roads transport were accelerated by Egypt's entry into the American postwar aid regime. While these efforts represented attempts by the U.S. government to use aid as a tool of Soviet containment, they were dwarfed by the arrangements that bound Egypt to American agricultural exports under the U.S. food aid program.

FROM TERRITORIALIZATION TO NATIONALIZATION

Under the Free Officers, the mechanisms by which cultivators sold their cotton were entirely reconfigured. The national institutions that earlier agrarian reformers—like Talʿat Harb, Yusuf Nahhas, and Ibrahim Rashad—had envisioned or created to deal with volatility were not clearly state institutions. They included cooperative societies, national banks, and agricultural syndicates that would work with the government without fully being part of it. By the 1950s, many of those institutions that provisioned seeds, fertilizers, and credit had become integrated into the formal apparatus of state power. What began as an interwar project to territorialize the ability to control the lives of cultivators within Egypt's borders turned into a project of full-blown nationalization.

The question of nationalization appeared in public discussions in the months before the officers seized power.[73] In 1950, the prices of Egyptian cotton started to rise due to a combination of growing European demand for postwar reconstruction, the outbreak of the Korean War, and the reopening of the cotton futures market two years earlier after it had been closed during the war. This prompted a handful of speculators to buy up Ashmouni cotton in the futures market, more than doubling its price. As postwar inflation affected domestic consumption, some observers argued that there existed a direct relationship between the high price of cotton and the rising cost of living. The ideal solution, they believed, was for the government to intervene more forcefully in the cotton trade.

The following year, the debate over nationalization intensified after an Egyptian senator submitted a bill to the legislative chamber's financial committee proposing the complete nationalization of the cotton trade.[74] The Iranian parliament's decision to nationalize the Anglo-Iranian Oil Company in March 1951 made the question even more pertinent in Egypt. The bill set off a controversy between its supporters and opponents in parliament.[75] The senate finance committee unanimously rejected the bill, with Wafdist Minister of Finance Fu'ad Siraj al-Din maintaining that the government opposed nationalization as a matter of principle. But his insistence only came after intense pressure by cotton merchants, like Muhammad Farghali, who defended the existing system.[76] While the senate bill was swiftly defeated, the debate over the role of the government in the cotton market continued.

In April 1951, M. M. Hamadi, an assistant professor of economics at Faruq University, delivered a lecture at the British Institute in Alexandria in which he called for a wholesale nationalization of the cotton trade.[77] He was careful to specify that he did not support the expropriation of landed property on which cotton was produced; rather, he encouraged the government to requisition the crop in order to stabilize cotton prices. Hamadi explained that soaring international prices for Egyptian cotton were a driving factor behind the high cost of living at home because the National Bank of Egypt issued notes in direct relation to cotton purchasing needs. The high price of cotton meant an increase in the money supply, which in turn led to growing inflation.[78] Correcting this situation, Hamadi argued, did not require the creation of new administrative machinery.[79] The Egyptian state had already acquired years of experience in controlling prices, especially during World War II. Key features of the wartime regulatory system—including collaboration between the state and big export houses, the creation of the Egyptian Cotton Commission (ECC), and methods for projecting future cotton prices—had already laid the groundwork for the nationalization of cotton.

Anticipating a harsh reaction from cotton traders, Hamadi insisted that his proposal did not run contrary to their professed commitment to free trade since they had a long history of supporting government intervention when it suited their interests. Moreover, any claims that government purchases of cotton violated the right to freely exchange in the market ignored the social character of the cash crop. "Cotton is a commodity which is produced to be sold and not to be kept," he said. "Therefore, the platitude that requisitioning infringes individual freedom and property rights can only be regarded as a surface irritation and not a serious conviction."[80] Because the lives of millions of producers, traders, and consumers were linked to cotton, state officials had a duty to stabilize prices and to rearrange the uneven flows of income that derived from the crop in a manner that would "[afford] the greatest happiness to the many and the least sacrifice to the few."[81] While the public debate over cotton nationalization fell quiet after the summer of 1951, the proposals that were put on the table would be revived after the Free Officers' Revolt.

During the first decade of the republic, the officers embarked on a gradual yet comprehensive effort to restructure the cotton trade in three phases.[82] In the first months of the officers' rule, prices were still determined on the cotton exchange and fluctuated wildly. From 1953 to 1961, the officers revived the ECC, and it quickly became a central player in cotton markets around the country.[83] Every season it would purchase cotton from cultivators or merchants at fixed prices and then sell it to local or international buyers based on quotations for American middling on the New York Cotton Exchange. As such, the government could guarantee a minimum level of income to producers and capture a portion of the spread between the two prices with merchants capturing the rest. In 1961, the Egyptian government responded to a major failure of the cotton crop by accelerating its program of nationalization.[84] It eliminated the spot and futures markets in Alexandria and required all cotton—whether for export or domestic use—to be bought and sold under fixed prices. The dozens of export firms that had once dominated the cotton trade were reorganized into six joint-stock companies in which public entities maintained at least a 50 percent share. The following year, the government introduced cooperative cotton marketing on a volunteer basis in four governorates—Munufiyya, Asyut, Bani Swayf, and Suhag. In 1963, Nasser issued a decree that placed all the ginneries in the country under the supervision of a public organization. Two years later, the government extended the system of exclusive cooperative marketing across the entire country, thereby completing the nationalization of the cotton trade.[85]

Under the compulsory delivery system, state-run cooperatives not only monopolized the provision of seeds, fertilizers, and credit to peasants on redistributed land, they also served as the only available outlet for all cultivators to sell their crops. Cultivators would deliver their cotton to their assigned cooperative that would then hand it over to state-run collection centers (*marakiz tajmi'*). The farmers would receive payment in installments as their crop was inspected and processed. Public companies would then pick up an assigned quota of cotton from the collection centers, gin it, and transport it to Alexandria. The ECC continued to set purchase prices for different grades of cotton and announced sale prices on a weekly basis until these tasks were taken over by the Egyptian General Cotton Organization.[86] The result was a massive transfer of wealth into the state's coffers; between 1953 and 1965, the value of cooperatively marketed cotton grew from L.E. 408,000 to L.E. 18,465,000.[87] An Egyptian expert on agrarian finance observed in the late 1960s that state intervention in all aspects of cotton marketing was necessary to "determine the farmer's net return from a *qintar* of cotton." But it also served a more important purpose that was aligned with the principal aims of the Nasserist state. "If one day we reach a high level among the major industrial countries," he remarked, "the basis for that will be the abundant foreign currency earnings that cotton provided for us and upon which all development projects were based."[88]

The bureaucratic apparatus that the officers constructed to control the cotton trade reorganized the circuits of accumulation that had existed for nearly a century in the Egyptian Nile Valley. The compulsory delivery system provided the officers a way to set favorable terms of trade with Egyptian cultivators by purchasing their cotton at fixed prices and selling it for more on international markets. It acted as a form of revenue collection without taxation as noncompetitive price setting became a primary means for the Nasserist state to appropriate rural surpluses. The value it extracted from the cotton trade would prove crucial for its ability to skillfully navigate the geopolitical landscape of the Cold War and secure resources and funds from other countries, especially those that had already industrialized, for a variety of political and economic projects.

COLD WAR COTTON

In the 1950s and 1960s, the production and trade of cotton continued to form the basis of Egypt's national economy, but its proportion relative to other areas of economic activity, its major buyers around the world, and the mechanisms through which it was exchanged were profoundly transformed. Although the country still accounted for 70 percent of the world's production of extra-long-staple cotton, its contribution to public revenues slowly diminished.[89] Between 1952 and 1970, the share of raw cotton in total Egyptian exports dropped from 84 percent to 49 percent (it was mainly replaced by rice and manufactured goods, especially textiles).[90] For the officers, however, cotton remained crucial for their development program and their ability to manage geopolitical alliances during the Cold War. It supplied raw materials to state-owned textile manufacturers in Egypt, it became a chief source of foreign exchange that was necessary for continued industrialization, it served as a form of barter repayment for imports from the Warsaw Pact countries, and it represented a potential threat to other major cotton producers that could exacerbate tensions between Egypt and its foreign patrons. These processes worked in tandem with all the changes to cotton production and trade described above. Cold War cotton was produced by disciplined peasant bodies; it was transported on a U.S.-promoted road network; it was traded through a system of centrally planned pricing that transferred value from farmers to the state; and it allowed the Free Officers to either acquire hard currency from abroad or to circumvent the need for it through international barter agreements.

In the two decades after the war, the political economy of Egyptian cotton underwent important structural transformations. First, the export of cotton to Britain waned significantly. Second, the Egyptian government became a major net importer of food from the United States, making it an important participant in the U.S. postwar aid regime. Third, the Free Officers intensified their commercial dealings with Warsaw Pact countries through a variety of bilateral agreements—centered around the exchange of raw materials for

Soviet arms and capital goods—that functioned as a program of "aid through trade."[91] Along with the expropriation of land and the tolls collected from the Suez Canal, these mechanisms facilitated many of the necessary political transfers of value upon which the Nasserist state depended. What follows is a closer examination of each one of these interrelated shifts.

The end of the Manchester trade began with a series of monetary rearrangements that happened during the interwar period. After the British government abandoned the gold standard in 1931, an informal currency bloc began to form through the activities of countries that maintained close trading relations with Britain, pegged their currencies to the pound sterling, and held most of their foreign exchange reserves in London. But it was only during the war that it acquired a more formal status.[92] As part of their wartime policies, British and French authorities suspended the convertibility of their currencies within their respective monetary zones. Many countries that were tied in various ways to the British Empire were brought under a single regime of exchange controls, managed by the Bank of England, that ultimately aimed to maintain the value of sterling as a world currency. In other words, the sterling bloc replaced gold bullion as a mechanism for the preservation of British monetary power on the global stage. Under the new system, members of the bloc would deposit their dollars, francs, and other hard currencies in an exchange pool in London, and in return, they would be granted sterling credits by the Bank of England. Those countries that needed non-sterling hard currencies to pay for their imports would obtain them from the pool and all payments to non-bloc members (with the exception of the United States, Switzerland, and Sweden) had to be made through special accounts in London.[93] According to Maylis Avaro, British authorities routinely subjected sterling area countries to exchange controls, commercial threats, and economic sanctions in order to compel them to keep their foreign exchange reserves in sterling and therefore limit their access to other hard currencies and precious metals.[94] In other words, they depended on overt forms of coercion and political intervention, rather than bilateral trade, to maintain the international status of sterling after the war.

Under the wartime regulatory system, the British soldiers who were stationed in Egypt played an outsized role in putting money into circulation through the purchase of supplies, labor, and other goods. As a result, the country began to accumulate so much sterling in London that it became the second largest holder after India. After the war, the Egyptian government hoped to convert these sterling balances into dollars to pay for growing imports from the United States, but the Bank of England refused and Egypt's sterling balances were frozen.[95] As a result, the Egyptian government was compelled to leave the sterling zone in 1947, and the following year it promulgated Law 119 which ensured that all bank notes would be backed by Egyptian securities.[96] This meant that the large sterling deposits the Egyptian government had kept in London were suddenly owed to it. Egypt's exit from the sterling area proved to be a major event that reduced its trade dependence on Britain. In 1938, one third of Egyptian exports—including the largest portion of its cotton crop—were destined for the United Kingdom. By 1954–55, the latter received only 5 percent of Egyptian cotton exports as it had been surpassed by France, India, Japan, the United States, and several continental European and Eastern bloc countries.[97] The end of the Manchester trade represented an important dimension in the twilight of British imperialism; the industrial and monetary hegemony that Britain once held was shifting to new centers of power.

During the Cold War, the United States and the Soviet Union emerged as global superpowers that competed for dominance on the world stage. In the 1950s and 1960s, they began to offer development aid and assistance to newly independent countries as a tool in their rivalry.[98] Under the auspices of Truman's Point Four program, Egypt started to become a beneficiary of the postwar American aid regime. In the same week that the officers seized power, a director of the program arrived in Cairo to solicit a request for assistance from the new government.[99] The first major tranche of aid started to arrive the following year to fund a joint U.S.-Egyptian program of land reclamation and resettlement. However, the fuller incorporation of Egypt into American-sponsored development programs began in 1954 and overwhelmingly took the form of food aid.[100] While the provision of financial and technical assistance was one part of American imperial strategy in the Middle East, the creation of military alliances was another. As part of its policy of anti-communist containment, the United States promoted the formation of the Baghdad Pact—a pro-Western military alliance that was created in February 1955 and that included Iran, Iraq, Turkey and Pakistan—as an extension of the North Atlantic Treaty Organization (NATO) in the Middle East. Understanding the dangers of being too firmly aligned in the Cold War, Nasser sought to ensure that newly independent states, like Egypt, could uphold their sovereignty, control their natural resources, and assist other nations in their own liberation. He refused to join the pact and instead pursued a policy of positive neutrality, which took clearer shape after the Bandung conference in April 1955. At the same time, the officers wanted to obtain advanced weapons, especially in light of an Israeli raid on the Egyptian-administered Gaza Strip a couple of months earlier that killed more than three dozen soldiers under Egyptian command. As Israel began to purchase French weapons on a large scale, Nasser unsuccessfully tried to convince American leaders to help him build up his military arsenal.[101] The refusal of the Eisenhower administration to authorize the sale of heavy weaponry to Egypt on grounds that it was unable to pay in hard currency prompted the Free Officers to seek assistance from the Soviet Union. In September 1955, they concluded the Egyptian-Czechoslovak arms deal whereby the officers purchased weapons that augmented Soviet influence in the region.[102] This marked the first time in modern history that the Western monopoly over the provision of military supplies to the Middle East was broken.

As the arrangements that linked Egypt to the sterling bloc fell into decline, Egypt became part of a new international monetary order that operated through a multiplicity of bilateral relations rather than integration into an imperial currency zone.[103] The U.S. food aid regime allowed governments, especially in the Global South, to purchase American surplus agricultural commodities without depleting their scarce reserves of hard currency. Because the purpose of the program was to promote U.S. strategic interests in the Cold War, aid was largely directed towards countries for the purpose of anti-Soviet containment. Under Public Law 480, the United States Department of Agriculture began to manage food assistance programs around the world. The most common form of aid, known as Title I, consisted of discounted sales of U.S. food in return for the local currencies of purchasing countries (i.e. counterpart funds). While emergency famine relief and barter trade also fell under the rubric of the program, these concessionary sales accounted for the vast majority of its activities. A sizeable portion of the money that Egypt paid to the United States for wheat imports was loaned back to the Egyptian government for the construction of roads, bridges, schools, and health clinics.[104] The massive growth of American food assistance reflected the country's rise to global superpower status in the postwar period, after which it replaced Western Europe as the center of international trade.[105] By 1956, food aid accounted for nearly half of U.S. economic assistance to foreign countries, and by the mid-1960s it accounted for one quarter of global wheat exports.[106] While the provision of cheap food was intended to promote industrialization in developing countries by feeding their growing urban labor forces, it ended up fostering long-term food dependency and agricultural underdevelopment for many participants in the program.[107]

As the officers pursued industrialization, Egypt became one of the most important countries that participated in the program. In the 1950s and 1960s, the number of industrial laborers in Egypt more than doubled, while its urban population increased steadily, even if the majority of Egyptians still lived in the countryside.[108] The growth of this sizeable workforce was sustained by the provision of cheap calories that mainly consisted of American wheat. While some of the grain was diverted to the countryside to mitigate against crop failures or to provide fodder for livestock, most of it was used to regulate urban food prices (especially for *baladi* bread) in order to keep wages down. Between 1962 and 1966, the United States was the largest single source of foreign loans to the country, and by 1963, Egypt had become the world's largest per capita consumer of American food aid.[109] Many of the workers who obtained American wheat worked in state-run textile factories, the heart of the country's growing industrial sector.[110] A few years into the officers' rule, the output of cotton yarn had increased by more than 50 percent from what it was before they had taken power.[111] By 1960, the manufacture of textiles employed more than half of Egypt's industrial workforce.[112]

The export of industrial goods, especially cotton textiles, was an important means of acquiring hard currency. But there was a limit to how much Egypt could rely on it to further the country's industrialization. First, the physical qualities of Egyptian cotton were not well suited for a country that was still incubating its domestic industries. Because farmers specialized in the cultivation of long- and extra-long-staple cotton that required high-quality processing with advanced machinery, its natural endowment demanded "very capital-intensive industrialization" whereas other countries that had opportunities for more labor-intensive manufacture could move a larger portion of their population into industrial employment.[113] Second, the export of Egyptian textiles was limited by the imposition of international trade restrictions that favored industrialized countries. Although states that engaged in commercial transactions with the capitalist bloc ostensibly participated in a regime of free trade—one that was liberalized through successive revisions to the General Agreement on Tariffs and Trade (GATT)—their ability to do so was always circumscribed by Western powers. For example, a series of agreements in 1961 and 1962—known as the Short- and Long-Term Arrangements Regarding International Trade in Cotton Textiles—limited the sale of mechanically produced cotton textiles to Western countries at a time when cotton goods (including yarn) made up at least 70 percent of Egypt's manufactured exports.[114] Third, global superpowers had the ability to withhold political transfers of value to developing states in order to discipline their nationalist leaders. Since food aid constituted 70 percent of American assistance to Egypt, the United States could use the "wheat weapon" to influence the policies of the Nasser government, as it did during the Tripartite Aggression and the Egyptian intervention in North Yemen.[115]

Another source of foreign exchange was the country's raw materials themselves. The export of cotton to the United States was a principal means for Egypt to acquire dollars. But Nasser's ability to expand cotton production and to access American markets faced political obstacles. Since 1942, U.S. congressmen from the American South ensured that restrictions were maintained on the importation of long-staple fibers, including from Egypt.[116] By the mid-1950s, Nasser's collaboration with the Soviet camp along with his decision to join the Bandung conference began to irk the Eisenhower administration. This prompted the U.S. Secretary of State John Foster Dulles to draft a secret policy briefing—known as the OMEGA memorandum—that sought to confront Nasser by, among other things, manipulating U.S. trade policies in a way that would seriously impede the export of Egyptian cotton.[117] Although it was never put into effect, American concerns with Egyptian cotton would continue to color their view of Nasser. His growing ties with the Soviet camp in the mid-1950s prompted the United States (in partnership with Britain and the World Bank) to present Nasser with a formal offer to help cover the costs of the Aswan High Dam, the centerpiece of his development project which required 30 percent payment in foreign exchange.[118] Nasser's program of agricultural growth, however, vexed politicians in the United States who continued to view Egyptian cotton as a potentially dangerous competitor. Those who opposed funding the dam included supporters of Israel, lawmakers who rejected Nasser's rapprochement with communist states, and Southern politicians who feared that the increased production of Egyptian cotton resulting from the dam would harm American cotton farmers. "Because of basic opposition from congressional representatives from cotton-growing areas," the deputy director of Near Eastern affairs at the State Department warned Dulles, "it is possible that the administration's hands will be tied in the implementation of the High Aswan Dam project."[119] In July 1956, the Eisenhower administration withdrew its offer to finance the construction of the dam, and in response, Nasser nationalized the Suez Canal Company and froze all of its assets. Three months later, Britain, France, and Israel invaded Egypt to reverse the nationalization and to remove Nasser from power, but the mission failed. Compensating the former shareholders of the company, however, contributed to the depletion of Egypt's foreign-exchange reserves. This was compounded by a cotton pest attack in 1961, after which Egypt turned to the IMF for the first time."[120]

While the U.S. food aid program operated as one pillar in the Free Officers' project of nationally scaled industrial growth, the Soviet program of "aid through trade" functioned as another. In the early years of the Cold War, the Soviet Union began to reassess the political landscape of the world amidst the intersecting dynamics of decolonization and superpower bipolarity. After Stalin's death, Soviet leaders and intellectuals who became increasingly concerned with countering the formation of American-led military alliances turned to national liberation movements that shared the Soviet Union's opposition to Western dominance. By the mid-1950s, they had started to revise Soviet doctrine on national revolutions and the historical role of their local bourgeoisies. Rather than insist that the Soviet Union only join forces with other communists abroad, they opened up to the possibility that national bourgeoisies who had suffered under colonialism could be potential allies in the Cold War.[121] In 1956, the first secretary of the Communist Party of the Soviet Union, Nikita Khrushchev, remarked that "the disintegration of the imperialist colonial system" had become the most important trend in the postwar era.[122] The Soviet Union could therefore find common cause with postcolonial states that were not necessarily communist in order to form a united front against Western imperialism.

When the Free Officers came to power, trade relations between Egypt and the Soviet Union had existed for almost two decades.[123] But they reached new heights in the mid-1950s. As a result of Khrushchev's reorientation towards the Third World, Soviet trade with non-communist states in Asia, Africa, and Latin America witnessed a fivefold expansion over the next decade.[124] During that time, Egypt became the first country outside of the Communist Bloc to receive significant assistance from the Soviet Union, and it soon became one of the top beneficiaries of Soviet aid in the world. This included the provision of soft loans that were serviced through a system of state-managed commerce whereby the two countries engineered an Egyptian trade surplus with the U.S.S.R as well as support for projects like iron and steel manufacturing and the Aswan High Dam.[125] Rather than taking the form of consumer goods, like American foodstuffs, Soviet aid largely financed the import of capital goods and weapons. During the first 13 years of Nasser's rule, the volume of Egyptian trade with the Soviet Union grew from $15 million to $380 million.[126] By 1970, Egypt was sending 61 percent of its exports to socialist countries and receiving 34 percent of its imports from them.[127]

The export of Egyptian cotton was at the center of the Soviet aid regime. Much of the cotton that was produced by disciplined peasant bodies was seized by the Egyptian government and exchanged for weapons, equipment, and machinery through preferential trade agreements with the countries in the Soviet camp. Even though some officers privately worried about the expansion of Soviet influence in the Middle East, turning raw cotton into necessary inputs for defense and industrialization became a signature feature of Nasser's development strategy.[128] While these deals were part of a policy of nonalignment (or positive neutrality), they were also appealing because of their specific terms. The Egyptian-Czechoslovak arms deal, which marked a turning point in the Cold War, was essentially a "cotton for arms" barter agreement that carried a discounted interest rate and required only 20 percent of the value of the weapons to be paid in hard currency. The remainder would be paid in raw materials—mainly cotton.[129] Over the course of the 1950s and 1960s, the Free Officers concluded dozens of barter agreements—both military and nonmilitary—with the U.S.S.R, Bulgaria, Czechoslovakia, East Germany, Hungary, North Vietnam, Poland, Romania, and China.[130] In 1957, Egypt and the U.S.S.R signed their first major technical cooperation agreement that saw the disbursement of Soviet credits for the import of capital goods with Egyptian repayment phased over 12 years at 2.5 percent interest. This agreement effectively financed Egypt's first five-year industrialization plan from 1960 to 1965—which required nearly L.E. 150 million, or 60 percent of its total cost, in foreign exchange—and it laid the groundwork for similar agreements in the future.[131] According to a Soviet source, more than three quarters of the credit that was granted to Egypt by the U.S.S.R went to industry and power engineering.[132] Rather than the provision of hard-currency loans, then, Soviet aid consisted of barter transactions on favorable terms that earned Egypt higher returns on exports than it would have received from trading on Western markets.

The Soviet aid regime reorganized the position of Egyptian cotton in world trade. Between 1954 and 1956, shipments of Egyptian cotton to Czechoslovakia quadrupled while those that went to mainland China, East Germany, and the Soviet Union doubled; by the end of this period, cotton exports to these countries had for the first time exceeded those that were destined for Western Europe.[133] Whereas in 1938 Egypt only exported 10 percent of its cotton to the Soviet Union, Eastern Europe, and China, by 1957 that share had jumped to 46 percent.[134] "For the sake of extensive shipments of military and industrial equipment from the Soviet bloc," a U.S. Senate report observed, "Egypt has pledged a substantial portion of its main export crop of cotton in payment."[135] The geopolitical impact of these arrangements spoke for themselves. According to one estimate, the total Soviet aid to Egypt between 1954 and 1974 was probably four times larger than Western aid.[136] To ensure favorable terms of trade for their ally, the Soviets either paid a premium for cotton that it bought from the Egyptian government or sold it arms and capital goods at discounted prices. Whereas in 1961 the Soviets purchased Egyptian extra-long-staple cotton at 6 percent more than its price on other markets, by 1971 that differential had reached 24 percent (and for lower quality cottons it was even higher).[137] One observer even surmised that "low prices for arms and high prices for cotton" allowed Egypt to obtain an abundance of weapons that it could not have obtained in similar transactions with Western countries.[138]

While these barter arrangements ensured a net transfer of value to Egypt through nonmarket mechanisms, they were not immune to controversy. A recurring subject of contention concerned the prices that the Egyptian government received for its cotton from the Soviet Union and the destination of the crop after it was sold. In 1962, for example, a Soviet trade representative learned that Egypt had been selling its cotton on Western markets even though it had not yet completed its deliveries to the Soviet Union as stipulated in an existing trade agreement. For their part, Egyptian officials did so to pressure the Soviets into reducing the prices at which they acquired Egyptian cotton and to deter them from reexporting the purchased crop to Western markets and thereby further driving down the price of future sales.[139] These kinds of disagreements were indicative of a growing dependence that had linked Nasser's Egypt to the Soviet Union. By the 1960s, Egypt had become one of the largest Soviet trade partners in the Third World—among developing countries it had become the top importer of spare parts from the Soviet Union, which buttressed Nasser's industrialization program.[140]

From the late 1950s to the mid-1960s, Egypt witnessed its highest growth rates under Nasser, partly because of American food aid and Soviet barter agreements.[141] According to one estimate, the country's GNP by the end of that period was more than 20 percent greater than it would have been without the contributions of foreign capital.[142] But the model of national development pursued by the officers proved unsustainable. In the decade after the July Revolution, the Egyptian state's net foreign exchange reserves declined by more than 90 percent, especially as government officials rapidly drew on their released sterling balances.[143] After a cotton-leafworm attack in 1961 reduced the crop by 40 percent, there were almost no holdings left except for gold.[144] This forced the government to devalue the Egyptian pound the following year and to resort to high-cost borrowing in order to maintain the country's pace of growth. By 1964–65, the Nasserist system entered a general crisis. The simultaneous pursuit of its two main objectives—promoting nationally planned industrial growth, on the one hand, and creating a mass consumer society financed by public spending, on the other—had become too expensive. As a percentage of national income, the rate of investment and the share of wages began to decline sharply.[145] Egyptian industrialization slowed down as state enterprises could not acquire sufficient export earnings through competitive production for overseas markets. Meanwhile, the costs of providing social welfare, financing industrialization, and intervening militarily in North Yemen became too burdensome for a state that relied heavily on international subsidies. By the middle of the decade, the IMF observed that "foreign exchange shortages have placed a brake on industrial expansion."[146] The vast majority of Egypt's debts were owed to foreign governments, nearly one-third of which came from the Soviet Union.[147] The country began to fall behind on its repayments, and servicing foreign debt consumed a significant portion of its hard currency.[148] At the same time, a new cabinet under the premiership of Zakariyya Muhi al-Din adopted the slogan "no consumption without production," and public concerns about dependence on foreign trade began to circulate in the state press.[149] "Why do we import finished textiles for 6 million pounds?" asked an author in the weekly *Ruz al-Yusuf*, urging greater reliance on the country's own cotton.[150] As its budget and balance-of-payments deficits continued to grow, the officers' regime was months away from a crisis from which it would not recover.

The country's military defeat by Israel in 1967 sounded the death knell for

FIGURE 9. "Oh my . . . the cotton has shined." Source: *Rūz al-Yūsuf*, vol. 1993, August 22, 1966.

Nasserism. The war resulted in a severe constriction of those flows of rent and aid upon which the Nasserist state depended.[151] At a time when the Egyptian state bore enormous costs of rebuilding its military, the United States halted its food aid to Egypt (a decision taken in 1966), the closure of the Suez Canal blocked the officers' ability to collect tolls from maritime traffic, and Israel's occupation of the Sinai Peninsula diminished revenues from both tourism and the production and sale of petroleum. Meanwhile, Egypt became one of the first countries to fall into protracted arrears to the IMF, even though those financial obligations were relatively small compared to its loans from foreign governments, and its debt service payments nearly doubled over the next five years.[152] Although grants from Arab oil exporters increased after 1967, and loans from the Soviet Union continued to arrive, they mostly went towards Egyptian military outlays that rose by more than 600 percent.[153] By 1973, the ratio of Egypt's foreign debt payments to the export of goods and nonfactor services was the largest in the world.[154] As it turned out, the success of the Nasserist project was contingent on the ability of the officers to access political transfers of value and the willingness of foreign countries to provide or withhold them. Just as the pursuit of national development enmeshed Egyptian cotton producers in a new web of power relations with the postcolonial state, it also locked the country into inescapable relationships of economic and technological dependence on global superpowers.

"A COMPLETE THEORY OF REVOLUTIONARY CHANGE"

The 1950s and 1960s witnessed a wave of historical revisionism the central purpose of which was to legitimize the arrival of the Free Officers. What distinguished Nasserist historiography from earlier traditions that were also shaped by presentism, however, was the particular standpoint from which it reinterpreted modern Egyptian history.[155] If its disseminators saw the past through the windows of their contemporary situation, then the particularities of the world they inhabited—one that had become saturated with concerns about nationally scaled growth and industrial development—are what made possible the kinds of stories they told. To present themselves as a force whose rise to power heralded a transition to modernity, the officers drew on the intellectual repertoire that Egyptian Marxists, socialists, and left-nationalists had constructed less than a decade earlier. It provided the basic terms and concepts that selectively permeated the early speeches and writings of the revolutionary leadership before they found more formal expression in its foundational documents. The six principles of the revolution—which included the "abolition of feudalism" and the "abolition of monopoly and the domination of capital over government"—were enshrined in the 1956 Constitution and, later, in the 1962 National Charter. As we have seen, the usage of the term "feudal" to describe the Egyptian countryside gained traction among opposition groups and intellectuals in the 1940s. Its deployment by Marxists, socialists, and left-nationalists represented a sophisticated albeit problematic attempt to understand the differences that separated economic life in the Egyptian Nile Valley from Western Europe and the United States. After the officers seized power, however, it turned into a denunciatory label used by writers, intellectuals, and policymakers who sought to prove their fidelity to the new regime.

The efforts at historical revision under the Free Officers were on display almost from the start. Six months after they took power, al-Barrawi declared that their actions heralded a necessary revolution against backwardness that would align the country with the spirit of the modern age.[156] After promulgating their first law for the distribution of landed property, the officers convened a series of festivals and celebrations in which they proclaimed the benefits of agrarian reform. In 1954, for example, Nasser spoke at a land redistribution ceremony in the town of Maʿmal al-Qazzaz. "Restricting property," he declared, "will rid us of the feudal system that lasted for many years in this country."[157] The officers soon began to fashion their own cohort of historians. They enthusiastically promoted the work of ʿAbd al-Rahman al-Rafʿi that analogized the officers to earlier historical figures, like Colonel Ahmad ʿUrabi, who they portrayed as national heroes.[158] The work of Muhammad Amin Hassuna re-narrated the history of modern Egypt as a series of popular struggles that culminated with the Free Officers' Revolt and in which "the people" gained their national consciousness.[159] Around the same time, Abd al-Rahman al-Sharqawi published his classic social realist novel, *Al-Ard* (The Land), in which he told the story of a struggle between insurgent peasants and an avaricious landowner in a prerevolutionary village.[160] Meanwhile, the state began to actively produce its own propaganda materials. An upsurge of official pamphlets and publications depicted modern Egyptian history as a succession of popular confrontations with Western imperialism and its local collaborators that reached its zenith in 1952. In a short treatise published by the HCAR, the authors retold the history of the country as an extended series of "silent struggles" by Egyptians against an uncompromising despotism that was most clearly embodied in the reign of Mehmed Ali.[161] Long portrayed as the founder of modern Egypt, Mehmed Ali now appeared as an antagonist whose primary misdeed was to turn peasants into "real slaves of the land" by introducing the *'izba* system in the nineteenth century. Within a few decades, Egyptians were unjustly subjected to an alliance of "feudalism and foreign occupation" which turned the country into a cash crop plantation that persistently suffered from overpopulation and agricultural stagnation.[162]

Those accounts of modern Egyptian history that made the boldest claims to advancing a novel interpretative framework belonged mostly to the Marxist tradition. These included works that were both laudatory and critical of the Free Officers.[163] The strongest faction within the Democratic Movement for National Liberation (DMNL) initially supported the Free Officers out of a belief that in order to reach socialism Egypt had to go through a national-democratic revolution. It only retracted its support one year into their rule, after the officers took repressive measures against the communist and independent trade union movement. Egyptian communists then united in opposing the regime until the mid-1950s when Nasser drew closer to the Soviet camp, nationalized the Suez Canal, and defended his country against the Tripartite Aggression. These actions won him the support of communists from inside Egyptian prisons. Over the next few years, they began to theorize the officers' regime in new ways, a process that was made easier by Khrushchev's reorientation of Soviet foreign policy towards the decolonizing world. By the late 1950s, the United Communist Party of Egypt—an alliance that brought together the majority of communists in the country—argued that the Nasserist state followed a path of "non-capitalist development" that would ultimately lead to socialism.[164] Their short-lived unity was followed by mass arrests of communist activists towards the end of the decade. Around the same time, the works of Shuhdi 'Atiyya, Fawzi Jirjis, and Ibrahim 'Amir offered careful examinations of both the country's historical development and the appropriate sociological categories through which it should be apprehended.[165] As the term "feudalism" became one of the regime's main legitimating categories, some Marxist intellectuals like Anouar Abdel-Malek and Ibrahim 'Amir eschewed it altogether;

instead, they suggested, directly or indirectly, that the country's twentieth-century realities were firmly rooted in capitalism.[166] While these thinkers laid the groundwork for generative forms of self-criticism by Egyptian Marxists in the 1970s and 1980s, they remained outliers for their time as both officers and communists kept tenaciously producing modernist accounts of the country's history. Both groups would once again draw closer together a few years later as the regime embarked on another reorientation.[167]

In the early 1960s, the officers responded to a set of challenges, like the unwillingness of private capitalists to invest in industry and the collapse of a union with Syria, by launching a new project that they termed Arab socialism. Their program involved a renewed drive towards planned industrialization, nationalization, and public sector expansion. However, they were careful to present it as an alternative to both capitalism and communism, and to insist on the compatibility of the country's Islamic heritage with its socialist transformation. After promulgating a series of socialist decrees and regulations, they adopted the National Charter in 1962 that reaffirmed the leadership's commitment to these goals without the complete elimination of private ownership.[168] The program would be undertaken by a new ruling party known as the Arab Socialist Union (ASU). As much as the charter prescribed future policies, it also called for a reinterpretation of the past. It charged that successive generations of young Egyptians were "taught that their country is not fit for industry, nor capable of it," and as a result, they misunderstood its national history. The problem was that the anti-colonial advance that had begun with the uprising of 1919 proceeded "without a complete theory of revolutionary change." The officers and their supporters understood themselves to have transcended the limits of the interwar nationalist movement by combining a national liberation struggle against foreign rule with a social revolution against backwardness. It would only be a matter of time before Egyptians realized that a socialist solution—by which the authors of the charter meant state-led industrialization combined with social redistribution—was a historical inevitability imposed by the realities of colonial underdevelopment and embodied by the Nasserist state.

Over the next few years, the theory of history that appeared in the National Charter was fleshed out by writers and historians, and the term "feudalism" began to appear with more regularity in Egyptian publications, speeches, and campaigns.[169] In 1963, the Ministry of Culture established a commission to supervise the rewriting of Egyptian history in accordance with the newly proclaimed socialist identity of the regime. The head of the project, historian Muhammad Anis, described the "socialist view of history" as an approach that examined the development of social forces, rather than the actions of great men who were often the focus of older nationalist accounts.[170] He divided the major social classes that shaped the country's modern history into six categories, including feudalists. As Nissim Rejwan argues, the project of rewriting history was understood by its advocates to be necessary for the intellectual modernization of Egyptians, and it would encourage an even greater proliferation of revisionism. Such efforts would gain further momentum after an infamous affair in the Nile Delta. In 1966, local activist Salah Husayn launched a struggle against a powerful landowning family from his village, Kamshish, in the Munufiyya governorate.[171] After being recruited into an ASU committee, Husayn used his position to rally peasants around a radical vision of socialism that emphasized local empowerment, rather than the one promoted by the regime that emphasized political-economic modernization and centralization. When Husayn was shot dead in 1966, Nasser visited his village and set up the Higher Committee for the Liquidation of Feudalism, which became overwhelmingly dominated by officers and landowners.[172] As Timothy Mitchell remarks, this response narrowly defined the problem in Kamshish as "the survival of individual 'feudalists,' meaning remnants of the old regime, rather than as the power of a landowning class nurtured by the new regime."[173] However, the anti-feudal posture of the officers was met with positive reactions from many Egyptian socialists. Four months after the incident, the newly founded leftist magazine, *al-Tali'a*, published a special issue in which its authors carefully examined social relations in the countryside and warned that feudal elements still prevailed.[174] At the same time, a new wave of revisionist histories began to emerge. In 1966, for example, Muhammad al-'Azab Musa published *Awwal Thawra 'Ala al- Iqta'* (The First Revolution Against Feudalism) in which he attempted to reveal a historical precedent for combating feudalism in Egypt that went back to the Pharaonic age.[175] The concepts to which the Nasserist state tethered its legitimacy did not only circulate among intellectuals; they also gained traction in the everyday consciousness of peasants across generations.[176] Its rhetoric proved to be trenchantly durable over time

FIGURE 10. Feudalists: "From the day the peasants exposed us our hands and legs have become tied . . . and we're unable to frighten them." Source: *Rūz al-Yūsuf*, vol. 1980, May 23, 1966.

as Husayn became remembered by his own family members and villagers as a noble warrior who waged a battle to "get rid of feudalism."[177]

CONCLUSION

A fundamental problem with Nasserist historiography is that it does not provide a way to understand the historical conditions that made its claims both possible and compelling. As this book has shown, the central tenets of Nasserism became appealing for two reasons. First, they acquired their plausibility in a world where industrial growth had become an overriding imperative of national development, and conditions in Egypt had made the country ripe for its reception. In that sense, Nasserism represented a local instantiation of a global development model that took hold in the three decades after the war. As a historically specific articulation of state-economy relations, the Free Officers' project had much in common with its counterparts in the Global South that pursued remarkably similar policies—many of which were avidly promoted by nationalist leaders, development experts, international organizations, and global superpowers alike. For that reason, Nasserism can only be fully grasped within the context of world history.

Second, Nasserist historiography was rooted in a kind of fetishization that exists widely within capitalist societies. The Free Officers anchored their political legitimacy in an ideology that represented a reversal from what Egyptian nationalists had proposed less than half a century earlier. Rather than identify the realm of circulation as the primary arena in which colonialism obstructed the ability of Egyptians to become independent, the officers presented the sphere of production as the central space in which the impact of colonial underdevelopment manifested itself. Overcoming this state of affairs required a revolutionary improvement of the nation's productive capacities. As such, national liberation could only be achieved through the pursuit of national development. In their private meetings and in international forums, the officers might have exhibited an awareness of the uneven forms of global trade within which their country was still locked, and they undoubtedly tried to confront the development paradox through some of their policies. But the critique of uneven exchange and its persistent legacies hardly appeared in their public campaigns. As a result, the officers did not anchor their political legitimacy in any claim to be skillfully navigating, let alone challenging, a world system that continued to disadvantage them. Instead, they largely described their project as a triumphant ascent from one stage of history to another. In their official discourse, then, the officers and their allies winnowed out the realm of production and isolated it from its related sphere of circulation, a maneuver that had several important consequences. It permitted the officers to sustain a belief that national development in a postwar world was both possible and desirable. It encouraged them to fix their attention on a problem that they could name but not solve because the capacity of the country to produce efficiently was always constrained by globally uneven forms of exchange. Most importantly, it allowed the officers to portray their own rise to power as a triumph over a traditional order in which an alliance of imperial forces and local collaborators had impeded the development of the country.

The Nasserist state presented itself as a force that moved the country forward in historical time rather than one that remained locked into relations of power and subordination within an unequal capitalist world economy. The extent to which the officers' pursuit of national development could succeed, however, had less to do with any confirmation of their own linear conception of history than it did with their unsustainable ability to leverage Cold War geopolitics to temporary advantage through various forms of subsidy. The officers' republic did not represent the completion of a historical mission that was previously arrested by colonialism; rather, it embodied one of many political-economic configurations in a longer history of capitalism in Egypt. The fetishization of production might have lent itself to a mode of historical narration in which the July Revolution marked a decisive break with the past. But if the regime that the officers built represented one episode in a longer history of capitalist transmutation, rather than a watershed in a history of ruptures, then understanding their ascent to power as a revolution against backwardness misrecognized both the historical conditions from which they emerged as well as the postwar environment in which they existed. The officers represented an outgrowth of the past from which they continuously sought to distance themselves more than an inevitable and uncompromising rebellion against it. Their preoccupation with national development, their control over peasant livelihoods, their inescapable dependence on global superpowers, and their efforts to justify these arrangements by retelling the modern history of their country in stagist terms have profoundly shaped both politics and historical memory in a formally independent Egypt and continue to do so until the present.

EPILOGUE

IN JANUARY 2013, Egyptian journalist ʿAbdullah al-Sinnawi offered a historical appraisal of Nasserism. "[I]n its entire history," he wrote, "Egypt has not witnessed . . . social justice similar to what happened in the Nasserist era."[1] As the chief editor of the country's leading Nasserist newspaper, *al-ʿArabi*, he had long been a public supporter of the regime that the officers built. Writing nearly six months before the military coup that would remove the popularly elected Muslim Brotherhood from power, al-Sinnawi's words were an indictment of the existing state of affairs in Egypt. By harkening back to an earlier moment, he repudiated the major political-economic tendencies that had prevailed in the country over the previous four decades. His praise for the social gains that were delivered under Nasser implied a rejection of neoliberalism—whose adherents had no conception of social justice outside of trickle-down economics—and Islamism—whose proponents anchored their understandings of social justice in frameworks of religious moral economy. To venerate the Nasserist past, then, was to simultaneously endorse what he believed to be a proven alternative to an objectionable present.

This kind of defensive admiration for Nasserism has long colored various strands of political dissent in Egypt. In a 2014 interview, Gilbert Achcar argued that Nasserism represented "the main form of progressive political consciousness in Egypt."[2] This was discernible during the period of flourishing opposition activity that existed over the previous decade. As part of a sustained anti-privatization campaign, for example, activists rallied to oppose the undervalued sale of Omar Effendi, an iconic department store chain that was nationalized in the late 1950s, to a Saudi trading company. After the 2011 revolution that unseated former Egyptian President Hosni Mubarak, an administrative court declared the decision to be unlawful.[3] The principal complaint by detractors was either that the privatization involved flagrant corruption—an objection rooted in liberal concerns about the rule of law—or that it surrendered the country to foreign capital—an objection rooted in nationalist concerns about Egyptian sovereignty. Absent from these efforts was any analysis of how transformations in the structure of class relations, the spatial organization of Egyptian capital, and the prevailing international conceptions of development made it difficult to simply revert to the way things were decades earlier. To these activists, the annulment of the sale represented the potential restoration of a more prosperous, just, and independent society that had gradually been surrendered by the country's leadership. As Amr Adly has remarked, "The only social contract present in the imagination of many Egyptians is purely Nasserist."[4] More than a relic of the past, Nasserism represented an aborted mission that had to be restored so that its ideals of anti-imperialism, independence, and social justice could be fully realized. As a result, a widespread romance for early independence leaders, like Nasser, has tenaciously pervaded many discussions about history and social change in the postcolonial world. Writing a critical history of Nasserism, then, is as much an exercise in reimagining the future as it is rethinking the past.

Outside of Egypt, the postwar golden age has also been a misplaced object of nostalgia. In the United States, it has often functioned as a normative reference point for a more benevolent and socially inclusive form of capitalism in the twenty-first century. For example, American economist Paul Krugman described the 1950s and 1960s as a "paradise lost" that was wrongly abandoned by successive waves of neoliberal restructuring since the 1970s.[5] Many Egyptian writers and thinkers have rehearsed similar arguments. In 2011, for example, Ahmad al-Sayyid al-Najjar published one of the first manifestos for a postrevolutionary economy. To address what he described as rampant corruption, stagnation, and rentierism, he promoted a mixed economy that harkened back to mid-century Keynesian welfare states. "It was this economic model . . . that helped capitalist countries overcome the crisis of the Great Depression in the

1930s," he wrote, "and to confront the period of World War II, and the period of rebuilding what was destroyed by the war, achieving major economic leaps."[6] As several commentators have pointed out, however, the postwar boom in the United States, Western Europe, and Japan was an aberration. The French economist Thomas Piketty endorsed this view in his account of wealth and income inequality in the modern world. "[W]hen viewed in historical perspective," he writes, "the thirty postwar years were the exceptional period, quite simply because Europe had fallen far behind the United States over the period 1914–1945 but rapidly caught up during the Trente Glorieuses."[7] The mass destruction of capital in Europe and Asia—in the form of factories, buildings, and infrastructure—and the postwar recovery that followed gave rise to what David Harvey has called "one of the greatest economic upswings in the history of capitalism."[8] Just as the experience of postwar recovery yielded an era of growth and prosperity in the West, the end of colonial rule did the same in many newly independent countries. But it did not offer a model to be faithfully replicated.

As this book has shown, the proponents of Nasserism consistently obscured their country's position in global space by misconstruing its place in historical time. First, they embellished the role of the Free Officers in Egyptian history. Over and over again, the Nasserist state anchored its legitimacy in a claim that by industrializing the country it was leading Egyptians to a higher stage of economic development. This historicist vision was shared by contemporary observers within the Egyptian communist movement. In the two decades after Nasser's death, some Egyptian Marxists revised what they considered to be their own conceptual errors during the struggle for national independence. Engaging in this kind of autocritique, Sadiq Sa'd concluded that Egyptian Marxists had fundamentally misdiagnosed the Nasserist state because they mistakenly took the Western European historical experience to be their classical reference point.[9] As a result, they understood Egypt to be following a historical script that had already been laid out by Western Europe—*'izba* owners were akin to feudal lords, the national bourgeoisie were their capitalist adversaries, and the petty bourgeoisie from which the Free Officers emerged stood outside this antagonism altogether and could therefore potentially become socialist. In presenting things this way, Sadiq Sa'd argued, Egyptian Marxists neglected the "specificity of the Egyptian situation" and instead grasped the social dynamics of their own country through theoretical categories that were derived from elsewhere. Citing Marx's correspondence with Zasulich in the 1880s (see chapter 2), Sadiq Sa'd argued that the transition to capitalism in Western Europe did not constitute a "typical model for the development of all countries."[10] Instead, he began to adopt the concept of an "Asiatic mode of production"—used by Marx in some of his writings—in order to apprehend Egypt's historical difference from the West. As part of this exercise in self-criticism, Sadiq Sa'd abandoned the concept of feudalism altogether.[11] As this book has shown, the particular way of viewing the past that left-nationalists, communists, and officers adopted from the late 1940s was itself tethered to the world that depression and war had created. The corpus of Egyptian Marxist writings from that period, which served as an intellectual repertoire for Nasserism, helped provide a basis for the Free Officers to understand themselves as a progressive force in history. They routinely justified the July Revolution by claiming that it had abolished feudalism and, in doing so, eliminated any residues of imperial rule, especially as they manifested themselves in the countryside. As the circumstances that made possible this way of interpreting history changed, so too did its appeal among some intellectuals in the post-Nasser era.

Second, the proponents of Nasserism often downplayed the constraints that the postwar international order placed on the Free Officers' ability to pursue national development. As they sought to modernize agriculture and build national industries, the officers embraced an ideological project, and created a sense of purpose for it, by shining a spotlight on some aspects of living in a capitalist world and ignoring others. While Egyptian nationalists in the 1910s and 1920s understood the sphere of unregulated circulation to be the main inhibitor to genuine independence, Nasserists often reversed this presupposition. They understood the realm of production to be the primary arena for social transformation; the central task of a nationalist government was to revitalize the productive capacities of the country that had stagnated under imperial rule. In an age of Fordist-Keynesian accumulation in the West and centrally planned modernization in newly independent countries, Nasserists largely adopted a production-centered understanding of capitalism which mirrored that of their counterparts in other parts of the world. But they had a far milder public critique, if any at all, of the uneven forms of exchange that continued to subordinate formally independent countries on a global scale. For that reason, some Marxist critics who distanced themselves from the regime in the 1960s insisted that the bureaucrats who oversaw the Nasserist state would never be able to truly liberate themselves from imperialist domination.[12] Reflecting on his own political trajectory, Samir Amin would later suggest that Nasserism was a "bourgeois project that was doomed to failure" because the polarizing dynamics of the world system necessarily gave it a comprador character.[13]

The unraveling of national development in the 1970s, along with the gradual onset of neoliberal restructuring, eventually gave way to new political and intellectual orientations among the Egyptian left. Until then, Egyptian Marxism had remained largely preoccupied with the question of historical transition from one mode of production to another. Only after Nasser's death did the center-periphery framework—which had been introduced more than two decades earlier in Latin America and offered the possibility of a less stagist account of capitalist development—begin to find a more systematic elaboration.[14] Those who adopted it did not simply replicate the concerns of an earlier generation of interwar nationalists. Rather than emphasize a distinction between wealth produced inside and outside the nation, Egyptian dependency theorists in the 1970s and 1980s sought to explain the persistence of global inequality by locating its roots in an international division of labor that was fundamentally uneven. They also mobilized the category of capitalism, rather than just colonialism, as an object of critical analysis. In doing so, they developed theories of accumulation by political means, like the one offered in this book, that again called into question the assumptions underlying pervasive transition narratives. In its more radical iterations, their thesis ran contrary to the Nasserist state's publicly stated commitments because it posited that national development within a geographically uneven world system would not lead to modernization, but rather to deepening forms of inequality and dependency. As such, the pursuit of self-sustained, nationally scaled growth was never an autonomous project; it was one that, in the form it existed, could only be organized within the strictures of the postwar economic order and the neoimperial rivalries that it unleashed between Cold War superpowers. While renewed attention to circulation on a global scale presented an effective critique of some of the underlying assumptions of Nasserism, it was also the byproduct of a moment in twentieth-century capitalism when national development, and the Bretton Woods system that underpinned it, had collapsed.[15]

The worldview that animated Nasserism acquired its conceptual plausibility and purchase within the context of postwar capitalism. Though the foundations of that world have long eroded, the ideological legacy of the July Revolution continues to survive in the Egyptian political imagination. Having an integrated conception of capitalism, one that treats production and circulation as differentiated moments in an accumulation process rather than as fetishized domains, can make it possible to transcend any lingering nostalgia for Nasserism. And recognizing how the entangled forms of political and economic domination that long existed in Egypt have evolved since the 1950s and 1960s can help foster a genuinely liberatory politics. Doing so will be a crucial step in imagining an alternative to the neoliberal order of the last four decades that does not simply entail a reversion to a romanticized golden age and a restoration of the Nasserist vision for national development. The historical circumstances that both enabled the Nasserist project and constrained its potential for success have fundamentally changed. Going forward, any visions for social justice in Egypt will have to keep pace with the transformations of capitalism itself.

NOTES

Introduction

1. Najīb, *Kuntu Ra'īsan li-Miṣr*, 157; 'Ukāsha, *Mudhakkirātī fī al-Siyāsa wa-l-Thaqāfa*, 97–98.

2. Gordon, *Nasser's Blessed Movement*, 62 and 94–95; Muḥī al-Dīn, *Wa-l-'Ān Atakallam*, 181.

3. "Marsūm bi-Qānūn Raqam 213 li-Sanat 1952 bi-Inshā' al-Majlis al-Dā'im li-Tanmiyyat al-Intāj al-Qawmi," *al-Waqā'i' al-Miṣriyya*, Special Edition (October 4, 1952): 1–3; Waterbury, *The Egypt of Nasser and Sadat*, 60.

4. Al-Barrāwī, *Haqīqat al-Inqilāb al-Akhīr fī Miṣr*, 37.

5. Al-Barrāwī, *Al-Falsafa al-Iqtiṣādiyya li-l-Thawra*, 156–168.

6. For a biographical account of al-Barrāwī, see Meijer, *The Quest for Modernity*, 66–95. For a comprehensive account of Egyptian political movements in the 1940s, see al-Bishrī, *Al-Ḥaraka al-Siyāsiyya fī Miṣr*.

7. Al-Barrāwī and 'Ulaysh, *Al-Taṭawwur al-Iqtiṣādī fī Miṣr fī al-'Aṣr al-Ḥadīth*.

8. Ibid., 134–182.

9. Injilz, *Al-Tafsīr al-Ishtirākī li-l-Tarīkh;* Linīn, *Al-Isti'mār A'lā Marāḥil al-Ra's Māliyya*; Mārks, *Ra's al-Māl: Al-Juz' al-Awwal.*

10. Meijer, *The Quest for Modernity*, 67.

11. Jakes, *Egypt's Occupation*, 219–245.

12. Al-Barrāwī, *Al-Falsafa al-Iqtiṣādiyya li-l-Thawra*, 156–168.

13. Al-Barrāwī and 'Alī, *Mushkilatunā al-Ijtimā'iyya*, 28; Al-Barrāwī, *Ḥaqīqat al-Inqilāb al-Akhīr fī Miṣr*, 70.

14. Al-Barrāwī, *Ḥaqīqat al-Inqilāb al-Akhīr fī Miṣr*, 68.

15. 'Abd al-Nāṣir, *Falsafat al-Thawra*, 28.

16. In their survey of Arab socialism, Abdel Razzaq Takriti and Hicham Safieddine observe that Nasser's primary aim was for Egypt to rapidly become an industrial power while

simultaneously eradicating political despotism, social injustice, and British colonialism. See Takriti and Safieddine, "Arab Socialism," 487.

17. Lacouture, *Nasser*; Nutting, *Nasser*; Vatikiotis, *Nasser and His Generation*; Ayubi, *Bureaucracy and Politics in Contemporary Egypt*, 339–436; Al-Bishrī, *Al-Dīmūqrāṭiyya wa-Niẓām 23 Yūlyū*.

18. Amin, *Re-reading the Postwar Period*, 152–153; Amin, *La Nation Arabe*, 68–70 and 86–107; Riad, *L'Égypte Nassérienne*, 85–130 and 240–224.

19. Abdel-Malek, *Egypt: Military Society*, 167–188 and 363–371; Fatḥī, "Ṭabī'at al-Sulṭa al-Burjwāziyya fī Miṣr"; Hussein, *Class Conflict in Egypt*, 95–241; Al-'Imarī, *Al-Nāṣiriyya fī al-Thawra al-Muḍāda*.

20. Beattie, *Egypt During the Nasser Years*; Yūnis, *Nidā' al-Sha'b*; Bier, *Revolutionary Womanhood*; Hatem, "Economic and Political Liberation and the Demise of State Feminism"; Salem, *Anticolonial Afterlives in Egypt*. Also see Shokr, "Reflections on Two Revolutions."

21. Beattie, *Egypt During the Nasser Years*, 59.

22. Owen, *Cotton and the Egyptian Economy*, 355.

23. Tignor, *State, Private Enterprise, and Economic Change in Egypt*, 246–247.

24. Arrighi, *The Geometry of Imperialism*, 10.

25. Vitalis, *When Capitalists Collide*, 170. Also see Vitalis, "The End of Third Worldism in Egyptian Studies."

26. Vitalis, *When Capitalists Collide*, 189 and 202–206.

27. Gordon, *Nasser's Blessed Movement*, 5 and 12.

28. Yūnis, *Nidā' al-Sha'b*, 666.

29. Sewell, "The Temporalities of Capitalism."

30. Marx, *Capital*, vol. 1, 915 and 925; Luxemburg, *The Accumulation of Capital*; Wallerstein, *The Modern World-System*, vols. I–IV; Williams, *Capitalism and Slavery*; Amin, *Accumulation on a World Scale*; James, *Black Jacobins*; Robinson, *Black Marxism*; Gilmore, *Golden Gulag*; Mies, *Patriarchy and Accumulation on a World Scale*; Federici, *Caliban and the Witch*; Fraser, "Behind Marx's Hidden Abode"; Moore, *Capitalism in the Web of Life*.

31. Marx, *Capital*, vol. 1, 899; Mau, *Mute Compulsion*; Postone, *Time, Labor, and Social Domination*. For important precursors to this reading of Marx, see Lukàcs, *History and Class Consciousness*; Adorno and Horkheimer, *Dialectic of Enlightenment*.

32. Marx, *Capital*, vol. 1, 168.

33. For accounts that identify earlier roots of capitalism in Egypt, see Cuno, "The Origins of Private Ownership of Land in Egypt"; Gran, *Islamic Roots of Capitalism*; Hanna, *Artisan Entrepreneurs in Cairo and Early-Modern Capitalism*; Bondioli, "Peasants, Merchants, and Caliphs: Capital and Empire in Fatimid Egypt."

34. Mitchell, *Rule of Experts*, 80–119.

35. McNeill, *Something New Under the Sun*, 236; Schmelzer, *The Hegemony of Growth*, 2. See also Arndt, *The Rise and Fall of Economic Growth*; Karbell, *The Leading Indicators*.

36. El Shakry, *The Great Social Laboratory*; Heydemann and Vitalis, "War, Keynesianism, and Colonialism: Explaining State-Market Relations in the Postwar Middle East"; Mitchell, *Rule of Experts*; Ramaḍān, *Al-Fikr al-Thawrī fī Miṣr Qabl Thawrat 23 Yūlyū*.

37. El Shakry, *The Great Social Laboratory*, 203.

38. Wahba, *The Role of the State in the Egyptian Economy*; Tignor, *State, Private Enterprise, and Economic Change in Egypt.*

39. For classical definitions of a plantation, see Mintz, "Caribbean Society," 311; Tomich, "Rethinking the Plantation."

40. Beckert, *Empire of Cotton.*

41. Cuno, *The Pasha's Peasants*, 179–197; Richards, "Primitive Accumulation in Egypt, 1798–1882."

42. Baer, *A History of Landownership in Modern Egypt*, 95–96.

43. Mitchell, *Rule of Experts*, 70–74; Esmeir, *Judicial Humanity*, 149–200.

44. Fraser, "Behind Marx's Hidden Abode."

45. Owen, *The Middle East in the World Economy*, 133.

46. Fritz Allemann, "Aims and Objects of the Alexandria General Produce Association," in International Federation of Master Cotton Spinners' and Manufacturers' Associations, *Official Report of the International Cotton Congress* (1927), 127. Some of these traders also owned companies that monopolized various aspects of the processing of cotton, like ginning and pressing. See El-Gritly, *The Structure of Modern Industry in Egypt*, 503–506.

47. Tignor, *State, Private Enterprise, and Economic Change in Egypt*, 20.

48. Cannon, "Mortgage Banking Strategies in Egypt," 37–40.

49. Ibid., 41; Société de Crédit Foncier Égyptien, *Crédit Foncier Égyptien*, 17–18; Saul, *La France et l'Égypte de 1882 à 1914*, 321–324.

50. Société de Crédit Foncier Égyptien, *Crédit Foncier Égyptien*, 35.

51. Tignor, *State, Private Enterprise, and Economic Change in Egypt*, 19; Tignor, "The Introduction of Modern Banking into Egypt, 1855–1920."

52. El-Gritly, *The Structure of Modern Industry in Egypt*, 502. Also see Vitalis, *When Capitalists Collide*, 17–26 and 32–41.

53. The term "commodity frontier" was coined by sociologist Jason Moore to describe areas where the geographical expansion of commodity production and trade, and the endless accumulation of capital that it facilitated, could proceed as an end onto itself. See Moore, "Sugar and the Expansion of the Early Modern World Economy."

54. Arrighi, *The Long Twentieth Century*, 163–179; Frieden, *Global Capitalism*, 13–27; Hobsbawm, *The Age of Empire*; Hobson, *Imperialism*; Osterhammel, *The Transformation of the World.*

55. Hobsbawm, *Nations and Nationalism Since 1780*, 132.

56. Getachew, *Worldmaking After Empire*; Manela, *The Wilsonian Moment*; Mayer, *Wilson vs. Lenin*; Mishra, *From the Ruins of Empire*; Tooze, *The Deluge*, 374–339.

57. Lenin, *Imperialism, The Highest Stage of Capitalism.*

58. Schumpeter, *Imperialism and Social Classes.*

59. Mishra, *From the Ruins of Empire.* See also Manela, *The Wilsonian Moment* and a critical response that can be found in Hussein A. H. Omar, "The Arab Spring of 1919."

60. Berque, *Egypt*, 300–303.

61. Jakes, *Egypt's Occupation*, 221–222.

Chapter 1

1. TNA, FO 371/4988: Report on the General Situation in Egypt for Period October 13 to 19, 1920 (October 26, 1920).

2. In 1921, the Egyptian government established agricultural rent commissions whose purpose was to ensure that rents were proportional to cotton prices, but its activities had a limited impact. See Shalabī, *Azmat al-Kasād al-'Ālamī al-Kubrā wa-In'ikāsuhā 'alā al-Rīf al-Miṣrī*, 64.

3. Beckert, *Empire of Cotton*, 274–311.

4. In the early to mid-1860s, roughly one-third of all cotton in Egypt was ginned using steam power. At the same time, steam ploughs were deployed in the Nile Delta for cotton growing, but they were later abandoned once cattle populations rebounded after the 1863 plague. Most ploughs were then refitted as steam irrigation pumps. See Ahmed, "Egypt Ignited," 152 and 179–226.

5. Owen, *Cotton and the Egyptian Economy*, 125.

6. Ibid., 199–200.

7. Owen, "The Rapid Growth of Egypt's Agricultural Output, 1890–1914, as an Early Example of the Green Revolutions of Modern South Asia,"; Richards, *Egypt's Agricultural Development*, 55–110.

8. TNA, FO 371/39999: H. E. Hussein Enan Bey, "Some Aspects of Agricultural Improvement in Egypt," in Middle East Supply Centre, "The Proceedings of the Conference on Middle East Agricultural Development" (February 1944).

9. Abdel-Fadil, *Development, Income Distribution and Social Change in Rural Egypt*, 3.

10. My account of how labor and land relations worked in the Egyptian countryside draws largely on Abbas and El-Dessouky, *The Large Landowning Class and the Peasantry in Egypt*, 108–126; 'Āmir, *Al-Arḍ wa-l-Fallāḥ*, 115–124; Cartwright, "Notes on Rent, Labour, and Joint Ownership in Egyptian Agriculture"; Richards, "Land and Labor on Egyptian Cotton Farms."

11. Richards, "Land and Labor on Egyptian Cotton Farms," 508–509.

12. Balls, *Egypt of the Egyptians*, 193.

13. Naḥḥās, *Al-Fallāḥ*, 75.

14. Tucker, *Women in Nineteenth-Century Egypt*, 43.

15. Baer, *A History of Landownership in Modern Egypt*, 76; Richards, *Egypt's Agricultural Development*, 82.

16. 'Āmir, *Al-Arḍ wa-l-Fallāḥ, 116.*

17. Richards, "Land and Labor on Egyptian Cotton Farms," 508; Jakes, *Egypt's Occupation*, 64–67.

18. Ayrout, *Moeurs et Coutumes des Fellahs*, 46; Richards, *Egypt's Agricultural Development*, 59.

19. Abbas and El-Dessouky, *The Large Landowning Class and the Peasantry in Egypt*, 113.

20. Abaza, *The Cotton Plantation Remembered*, 174.

21. Goldberg, *Trade, Reputation, and Child Labor in Twentieth-Century Egypt*, 65.

22. Jakes, "Boom, Bugs, Bust: Egypt's Ecology of Interest."

23. For an overview of how agricultural rents were determined in the interwar years, see

Abbas and El-Dessouky, *The Large Landowning Class and the Peasantry in Egypt*, 115–126.

24. Edwards, "The Egyptian Rural Problem," 192. Edwards was one of the last two British inspectors in the Ministry of Finance to be withdrawn from the Egyptian countryside after the Unilateral Declaration of Egyptian Independence in 1922. He remained a staunch defender of the British occupation.

25. 'Āmir, *Al-Arḍ wa-l-Fallāḥ*, 123.

26. Abbas and El-Dessouky, *The Large Landowning Class and the Peasantry in Egypt*, 121.

27. Edwards, "The Egyptian Rural Problem," 194.

28. Owen, *Cotton and the Egyptian Economy*, 128–129.

29. Baer, *A History of Landownership in Modern Egypt*, 99–111.

30. El-Gritly, *The Structure of Modern Industry in Egypt*, 426–427.

31. Jakes, *Egypt's Occupation*, 101–103 and 214–217.

32. Owen, *Cotton and the Egyptian Economy*, 105–106.

33. Owen, "Egypt and Europe: From French Expedition to British Occupation."

34. Barak, *On Time*, 21–52; Owen, *Cotton and the Egyptian Economy*, 92; "The Construction, Development, and Organization of the Egyptian State Railways, Telegraphs, and Telephone Systems," *L'Egypte Contemporaine* XXIV, no. 139 (January 1933): 87–138.

35. Administration des Chemins de Fer de l'État, de Télégraphes et du Port d'Alexandrie, *Rapport du Conseil d'Administration sur L'Exercice 1897*, 30; Wiener, *L'Egypte et Ses Chemins de Fer*, 393.

36. Abaza, *The Cotton Plantation Remembered*, 94–95.

37. Jakes, "The Scales of Public Utility."

38. Owen, *Cotton and the Egyptian Economy*, 213–215.

39. "The Egyptian Delta Light Railway Company Limited," *L'Egypte Contemporaine* XXIV, no. 139 (January 1933): 139–140.

40. Wright, ed., *Twentieth Century Impressions of Egypt*, 186.

41. Ibid., 187.

42. Beckert, "Emancipation and Empire: Reconstructing the Worldwide Web of Cotton Production in the Age of the American Civil War"; Roger Owen, *Cotton and the Egyptian Economy*, 89–121.

43. Barak, *On Time*, 53.

44. A. E. Crouchley, "A Century of Economic Development, 1837–1937 (A Study in Population and Production in Egypt)," *L'Egypte Contemporaine* XXX, no. 182/183 (Feb./Mar. 1939), 147; Issawi, "Asymmetrical Development and Transport in Egypt," 394–398; Owen, *Cotton and the Egyptian Economy*, 127–128 and 141; Wiener, *L'Egypte et Ses Chemins de Fer*, 83–93.

45. Goldfinch, *Steel in the Sand*, 22.

46. Luxemburg, *The Accumulation of Capital*, 399.

47. Ibid., 401–402.

48. Marx appeared to be ambivalent on the status of primitive accumulation in the history of capitalism. On the one hand, he wrote that the Iberian conquest of the Americas, the European enslavement of Africans, and the colonial plunder of South Asia signaled "the dawn of the era of capitalist production." On the other hand, he wrote that "the veiled

slavery of the wage-labourers in Europe needed the unqualified slavery of the New World as its pedestal." The former description suggests that primitive accumulation was historically anterior to the emergence of capitalism proper, while the latter implies that forms of extra-economic coercion were ongoing features of capitalism even after it emerged. See Marx, *Capital*, vol. 1, 915 and 925.

49. Luxemburg, *The Accumulation of Capital*, 433.

50. Ibid., 409–419.

51. West, "Report by Consul George West on the Trade and Commerce of the Port of Suez for 1872," 69.

52. Ibid., 61.

53. Owen, *The Middle East in the World Economy*, 128–131.

54. Luxemburg, *The Accumulation of Capital*, 408. Her reference here was to Argentina, but the quote is equally applicable to Egypt.

55. TNA, FO 78/4247: W. F. Halton to Marquis of Salisbury (January 5, 1889).

56. A branch office under the supervision of the London Office was established in Brussels in 1921 to inspect continental manufactures. In 1923, the Sudanese government created a separate office in London for its own orders.

57. TNA, FO 141/442/2: Mr. Henderson to Sir Austen Chamberlain (November 21, 1927).

58. Tignor, "Dependency Theory and Egyptian Capitalism, 1920–1950," 111–112.

59. TNA, FO 141/619/3: Memorandum by the Chief Inspecting Engineer on the Inspection Offices of the Egyptian Government in London and Brussels with Special Reference to Continental Complaints (March 15, 1930).

60. Wiener, *L'Egypte et Ses Chemins de Fer*, 133.

61. Egypt. No. 1 (1901), *Reports by His Majesty's Agent and Consul-General on the Finances, Administration, and Condition of Egypt and the Soudan in 1900*, 4–5.

62. Ibid., 5.

63. Wiener, *L'Egypte et Ses Chemins de Fer*, 368.

64. Ibid., 135.

65. For the first time, the ESR drew up estimates of the value of its capital (its existing lines, buildings, stocks, etc.). The capital of the state railways was estimated based on figures that were arbitrarily fixed by Lord Farrer's commission in 1886. See Egyptian State Railways, Telegraphs, and Port of Alexandria, *Report on the Egyptian State Railways and Telegraphs for 1907*, 6.

66. Sharaf al-Dīn, al-Mirghanī, and Barakāt, "Kifāḥ 'Ummāl al-Sikka al-Ḥadīd fī Thamānīn 'Āman, 1906–1986"; Beinin and Lockman, *Workers on the Nile*, 72–76.

67. El-Gritly, *The Structure of Modern Industry in Egypt*, 519.

68. Todd, *The Marketing of Cotton*, 162.

69. TNA, FO 141/636: Note by L. G. Roussin (July 2, 1917).

70. TNA, FO 141/636: Buying Cotton on Samples (November 1, 1923).

71. Jules Klat, "Organization of the Royal Bourse at Alexandria," in International Federation of Master Cotton Spinners' and Manufacturers' Associations, *Official Report of the International Cotton Congress* (1927), 130.

72. Owen, *Cotton and the Egyptian Economy*, 225.

73. TNA, FO 141/636: Buying Cotton on Samples.

74. Herbert B. Carver, "System of Cotton Purchase in the Interior and the Ginning of Cotton," in International Federation of Master Cotton Spinners' and Manufacturers' Associations, *Official Report of the International Cotton Congress* (1927), 136–38; Owen, *Cotton and the Egyptian Economy*, 207–11.

75. Owen, *Cotton and the Egyptian Economy*, 113.

76. Ibid., 221 and 386; Wright, *Twentieth-Century Impressions of Egypt*, 289. For a list of the most important export firms in the 1940s, see TNA, FO 371/24617: British Government Cotton Buying Commission: Instructions to Delegated Buying Firms (September 15, 1940); Dunn, *Cotton in Egypt*, 77.

77. Goldberg, *Trade, Reputation, and Child Labor in Twentieth-Century Egypt*, 77.

78. Allemann, "Aims and Objects of the Alexandria General Produce Association," 127.

79. TNA, FO 141/636: Buying Cotton on Samples.

80. Owen, *Cotton and the Egyptian Economy*, 222.

81. Ibid., 225; Klat, *Les Opérations de Bourse En Egypte*, 11. For a careful study of how new technologies of calculation and valuation in the early twentieth century produced the "cotton market" as an abstract site of exchange, see Primel, "Calculating Futures: Debt, Markets, and the Science of Prices in Colonial Egypt."

82. TNA, FO 141/636: Note by L. G. Roussin.

83. Klat, "Organization of the Royal Bourse at Alexandria," 130.

84. Ibid., 131.

85. Abdel Wahab, *Memorandum on the Bases of a Stable Cotton Policy*, 42–43; Klat, "Organization of the Royal Bourse at Alexandria," 131–132; Klat, *Les Opérations de Bourse en Egypte*, 29–40; TNA, FO 141/636: Note by L. G. Roussin.

86. TNA, FO 141/636: Note by L. G. Roussin.

87. Before the establishment of the futures market, the prices of Egyptian cotton in Mīnā al-Baṣal were more or less a reflection of prices of Egyptian cotton in the Liverpool spot market, especially after the construction of a telegraph between Europe and Egypt in 1861 allowed week-to-week fluctuations in the Liverpool market to be immediately transmitted and reproduced in Egypt. See Owen, *Cotton and the Egyptian Economy*, 165.

88. Léon Polier, "La Bourse d'Alexandrie et la Marché de Cotons Égyptiens," *Revue Économique Internationale* (Décembre 1912): 476–481; "Bulletin Bibliographique," *L'Égypte Contemporaine* IV, no. 13 (1913): 456–460.

89. Hussein K. Teymur, "De la Nécessité d'une Réforme de la Bourse de Commerce d'Alexandrie," *L'Égypte Contemporaine* VI, no. 21 (1914–15): 74–75.

90. Zaki Abd El Motaal, "La Nouvelle Réforme du Marché en Disponible," *L'Égypte Contemporaine* XXIII, no. 135 (April 1932): 370–371; Constantino Bresciani-Turroni, "L'Influence de la Spéculation sur les Fluctuations des Prix du Coton," *L'Égypte Contemporaine* XXII, no. 127 (March 1931): 308–309; Jules Klat, *Les Opérations de Bourse En Egypte*, 12–13; Klat, "Organization of the Royal Bourse at Alexandria," 130.

91. Owen, *Cotton and the Egyptian Economy*, 228 and 368.

92. Keynes, *Indian Currency and Finance*, 71.

93. Rifaat, *The Monetary System of Egypt*, 52; Bresciani-Turroni, "Egypt's Balance of Trade," 374–375.

94. Keynes, *Indian Currency and Finance*, 117.

95. Polanyi, *The Great Transformation*, 13.

96. Owen, *Cotton and the Egyptian Economy*, 222.

97. Ralph A. Harari, "Banking and Financial Business in Egypt," *L'Egypte Contemporaine* XXVII, no. 161 (February 1936): 135–137.

98. Coggan, *Paper Promises*, 80.

99. Arrighi, *The Long Twentieth Century*, 179 and 282–283.

100. L. G. Roussin, "Le Régime Monétaire Actuel de l'Egypte," *L'Égypte Contemporaine* XV, no. 77 (February 1924): 96.

101. Rifaat, *The Monetary System of Egypt*, 54.

102. *National Bank of Egypt*, 36–37.

103. Ibid.

104. Ibid., 42–43.

105. Rifaat, *The Monetary System of Egypt*, 55.

106. Jakes, *Egypt's Occupation*, 246–254.

107. Rifaat, *The Monetary System of Egypt*, 52.

108. *National Bank of Egypt*, 51.

Chapter 2

1. One observer even expressed his disappointment that the conference "dealt almost exclusively with manufacturing and financial problems" over other aspects of cotton production and trade. See Cotton Research Board, *Second Annual Report, 1921*, 169; International Institute of Agriculture, Statistical Service, *International Yearbook of Agricultural Statistics 1909 to 1921*, LXXI.

2. DWQ, WA 0069-004958: "Rapport Présente par les Délégués Égyptiens à la Conférence Cotonnière Mondiale," (June 1921); World Cotton Conference, *Official Report of the World Cotton Conference*, 239.

3. World Cotton Conference, *Official Report of the World Cotton Conference*, 240.

4. *National Bank of Egypt*, 49–50.

5. Emile Minost, "L'Action Contre la Crise Cotonnière en Égypte," *L'Égypte Contemporaine* XXII, no. 128 (April 1931): 412. See also United Nations, Department of Economic Affairs, *Instability in Export Markets of Under-Developed Countries*, 12.

6. Owen, "The Ideology of Economic Nationalism in its Egyptian Context," 3.

7. Beckert, *Empire of Cotton*, 381.

8. Ibid., 409. For a critique of Beckert's account of non-Western economic nationalisms in the early twentieth century, see Jakes and Shokr, "Finding Value in *Empire of Cotton*," 128–30.

9. Vitalis, *When Capitalists Collide*, 41–49.

10. Tignor, "The Egyptian Revolution of 1919: New Directions in the Egyptian Economy."

11. Writing about the years immediately prior to World War I, Aaron Jakes argues in a similar vein that the central concern of Egyptian economic nationalists in that period was to shield Egyptians from their exposure to the volatile flows of foreign finance, not to industrialize Egypt. See Jakes, *Egypt's Occupation*, 221–224.

12. Beinin, "Egypt: Society and Economy, 1923–1952," 324; Tignor, "The Egyptian Revolution of 1919," 49–50.

13. Badrawi, *Isma'il Sidqi*, 7–11; Tignor, *State, Private Enterprise, and Economic Change in Egypt*, 55–58; Sidqī, *Mudhakkirātī*, 43.

14. Egyptian Government, *Rapport de la Commission du Commerce et de l'Industrie*, 6–8.

15. Tignor, *Egyptian Textiles and British Capital*, 10 and 16; Wahba, *The Role of the State in the Egyptian Economy*, 26–33 and 202–209.

16. Egyptian Government, *Rapport de la Commission du Commerce et de l'Industrie*, 60–61.

17. Jakes, *Egypt's Occupation*, 236–239.

18. Ḥarb, *Majmū'at Khuṭab Muḥammad Ṭal'at Ḥarb*, 13 and 44.

19. Ibid., 57.

20. Davis, *Challenging Colonialism*, 129.

21. Ḥarb, *Majmū'at Khuṭab Muḥammad Ṭal'at Ḥarb*, 112–118.

22. Davis, *Challenging Colonialism*, 129.

23. Ḥarb, *Majmū'at Khuṭab Muḥammad Ṭal'at Ḥarb*, 195. For a brilliant social history of al-Maḥalla al-Kubrā, the city in which Egypt's largest textile factory was built, see Hammad, *Industrial Sexuality*.

24. Reynolds, *A City Consumed*, 78–98.

25. Vitalis, *When Capitalists Collide*, 63–103.

26. Tignor, "The Economic Activities of Foreigners in Egypt," 436–437.

27. For some biographical details about Levi, see Beinin, *The Dispersion of Egyptian Jewry*, 262; Tignor, "The Egyptian Revolution of 1919," 59.

28. I. G. Levi, "L'Industrie et l'Avenir Économique de l'Égypte," *L'Égypte Industrielle* 3e Année, no. 5 (May 1927): 35.

29. H. Clayton Hartley, "Some Aspects of the Prospective Establishment of Textile Factories in Egypt," *L'Égypte Contemporaine* XIX, no. 110 (December 1928): 599.

30. Ibid., 604.

31. "Al-Niẓām al-Jumrukī al-Jadīd wa-Mashākil al-Imtiyāzāt al-'Ajnabiyya: Tabajjuḥ ba'ḍ al-Tujjār al-'Ajānib bi-l-Iskandariyya," *al-Yawm* (February 16, 1930).

32. Owen, "The Ideology of Economic Nationalism in its Egyptian Context," 8; Tignor, *State, Private Enterprise, and Economic Change in Egypt*, 109–112.

33. "Ra'y Tājir Kabīr fī al-Ta'rīfa al-Jumrūkiyya al-Jadīda: Min Sam'ān Siḍnāwī Bih ilā Wazīr al-Māliyya," *al-Balāgh* (January 15, 1930).

34. Davis, *Challenging Colonialism*, 157–158.

35. Ibid., 138; Mabro and Radwan, *The Industrialization of Egypt*, 26–29; Wahba, *The Role of the State in the Egyptian Economy*, 32.

36. "A Propos de la Réforme Douannière: Opinions de La Presse," *L'Égypte Industrielle* 6e Année, no. 1, (January 1930): 83.

37. Owen, *Cotton and the Egyptian Economy*, 312.

38. Richards, *Egypt's Agricultural Development*, 81; McKillop, *Note on the Readjustment of the Land Tax in Egypt 1895–1907*, 6. In conventional scholarship, the large landholding class are portrayed as the major beneficiaries of British rule. While there is some truth to

this characterization, Aaron Jakes complicates it by pointing out that the growing power of large landowners was often an unintended consequence of British policies—which instead sought to bolster peasant smallholders—rather than the result of a deliberate strategy. See Jakes, *Egypt's Occupation*, 33–34.

39. "L'Opinion de S. E. Ismail Sidky Pacha Sur le Programme Économique du Gouvernement," *L'Égypte Industrielle* 4e Année, no. 8 (December 1928): 53.

40. TNA, FO 371/24618: Sir Miles Lampson to the Right Honorable Viscount Halifax (December 27, 1939).

41. DWQ, WA 0069-004963: "Note sur l'Amélioration de Système de la Vente du Coton" (May 4, 1916); DWQ, MNW 0075-008410: Draft Resolution for the Composition of an Agricultural Committee (April 8, 1916); "Majlis al-Tijāra al-Zirā'iyya," *al-Muqaṭṭam* (May 25, 1916), 5.

42. For a detailed examination of Naḥḥās' career, see Goldberg, *Trade, Reputation, and Child Labor in Twentieth-Century Egypt*, 94–104.

43. Jakes, *Egypt's Occupation*, 233–235.

44. DWQ, WA 0069-004958: "Rapport au Conseil d'Administration du Syndicat Agricole Général D'Égypte, 1920."

45. Ibid. See also Deeb, *Party Politics in Egypt*, 22–26.

46. Youssef Nahhas, "Price Margins Between Egyptian and American Cotton," in International Federation of Master Cotton Spinners' and Manufacturers' Associations, *Official Report of the International Cotton Congress* (1927), 44.

47. Goldberg, *Trade, Reputation, and Child Labor in Twentieth-Century Egypt*, 33–62.

48. Ibid., 44–46.

49. Balls, "Researches on Egyptian Cotton," 664–665; "Majlis Mabāḥith al-Quṭn," *al-Majalla al-Zirā'iyya al-Miṣriyya*, Special Issue (February/March, 1931): 3.

50. TNA, FO 141/587: Restriction of Cotton Growing in Egypt (December 1920). See also Owen, *Cotton and the Egyptian Economy*, 202–204.

51. DWQ, WA 0069-004958: "Rapport au Conseil d'Administration du Syndicat Agricole Général D'Égypte, 1920."

52. TNA, FO 141/587: Note on the Law Restricting the Cotton Area (March 10, 1921).

53. Ibid.

54. Naḥḥās, *Juhūd al-Niqāba al-Zirā'iyya al-Miṣriyya al-'Āmma fī Thalāthīna 'Āman*, 43.

55. DWQ, WA 0069-012844: Telegrams from Tenant Farmers to the King (February 22–27, 1921).

56. For more on government cotton purchasing campaigns, see DWQ, MNW 0075-008428: "Report on Cotton Market Conditions" (March 24, 1921); DWQ, WA 0069-020684: "Memoranda from the Ministry of Finance on Government Intervention into the Cotton Market" (n.d.).

57. *National Bank of Egypt, 1898–1948*, 53.

58. Emile Minost, "L'Action Contre la Crise Cotonnière," *L'Égypte Contemporaine* XXII, no. 128 (April 1931): 414; Abdel Wahab, *Memorandum on the Bases of a Stable Cotton Policy*, 1.

59. Goldberg, *Trade, Reputation, and Child Labor in Twentieth-Century Egypt*, 70–71.

60. Selous, *Economic Conditions in Egypt*, 13–15; Tignor, *State, Private Enterprise, and Economic Change in Egypt*, 114–115.

61. DWQ, RMW 0081-075524: "Opinion Surveys on the Status of Egyptian Cotton in the Face of the Economic Crisis," (January 1, 1927).

62. TNA, FO 371/14647: J. J. Shute to John Murray (April 1, 1930); Arno S. Pearce, "Egyptian Cotton from the Points of View of the Spinning Industry," *L'Égypte Contemporaine* XXII, no. 127 (March 1931): 393. For a breakdown of Egyptian cotton exports by country, see Selous, *Economic Conditions in Egypt*, 123–124.

63. DWQ, WA 0069-004958: "Rapport au Conseil d'Administration du Syndicat Agricole General D'Égypte, 1920."

64. DWQ, WA 0069-004958: "L'Égypte à la Conférence Cotonnière Mondiale," (June 24, 1921). Naḥḥās's calculations are comparable to those made by Roger Owen. Based on limited data, Owen estimates that large landowners in the 1910s—who were powerful enough to secure a sizeable share of the revenue from selling their crops—obtained between 75 and 90 percent of the average export price of cotton, while smaller producers likely got between 55 and 65 percent. See Owen, *Cotton and the Egyptian Economy*, 227–230 and 368.

65. Naḥḥās, *Juhūd al-Niqāba al-Zirā'iyya al-Miṣriyya al-'Āmma fī Thalāthīna 'Āman*, 78.

66. Ibid.

67. Naḥḥās, *Al-Quṭn Fī Khamsīn 'Ām*, 100.

68. Ibid., 107–108.

69. Carver, "System of Cotton Purchase in the Interior and the Ginning of Cotton," 138; Goldberg, "Marketing Commodities Does Not Happen on Commodity Markets," 87–88; Issawi, *Egypt*, 108; Naḥḥās, *Juhūd al-Niqāba al-Zirā'iyya al-Miṣriyya al-'Āmma fī Thalāthīna 'Āman*, 109–110, 116, and 179; Owen, *Cotton and the Egyptian Economy*, 207; Todd, *The Marketing of Cotton*, 78–79, 108–110 and 163; Zannis, *Le Crédit Agricole en Egypte*, 28. See also Hubbard, "Hedging in the Cotton Market," 36–37.

70. TNA, FO 141/636: Buying over Contracts in Villages (November 1, 1923).

71. TNA, FO 141/636: K.P Birley (Peel & Company) to the High Commissioner (November 1, 1923).

72. Naḥḥās, *Al-Quṭn Fī Khamsīn 'Ām*, 123–124.

73. Ibid., 99.

74. The 1923 draft law included provisions to both eliminate on-call sales as well as to abolish merchants' option to refuse purchases of cotton to which they had committed if they felt the quality of the cotton did not match the samples they had seen. See TNA, FO 141/636: Projet de Loi Concernant Les Ventes de Coton (December 1, 1923). According to British sources, the Egyptian government's decision to propose the draft law was prompted in part by an episode in which a European merchant refused to purchase cotton from King Fu'ād by invoking a clause in their contract that allowed buyers to reject cotton that did not meet the quality standards of its sample.

75. TNA, FO 141/636: Minute on Residency Paper No. 219 (November 8, 1923).

76. TNA, FO 141/636: Minutes of a Meeting Held at the Residency on the Subject of the Proposed Law Prohibiting Certain Stipulations in Transaction in Respect of Sales of Cotton (n.d).

77. TNA, FO 141/636: SRP Carver to the High Commissioner (October 31, 1923).

78. TNA, FO 141/636: High Commissioner to the Residency (January 12, 1924).

79. Naḥḥās, *Al-Quṭn Fī Khamsīn 'Ām*, 154–168.

80. Abdel Wahab, *Memorandum on the Bases of a Stable Cotton Policy*, 43.

81. Klat, *Les Opérations de Bourse en Egypte*, 38.

82. Nahhas, "Price Margins Between Egyptian and American Cotton," 44.

83. "Egyptian Cotton Trade and Co-operation," *Birmingham Post* (August 27, 1928). See also "Central Selling Scheme for Egyptian Cotton," *Financial Times* (September 5, 1928). An official in the British Residency in Cairo later called Youssef a propagandist who "carries with him a large press-cutting album, gorged with references to himself" and quoted Youssef telling him privately that "he was more popular in England than in Egypt." See TNA, FO 141/480: Amin Bey Youssef (September 26, 1928).

84. Naḥḥās, *Al-Quṭn Fī Khamsīn 'Ām*, 154–168.

85. Shaṭā, *Al-Dā'iya Duktūr Ibrāhīm Rashād*, 56.

86. Walsh, *Bitter Freedom*, 104–126; Omar, "The Irish Were Egyptians Long Ago."

87. Rashād, *Mudhakkirāt Mujāhid Ta'āwunī*, 65.

88. For an overview of earlier cooperative advocacy in Egypt, see Jakes, *Egypt's Occupation*, 235–236 and 239–244. See also Bernard Michel, "Note Sur les Syndicats-Coopératives Agricoles Fonctionnant En Egypte," *L'Egypte Contemporaine* VI, no. 15 (1913): 376–386.

89. Rashād, *Mudhakkirāt Mujāhid Ta'āwunī*, 67; Shaṭā, *Al-Dā'iya Duktūr Ibrāhīm Rashād*, 24.

90. Rashād, *Mudhakkirāt Mujāhid Ta'āwunī*, 89.

91. Rashad, *An Egyptian in Ireland*, 14.

92. For a study of how the cooperative movement attracted students from across the British Empire, see Mo Moulton, "Co-opting the Cooperative Movement?"

93. Rodgers, *Atlantic Crossings*, 321.

94. Ibid., 324–331.

95. Marx, "The 'First' Draft," 106.

96. Arndt, "Economic Development: A Semantic History," 458–460; d'Encausse and Schram, *Marxism and Asia*.

97. Roy, "An Indian Communist Manifesto," 164. Adopting a different perspective, Indian nationalist Mohandas Karamchand Gandhi eschewed developmental thinking and became widely known for his critique of modern, industrial societies. He launched a noncooperation campaign that encouraged Indians to boycott British goods and to spin their own cloth (*khadi*) by hand—in other words, he called upon Indians to emulate the methods of the small peasantry rather than discipline them.

98. Chayanov, *The Theory of Peasant Economy*.

99. Rashad, *An Egyptian in Ireland*, 23–24.

100. Rashād, *Kitāb al-Ta'āwun al-Zirā'ī*, 202.

101. Rashad, *An Egyptian in Ireland*, 307.

102. Rashād, *Mudhakkirāt Mujāhid Ta'āwunī*, 123–125.

103. For a printed copy of the law, see DWQ, WSI 4029-000159: "Inshā' Majlis al-Ta'āwun al-A'lā," (1927).

104. TNA, FO 922/94: The Cooperative Movement in Egypt (December 24, 1942).

105. Bianchi, *Unruly Corporatism*, 67–68; Goldberg, *Trade, Reputation, and Child Labor in Twentieth-Century Egypt*, 67.

106. Ibrāhīm Rashād, "Al-Ta'āwun al-Zirā'ī wa-Atharuhu fī Istiqlālnā al-Iqtisādī wa-Ruqiyyinā al-Ijtimā'ī," *al-Majalla al-Zirā'iyya al-Miṣriyya* (October 1924): 19.

107. Ibid., 20.

108. Rashād, *Kitāb al-Ta'āwun al-Zirā'ī*, 199–200.

109. In 1927, there were 142 ginning factories in Egypt, of which 109 were in the Nile Delta and 33 in Upper Egypt. The smallest of these factories possessed 15 gins while the largest operated as many as 180. The most important ginning company in the country was the Associated Cotton Ginners of Egypt Ltd., which owned 10 factories in Lower Egypt with a total of 1,048 gins. The most important ginning centers in the Delta were al-Maḥalla al-Kubrā, Kafr al-Zayyāt, and Zifta in Gharbiyya province; Mansūra in Daqahliyya province; Zaqāzīq in Sharqiyya province; Damanhūr in Buḥayra province; and Banhā and Qanāṭir in Qalyūbiyya province. The main centers in Lower Egypt were Wasṭā, Bani Swayf, Maghāgha, al-Minyā, Dayrūṭ, and al-Fayyūm. See International Federation of Master Cotton Spinners' and Manufacturers' Associations, *Official Report of the International Cotton Congress* (1927), 138–139.

110. Rashad, *An Egyptian in Ireland*, 15.

111. Jakes, *Egypt's Occupation*, 219–245.

112. DWQ, WA 0069-009884-0016: Petition from Tenants of the Land of Muḥammad Badrāwī 'Ashūr (no date).

113. DWQ, WA 0069-009862: Petition from Peasants in al-Minyā (March 8, 1922).

114. Esmeir, *Juridical Humanity*, 149–200; Mitchell, *Rule of Experts*, 54–79.

115. Although they did not use the term "comprador" to describe cotton merchant-financiers in Alexandria, Egyptian landowning nationalists portrayed them in similar fashion as agents of imperialism whose activities harmed the interests of the majority of Egyptian cultivators. Robert Vitalis has convincingly argued that the deployment of this class-analytic category to understand the activities of interwar business tycoons, like Ahmad 'Abbud, yields a misleading interpretation of the history of capitalism in Egypt. See Vitalis, "On the Theory and Practice of Compradors."

116. For an account of Naḥḥās's earlier critiques of foreign banks, see Jakes, *Egypt's Occupation*, 233–236.

117. Abbas and El-Dessouky, *The Large Landowning Class and the Peasantry in Egypt*, 156–161.

118. Gasper, *The Power of Representation*, 108–147.

119. Jakes, *Egypt's Occupation*, 122–126.

120. For a similar account of how interwar Chinese nationalists and communists began to portray Chinese employees of foreign-owned banking, insurance, and shipping companies as imperialist collaborators who undermined large-scale agrarian production, see Liu, *Tea War*, 234–238. For similar accounts of how twentieth-century American, Soviet, German, and Italian political and business leaders celebrated productive engineers and industrialists over parasitic financiers and rentiers, see Link, *Forging Global Fordism*, 19–89; Maier, *In Search of Stability*, 76–79.

121. Marx argued that the thing-like character of a commodity—or what he called the fetishism of commodities—conceals the capitalist social relations that go into the production and distribution of any good or service for sale on a market. According to Marx, this

misapprehension is a social process, rather than a subjective illusion. See Marx, *Capital*, vol. 1, 163–177.

122. This formulation draws on Postone, "Anti-Semitism and National Socialism: Notes on the German Reaction to the 'Holocaust.'"

Chapter 3

1. For an effort to theorize historical events as a sequence of occurrences that result in the transformation of durable social practices, see Sewell, *Logics of History*, 225–270.

2. *National Bank of Egypt*, 55.

3. TNA, T 188/178: Memorandum on the Cotton Situation" (October 21, 1937); Taylor and Taylor, *World Trade in Agricultural Products*, 10–12; Kindleberger, *The World Depression*, 90.

4. G. Blanchard, "La Crise en Egypte," *L'Égypte Contemporaine* XXII, no. 127 (March 1931): 344.

5. Ibid., 384; Al-Shirbīni, *Tijārat Miṣr al-Khārijiyya*, 143–169; TNA, T 188/178: Extract from Address by Henry A. Wallace, Secretary of Agriculture, Before Meeting of Farmers at Memphis, Tennessee (October 1, 1937).

6. *National Bank of Egypt*, 52.

7. Tignor, *State, Private Enterprise, and Economic Change in Egypt*, 116; Owen, "Egypt in the World Depression," 137 and 145.

8. Owen, "Egypt in the World Depression," 137 and 145.

9. Edwards, "The Egyptian Rural Problem," 192 (emphasis in original text).

10. "Al-Azma al-Iqtiṣādiyya wa-Ṣadāha fī Anḥā' al-Bilād," Letter 5, *al-Ahrām* (September 1, 1931).

11. "Al-Azma al-Iqtisādiyya wa-Ṣadāha fī Anhā' al-Bilād," Letter 2, *al-Ahrām* (September 2, 1931).

12. Bresciani-Turroni, "L'Influence de la Spéculation sur les Fluctuations des Prix du Coton," 341–342.

13. Pearce, "Egyptian Cotton from the Points of View of the Spinning Industry," 391.

14. Greaves, "Competition, Collusion, and Confusion," 52.

15. International Institute of Agriculture, *World Cotton Production and Trade*, 336–337. In the years immediately after the war, the share of exports from Lancashire to key international markets had already begun to suffer from competition with Japanese textiles. See Daniels and Jewkes, "The Crisis in the Lancashire Cotton Industry," 40.

16. Sandberg, *Lancashire in Decline*, 5; Beckert, *Empire of Cotton*, 381–382.

17. International Institute of Agriculture, *World Cotton Production and Trade*, 338–339.

18. One cotton exporter in Egypt even blamed the English trade union movement for driving up labor costs in spinning to the point where they represented over 40 percent of the total cost of yarns made from Egyptian cotton. See Pearce, "Egyptian Cotton from the Points of View of the Spinning Industry," 392.

19. "Al-Azma al-Iqtisādiyya wa-Ṣadāha fī Anhā' al-Bilād," Letter 4, *al-Ahrām* (September 1, 1931).

20. "Al-Azma al-Iqtisādiyya wa-Ṣadāha fī Anhā' al-Bilād," Letter 1, *al-Ahrām* (September 4, 1931).

21. Owen, *Cotton and the Egyptian Economy*, 165.

22. "Discussion de la Conférence de Professeur Bresciani-Turroni," *L'Égypte Contemporaine* XXI, no. 124 (December 1930): 705. J. I. Craig also made similar calculations for the Scottish economist, John A. Todd. See Todd, *The World's Cotton Crops*, 299.

23. Owen, *Cotton and the Egyptian Economy*, 162–165 and 202.

24. Constantino Bresciani-Turroni, "Relations Entre La Récolte et le Prix du Coton Égyptien," *L'Égypte Contemporaine* XXI, no. 124 (December 1930): 633–689; Zahra, M. A., and M. El-Darwish, *A Statistical Study of Some of the Factors Affecting the Price of Egyptian Cotton*; Abdel Wahab, *Memorandum on the Bases of a Stable Cotton Policy*.

25. In the interwar period, Bresciani-Turroni built a reputation as an exponent of the quantity theory of money. See Constantino Bresciani-Turroni, *The Economics of Inflation*. He spent his early career teaching at universities in Italy except for a brief period in the 1930s when he resigned in opposition to Mussolini. By the 1940s and 50s, Bresciani-Turroni went on to lead important national and international financial institutions, including the Bank of Rome and the International Bank for Development and Reconstruction.

26. "Discussion de la Conférence de Professeur Bresciani-Turroni," 706.

27. On the Sidqī dictatorship in the 1930s, see al-Sayyid-Marsot, *Egypt's Liberal Experiment*, 138–170; Badrawi, *Isma'il Sidqi*, 58–107.

28. Abdel Wahab, *Memorandum on the Bases of a Stable Cotton Policy*. There is a detailed and insightful discussion of the Abdel Wahab memorandum and the politics surrounding it in Goldberg, *Trade, Reputation, and Child Labor in Twentieth-Century Egypt*, 77–83.

29. *National Bank of Egypt*, 53–54.

30. Abdel Wahab, *Memorandum on the Bases of a Stable Cotton Policy*, 11–13.

31. SM/47/156, Survey of the Economy of Egypt, 12/23/1947, IMF Archives, 5. Tignor argues that Egypt maintained a high volume of exports by the late 1930s and that its earnings from abroad suffered less than other cotton-exporting countries. See Tignor, *State, Private Enterprise, and Economic Change in Egypt*, 114. For a different perspective that challenges prevailing assumptions in the 1930s that the Egyptian crop was too small to influence world prices, see Yousef, "The Political Economy of Interwar Egyptian Cotton Policy," 301–325.

32. Bresciani-Turroni, "Relations Entre La Récolte et le Prix du Coton Égyptien," 636.

33. Naḥḥās, *Al-Quṭn fī Khamsīn 'Ām*, 245. For a comprehensive repudiation of acreage restrictions, cotton buying campaigns, and advances to cultivators as methods to artificially bolster the price of Egyptian cotton, see Emile Minost, "L'Action Contre la Crise Cotonnière," *L'Égypte Contemporaine* XXII, no. 128 (April 1931): 419–425.

34. Goldberg, *Trade, Reputation, and Child Labor in Twentieth-Century Egypt*, 81.

35. Grubbs, *Cry From the Cotton*, 17–29; Patel, *The New Deal*, 56–65.

36. "Too Much Cotton," *The Economist* (November 27, 1937).

37. Ibid.

38. TNA, T 188/178: Memorandum on the Cotton Situation (October 21, 1937).

39. "Too Much Cotton."

40. TNA, T 188/178: Pietro Stoppani to Mr. Henry F. Grady (April 9, 1938).

41. Ayrout, *Moeurs et Coutumes des Fellahs*, 46; Issawi, *Egypt at Mid-Century*, 223.

42. Selous, *Economic Conditions in Egypt*, 9; James, "L'Organisation du Crédit en Égypte," 571.

43. TNA, FO 371/17015: Sir Percy Loraine to Sir John Simon (November 20, 1933).

44. TNA, FO 141/638/1: Ahmad Abdel Wahab, "The Farm Debt Problem" (February 15, 1935).

45. Minost, "L'Action Contre la Crise Cotonnière," 451.

46. "Transactions Foncières Rurales," *Bulletin de l'Union des Agriculteurs d'Égypte* 32, no. 249 (January 1934): 58.

47. DWQ, WA, 0069-009867: Petition from al-Mansūra al-Maḥaṭṭa (December 6, 1930).

48. Selous, *Economic Conditions in Egypt*, 9.

49. Deeb, *Party Politics in Egypt*, 222–223.

50. Abbas and El-Dessouky, *The Large Landowning Class and the Peasantry in Egypt*, 136–37; Selous, *Economic Conditions in Egypt*, 37.

51. TNA, FO 371/17989: Collection of Land Tax from Members of Parliament and the Provincial Councils (May 17, 1934); TNA, FO 371/17015: Minute on the Land Tax by the Financial Adviser (November 28, 1933). The portion of the land tax that was remitted came from the provincial council tax that was a percentage addition to the land tax.

52. Selous, *Economic Conditions in Egypt*, 38; "Transactions Foncières Rurales," 59 and 67–72. For a brief summary of these measures, see Tignor, *State, Private Enterprise, and Economic Change in Egypt*, 119–121.

53. Tignor, *State, Private Enterprise, and Economic Change in Egypt*, 120–121.

54. "Crédit Foncier Égyptien: Assemblée Générale Ordinaire du 22 Janvier 1934," *Bulletin de l'Union des Agriculteurs d'Égypte* 32, no. 249 (January 1934): 64.

55. Zannis, *Le Crédit Agricole en Egypte*, 166.

56. TNA, FO 371/17015: Sir Percy Loraine to Sir John Simon.

57. "Ma' Mudīr al-Bank al-'Aqārī: Mā Yaqūluhu 'an Khiṭaṭ al-Bank Izā' al-Aqsāṭ al-Mustaḥaqa," *al-Ahrām* (October 23, 1933); "Mudhakkira 'an al-Mushkila al-'Aqāriyya bi-Wajh 'Ām," *al-Ahrām* (December 10, 1933); "Crédit Foncier Égyptien: Assemblée Générale Ordinaire du 22 Janvier 1934," 63; Politi, *L'Egypte de 1914 à "Suez,"* 168–170. For more biographical information on Politi, see Beinin, *The Dispersion of Egyptian Jewry*, 262.

58. "Al-Dayn al-'Aqārī wa-l-Amlāk fi Miṣr," *al-Ahrām* (August 12, 1931).

59. Naḥḥās, *Al-Quṭn fī Khamsīn 'Ām*, 327.

60. "Mu'tamar al-A'yān fī al-Munūfiyya," *al-Fallāḥ al-Iqtiṣādī*, vol. 5 (February, 1934): 26.

61. Ibid., 27.

62. "Mushkilat al-Duyūn al-'Aqāriyya," *al-Fallāḥ al-Iqtiṣādī*, vol. 5 (February, 1934): 44–47; Naḥḥās, *Al-Quṭn fī Khamsīn 'Ām*, 330.

63. DWQ, WA, 0069-009870: Petitions from Gharbiyya (March-April 1935).

64. Ibid.

65. Ayrout, *Moeurs et Coutumes des Fellahs*, 46–47. This section of Ayrout's study that appears in the original French edition was omitted from subsequent translations into English.

66. TNA, FO 141/638/1: The Farm Debt Problem.

67. Ibid.

68. TNA, FO 141/638: G. H. Selous, "Memorandum on the Mortgage Debts of Egypt" (April 6, 1935).

69. "Al-Duyūn al-'Aqāriyya wa-l-Da'wa ilā Qarḍ Ahlī 'Ām," *al-Ahrām* (March 5, 1935).

70. Emile James, "L'Organisation du Crédit en Égypte," *L'Égypte Contemporaine* XXX, no. 186/187 (November/December 1939), 569; Peck, "Mortgage Banking and Tenure Security in Egypt," 218–226.

71. Deeb, *Party Politics in Egypt*, 224.

72. Peck, "Mortgage Banking and Tenure Security in Egypt," 263.

73. Issawi, *Egypt at Mid-Century*, 224.

74. Peck, "Mortgage Banking and Tenure Security in Egypt," 200–231.

75. Tignor, *State, Private Enterprise, and Economic Change in Egypt*, 118.

76. "Al-Bank al-'Aqārī al-Miṣrī: Taqrīr Majlis al-Idāra 'an 1939," *al-Ahrām* (January 18, 1940).

77. Tignor, *State, Private Enterprise, and Economic Change in Egypt*, 122–123; Zannis, *Le Crédit Agricole en Egypte*, 168–169.

78. James, "L'Organisation du Crédit en Égypte," 568.

79. Issawi, *Egypt at Mid-Century*, 224; Charles Issawi and Felix Rosenfeld, "Company Profits in Egypt, 1929–1939," *L'Egypte Contemporaine* XXXII, no. 200 (November 1941): 682.

80. Tignor, *State, Private Enterprise, and Economic Change in Egypt*, 121.

81. The congress was established in Brussels in 1885 as an international forum for discussions about railway development and improvement.

82. International Railway Congress Association, "Opening Ceremony of the 12th Session," *Monthly Bulletin of the International Railway Congress Association* XV, no. 5 (May 1933): 470.

83. Abdel Wahab, *The Railway Crisis and the Conflict Between the Rail and the Road*.

84. El-Gritly, *The Structure of Modern Industry in Egypt*, 519.

85. "Comité de la Chambre de Navigation Fluviale d'Égypte," *L'Égypte Industrielle* 4e Année, no. 3 (March 1928): 17; "Chambre de Navigation Fluviale d'Egypte," *L'Égypte Industrielle* 12e Année, no. 1 (January 1, 1936): 11; Crouchley, *The Investment of Foreign Capital in Egyptian Companies and Public Debt*, 112–113.

86. "Rapport Présenté par la Chambre de Navigation Fluviale à S.E le Ministre des Communications au Sujet des Taxes que le Gouvernement se Propose d'Appliquer à la Navigation Fluviale," *L'Égypte Industrielle* 8e Année, no. 13 (November 1, 1932): 27.

87. "Transport from Field to Market," *Egyptian Gazette*, Cotton Supplement (March 31, 1948). Cited in Dunn, *Cotton in Egypt*, 80–81.

88. TNA, FO 141/733/10: A Review of the Development of Transport in Egypt (June 28, 1934).

89. Harvey, *Cosmopolitanism and the Geographies of Freedom*, 135–141; White, *Railroaded*, 146.

90. TNA, FO 141/592/7: Note sur le Projet de Réglementation de la Navigation Fluviale

et sur le Projet de Taxe sur la Navigation Fluviale (November 9, 1934). Reed was a British civil engineer who had recently worked for the Manchester Ship Canal (once the largest river navigation canal in the world). He gained experience working with a variety of international transport endeavors, including the Suez Canal Consultative Working Commission and several navigation congresses. See Institution of Civil Engineers, "Obituary," 789–790.

91. "La Crise du Transport Automobile en Egypte" *L'Égypte Industrielle* 8e Année, no. 12 (June 15, 1932): 28.

92. "Rapport Présenté par la Chambre de Navigation Fluviale à S. E le Ministre des Communications," 29.

93. Arthur D. Little, Inc., *Economic Study of Inland Transportation in Egypt*, 8. Even though this estimate is from 1954, there is no reason to believe that the same obstacles to navigation along the Mahmūdiyya Canal, which was constructed between 1817 and 1820, did not exist in the 1930s and 1940s.

94. Issawi, *Egypt at Mid-Century*, 184.

95. El-Gritly, *The Structure of Modern Industry in Egypt*, 514.

96. DWQ, RMW 0081-035430: Memorandum to the Administration of the State Railways, Telegraphs, and Telephones (March 13, 1947); TNA, FO 141/592/7: Note sur le Projet de Réglementation de la Navigation Fluviale et sur le Projet de Taxe sur la Navigation Fluviale.

97. Abdel Wahab, *Memorandum on the Bases of a Stable Cotton Policy*, 38. These calculations only included rates for cotton transported at the risk of the railway department, which were more expensive than rates for transportation at the risk of the owner.

98. "Takhfīḍ 'Ujūr Naql al-Quṭn wa-l-Bidhra," *al-Ahrām* (July 9, 1931).

99. "'Ujūr Naql al-Quṭn 'alā al-Sikka al-Ḥadīdiyya al-'Āmiriyya," *al-Ahrām* (August 15, 1931); "Naql al-Quṭn 'alā al-Sikka al-Ḥadidiyya," *al-Ahrām* (October 1, 1931); TNA, FO 141/442/2: Draft Decree to Constitute the Supreme Railway Board (February 17, 1927); TNA, FO 141/442/2: From Tottenham to Griffith (January 23, 1928); TNA, FO 141/442/2: Report on Egyptian State Railways (February 21, 1928).

100. DWQ, RMW 0081-035419: Memorandum 64 to the Administration of the State Railways, Telegraphs, and Telephones, Appendix 2 (August 13, 1931).

101. DWQ, RMW 0081-035419: Memorandum 16 to the Administration of the State Railways, Telegraphs, and Telephones (July 15, 1933).

102. DWQ, RMW 0081-035419: Chambre de Navigation Fluviale d'Egypte à S. E. le Directeur General de l'Administration des Chemins de Fer (July 27, 1933). The only exemption in the Nile Delta was Banhā where Misr Transport and Navigation Company was authorized to transport up to 100,000 *qintars* of cotton from its factory owned by Misr Cotton Ginning and Trading Company.

103. TNA, FO 141/592/7: "Note sur le Projet de Réglementation de la Navigation Fluviale et sur le Projet de Taxe sur la Navigation Fluviale."

104. TNA, FO 141/733/10: A Review of the Development of Transport in Egypt (July 2, 1934).

105. "Les Chemins de Fer de L'État et le Transport du Coton et de la Graine," *L'Égypte Industrielle* 12e Année, no. 4 (February 15, 1936): 33–34.

106. El-Gritly, *The Structure of Modern Industry in Egypt*, 514.

107. Issawi, *Egypt at Mid-Century*, 185.

108. Politi, *L'Egypte de 1914 à "Suez,"* 126.

109. Rafaat, "The Rise and Fall of Alexandria's Cotton Exchange."

110. Davis, *Challenging Colonialism*, 129 and 135.

111. TNA, FO 141/533/17: Biography of Mohamed Farghaly (March 20, 1935); TNA, FO 141/533/17: Particulars of Mohamed Farghaly (March 21, 1935). On the Egyptian trade mission to England, see Egypt. No. 1 (1935), *Correspondence with the Egyptian Mission of Economic Enquiry Regarding Trade Relations*. Farghalī served as president of the Alexandria Cotton Exporters Association (est. 1932) from 1941 to 1945 and 1954 to 1960. Today the association—better known by its acronym ALCOTEXA—includes in its membership every company in Egypt that is involved in the export of cotton.

112. DWQ, MNW 0075-008429: Note to the Council of Ministers (July 19, 1923); DWQ, MNW 0075-008505: Letter from the Minister of Finance (July 31, 1923).

113. Alleman, "Aims and Objects of the Alexandria General Produce Association," 129.

114. An example of a monthly report can be found in International Federation of Master Cotton Spinners' and Manufacturers' Associations, *International Cotton Bulletin*, vol. 4 (October 1925): 565.

115. "Government Crop Forecasts and the Crop Recording System," in International Federation of Master Cotton Spinners' and Manufacturers' Associations, *Official Report of the International Cotton Congress* (1927): 112–113. Prior to 1911, village-level tax collectors (*ṣarrāfs*) would record the area grown in cotton for each subprovincial district (*markaz*) and any details about amounts produced of each variety of cotton were recorded by the AGPA. For example, see Ministry of Finance, *Statistical Yearbook of Egypt for 1909*, 114–115.

116. Todd, *The Marketing of Cotton*, 205.

117. S. Lackany Bey, "Cotton: Estimation of the Crop and Measurement of its Elasticity," *L'Égypte Contemporaine* XVII, no. 93/94 (April/May 1926): 267–269.

118. "Government Crop Forecasts and the Crop Recording System," 119.

119. TNA, FO 141/587: From A. T. McKillop to the Residency in Cairo (December 21, 1920).

120. For a comparison of preliminary estimates by the Egyptian government and by the AGPA between 1910/11 and 1925/26, see Economou and Co., *Some Information About the Egyptian Cotton Market*, 52–53.

121. Todd, *The Marketing of Cotton*, 205.

122. Abdel Wahab, *Memorandum on the Bases of a Stable Cotton Policy*, 36.

123. Ibid., 40–41; Hugo Lindemann, "Le Coton Égyptien du Point de Vue de l'Exportateur," *L'Égypte Contemporaine* XXII, no. 127 (March 1931): 404.

124. Abdel Wahab, *Memorandum on the Bases of a Stable Cotton Policy*, 39; TNA, FO 371/14647: Acting High Commissioner to the Residency (October 24, 1930). For a report on cotton costs after ginning, see "Takālīf al-Quṭn ba'd Janyuh: Taqrīr al-Lajna al-Mukhtaṣṣa," *al-Ahrām* (September 17, 1931).

125. Abdel Wahab, *Memorandum on the Bases of a Stable Cotton Policy*, 40; Goldberg, *Trade, Reputation, and Child Labor in Twentieth-Century Egypt*, 68; Lindemann, "Le

Coton Égyptien du Point de Vue de l'Exportateur," 404–405; Owen, *Cotton and the Egyptian Economy*, 209–210; Todd, *The Marketing of Cotton*, 162–163.

126. TNA, FO 371/14647: Egyptian Legislation to Prevent Mixing of Cotton (June 14, 1930); Abdel Wahab, *Memorandum on the Bases of a Stable Cotton Policy*, 42.

127. TNA, FO 141/719/19: Note Explicative sur le Projet de Loi pour Empêcher la Mélange des Variétés de Coton (June 7, 1934).

128. Naḥḥās, *Juhūd al-Niqāba al-Zirā'iyya al-Miṣriyya al-'Āmma fī Thalāthīna 'Āman*, 212–224.

129. "La Mélange des Cotons," *La Réforme* (July 28, 1934).

130. Politi, *L'Egypte de 1914 à "Suez,"* 125–126.

131. Goldberg, *Trade, Reputation, and Child Labor in Twentieth-Century Egypt*, 68–69.

132. Pearce, "Egyptian Cotton from the Points of View of the Spinning Industry," 395; Naḥḥās, *Al-Quṭn fī Khamsīn 'Ām*, 318.

133. Politi, *L'Egypte de 1914 à "Suez,"* 126.

134. Lindemann, "Le Coton Égyptien du Point de Vue de l'Exportateur," 405.

135. Abdel Wahab, *Memorandum on the Bases of a Stable Cotton Policy*, 44.

136. TNA, FO 371/14647: A. W. Jessop to the Residency (October 22, 1930).

137. "Iḍrāb 'Ummāl al-Naql fī Mīnā al-Baṣal," *al-Ahrām* (September 3, 1931).

138. Curry, *The Control of Weights and Measures in Egypt*, 5–6. In 1914, the Legislative Council passed the Weights and Measures Law with the approval of the Mixed Courts. The law defined those weights and measures that could be used in trading and stipulated their equivalence in international meter-kilogram units. This spawned a class of officially licensed weighers who played an important role in the cotton trade.

139. Ibid., 13.

140. TNA, FO 141/763/15: L. B. Grafftey-Smith to the Acting High Commissioner (September 26, 1931).

141. Curry, *The Control of Weights and Measures in Egypt*, 7.

142. Beinin and Lockman, *Workers on the Nile*, 189–206.

143. "Iḍrāb al-Shayālīn fī Mīnā al-Baṣal," *al-Ahrām* (April 1, 1931).

144. TNA, FO 141/763/15: L. B. Grafftey-Smith to the Acting High Commissioner.

145. Ibid.

146. "Iḍrāb 'Ummāl al-Naql fī Mīnā al-Baṣal," *al-Ahrām*.

147. TNA, FO 141/763/15: L. B. Grafftey-Smith to the Acting High Commissioner. For an account of the creation of the Labor Conciliation Board in 1919, see Lockman, "British Policy Toward Egyptian Labor Activism, 1882–1936," 274–275.

148. Beinin and Lockman, *Workers on the Nile*, 203.

149. "Fī Muḥīṭ al-'Ummāl fī al-Iskandariyya," *al-Ahrām* (December 2, 1934).

150. "Sūq al-Quṭn," *al-Ahrām* (November 15, 1931); Todd, *The Marketing of Cotton*, 162.

151. Ministère des Finances, *Annuaire Statistique de l'Egypte 1920*, 104–109; Ministère des Finances, *Annuaire Statistique de l'Egypte 1921–22*, 138–143.

152. "La Mélange du Coton: Une Interview du Ministre de l'Agriculture," *La Réforme* (August 4, 1934).

153. Ṣufayr, *Muḥīṭ al-Sharā'i' 1856–1952*, vol. 3, 3227–3230.

154. Goldberg, *Trade, Reputation, and Child Labor in Twentieth-Century Egypt*, 82.
155. Arrighi, *The Long Twentieth Century*, 179.
156. Cain and Hopkins, *British Imperialism*, 501–525; Drummond, *Imperial Economic Policy*.
157. Harari, "Banking and Financial Business in Egypt," 149.
158. Selous, *Economic Conditions in Egypt*, 43 and 128.
159. Bresciani-Turroni, "Egypt's Balance of Trade," 376.
160. Aḥmad Ṣadiq Sa'd, "Taṭawwur Miṣr al-Ra'smālī, 1919–1945," *al-Fajr al-Jadīd*, No. 13 (November 16, 1945): 5–7. Republished in Sa'd, *Ṣafaḥāt Min al-Yasār al-Miṣrī fī A'qāb al-Ḥarb al-'Ālamiyya al-Thānya*, 176–182. In the 1940s, Ṣadiq Sa'd wrote prolifically about capitalism in Egypt from a Marxist perspective.
161. Eichengreen and Temin, "The Gold Standard and the Great Depression."
162. *National Bank of Egypt*, 56–58.
163. Hansen, *The Political Economy of Poverty, Equity, and Growth*, 79.
164. TNA, FO 141/728: Memorandum from Edward Cook to the Residency (November 19, 1931). Cook was the last British governor of the National Bank of Egypt.
165. Wadia and Joshi, *A Plea for an Effective Gold Standard in India*; Balachandran, "Britain, USA, and Indian Gold Standard."
166. "Ḥarrarū al-Junayh al-Miṣri min Ḥimāyat al-Junayh al-Injilīzī," *al-Ahrām* (September 8, 1931).
167. Rifaat, *The Monetary System of Egypt*.
168. Ibid., 59.
169. Issawi, *Egypt at Mid-Century*, 228.
170. Strange, *Sterling and British Policy*, 4–5. On the concept of world money, see Marx, *Capital*, vol. 1, 240–244.

Chapter 4

1. TNA, FO 371/39999: Ahmed Hussein, "Rural Social Improvement in Egypt," in Middle East Supply Centre, "The Proceedings of the Conference on Middle East Agricultural Development" (February 1944).
2. The Royal Government of Egypt, *The Fallāḥ Department*, 7.
3. Hansen, "Income and Consumption in Egypt, 1886/1887 to 1937," 29.
4. Hansen, *The Political Economy of Poverty, Equity, and Growth: Egypt and Turkey*, 75.
5. El-Gritly, *The Structure of Modern Industry in Egypt*, 571.
6. Tignor, *State, Private Enterprise, and Economic Change in Egypt*, 115–116.
7. TNA, FO 141/723/19: Memorandum on the Situation of the Fellaheen (October 28, 1933).
8. Abdel Wahab, *Memorandum on the Bases of a Stable Cotton Policy*, 3–5.
9. DWQ, WA, 0069-009908: Petition from Mīnā al-Qamḥ, Sharqiyya (September 6, 1930).
10. TNA, FO 141/560/23: No. 897/30 from the Director General, European Department, Ministry of Interior (August 28, 1930).
11. Shalabī, *Azmat al-Kasād al-'Ālamī al-Kubrā wa-In'ikāsuhā 'alā al-Rīf al-Miṣrī*, 65–66.

12. DWQ, WA, 0069-009867: Petition from Daqahliyya (October 11, 1930).

13. For a careful examination of the sophisticated ways in which peasants could use petitions to engage the state, see Chalcraft, "Engaging the State," 303–325.

14. Postone, *Time, Labor, and Social Domination*, 29–34.

15. Minost, "L'Action Contre la Crise Cotonnière," 443–444.

16. "Al-'Ījārāt al-Zirā'iyya fī Sanat 1931," *al-Ahrām* (September 9, 1931); "Fī Majlis al-Nuwwāb: Takhfīḍ al-'Ījārāt al-Zirā'iyya," *al-Ahrām* (April 6, 1931).

17. TNA, FO 141/560/23: R. H. Hoare to the Residency (September 13, 1930); Deeb, *Party Politics in Egypt*, 226–227.

18. TNA, FO 141/763/2: Mr. Job to Martin (July 6, 1931).

19. Edwards, "The Egyptian Rural Problem," 195.

20. TNA, FO 141/763/2: Hajj Mahmoud Allam, 1st Substitute of Parquet, Tanta Native Court, "A Note on Usury in Egypt" (February 11, 1931).

21. Edwards, "The Egyptian Rural Problem," 195.

22. TNA, FO 141/763/2: "A Note on Usury in Egypt"; "Al-Azma al-Iqtiṣādiyya wa-Ṣadāha fī Anḥā' al-Bilād," Letter 3, *al-Ahrām* (September 1, 1931).

23. Minost, "L'Action Contre la Crise Cotonnière," 439.

24. TNA, FO 371/14647: Acting Financial Advisor to the Residency (August 17, 1930); DWQ, MS 3019-000112: "Bank al-Taslīf al-Zirā'ī wa-l-Ta'āwunī" (1948–1953). For a detailed account of the Crédit Agricole, see Iyer, *Agrarian Superpower*, chapter 2.

25. DWQ, MS 3019-000111: "Taqārīr Bank al-Taslīf al-Zira'ī wa-l-Ta'āwunī, 1948–1953"; Zannis, *Le Crédit Agricole en Egypte*, 99–100; "Bank al-Taslīf al-Zirā'ī: Al-Marsūm al-Saḍir bi-Ta'sīsahu," *al-Ahrām* (July 26, 1931).

26. Eshag and Kamal, "A Note on the Reform of the Rural Credit System in U.A.R (Egypt)," 99.

27. DWQ, RMW 0081-023720: "Taqrīr al-Lajna al-Far'iyya al-Mukallafa bi-Baḥth Mashrū' Inshā' Bank Zirā'ī" (1930); TNA, FO 371/14647: Conseil Économique, "Rapport du Sous-Commission Chargée de l'Étude d'un Projet de Création d'une Banque Agricole" (July 16, 1930).

28. Jakes, *Egypt's Occupation*, 101–103 and 214–217.

29. *National Bank of Egypt*, 52–54.

30. Issawi, *Egypt*, 24 and 144–145; Tignor, *State, Private Enterprise, and Economic Change in Egypt*, 115.

31. "Bank al-Taslīf al-Zirā'ī," *al-Ahrām* (September 1, 1931).

32. TNA, FO 371/14647: A. W. Jessop to the Residency (October 22, 1930).

33. TNA, FO 371/14647: Acting Financial Advisor to the Residency (September 13, 1930).

34. Eshag and Kamal, "A Note on the Reform of the Rural Credit System in U.A.R (Egypt)," 99; Richards, *Egypt's Agricultural Development*, 154.

35. Zannis, *Le Crédit Agricole en Egypte*, 165–166.

36. "Lamḥa Iqtiṣādiyya: Al-Azma al-Ḥāḍira wa-l-Duyūn," *al-Ahrām* (July 16, 1931); "Al-Azma al-Iqtiṣādiyya wa-l-Duyūn al-Maḍmūna bi-Ruhūn Amwāl Thābita," *al-Ahrām* (July 20, 1931); "Al-Azma al-Iqtiṣādiyya wa-Ḥall Mushkilat Duyūn al-Zurrā'," *al-Ahrām* (July 24, 1931).

37. "Al-Tharwa al-Aqāriyya wa-l-Muḥāfaẓa 'Alayhā," *al-Ahrām* (September 9, 1931).

38. Eshag and Kamal, "A Note on the Reform of the Rural Credit System in U.A.R (Egypt)," 99–100.

39. TNA, FO 371/15428: Note by Acting Financial Advisor (August 18, 1931); Tignor, *State, Private Enterprise, and Economic Change in Egypt*, 119.

40. "Al-Muḥāfaẓa 'alā al-Tharwa al-'Aqāriyya: Mudhakkirat Mudīr Bank al-Taslīf al-Zirā'ī," *al-Ahrām* (September 2, 1931).

41. "Ra'y fī Ḥall Mushkilat al-Duyūn al-'Aqāriyya," *al-Ahrām* (September 3, 1931).

42. "Taswiyyat al-Duyūn al-'Aqāriyya: Lā Yurjā Inqādh al-Tharwa al-'Aqāriyya illā bi-Tashrī' wa-Lijān Taḥkīm," *al-Ahrām* (September 29, 1931).

43. Rifaat, *The Monetary System of Egypt*, 41–42.

44. "Fī al-Ḥāla al-Ḥaḍira: Iltimās ilā Bank al-Taslīf," *al-Muqaṭṭam* (September 6, 1931).

45. Selous, *Economic Conditions in Egypt*, 37–38; Zannis, *Le Crédit Agricole en Egypte*, 166–172.

46. Selous, *Economic Conditions in Egypt*, 43 and 76–77.

47. Zannis, *Le Crédit Agricole en Egypte*, 38.

48. DWQ, WA 0069-009912: Petition from Kafr Khuzām, Asyūṭ (January 17, 1938).

49. DWQ, WA 0069-009911: Petition from Al-'Ayyāṭ, Giza (August, 1937).

50. TNA, FO 141/723/19: Report from Bani Swayf (October 15, 1933).

51. TNA, FO 141/723/19: Nelson Shuter to Larkins (October 9, 1933).

52. TNA, FO 141/723/19: Memorandum on the Situation of the Fellaheen.

53. Richards, *Egypt's Agricultural Development*, 155.

54. Martinez-Matsuda, *Migrant Citizenship*; Olsson, *Agrarian Crossings*; Palacios, "Postrevolutionary Intellectuals, Rural Readings, and the Shaping of the 'Peasant Problem' in Mexico"; Roberts, *The Farm Security Administration and Rural Rehabilitation in the South*; Vaughn, *Cultural Politics in Revolution*.

55. Cole, "To Save the Village"; Chiang, *Social Engineering and the Social Sciences in China*; Douw, "The Representation of China's Rural Backwardness"; Ekbladh, "To Reconstruct the Medieval: Rural Reconstruction in Interwar China and the Rise of an American Style of Modernization"; Shiroyama, *China During the Great Depression: Market, State, and the World Economy*.

56. Petrie, "Village Visions: Science and Technology in the Bengal Countryside."

57. Foucault, "Governmentality"; Foucault, *Society Must Be Defended*, 34–36.

58. El Shakry, *The Great Social Laboratory*, 113–142.

59. Derr, *The Lived Nile*, 127–156.

60. Jacques Berque claims that American psychologist Wendel Cleland, a professor at the American University in Cairo, was one of the first people to employ the phrase in the 1930s. Berque, *Egypt*, 487.

61. Cromer, *Modern Egypt*, vol. II, 453.

62. See J. I. Craig, "The Census of Egypt," *L'Égypte Contemporaine* VIII, no. 32 (April 1917): 209–234; J. I. Craig, "The Census of Egypt," *L'Égypte Contemporaine* XVII, no. 26 (December 1926): 434–455; Macdonald, *Nile Control*.

63. El Shakry, *The Great Social Laboratory*, 147. The first study of population control in Egypt was Cleland, *The Population Problem in Egypt*.

64. For similar observations about China, see Thompson, "The Birth of the Chinese Population: A Study in the History of Governmental Logics."

65. Carr-Saunders, *World Population, Past Growth and Present Trends*; Thompson, "Population"; Iyer, "Colonial Population and the Idea of Development."

66. Ḥāfiẓ 'Afīfī, "Al-Ṣinā'āṭ al-Miṣriyya: Atharuhā fī al-Rakhā' al-Qawmī fī Zaman al-Silm wa-l-Ḥarb," *al-Muqtaṭaf* 104, no. 2 (February 1944): 114–126; Ghālī, *Siyāsat al-Ghad*, 40. See also al-Barrāwī and Ulaysh, *Al-Taṭawwur al-Iqtiṣādī fī Miṣr fī al-'Aṣr al-Hadīth*, 301.

67. Al-Hakīm, *Yawmiyyāt Nā'ib fī al-Aryāf*; Selim, *The Novel and the Rural Imaginary in Egypt*, 117–126.

68. Kholoussi, "Fallāḥin."

69. Deeb, *Party Politics in Egypt*, 272–275.

70. Al-Shāṭi', *Al-Rīf al-Miṣrī*; Al-Shāṭi', *Qaḍiyyat al-Fallāḥ*.

71. Al-Shāṭi', *Al-Rīf al-Miṣrī*, 8.

72. 'Afīfī, *'Alā Hāmish al-Siyāsa*; Ghālī, *Siyāsat al-Ghad*; Ḥusayn, *Musṭaqbal al-Thaqāfa fī Miṣr*.

73. Minost, "L'Action Contre la Crise Cotonnière," 409–410. Minost was responding to a metaphor presented by Italian agricultural economist Umberto Ricci, who taught at Cairo University for more than a decade, that "the microbes of depression work during periods of prosperity and the leukocytes of recovery work during periods of depression."

74. Meijer, *The Quest for Modernity*, 37–65.

75. Ghālī, *Siyāsat al-Ghad*, 75.

76. El Shakry, *The Great Social Laboratory*, 132–137.

77. Muḥammad al-'Ashmāwī, "Tansīq al-Iṣlāḥ al-Ijtimā'ī fī Miṣr," *Majallat al-Shu'ūn al-Ijtimā'iyya* 12 (December 1940): 12–18.

78. "Al-Dayn al-'Aqārī wa-l-Amlāk fī Miṣr," *al-Ahrām* (August 17, 1931).

79. Edwards, "The Egyptian Rural Problem," 194.

80. Ayrout, *Moeurs et Coutumes des Fellahs*, 47. Translations from French in this paragraph are taken from Henry Ayrout, *The Egyptian Peasant*, 19.

81. Ayrout, *Moeurs et Coutumes des Fellahs*, 47.

82. Ibid., 48.

83. Selous, *Economic Conditions in Egypt*, 77.

84. Minost, "L'Action Contre la Crise Cottonière en Egypte," 447.

85. Eshag and Kamal, "A Note on the Reform of the Rural Credit System in U.A.R (Egypt)," 99; Richards, *Egypt's Agricultural Development*, 154.

86. Zannis, *Le Crédit Agricole en Egypte*, 173.

87. Ibrahim Rashad, "The Cooperative Movement: Another Democratic Institution Introduced into Egypt," *L'Égypte Contemporaine* XXX, No. 185 (May 1939): 488.

88. Ibid., 489; Ministry of Social Affairs, *Co-operative Societies in Egypt*, 8–9.

89. Ministry of Social Affairs, *Co-operative Societies in Egypt*, 2.

90. Rashād, *Wājibnā al-Ta'āwunī ba'd al-Mu'āhada*, 4 and 7.

91. Rashad, "The Cooperative Movement," 490.

92. Ministry of Social Affairs, *Co-operative Societies in Egypt*, 2 and 12.

93. Ibid., 2.

94. Mar'ī, *Tarīkh al-Sīnimā al-Tasjīliyya fī Miṣr*, 9.
95. Ministry of Agriculture, *Zamīl al-Fallāḥ* 1, no. 1 (1930): 2.
96. Ibid., 5–6.
97. *Al-Fallāḥ al-Iqtiṣādī* 1, no. 1 (October 1933).
98. Johnson, *Reconstructing Rural Egypt*, xix–xx.
99. Ibid., 55.
100. The Royal Government of Egypt, *Social Welfare in Egypt*, 33.
101. Johnson, *Reconstructing Rural Egypt*, 83.
102. Ibid., 86.
103. Ministry of Social Affairs, *Social Welfare in Egypt*, 13–14.
104. TNA, FO 371/39999: Middle East Supply Centre, "The Proceedings of the Conference on Middle East Agricultural Development."
105. Gasper, *The Power of Representation*; Jacob, *Working Out Egypt*; Pollard, *Nurturing the Nation.*
106. David Scott, "Colonial Governmentality," 214.
107. Jakes, *Egypt's Occupation*, 25–27.
108. Owen, "The Rapid Growth of Egypt's Agricultural Output, 1890–1914, as an Early Example of the Green Revolutions of Modern South Asia," 81–99; Richards, *Egypt's Agricultural Development,* 55–110.
109. Jakes, *Egypt's Occupation*, 201–202.
110. Brown, "Brigands and State Building"; Richards, *Egypt's Agricultural Development, 56-58.*
111. Pursley, *Familiar Futures*, 31–33.
112. Stokes, *The English Utilitarians and India*, 81-139. See also Macaulay, "Minute on Indian Education (2 February 1835)."
113. Mitchell, *Colonizing Egypt.*
114. Jacob, *Working Out Egypt.*
115. An exception is where Mitchell discusses government inspections of peasant farming activities in the 1830s and 1840s. However, the system of meticulous supervision that he describes was primarily intended to penalize infractions—for example, peasants who abandoned their villages or failed to cultivate their fields in accordance with the requirements of state officials—through forms of corporeal punishment. Its principal aim was not to instruct, educate, and rehabilitate peasants. See Mitchell, *Colonizing Egypt*, 40–43.
116. Foucault writes, "Maybe what is really important for our modernity—that is, for our present—is not so much the *étatisation* of society, as the 'governmentalization' of the state." See Foucault, "Governmentality," 103.
117. Chatterjee, *Nationalist Thought and the Colonial World.*
118. Jessop, "From Micro-powers to Governmentality," 34–40.

Chapter 5

1. Sa'd, *Mushkilat al-Fallāḥ*, 50–51.
2. Mulattam, *Al-Ḥizb al-Shīyū'ī al-Miṣrī*, 81–84.
3. Minost, "L'Action Contre la Crise Cotonnière," 452.
4. Schewe, "State of Siege"; Tripp, "Ali Maher and the Politics of the Egyptian Army."

According to the 1936 Anglo-Egyptian treaty, all restrictions on the presence of British troops in Egypt would be lifted if there were an "imminent menace of war or apprehended international emergency"—namely in the case of German or Italian aggression.

5. Martin, "The Global Crisis of the Commodity Glut During the Second World War."

6. TNA, FO 371/24617: Disposal of Egyptian Cotton Surplus (December 23, 1940).

7. "Al-Quṭn wa-Buyūt al-Isdār: I'tirāḍāt lā Maḥal lahā fī al-Waqt al-Ḥāḍir," *al-Balāgh* (October 21, 1939).

8. TNA, FO 371/24617: Disposal of Egyptian Cotton Surplus.

9. TNA, FO 371/24617: British Government Cotton Buying Commission, "Operation Scheme" (September 15, 1940).

10. *National Bank of Egypt*, 67.

11. Richards, *Egypt's Agricultural Development*, 168–169; Vitalis, *When Capitalists Collide*, 112–113.

12. Heydemann and Vitalis, "War, Keynesianism, and Colonialism: Explaining State-Market Relations in the Postwar Middle East"; Wilmington, *The Middle East Supply Center.*

13. *National Bank of Egypt*, 68; Dunn, *Cotton in Egypt*, 29; and Richards, *Egypt's Agricultural Development*, 170.

14. Anouar Abdel-Malek, *Egypt: Military Society*, 14. See also Abū al-'Azm, *Awḍā' Miṣr al-Ṣinā'iyya min 1945 ilā 1961.*

15. Al-Barrāwī and 'Ulaysh, *Al-Taṭawwur al-Iqtiṣādī fī Miṣr fī al-'Aṣr al-Hadīth*, 309.

16. Beinin and Lockman, *Workers on the Nile*, 261–264.

17. Tignor, *State, Private Enterprise, and Economic Change in Egypt*, 180–181.

18. El-Gritly, *The Structure of Modern Industry in Egypt*, 502.

19. Gallagher, *Egypt's Other Wars*, 20–39; Richards, *Egypt's Agricultural Development*, 172.

20. Ministry of Finance, *Population Census of Egypt* (1937); Ministry of Finance, *Population Census of Egypt* (1947); Janet Abu Lughod, *Cairo: 1001 Years of the City Victorious*, 129.

21. Yaḥyā Huwaydī, "Al-Hijra Min al-Qarya ilā al-Madīna," *Majallat al-Shu'ūn al-Ijtimā'iyya* (June 1945): 16.

22. Ibid, 18–19; Ministry of Social Affairs, *Note on Questions Relating to Agriculture*, 3; Richards, *Egypt's Agricultural Development*, 228.

23. Richards, *Egypt's Agricultural Development*, 173–174.

24. Ghonemy, "Resource Use and Income in Egyptian Agriculture," 43.

25. Ibid, 45–49. Although Ghonemy questioned the accuracy of statistics for rented areas that appeared in the 1939 agricultural census, he still concluded that rural tenancy did increase substantially in this period. Similar statistics are reproduced in a variety of other sources that were published later. These include Abbas and El-Dessouky, *The Large Landowning Class and the Peasantry in Egypt*, 125; Abdel-Malek, "La Question Agraire en Égypte et la Réforme de 1952," 189; and Richards, *Egypt's Agricultural Development*, 172–173.

26. Ghonemy, "Resource Use and Income in Egyptian Agriculture," 58.

27. Ministry of Social Affairs, *Note on Questions Relating to Agriculture*, 5; Richards, *Egypt's Agricultural Development*, 173.

28. El Mallakh, "The Effects of the Second World War on the Economic Development of Egypt," 102.

29. Abbas and El-Dessouky, *The Large Landowning Class and the Peasantry in Egypt*, 125; Abdel-Malek, "La Question Agraire en Égypte et la Réforme de 1952," 189; ʿĀmir, *Al-Arḍ wa-l-Fallāḥ*, 106; Dunn, *Cotton in Egypt*, 35; Ghonemy, "Resource Use and Income in Egyptian Agriculture," 57–58.

30. Dunn, *Cotton in Egypt*, 35. The National Cotton Council is an American trade organization that was created during the Great Depression.

31. DWQ, WA 0069-009877-0013: "Petition from Markaz Mīt Ghamr, Daqahliyya Governorate" (April 25, 1942); DWQ, WA 0069-009879-0006: "Petition from Markaz Tūkh, Munūfiyya Governorate" (August 10, 1946).

32. Al-Barrāwī, *Haqīqat al-Inqilāb al-Akhīr fī Miṣr*, 87; Beinin and Lockman, *Workers on the Nile*, 291–294; Richards, *Egypt's Agricultural Development*, 160.

33. Ministry of Social Affairs, *Note on Questions Relating to Agriculture*, 3.

34. Abbas and Dessouky, *The Large Landowning Class and the Peasantry in Egypt*, 125; Abdel-Malek, "La Question Agraire en Égypte et la Réforme de 1952," 189.

35. DWQ, WA 0069-009926-0014: "ʿAqd Ījār Aṭyān," (undated).

36. Dunn, *Cotton in Egypt*, 34.

37. Ghonemy, "Economic and Institutional Organization of Egyptian Agriculture Since 1952," 67.

38. Ministry of Social Affairs, *Note on Questions Relating to Agriculture*, 5.

39. Ghonemy, "Resource Use and Income in Egyptian Agriculture," 33–36 and 57.

40. DWQ, WSI 4029-000180: "Petition from Muḥammad al-Jammāl to the Minister of Social Affairs" (October 5, 1947).

41. Ghonemy, "Resource Use and Income in Egyptian Agriculture," 61–62.

42. Davis, *Challenging Colonialism*, 136; Tignor, *State, Private Enterprise, and Economic Change in Egypt*, 177–179.

43. Muḥammad ʿAbd al-Karīm, "Fī al-Maḥalla al-Kubrā," *Majallat al-Shu'ūn al-Ijtimāʿiyya* (November 1943): 52.

44. Ibid., 51. By the end of the 1930s, Bank Misr faced a financial crisis that resulted from competition with Japanese textile imports, excessive funds that it devoted to its subsidiary companies, contributions to the country's defense budget after the conclusion of the Anglo-Egyptian Treaty of 1936, and sudden withdrawals by clients of its subsidiary savings bank at the start of the war. But the war presented the bank with renewed opportunities to make profits. See Davis, *Challenging Colonialism*, 134–168; Sharikat Miṣr li-l-Ghazl wa-l-Nasīj, *Taqrīr Majlis al-Idāra*.

45. For a detailed account of how lower-class women in *al-Maḥalla al-Kubrā* took advantage of the high demand for affordable housing that resulted from the city's unprecedented population growth, see Hammad, *Industrial Sexuality*, 106–138.

46. Mūsā, *Ghandī wa-l-Ḥaraka al-Hindiyya*, 75. See also "Mānshistar fī Miṣr" *al-Fallāḥ al-Iqtiṣādī* (November 1933), 27–29.

47. For a fuller account of how Gandhi was received by different segments of the Egyptian nationalist movement, see Khan, *Egyptian-Indian Nationalist Collaboration and the British Empire*, 111–128.

48. Mustṭafa Nuṣrat, "Siyāsat Miṣr al-Zirā'iyya ba'd al-Ḥarb," *Majallat al-Shu'ūn al-Ijtimā'iyya* (March, 1944): 7.

49. Muḥammad Subḥī al-Daghashī, "Al-Sinā'a wa-Atharuhā fī Kiyāninā al-Qawmī," *Majallat al-Shu'ūn al-Ijtimā'iyya* (November 1945): 51.

50. Muḥammad Rushdī, "Al-Ṣinā'a al-Hadītha: Sabīl Miṣr ilā al-Raf'a wa-l-Majd," *al-Mujtama' al-Jadīd* (February 1948).

51. "Al-Tawsī' fī Istikhdām al-Khuyūṭ al-Ṣinā'iyya," *al-Miṣrī*, (1950).

52. Zakariyya Mahrān, "Al-Ṣinā'a fī Miṣr," *Majallat al-Shu'ūn al-Ijtimā'iyya* (May 1944): 45.

53. Ghālī, *Siyāsat al-Ghad*, 41–53.

54. 'Aryān Yūsuf Sa'd, "Intāj al-'Āmil al-Zirā'ī fī Miṣr," *Majallat al-Shu'ūn al-Ijtimā'iyya* (May 1945): 51–53.

55. Eman, *L'Industrie du Coton en Egypte*, 203.

56. Mahrān, "Al-Ṣinā'a fī Miṣr," 43.

57. Ismā'īl Sidqī, "Al-Taṭawwur al-Ṣinā'ī fī Miṣr," *Majallat al-Shu'ūn al-Ijtimā'iyya* (September 1944): 8.

58. Iyer, "Colonial Population and the Idea of Development," 88–89; Lewis, "Reflections on South-East Asia," 9–13; Lewis, "Economic Development with Unlimited Supplies of Labor," 143–144. For a detailed biography of W. Arthur Lewis from the 1930s to the 1950s, see Tignor, *W. Arthur Lewis and the Birth of Development Economics*, 42–108.

59. El-Gritly, *The Structure of Modern Industry in Egypt*, 575.

60. Ibid., 577. See Rosenstein-Rodan, "Problems of Industrialization of Eastern and South-Eastern Europe."

61. Sidky, "Industrialization of Egypt and a Case Study of the Iron and Steel Industry," 7–8.

62. On the electrification of the Aswan dam, see Aḥmad, *Al-Khuṭūṭ al-'Arīḍa fī Kahrabat Miṣr*, 31–32 and Vitalis, *When Capitalists Collide*, 63–103.

63. Anise, *A Study of the National Income of Egypt*; Mitchell, *Rule of Experts*, 112–113. Various estimates of national income, by people like Maḥmūd Anīs, Munīr Ḥabashī, and 'Abd al-Mun'im al-Shāf'ī were in circulation by the early 1950s. See Charles Issawi, *Egypt at Mid-Century*, 81–85.

64. Al-Daghashī, "Al-Sinā'a wa-Athāruhā fī Kiyāninā al-Qawmī," 52.

65. Abdel-Malek, *Egypt: Military Society*, 42–43.

66. Waḥīda, *Fī 'Uṣūl al-Mas'ala al-Miṣriyya*, 180–181.

67. Ibid., 186.

68. Baer, *A History of Landownership in Modern Egypt*, 77–90; Richards, *Egypt's Agricultural Development*, 153.

69. Hamrūsh, *Thawrat 23 Yūlyū*, vol. 1, 254–256.

70. Ghālī, *Al-Iṣlāḥ al-Zirā'ī*; Sa'd, *Mushkilat al-Fallāḥ*.

71. Ghālī, *Siyāsat al-Ghad*, 73–75.

72. Ghālī, *Al-Iṣlāḥ al-Zirā'ī*, 33 and 57.

73. Ibid., 60.

74. Botman, "The Rise and Experience of Egyptian Communism: 1919–1952," 60–61.

75. Aḥmad Sa'īd, "Al-Iṣlāḥ al-Zirā'ī," *Al-Fajr al-Jadīd*, no. 7 (August 16, 1945): 16–17. Re-

published in Sa'd, *Ṣafaḥāt min al-Yasār al-Miṣrī fī A'qāb al-Ḥarb al-'Ālamiyya al-Thānya*, 161–164. The reviewer was reportedly Aḥmad Ṣādiq Sa'd writing under a pseudonym. See al-Sibā'ī, "Ṣāḍiq Sa'd: Biyūājrāfyā Mūjaza."

76. Sa'd, *Mushkilat al-Fallāḥ*, 3.

77. Ghālī, *Al-Iṣlāḥ al-Zirā'ī*, 4.

78. Ibid., 58.

79. Ibid., 73.

80. Ibid., 74–75.

81. Ibid., 75–76.

82. Sa'd, *Mushkilat al-Fallāḥ*, 45–46.

83. Ṣādiq Sa'd relied on a Ricardian theory of rent that understood it to be unearned income that was largely determined by natural bounty or monopoly privilege, rather than by the law of value. For Marx's critique of Ricardo, see Marx, *Capital*, vol. 3, 751–950.

84. Sa'd, *Mushkilat al-Fallāḥ*, 38.

85. Ibid., 31.

86. Sa'd, *Mushkilat al-Fallāḥ*, 65–66.

87. Al-Barrāwī and 'Alī, *Mushkilatunā al-Ijtimā'iyya*, 33.

88. Rashād, *Mashrū' al-Mazāri' al-Ta'āwuniyya*. In the 1940s, George Bernard Shaw visited Egypt and convinced Rashād that collectivization, along the lines of what Joseph Stalin had accomplished in the Soviet Union, would be more effective than the existing cooperatives movement in Egypt. See Rashād, *Mudhakkirāt Mujāhid Ta'āwunī*, 89–94; *The Letters of Bernard Shaw to the Times*, 261–265.

89. Sa'd, *Mushkilat al-Fallāḥ*, 48–51.

90. Ikeda, "Sociopolitical Debates in Late Parliamentary Egypt, 1944–1952," 88–93.

91. Ibid., 94–95. Fatḥī 'Abd al-Fattāḥ claims that the Egyptian Socialist Party first used this slogan in the 1920s. See 'Abd al-Fattāḥ, *Al-Nāṣiriyya wa-Tajribat al-Thawra min A'lā: Al-Mas'ala al-Zirā'iyya*, 38. Muriam Haleh-Davis examines the use of the slogan in Algeria under the rule of Ahmed Ben Bella, the country's first president. See Haleh-Davis, *Markets of Civilization*, 123–126.

92. Ghonemy, "Resource Use and Income in Egyptian Agriculture," 146–147.

93. Hamrūsh, *Thawrat 23 Yūlyū*, vol. 1, 257–258; 'Ashmāwī, *Al-Fallāḥūn wa-l-Sulṭa 'Alā Ḍaw' al-Ḥarakāt al-Fallāḥiyya al-Miṣriyya*, 86; Al-Barrāwī, *Ḥaqīqat al-Inqilāb al-Akhīr fī Miṣr*, 88; Baer, *Studies in the Social History of Modern Egypt*, 102–103; Al-Nūr, *Al-Arḍ wa-l-Fallāḥ wa-l-Mustathmir*, 59; Richards, *Egypt's Agricultural Development*, 174–75.

94. Abdel-Malek, *Egypt, Military Society*, 68–69.

95. "Ma'raka fī 'Izbat al-Badrāwi Bāshā," *al-Ahrām* (June 24, 1951).

96. Abdel Hamid Nazmy, "The Land is a Bottomless Sink for Egyptian Capital," *L'Egypte Contemporaine* XXXV, no. 218/219 (March/April 1944): 239–241.

97. Meijer, *The Quest of Modernity*, 68–69.

98. Al-Barrāwī and 'Ulaysh, *Al-Taṭawwur al-Iqtiṣādī fī Miṣr fī al-'Aṣr al-Ḥadīth*, 59. Similar accounts that began to appear in the 1940s can be found in Ḥāfiẓ 'Afīfī, "Nahḍat Miṣr al-Ṣinā'iyya," *Majallat al-Shu'ūn al-Ijtimā'iyya* (December, 1943): 15–18; Eman, "L'Industrie Égyptienne Sous la Dynastie de Mohamed Aly"; Ghurbāl, *Muḥammad 'Alī al-Kabīr*, 39 and 69–70. For an account of the wider debates between Egyptian historians

in the 1930s about the role of Mehmed Ali in their country's modern history, see Di-Capua, *Gatekeepers of the Arab Past*, 155–159.

99. Al-Barrāwī and 'Ulaysh, *Al-Taṭawwur al-Iqtiṣādī fī Miṣr fī al-'Aṣr al-Ḥadīth*, 105–182. Similar accounts that began to appear in the 1940s can be found in El-Gritly, *The Structure of Modern Industry in Egypt*, 363–368; Ṣāliḥ, *Krūmar fī Miṣr.*

100. Al-Barrāwī and 'Ulaysh, *Al-Taṭawwur al-Iqtiṣādī fī Miṣr fī al-'Aṣr al-Ḥadīth*, 183–210. Similar accounts that began to appear in the 1940s can be found in Sidqī, "Al-Taṭawwur al-Ṣinā'ī fī Miṣr," 6–9; Mahrān, "Al-Ṣinā'a fī Miṣr," 42–46; Luhayṭa, *Tarīkh Fu'ād al-Awwal al-Iqtiṣādī*, vols. 1–3; Sa'd, "Taṭawwur Miṣr al-Ra'smālī, 1919–1945."

101. Al-Barrāwī and 'Ulaysh, *Al-Taṭawwur al-Iqtiṣādī fī Miṣr fī al-'Aṣr al-Ḥadīth*, 302.

102. Meek, "Smith, Turgot, and the 'Four Stages' Theory."

103. Barendse, "The Feudal Mutation: Military and Economic Transformations of the Ethnosphere in the Tenth to Thirteenth Centuries," 504–508; Brown, "The Tyranny of a Construct: Feudalism and Historians of Medieval Europe"; Reynolds, *Fiefs and Vassals*, 3–14.

104. Al-Māwardī, *Al-Aḥkām al-Ṣulṭāniyya.*

105. Al-Ṭahṭāwī, *Kitāb al-Jughrāfyā al-'Umūmiyya*; Heyworth-Dunne, "Rifā'ah Badawī Rāfi' aṭ-Ṭahṭāwī: The Egyptian Revivalist (Continued)," 412.

106. "Al-Niẓām al-Iqṭā'ī—Al-Mujtama' al-Iqṭā'ī," *al-Muqtabas*, No. 4 (April 1912): 321–332.

107. Naḥḥās, *Al-Fallāḥ*, 9–10, 12–14, 108–109, and 118.

108. Mai Ziāda, "Al-Musāwā," *al-Muqtaṭaf* LVIX (June–December 1921): 453.

109. "Fī al-Rīf al-Miṣrī 9: Warā' al-Sitār," *al-Ahrām* (August 22, 1935).

110. For a critical assessment of Poliak's use of the term "serfdom," see Heyworth-Dunne, Review of *Feudalism in Egypt, Syria, Palestine and the Lebanon, 1250–1900.*

111. Poliak, *Feudalism in Egypt, Syria, Palestine, and the Lebanon*, 78.

112. Al-Barrāwī, *Ḥālit Miṣr al-Iqtiṣādiyya fī 'Aṣr al-Fāṭimiyyīn*, 55–56.

113. Al-Barrāwī and 'Ulaysh, *Al-Taṭawwur al-Iqtiṣādī fī Miṣr fī al-'Aṣr al-Ḥadīth*, 10.

114. Ibid., 13.

115. Ibid., 48 and 53–59.

116. Meijer, *The Quest of Modernity*, 78.

117. Injilz, *Al-Tafsīr al-Ishtirākī li-l-Tarīkh*, 1.

118. Ibid.

119. Al-Barrāwī, *Mashrū'āt al-Sanawāt al-Khams*, 18–20.

120. Ibid., 446; Richards, *Egypt's Agricultural Development*, 65–66.

121. Botman, *The Rise of Egyptian Communism*, 33–113; Ismael and El-Said, *The Communist Movement in Egypt*, 32–67.

122. Abbās, *Awrāq Hinrī Kūryal wa-l- Ḥaraka al-Shīyū'iyya al-Miṣriyya*, 47, 62, and 177; Abdel-Malek, *Egypt: Military Society*, 85.

123. Salih, *Krōmar fi Miṣr*, 103.

124. Ibid.

125. Mursī, *Taṭawwur al-Ra'smāliyya wa-Kifāḥ al-Tabaqāt fī Miṣr.*

126. Sa'd, "Taṭawwur Miṣr al-Ra'smālī," 180.

127. Sa'd, *Mushkilat al-Fallāḥ*, 47–48.

128. Ibid., 51.

129. Ibid., 48. The concept of "semi-feudalism" was debated by Chinese communists in the 1930s and gained traction after the 1949 revolution. See Karl, *The Magic of Concepts*, 31; Cole, "To Save the Village: Confronting Chinese Rural Crisis in the Global 1930s," 14–19; Brass, *Labour Regime Change in the Twenty-First Century*, 75–103.

130. Sa'd, *Mushkilat al-Fallāḥ*, 55–56.

131. Ministry of Social Affairs, *Note on Questions Relating to Agriculture*, 4.

132. Dunn, *Cotton in Egypt*, 36.

133. Ghālī, *Al-Iṣlāḥ al-Zirā'ī*, 74–75. For a similar observation, see Sa'd, *Mushkilat al-Fallāḥ*, 55–56.

134. DWQ, WA 0069-009877: Petition from Mīt Ghamr, Daqahliyya (April 25, 1942).

135. DWQ, WA 0069-009921: Petition from al-'Uqṣur (June 18, 1947).

136. Karl, *The Magic of Concepts*, 46.

137. Ṣādiq Sa'd would adopt the concept of Asiatic mode of production in the 1970s. See Sa'd, *Tarīkh Miṣr al-Ijtimā'ī—al-Iqtṣādī*.

138. Muḥī al-Dīn, *Wa-l-'Ān Atakallam*, 91.

139. Gordon, *Nasser's Blessed Movement*, 54–55; Muḥī al-Dīn, *Wa-l-'Ān Atakallam*, 93. See also Ginat and Alon, "En Route to Revolution."

140. Muḥī al-Dīn, *Wa-l-'Ān Atakallam*, 94.

141. Beinin, *Was There a Red Flag Flying There?*, 107 and 111. Every other Egyptian communist group denounced the officers' seizure of power. The most vociferously opposed was al-Raya, one of the smaller communist groups in the country. Following the line of the rigidly orthodox Communist Party of France, their members called the Free Officers' Revolt a "fascist coup"—a position that derived from Mursi's thesis that conditions in Egypt were already ripe for a socialist revolution.

142. Hamrūsh, *Thawrat 23 Yūlyū*, vol. 1, 238–239 and 259.

Chapter 6

1. Sidky, *The Agricultural Policy in the New Era*, 6.

2. Ibid., 3.

3. O'Brien, "The Long-Term Growth of Agricultural Production in Egypt," 190–193.

4. Sidky, *The Agricultural Policy in the New Era*, 7.

5. Ibid., 26.

6. Kardouche, *The U.A.R in Development*, 9.

7. Waterbury, *The Egypt of Nasser and Sadat*, 5.

8. Truman, "Inaugural Address."

9. Al-Barrāwī, Al-*Nuqṭa al-Rābi'a fī al-Mīzān*, 12–23.

10. Issawi, *Egypt at Mid-Century*, 227–229; Mitchell, *Rule of Experts*, 80–119.

11. Keyder, *State and Class in Turkey*, 165–167; Richards and Waterbury, *A Political Economy of the Middle East*, 196.

12. Zaki Hashem, "An Inquiry into the Problem of Economic Underdevelopment," *L'Égypte Contemporaine* LXII, no. 226 (October 1951): 87. Hāshim was the first Egyptian to produce a full-length study of the United Nations after it was created. See Hāshim, *Al-'Umam al-Mutaḥida*.

13. Hashem, 88.

14. Prebisch, *The Economic Development of Latin America and Its Principal Problems*, 1. This manifesto was originally published in Spanish in 1949. See Love, "Raúl Prebisch and the Origins of the Doctrine of Unequal Exchange."

15. Fajardo, *The World That Latin America Created*, 43.

16. Fajardo, 42–43; Fishlow, "Comment." In the 1970s, Greek-French Marxian economist Arghiri Emmanuel critiqued the Prebisch-Singer thesis that market demand for raw materials, especially from the Global South, drove their long-term price decline relative to industrial exports from the Global North. What explained unequal exchange on a world scale, Emmanuel countered, was "that prices are determined by wages." See Emmanuel, *Unequal Exchange*, 87; Amin, *Accumulation on a World Scale*, 81–85.

17. Walter Lippman, "The Richer and the Poorer Nations," *New York Herald Tribune* (October 5, 1965).

18. In Latin America, radical critics of the *cepalinos* in the 1960s challenged the premise that cooperation between center and periphery, along with the empowerment of national bourgeoisies, could lead to development. See Cardoso, "The Entrepreneurial Elites in Latin America"; Frank, *Capitalism and Underdevelopment in Latin America*; Love, "The Origins of Dependency Analysis," 143–168; Fajardo, *The World That Latin America Created*, 140–165.

19. Fajardo, *The World That Latin America Created*, 178–182; Dosman, *The Life and Times of Raúl Prebisch*, 381–382; United Nations Conference on Trade and Development, *The History of UNCTAD*, 10 and 182–183.

20. Economic Commission for Africa, United Nations Economic and Social Council, "Cairo Declaration of Developing Countries."

21. Efforts by Third-World states to collectively push for a reorganization of the international trade, monetary, and financial system continued to happen in the late 1960s and 1970s—for example, the G77 and the New International Economic Order (NIEO). Before then, UNCTAD and the Non-Aligned Movement both played a key role in generating alternative and more equitable ideas about development and global trade.

22. Kardouche, *The U.A.R in Development*, 13–15. That the officers seized power when cotton prices were inflated because of the Korean War might partly explain their subsequent decline.

23. Ibid., 11.

24. Warriner, *Land Reform and Development in the Middle East: A Study of Egypt, Syria, and Iraq*, 31–41.

25. ʿAbd al-Nāṣir, *Falsafat al-Thawra*, 28.

26. Abdel-Malek, *Egypt, Military Society*, 67–68; United States, *Land Reform, A World Challenge*.

27. El Shakry, *The Great Social Laboratory*, 208–212; Hasanayn, *Al-Ṣaḥrā'—Al-Thawra wa-l-Tharwa*.

28. Springborg, *Family, Power, and Politics in Egypt*, 147–154.

29. Ibid., 154.

30. Muḥī al-Dīn, *Wa-l-'Ān Atakallam*, 328.

31. ʿAbd al-Fattāḥ, *Al-Nāṣiriyya wa-Tajribat al-Thawra min Aʿlā*, 11.

32. Marei, *Agrarian Reform in Egypt*, 108.

33. Ibid., 105–106.

34. Ibid., 115.

35. Ibid., 105.

36. Ibid., 109.

37. Ladejinsky, *Agrarian Reform as Unfinished Business*, 364.

38. Rashād, "Mudhakkira 'an Bank al-Taslīf al-Zirā'ī wa-l-Ta'āwunī wa-Iqrāḍ Kibār al-Muzāri'īn."

39. See Ibrāhīm Rashād's short articles in *al-Risāla al-Ta'āwuniyya* in November 1953 and October 1955.

40. O'Brien, *The Revolution in Egypt's Economic System*, 165.

41. Adams, *Development and Social Change in Rural Egypt*, 23–27; O'Brien, "The Long-Term Growth of Agricultural Production in Egypt," 189.

42. Saad, *Social History of an Agrarian Reform Community in Egypt*, 75.

43. Adams, *Development and Social Change in Rural Egypt*, 50–77.

44. Abdel-Fadil, *Development, Income Distribution and Social Change in Rural Egypt*, 7–10 and 83–89.

45. Richards, "Egypt's Agriculture in Trouble"; Richards, *Egypt's Agricultural Development*, 179.

46. Batatu, *The Egyptian, Syrian, and Iraqi Revolutions*, 18–20.

47. Radwan, *Agrarian Reform and Rural Poverty*, 28–31; Mīshīl Kāmil, "Ṭaqrīr Siyāsī: Ḥawl Ḥarakat wa-Ittijāhāt al-Ṣirā' al-Ṭabaqī fī al-Rīf al-Miṣrī," *al-Ṭalī'a*, vol. 9 (September, 1966): 54–65.

48. Abdel-Fadil, *Development, Income Distribution and Social Change in Rural Egypt*, 44.

49. Toth, *Rural Labor Movements in Egypt and Their Impact on the State.*

50. 'Abd al-Fattāḥ, *Al-Nāṣiriyya wa-Tajribat al-Thawra Min A'lā*, 66; Kardouche, *The U.A.R in Development*, 22–25.

51. Abdel-Fadil, *Development, Income Distribution and Social Change in Rural Egypt*, 44 and 84–85. Samir Radwan adds that the objective of these policies was "to squeeze as much of the agricultural surplus as possible in order to finance the process of accumulation in other sectors of the economy and redress the deficit in the balance of payments." See Radwan, *Agrarian Reform and Rural Poverty*, 70.

52. Jumhūriyyat Miṣr, *Al-Majlis al-Dā'im li-Tanmiyyat al-Intāj al-Qawmī*, 343.

53. DWQ, WA 0069-005355: Awrāq Khāṣa bi Inshā' Tarīq Malāḥi Nahari Yarbuṭu Madinat Ṭanṭa bil Qāhira wa-l-Iskandariyya Sanat 1937 (1936); Schewe, "State of Siege: The Development of the Security State in Egypt During the Second World War," 130–132.

54. Arthur D. Little, Inc., *Economic Study of Inland Transportation in Egypt*, 4 and 16.

55. On the restriction of commercial automobile transportation in the 1930s, see Selous, *Economic Conditions in Egypt*, 42.

56. Egyptian State Railways, Telegraphs, and Telephones, *Annual Report on the Working of the Egyptian State Railways, Telegraphs, and Telephones, Financial Year 1943–44*, 4–5; TNA, FO 371/27486: Note by the Ministry of Shipping: Partial Conversion of the Egyptian State Railways to Oil (April 10, 1941).

57. ʿUthmān, *Al-Bitrūl wa-Iqtiṣādunā al-Qawmī*, 4.

58. NARA, Record Group 59, Department of State, Box 6089, 974.512/9-252.

59. NARA, Record Group 59, Department of State, Box 6089, 974.512/6-553.

60. Ibid.

61. Goldfinch, *Steel in the Sand*, 46.

62. "Les Voies Fluviales en Egypte," *L'Egypte Industrielle* 33, no. 7 (July 1957), 8.

63. DWQ, WA 0069-006221: Memorandum to the Administration of the State Railways, Telegraphs, and Telephones (August 23, 1952).

64. Claussen, Lee, and Raether, eds., *Foreign Relations of the United States*, vol. IV.

65. Al-Barrāwī, *Al-Nuqṭa al-Rābiʿa fī al-Mīzān*, 109–113.

66. Arthur D. Little, Inc., *Economic Study of Inland Transportation in Egypt*. The FAO was created in 1953 to promote the "cooperative development of economic and military strength among the nations of the free world." Two years later, it would be abolished and its operations transferred to the U.S. State Department, with the exception of certain military functions that were transferred to the U.S. Department of Defense. See Eisenhower, "Letter to Secretary Dulles Regarding Transfer of the Affairs of the Foreign Operations Administration to the Department of State, April 17, 1955," 400.

67. Arthur D. Little, Inc., *Economic Study of Inland Transportation in Egypt*, 34.

68. Ibid., 16.

69. Ibid., 1.

70. Tanksy, *U.S. and U.S.S.R Aid to Developing Countries*, 183.

71. Goldfinch, *Steel in the Sand*, 48.

72. NARA, Record Group 59, Department of State, Box 5337, 986B.712/I-959.

73. Ikeda, "Sociopolitical Debates in Late Parliamentary Egypt," 315–322.

74. "Ta'mīm al-Quṭn bi-Miṣr," *al-Ahrām* (February 21, 1951).

75. "Ta'mīm Quṭn Miṣr," *al-Ahrām* (March 16, 1951).

76. "Ishāʿat Ta'mīm al-Quṭn Tahbiṭu bi-Asʿārihi Hubūṭan Kabīran," *al-Miṣrī* (March 17, 1951).

77. M. M. Hamadi, "Nationalization of Cotton," *L'Egypte Contemporaine* LXII, no. 265 (July 1951): 57–71.

78. Ibid., 65. For an account of inflation in Egypt during World War II, see DWQ, RMW 0081-054511: "Mudhakkira Marfūʿa ilā Majlis al-Wuzarā' bi-Sha'n Mukāfaḥat al-Ghalā' wa-Khafḍ Takālīf al-Maʿīsha," (October, 21, 1949).

79. Hamadi, "Nationalization of Cotton," 68.

80. Ibid., 68–69.

81. Ibid., 62.

82. Abdel-Fadil, *Development, Income Distribution and Social Change in Rural Egypt*, 90.

83. SM/54/110, 1954 Consultations – Egypt, Part I, 10/25/1954, IMF Archives, 3–4.

84. SM/63/51, United Arab Republic, 1962 Article XIV Consultations, Part I, 5/23/1963, IMF Archives, 15.

85. SM/64/34, United Arab Republic, 1963 Article XIV Consultations, Part II, 4/9/1964, IMF Archives, 15.

86. "The Reorganization of the Cotton Sector," *Egyptian Cotton Gazette*, 48 (June 1965): 64–67.

87. National Bank of Egypt, "Agricultural Cooperation in the U.A.R.," *Economic Bulletin* XIX, no. 4 (1966): 361.

88. Aḥmad, *Al-Taswīq al-Taʿāwunī li-l-Quṭn*, 6 and 11.

89. Mallakh, "Economic Integration in the United Arab Republic," 255.

90. Mabro, *The Egyptian Economy*, 180; Mabro and Radwan, *The Industrialization of Egypt*, 218; Waterbury, *The Egypt of Nasser and Sadat*, 30.

91. Kardouche, *United Arab Republic*.

92. Drummond, *The Floating Pound and the Sterling Area*, 3–14.

93. Mikesell, "Sterling Area Currencies of the Middle East," 164–165.

94. Avaro, "Zombie International Currency."

95. Ibid., 20–22.

96. Issawi, *Egypt at Mid-Century*, 212; Tignor, *State, Private Enterprise, and Economic Change in Egypt*, 197; Frederick Leith-Ross, "Financial and Economic Developments in Egypt," *International Affairs* 28, no. 1 (January 1952): 29–37.

97. Mabro, "Egypt's Economics Relations with the Socialist Countries," 55; EBS/57/8, Egypt – Recent Economic Developments and Changes in the Restrictive System, 1/30/1957, IMF Archives, 8.

98. Escobar, *Encountering Development*, 21–54; Lorenzini, *Global Development*, 22–32; Maier, *In Search of Stability*, 121–152; Westad, *The Global Cold War*, 25–27 and 32–38.

99. Alterman, "American Aid to Egypt in the 1950s."

100. El-Biali, "U.S.A and U.S.S.R. Styles in Economic Aid," 42.

101. Burns, *Economic Aid and American Policy Toward Egypt*, 25–26; Sadat, *In Search of Identity*, 135.

102. Abou-El-Fadl, *Foreign Policy as Nation Making*, 204–233; Dawisha, *Egypt in the Arab World*, 12–13; Ismāʿīl, *Amn Miṣr al-Qawmī fī ʿAṣr al-Taḥadiyyāt*, 44–48; Sanchez-Sibony, *Red Globalization*, 219–22; Yaqub, *Containing Arab Nationalism*, 39–40.

103. Muḥammad ʿAlī Rifʿat, "Al-Junayh al-Miṣrī fī ʿAhdahu al-Jadīd," *Al-Thaqāfa* 450 (August 12, 1947): 828–830.

104. Abdalla, "The Role of Foreign Capital in Egypt's Economic Development," 89; Iyer, *Agrarian Superpower*, chapter 7.

105. Friedmann, "The Political Economy of Food"; Iyer, *Agrarian Superpower*, chapters 5 and 6.

106. McMichael, *Development and Social Change*, 60.

107. Friedmann, "The Political Economy of Food," S271; McMichael, *Development and Social Change*, 63–64.

108. Batatu, *The Egyptian, Syrian, and Iraqi Revolutions*, 14–16; Waterbury, *The Egypt of Nasser and Sadat*, 42.

109. Abdalla, "The Role of Foreign Capital in Egypt's Economic Development," 89; Dethier and Funk, "The Language of Food: PL 480 in Egypt," 23.

110. Mabro, *The Egyptian Economy*, 144–146; Waterbury, *The Egypt of Nasser and Sadat*, 104.

111. United Nations, *The Development of Manufacturing Industry in Egypt, Israel and Turkey*, 62.

112. Mabro and Radwan, *The Industrialization of Egypt*, 103.

113. Mabro, *The Egyptian Economy*, 150.

114. SM/66/29, United Arab Republic, 1965 Article XIV Consultations, Part II, Appendix II, 2/25/1966, IMF Archives, 57; United States International Trade Commission, *The History and Current Status of the Multifiber Arrangement*, 44–45.

115. Dethier and Funk, "The Language of Food: PL 480 in Egypt," 23–24.

116. Hahn, *The United States, Great Britain, and Egypt*, 56–58.

117. Yaqub, *Containing Arab Nationalism*, 43.

118. Burns, *Economic Aid and American Policy Toward Egypt*, 36–75.

119. Hahn, *The United States, Great Britain, and Egypt*, 203.

120. Toth, *Rural Labor Movements in Egypt and Their Impact on the State*, 109–112.

121. Kanet, "Soviet Attitudes Toward Developing Nations Since Stalin," 28.

122. Gruliow, ed., *Current Soviet Policies—II: The Documentary Record of the 20th Communist Party Congress and Its Aftermath*, 33.

123. TNA, FO 141/619/4: Letter from Kalnine in Moscow—the Director of Textile Import—to Léon Meltz—Agent, Textile Import in Alexandria (November 29, 1930); "Mandūb Rūsi li-Shirā' al-Quṭn," *al-Ahrām* (July 12, 1931); Sanchez-Sibony, *Red Globalization*, 76.

124. Kanet, "The Soviet Union and the Developing Countries," 338.

125. Mabro, "Egypt's Economics Relations with the Socialist Countries," 72–73; Waterbury, *The Egypt of Nasser and Sadat*, 395–399.

126. Laqueur, *The Struggle for the Middle East*, 139.

127. Hansen and Nashashibi, *Foreign Trade Regimes and Economic Development*, 22. See also Owen, "The Economic Consequences of the Suez Crisis for Egypt."

128. Ismā'īl, *Amn Miṣr al-Qawmī fī 'Aṣr al-Taḥadiyyāt*, 49.

129. Ferris, "Guns for Cotton?" 14.

130. Abdalla, "The Role of Foreign Capital in Egypt's Economic Development," 89; Allen, *Middle Eastern Economic Relations with the Soviet Union, Eastern Europe, and Mainland China*, 86–93.

131. El-Biali, "U.S.A and U.S.S.R. Styles in Economic Aid," 49; Ferris, "Guns for Cotton?" 13; Laqueur, *The Struggle for the Middle East*, 139–140; Mabro, "Egypt's Economics Relations with the Socialist Countries," 71; Waterbury, *The Egypt of Nasser and Sadat*, 397; Mallakh, "Economic Integration in the United Arab Republic," 262.

132. Ro'i and Ronel, "The Soviet Economic Presence in Egypt and Its Political Implications," 15.

133. Allen, *Middle Eastern Economic Relations with the Soviet Union, Eastern Europe, and Mainland China*, 20–23.

134. United States, *The Sino-Soviet Economic Offensive in the Less Developed Countries*, 48.

135. Hoskins, *Soviet Economic Penetration in the Middle East*, 6.

136. Mabro, "Egypt's Economics Relations with the Socialist Countries," 72.

137. Ibid., 68.

138. Allen, *Middle Eastern Economic Relations with the Soviet Union, Eastern Europe, and Mainland China*, 53; El-Biali, "U.S.A and U.S.S.R. Styles in Economic Aid," 65.

139. Sanchez-Sibony, *Red Globalization*, 126.

140. Ro'i and Ronel, "The Soviet Economic Presence in Egypt and its Political Implications," 16.

141. Mabro, "Egypt's Economics Relations with the Socialist Countries," 58

142. Abdalla, "The Role of Foreign Capital in Egypt's Economic Development," 93–94.

143. Hansen and Nashashibi, *Foreign Trade Regimes and Economic Development*, 73; United States, *Special Report*, 3.

144. Hansen and Nashashibi, *Foreign Trade Regimes and Economic Development*, 50 and 89.

145. Goldberg and Beinin, "Egypt's Transition Under Nasser," 25–26.

146. SM/66/29, United Arab Republic, 1965 Article XIV Consultations, Part I, 2/25/1966, IMF Archives, 23.

147. Abdalla, "The Role of Foreign Capital in Egypt's Economic Development," 87–88.

148. Cooper, *The Transformation of Egypt*, 44-63; Ferris, "Guns for Cotton?" 15–16; Kanovsky, *The Economic Impact of the Six Day War*, 254; Laqueur, *The Struggle for the Middle East*, 139–140; Ro'i and Ronel, "The Soviet Economic Presence in Egypt and Its Political Implications," 11.

149. "Ḥadīth Khaṭīr li-Zakariyya Muḥī al-Dīn," *al-Ahrām* (October 18, 1965).

150. "Imnaʿū istīrād hādhihi al-silaʿ," *Rūz al-Yūsuf*, Issue 1993 (August 22, 1966): 8–9.

151. Jakes and Shokr, "Capitalism in Egypt, not Egyptian Capitalism," 134–138; Kanovsky, *The Economic Impact of the Six Day War*, 279–325.

152. Abdalla, "The Role of Foreign Capital in Egypt's Economic Development," 94.

153. Ibid., 90 and 95; Bush, *Economic Crisis and the Politics of Reform in Egypt*, 15.

154. Abdalla, "The Role of Foreign Capital in Egypt's Economic Development," 95.

155. Di-Capua, *Gatekeepers of the Arab Past*, 248.

156. Al-Barrāwī, *Ḥaqīqat al-Inqilāb al-Akhīr fī Miṣr*, 28 and 68; Meijer, *The Quest for Modernity*, 85–88.

157. ʿAbd al-Nāṣir, "Kalimat al-Raʾīs Jamāl ʿAbd al-Nāṣir bi-Baldat Ma ʿmal al-Qazzāz fī Ḥafl Tawzīʿ al-Arāḍī."

158. Di-Capua, *Gatekeepers of the Arab Past*, 251–253; Mayer, *The Changing Past*, 32. See also al-Rāfʿī, *Miṣr al-Mujāhida fī al-ʿAṣr al-Hadīth.*

159. Ḥassūna, *Kifāḥ al-Shaʿb min ʿUmar Makram ilā Jamāl ʿAbd al-Nāṣir*; Ḥassūna, *Jumhūriyyat Miṣr fī ʿĀmaha al-Awwal*; Ḥassūna, *Jumhūriyyat Miṣr fī ʿĀmaha al-Thānī.*

160. Al-Sharqāwī, *Al-Arḍ*; Selim, *The Novel and the Rural Imaginary in Egypt*, 159–184.

161. Egypt, *Silent Struggle Between the Egyptian Fellah and Mohamed Aly Dynasty.*

162. Ibid., 10. The claim that the Free Officers dislodged a reactionary alliance of imperialism and local feudalists was originally made by al-Barrāwī. See al-Barrāwī, *Ḥaqīqat al-Inqilāb al-Akhīr fī Miṣr*, 70–71.

163. Botman, *The Rise of Egyptian Communism*, 115–147; Beinin, "The Communist Movement and Nationalist Political Discourse in Nasirist Egypt"; Beinin, *Was There a Red Flag Flying There?*, 177–190 and 205–212; Ismael and El-Said, *The Communist Movement in Egypt*, 106–126; Al-Mulla, *Al-Yasār al-Miṣrī Bayn ʿAbd al-Nāṣir wa-l-Sādāt*; Labīb, *Al-Shīyūʿiyyūn wa-ʿAbd al-Nāṣir.*

164. In 1958, the party briefly adopted the perspective that Nasserism represented a form

of "state monopoly capitalism"—a system in which a ruling class used the instruments of the state to protect monopolistic forms of capital accumulation—but the leadership soon reverted back to the party's original position. See Beinin, "The Communist Movement and Nationalist Political Discourse in Nasirist Egypt," 583; Botman, *The Rise of Egyptian Communism*, 144.

165. Di-Capua, *Gatekeepers of the Arab Past*, 272–278. See 'Āmir, *Al-Arḍ wa-l-Fallāḥ*; Al-Shāfi'ī, *Taṭawwur al-Ḥaraka al-Waṭaniyya al-Miṣriyya*; Jirjis, *Dirāsāt fī Tārīkh Miṣr al-Siyāsī Mundhu al-'Aṣr al-Mamlūkī*.

166. Abdel-Malek, *Egypt: Military Society*, 85–86; 'Āmir, *Al-Arḍ wa-l-Fallāḥ*, 13–16 and 70–92.

167. 'Abd al-Fattāḥ, *Shīyū'iyyūn wa-Nāṣiriyyūn*, 162–163. 'Abd al-Fattāḥ writes that imprisoned communists were divided over Nasser's socialist laws. The first (and smallest) tendency believed that the Nasserist regime represented a form of state capitalism; they would go on to form a group, known as Wiḥdat al-Shīyū'iyyīn, that rejected the dissolution of the two communist parties in 1964. A second tendency believed that the regime had indeed become socialist. A third tendency continued to believe that the regime represented a non-capitalist path of development.

168. Ginat, *Egypt's Incomplete Revolution*, 19–23 and 134–142.

169. Rejwan, *Nasserist Ideology*, 11–28; Di-Capua, *Gatekeepers of the Arab Past*, 282–310.

170. "Al-Naẓra al-Ishtirākiyya li-Tārīkh Mujtama'nā," *al-Ahrām* (July 10, 1963).

171. Ansari, *Egypt: The Stalled Society*; Ṣaqr, *Al-Fallāḥūn wa-l-Iqṭā'*.

172. Rashād, *Sirrī Jiddan*.

173. Mitchell, *Rule of Experts*, 169–170.

174. *Al-Ṭalī'a*, vol. 9 (September, 1966).

175. Mūsā, *Awwal Thawra 'Alā al-Iqṭā'*.

176. Saad, "The Two Pasts of Nasser's Peasants: Political Memories and Everyday Life in an Egyptian Village," 127–148.

177. Maklad, Ahmed, and Saad, "Interview with Shahenda Maklad."

Epilogue

1. 'Abdullāh al-Sinnāwī, "Limādhā 'Āsh Jamāl 'Abd al-Nāṣir?" *al-Shurūq* (January 14, 2013).

2. Magdy, "The People Want—But Do They Have a Chance?"

3. Kupferschmidt, "Who Needed Department Stores in Egypt? From Orosdi-Back to Omar Effendi"; Steve Negus, "Omar Effendi: A Flashpoint in the Privatisation Debate" *Financial Times* (December 11, 2006); Shenker, *The Egyptians*, 290 and 294.

4. Amr Adly, "The Problematic Continuity of Nasserism," *Jadaliyya* (March 18, 2014), accessed May 9, 2023, https://www.jadaliyya.com/Details/30469.

5. Krugman, *The Conscience of a Liberal*, 3.

6. Al-Najjār, "Al-Thawra wa-Muwājahat Mu'ḍilāt al-Iqtiṣād al-Miṣrī," 6.

7. Piketty, *Capital in the Twenty-First Century*, 96–97.

8. Harvey, *Spaces of Capital*, 310. See also Stiglitz, "The Myth of America's Golden Age."

9. Sa'd, "Ḥawl al-'Alāqa Bayn Namaṭay al-Intāj: Al-Kūlūnyālī wa-l-Asyāwī," 139.

10. Sa'd, *Tārīkh Miṣr al-Ijtimā'ī—al-Iqtiṣādī*, 10–11.

11. Ibid., 19–22 and 29. For other Egyptian Marxist and left-nationalist scholars who have similarly questioned or abandoned the concept, see 'Abd al-Fattāḥ, *Al-Qarya al-Miṣriyya*; Al-Disūqī, *Naḥwa Fihm Tārīkh Miṣr al-Iqtiṣādī al—Ijtimā'ī*; Ṣāliḥ, *Al-Iqṭā' wa-l-Ra'smāliyya al-Zirā'iyya fī Miṣr min 'Ahd Muḥammad 'Alī ilā 'Ahd 'Abd al-Nāṣir*. In addition to Marxists, there are also Orientalists and other historians who have questioned or rejected the application of the term "feudalism" and its related concepts to the Middle East, past or present. See Cahen, "L'évolution de l'Iqta' du IXe au XIIIe Siècle"; al-Duri, "The Origins of 'Iqtā' in Islam"; Dupree, "Medieval European Feudalism and the Contemporary Middle East: A Clarification of Terms"; Lambton, "The Evolution of the 'Iqṭā' in Medieval Iran." Similar efforts to abandon feudalism as a category to apprehend the colonial past in South Asia can be found in several contributions to Patnaik, *Agrarian Relations and Accumulation*.

12. Riad, *L'Égypte Nassérienne*, 240.

13. Amin, *A Life Looking Forward*, 97–98.

14. Amin, *Uneven Development*; Dowidar, "The Self-Reliance Strategy of Development and the New International Economic Order"; Mansour, "Third World Revolt and Self-Reliant Auto-Centered Strategy of Development"; Ḥusayn, *Al-Iqtiṣād al-Miṣrī min al-Istiqlāl ilā al-Taba'iyya*. In Latin America, the core-periphery framework that the *cepalinos* had inaugurated in the 1940s and 1950s eventually fused with Marxism in the works of *dependentistas* and world-systems analysis by the late 1960s and 1970s.

15. Liu, "Production, Circulation, and Accumulation."

BIBLIOGRAPHY

Archival Sources

EGYPT

DWQ: *Dār al-Wathā'iq al-Qawmiyya* (Egyptian National Archives), Cairo
- WA (0069) *Wathā'iq 'Ābdīn* (Papers of the 'Ābdīn Palace)
- MNW (0075) *Majlis al-Nuẓẓār wa-l-Wuzarā'* (The Council of Ministers)
- RMW (0081) *Ri'āsat Majlis al-Wuzarā'* (The Presidency of the Council of Ministers)
- MS (3019) *Maṣlaḥat al-Sharikāt* (Companies Department)
- WSI (4029) *Wizārat al-Shu'ūn al-Ijtimā'iyya* (The Ministry of Social Affairs)

ENGLAND

TNA: The National Archives
- FO Foreign Office Papers
- T Treasury

UNITED STATES

NARA: National Archives and Records Administration
- Record Group 59 (General Records of the Department of State)

IMF Archives: International Monetary Fund Archives
- SM Staff Memorandum
- EBS Executive Board Specials

Selected Newspapers and Journals

ARABIC

al-Ahrām
al-Balāgh
al-Fajr al-Jadīd
al-Fallāḥ al-Iqtiṣādī

al-Majalla al-Zirāʿiyya al-Miṣriyya
Majallat al-Shuʾūn al-Ijtimāʿiyya
al-Miṣrī
al-Mujtamaʿ al-Jadīd
al-Muqaṭṭam
al-Muqtabas
al-Muqtaṭaf
al-Risāla al-Taʿāwuniyya
Rūz al-Yūsuf
al-Shurūq
al-Ṭalīʿa
al-Thaqāfa
al-Waqāʾiʿ al-Miṣriyya
al-Yawm
Zamīl al-Fallāḥ

OTHER
Birmingham Post
Bulletin de l'Union des Agriculteurs d'Égypte
Economic Bulletin
The Economist
L'Egypte Contemporaine
Egyptian Gazette
The Egyptian Cotton Gazette
L'Égypte Industrielle
The Financial Times
International Affairs
Monthly Bulletin of the International Railway Congress Association
New York Herald Tribune
La Réforme
Revue Économique Internationale

Other Published Sources Cited

Abaza, Mona. *The Cotton Plantation Remembered: An Egyptian Family Story*. Cairo: American University of Cairo Press, 2013.

Abbās, Raʾūf. *Awrāq Hinrī Kūryal wa-l-Ḥaraka al-Shīyūʿiyya al-Miṣriyya*. Translated by ʿAzza Riyāḍ. Cairo: Sīnāʾ li-l-Nashr, 1988.

Abbas, Raouf, and Assem El-Dessouky. *The Large Landowning Class and the Peasantry in Egypt, 1837–1952*. Translated by Amer Mohsen and Mona Zikri, edited by Peter Gran. Syracuse, NY: Syracuse University Press, 2012.

Abdalla, Nazem. "The Role of Foreign Capital in Egypt's Economic Development: 1960–1972," *International Journal of Middle East Studies* 14, no. 1 (February 1982): 87–97.

Abdel-Fadil, Mahmoud. *Development, Income Distribution and Social Change in Rural*

Egypt, 1952–1970: A Study in the Political Economy of Agrarian Transition. Cambridge: Cambridge University Press, 1975.

ʿAbd al-Fattāḥ, Fatḥī. *Al-Nāṣiriyya wa-Tajribat al-Thawra min Aʿlā: Al-Masʾala al-Zirāʿiyya*. Cairo: Dār al-Fikr li-l-Dirāsāt wa-l-Nashr wa-l-Tawzīʿ, 1987.

ʿAbd al-Fattāḥ, Fatḥī. *Al-Qarya al-Miṣriyya: Dirāsa fī al-Milkiyya wa-ʿAlāqāt al-Intāj*. Cairo: Dār al-Thaqāfa al-Jadīda, 1973.

ʿAbd al-Fattāḥ, Fatḥī. *Shīyūʿiyyūn wa-Nāṣiriyyūn*. Cairo: Rūz al-Yūsuf, 1975.

Abdel-Malek, Anouar. *Egypt: Military Society: The Army Regime, the Left, and Social Change Under Nasser*. Translated by Charles Lam Markman. New York: Random House, 1968.

Abdel-Malek, Anouar. "La Question Agraire en Égypte et la Réforme de 1952." *Tiers-Monde*, Tome 3, no. 9/10 (1962): 181–216.

ʿAbd al-Nāṣir, Jamāl. *Falsafat al-Thawra*. Cairo: Dār al-Maʿārif, 1954.

ʿAbd al-Nāṣir, Jamāl. "Kalimat al-Raʾīs Jamāl ʿAbd al-Nāṣir bi-Baldat Ma ʿmal al-Qazzāz fī Ḥafl Tawzīʿ al-Arāḍī." Speech. Maʿmal al-Qazzāz, Kafr al-Dawār, Buḥayra Governorate, April 19, 1954. Accessed April 20, 2023. http://nasser.bibalex.org/Data/GR09_1/Speeches/1954/540419_2.htm.

Abdel Wahab, Ahmad. *Memorandum on the Bases of a Stable Cotton Policy; Submitted to H. E. the Minister of Finance*. Cairo: Government Press, 1930.

Abdel Wahab, Ahmad. *The Railway Crisis and the Conflict Between the Rail and the Road*. Cairo: Government Press, 1933.

Abou-El-Fadl, Reem. *Foreign Policy as Nation Making: Turkey and Egypt in the Cold War*. Cambridge: Cambridge University Press, 2019.

Abū al-ʿAzm, Munā ʿAlī. *Awḍāʿ Miṣr al-Ṣināʿiyya min 1945 ilā 1961*. Cairo: Al-Hayʾa al-Miṣriyya al-ʿĀma li-l-Kitāb, 2021.

Abu Lughod, Janet. *Cairo: 1001 Years of the City Victorious*. Princeton, NJ: Princeton University Press, 1971.

Adams, Richard. *Development and Social Change in Rural Egypt*. Syracuse, NY: Syracuse University Press, 1986.

Al-ʿAdawī, Zuhdī. *Bidāyat al-Maʿraka*. Cairo: Dār al-Fann al-Ḥadīth, 1952.

Administration des Chemins de Fer de l'État, de Télégraphes et du Port d'Alexandrie. *Rapport du Conseil d'Administration sur L'Exercice 1897*. Le Caire: Imprimérie de l'Administration, 1898.

Adorno, Theodor, and Max Horkheimer. *Dialectic of Enlightenment*. Translated by John Cumming. New York: Continuum Publishing Company, 2002. Reprint of 1944 edition.

Adly, Amr. "The Problematic Continuity of Nasserism." *Jadaliyya*, March 18, 2014. Accessed May 9, 2023. https://www.jadaliyya.com/Details/30469.

ʿAfīfī, Ḥāfiẓ. *ʿAlā Hāmish al-Siyāsa*. Cairo: Maṭbaʿat Dār al-Kutub al-Miṣriyya, 1938.

Aḥmad, Ḥasan Zaki. *Al-Taswīq al-Taʿāwunī li-l-Quṭn*. Cairo: Dār wa-Maṭābiʿ al-Shaʿb, 1968.

Aḥmad, ʿAbd al-ʿAzīz. *Al-Khuṭūṭ al-ʿArīḍa fī Kahrabat Miṣr*. Cairo: Al-Maṭbaʿa al-Amīriyya, 1955.

Ahmed, Amr Khairy. "Egypt Ignited: How Steam Power Arrived on the Nile and Integrated Egypt into Industrial Capitalism, 1820s–1976." PhD diss., Lund University, 2023.

Allen, Robert Loring. *Middle Eastern Economic Relations with the Soviet Union, Eastern Europe, and Mainland China*. Charlottesville: University of Virginia, 1958.

Alterman, Jon B. "American Aid to Egypt in the 1950s: From Hope to Hostility." *Middle East Journal* 52, no. 1 (Winter 1998): 51–69.

Amin, Samir. *A Life Looking Forward: Memoirs of an Independent Marxist*. London: Zed Books, 2006.

Amin, Samir. *Accumulation on a World Scale*. New York: Monthly Review Press, 1974.

Amin, Samir. *La Nation Arabe: Nationalism et Luttes de Classes*. Paris: Les Editions de Minuit, 1976.

Amin, Samir. *Re-reading the Postwar Period: An Intellectual Itinerary*. Translated by Michael Wolfers. New York: Monthly Review Press, 1994.

Amin, Samir. *Uneven Development: An Essay on the Social Formations of Peripheral Capitalism*. Translated by Brian Pearce. Sussex: Harvester Press, 1976.

ʿĀmir, Ibrāhīm. *Al-Arḍ wa-l-Fallāḥ: Al-Masʾala al-Zirāʿiyya fī Miṣr*. Cairo: Matbaʿat al-Dār al-Miṣriyya, 1958.

Ansari, Hamied. *Egypt: The Stalled Society*. Albany: State University of New York Press, 1986.

Anise, Mahmoud. *A Study of the National Income of Egypt*. Monograph, published as *L'Égypte Contemporaine*, nos. 261/262. Cairo: Société Fouad 1er d'Économie Politique, de Statistique et de Législation, 1950.

Arndt, Heinz W. "Economic Development: A Semantic History." *Economic Development and Cultural Change* 29, no. 3 (April 1981): 457–466.

Arndt, Heinz W. *The Rise and Fall of Economic Growth: A Study in Contemporary Thought*. Melbourne: Longman Cheshire, 1978.

Arrighi, Giovanni. *The Geometry of Imperialism: The Limits of Hobson's Paradigm*. London: NLB, 1978.

Arrighi, Giovanni. *The Long Twentieth Century: Money, Power, and the Origins of Our Times*. New York: Verso, 2010.

Arthur D. Little, Inc. *Economic Study of Inland Transportation in Egypt*. Cambridge, MA, 1954.

ʿAshmāwī, Sayyid. *Al-Fallāḥūn wa-l-Sulṭa ʿAla Dawʾ al-Ḥarakāt al-Fallāḥiyya al-Miṣriyya, 1919–1999*. Cairo: Mīrīt li-l-Nashr wa-l-Maʿlūmāt, 2001.

Avaro, Maylis. "Zombie International Currency: The Pound Sterling, 1945–1973." Graduate Institute of International and Development Studies, International Economics Department, Working Paper Series (February 2020). Accessed June 23, 2024. https://repec.graduateinstitute.ch/pdfs/Working_papers/HEIDWP03-2020.pdf.

Ayrout, Habib. *The Egyptian Peasant*. Translated by John Alden Williams. Cairo: American University in Cairo Press, 2005.

Ayrout, Henry Habib. *Moeurs et Coutumes des Fellahs*. Paris: Payot, 1938.

Ayubi, Nazih M. *Bureaucracy and Politics in Contemporary Egypt*. London: Ithaca Press, 1980.

Badrawi, Malak. *Isma'il Sidqi (1875–1950): Pragmatism and Vision in Twentieth Century Egypt*. Richmond, Surrey: Curzon Press, 1996.
Baer, Gabriel. *A History of Landownership in Modern Egypt, 1800–1950*. London: Oxford University Press, 1962.
Baer, Gabriel. *Studies in the Social History of Modern Egypt*. Chicago: University of Chicago Press, 1969.
Balachandran, Gopalan. "Britain, USA, and Indian Gold Standard." *Economic and Political Weekly* 24, no. 35/36 (September 2–9, 1989): 2015–2023.
Balls, William Lawrence. *Egypt of the Egyptians*. New York: Charles Scriber's Sons, 1916.
Balls, William Lawrence. "Researches on Egyptian Cotton." *Nature* (July 22, 1920): 664–665.
Barak, On. *On Time: Technology and Temporality in Modern Egypt*. Berkeley: University of California Press, 2013.
Barendse, R. J. "The Feudal Mutation: Military and Economic Transformations of the Ethnosphere in the Tenth to Thirteenth Centuries." *Journal of World History* 14, no. 4 (December 2003): 503–529.
Al-Barrāwī, Rāshid. *Al-Falsafa al-Iqtiṣādiyya li-l-Thawra: Min al-Nāḥyatayn al-Naẓariyya wa-l-ʿAmaliyya*. Cairo: Maktabat al-Nahḍa, 1955.
Al-Barrāwī, Rāshid. *Ḥālit Miṣr al-Iqtiṣādiyya fī ʿAṣr al-Fāṭimiyyīn*. Cairo: Maktabat al-Nahḍa al-Miṣriyya, 1948.
Al-Barrāwī, Rāshid. *Haqīqat al-Inqilāb al-Akhīr fī Miṣr*. Cairo: Maktabat al-Nahḍa al-Miṣriyya, 1952.
Al-Barrāwī, Rāshid. *Mashrūʿāt al-Sanawāt al-Khams*. Cairo: Maktabat al-Nahḍa al-Miṣriyya, 1948.
Al-Barrāwī, Rāshid, and Dalāwir ʿAlī. *Mushkilatunā al-Ijtimāʿiyya: al-Faqr, al-Fallāh, al-Taʾmīm, al-ʿUmmāl*. Cairo: Maktabat al-Nahḍa al-Miṣriyya, 1948.
Al-Barrāwī, Rāshid. *Al-Nuqṭa al-Rābiʿa fī al-Mīzān*. Cairo: Maktabat al-Nahḍa al-Miṣriyya, 1953.
Al-Barrāwī, Rāshid, and Muḥammad Ḥamza ʿUlaysh. *Al-Taṭawwur al-Iqtiṣādī fī Miṣr fī al-ʿAṣr al-Ḥadīth*, 3rd edition. Cairo: Maktabat al-Nahḍa al-Miṣriyya, 1948.
Batatu, Hanna. *The Egyptian, Syrian, and Iraqi Revolutions: Some Observations on Their Underlying Causes and Social Character*. Washington, DC: Georgetown University, 1984.
Beattie, Kirk J. *Egypt During the Nasser Years: Ideology, Politics, and Civil Society*. Boulder, CO: Westview Press, 1994.
Beckert, Sven. "Emancipation and Empire: Reconstructing the Worldwide Web of Cotton Production in the Age of the American Civil War." *American Historical Review* 109, no. 5 (December 2004): 1405–1438.
Beckert, Sven. *Empire of Cotton: A Global History*. New York: Alfred A. Knopf, 2014.
Beinin, Joel. "Egypt: Society and Economy, 1923–1952." In *The Cambridge History of Egypt*, Vol. 2, *Modern Egypt from 1517 to the End of the Twentieth Century*. Edited by M. W. Daly, 309–333. Cambridge: Cambridge University Press, 1998.
Beinin, Joel. "The Communist Movement and Nationalist Political Discourse in Nasirist Egypt." *Middle East Journal* 41, no. 4 (Autumn 1987): 568–584.

Beinin, Joel. *The Dispersion of Egyptian Jewry: Culture, Politics, and the Formation of a Modern Diaspora*. Berkeley and Los Angeles: University of California Press, 1998.

Beinin, Joel. *Was There a Red Flag Flying There? Marxist Politics and the Arab-Israeli Conflict in Egypt and Israel, 1948–1965*. Berkeley and Los Angeles: University of California Press, 1990.

Beinin, Joel, and Zachary Lockman. *Workers on the Nile: Nationalism, Communism, Islam, and the Egyptian Working Class, 1882–1954*. Princeton, NJ: Princeton University Press, 1987.

Berque, Jacques. *Egypt: Imperialism and Revolution*. London: Faber and Faber Ltd., 1972.

Bianchi, Robert. *Unruly Corporatism: Associational Life in Twentieth-Century Egypt*. New York: Oxford University Press,1989.

Bier, Laura. *Revolutionary Womanhood: Feminisms, Modernity, and the State in Nasser's Egypt*. Stanford, CA: Stanford University Press, 2011.

Al-Bishrī, Ṭāriq. *Al-Dīmūqrāṭiyya wa-Niẓām 23 Yūlyū, 1952–1970*. Cairo: Dār al-Shurūq, 2013.

Al-Bishrī, Ṭāriq. *Al-Ḥaraka al-Siyāsiyya fī Miṣr, 1945–1953*, second edition. Cairo: Dār al-Shurūq, 2002.

Bondioli, Lorenzo. "Peasants, Merchants, and Caliphs: Capital and Empire in Fatimid Egypt." PhD diss., Princeton University, 2020.

Botman, Selma. "The Rise and Experience of Egyptian Communism: 1919–1952." *Studies in Comparative Communism* 18, no. 1 (Spring 1985): 49–66.

Botman, Selma. *The Rise of Egyptian Communism, 1939–1970*. Syracuse, NY: Syracuse University Press, 1988.

Brass, Tom. *Labour Regime Change in the Twenty-First Century*. Leiden: Brill, 2011.

Bresciani-Turroni, Constantino. "Egypt's Balance of Trade." *Journal of Political Economy* 42, no. 3 (June 1934): 371–384.

Bresciani-Turroni, Constantino. *The Economics of Inflation*. London: Allen and Unwin, 1937.

Brown, Nathan. "Brigands and State Building: The Invention of Banditry in Modern Egypt." *Comparative Studies in Society and History* 32, no. 2 (April 1990): 258–281.

Brown, Elizabeth A. R. "The Tyranny of a Construct: Feudalism and Historians of Medieval Europe." *American Historical Review* 79, no. 4 (October 1974): 1063–1088.

Burns, William J. *Economic Aid and American Policy Toward Egypt, 1955–1981*. Albany: State University of New York Press, 1985.

Bush, Ray. *Economic Crisis and the Politics of Reform in Egypt*. Boulder, CO: Westview, 1999.

Cain, P. J., and A. G Hopkins. *British Imperialism, 1688–2015*, 3rd ed. London: Routledge, 2016.

Cannon, B. "Mortgage Banking Strategies in Egypt, 1800–1914: Crédit Foncier Egyptien Investment and Local Borrowing." *Business History* 43, no. 4 (2001): 29–47.

Cahen, Claude. "L'évolution de l'Iqta' du IXe au XIIIe Siècle: Contribution à une Histoire Comparée des Sociétés Médiévales." *Annales*, 8e Année, no. 1 (January–March 1953): 25–52.

Cardoso, Fernando Henrique. "The Entrepreneurial Elites in Latin America." *Studies in Comparative International Development* 2, no. 10 (1966): 147–159.

Carr-Saunders, A. M. *World Population, Past Growth and Present Trends*. Oxford: Clarendon Press, 1936.

Cartwright, W. "Notes on Rent, Labour, and Joint Ownership in Egyptian Agriculture." *Cairo Scientific Journal* 4, no. 41 (February 1910): 29–38.

Chalcraft, John. "Engaging the State: Peasants and Petitions in Egypt on the Eve of Colonial Rule." *International Journal of Middle East Studies* 37, no. 3 (August 2005): 303–325.

Chatterjee, Partha. *Nationalist Thought and the Colonial World: A Derivative Discourse*. London: Zed Books, 1986.

Chayanov, Alexander V. *The Theory of Peasant Economy*. Edited by Daniel Thorner, Basile Kerblay, and R.E.F. Smith. Homewood, IL: Richard D. Irwin, 1966.

Chiang, Yung-chen. *Social Engineering and the Social Sciences in China, 1919–1949*. New York: Cambridge University Press, 2001.

Claussen, Paul, Joan M. Lee, and Carl N. Raether, eds. *Foreign Relations of the United States, 1952–1954*, Vol. IV, *The Near and Middle East*, Parts 1 and 2. Washington DC: U.S. Government Printing Office, 1986.

Cleland, Wendel. *The Population Problem in Egypt: A Study of Population Trends and Conditions in Modern Egypt*. Lancaster, PA: Science Press Printing Company, 1936.

Coggan, Phillip. *Paper Promises: Debt, Money, and the New World Order*. New York: PublicAffairs, 2013.

Cole, Robert William. "To Save the Village: Confronting Chinese Rural Crisis in the Global 1930s." PhD diss., New York University, 2018.

Cotton Research Board, Ministry of Agriculture, Egypt. *Second Annual Report, 1921*. Cairo: Government Press, 1922.

Cooper, Mark N. *The Transformation of Egypt*. New York: Routledge, 1982.

Earl of Cromer. *Modern Egypt*, Vol. II. New York: Macmillan and Co., 1908.

Crouchley, Arthur Edwin. *The Investment of Foreign Capital in Egyptian Companies and Public Debt*. Bulaq, Cairo: Government Press, 1936.

Cuno, Kenneth M. "The Origins of Private Ownership of Land in Egypt: A Reappraisal." *International Journal of Middle East Studies* 12, no. 3 (November 1980): 245–275.

Cuno, Kenneth M. *The Pasha's Peasants: Land, Society, and Economy in Lower Egypt, 1740–1858*. Cambridge: Cambridge University Press, 1992.

Curry, P. A. *The Control of Weights and Measures in Egypt*, Physical Department Paper 34. Cairo: Government Press, 1939.

Daniels, G. W., and J. Jewkes. "The Crisis in the Lancashire Cotton Industry." *Economic Journal* 37, no. 145 (March 1927): 33–46.

Davis, Eric. *Challenging Colonialism: Bank Misr and Egyptian Industrialization, 1920–1941*. Princeton, NJ: Princeton University Press, 1983.

Dawisha, Adeed. *Egypt in the Arab World: The Elements of Foreign Policy*. New York: John Wiley & Sons, 1976.

Deeb, Maurius, *Party Politics in Egypt: The Wafd and its Rivals, 1919–1939*. London: Ithaca Press, 1979.

d'Encausse, Helène Carrère, and S. R. Schram. *Marxism and Asia*. London: Penguin Press, 1969.

Derr, Jennifer. *The Lived Nile: Environment, Disease, and Material Colonial Economy in Egypt*. Stanford, CA: Stanford University Press, 2019.

Dethier, Jean-Jacques, and Kathy Funk. "The Language of Food: PL 480 in Egypt." *Middle East Report*, no. 145 (March–April, 1987): 22–28.

Di-Capua, Yoav. *Gatekeepers of the Arab Past: Historians and History Writing in Twentieth-Century Egypt*. Berkley and Los Angeles: University of California Press, 2009.

Al-Disūqī, ʿĀṣim. *Naḥwa Fihm Tārīkh Miṣr al-Iqtiṣādī al-Ijtimāʿī*. Cairo: Dār al-Kitāb al-Jāmiʿī, 1981.

Dosman, Edgar J. *The Life and Times of Raúl Prebisch, 1901–1986*. Montreal and Kingston: McGill-Queen's University Press, 2008.

Dowidar, Mohamed. "The Self-Reliance Strategy of Development and the New International Economic Order." *Mondes En Développement* 26 (1979): 249–254.

Douw, Leo. "The Representation of China's Rural Backwardness, 1932–1937." PhD diss., Leiden University, 1991.

Drummond, Ian M. *Imperial Economic Policy, 1917–1939: Studies in Expansion and Protection*. London: George Allen & Unwin Ltd., 1974.

Drummond, Ian. *The Floating Pound and the Sterling Area, 1931–39*. New York: Cambridge University Press, 1981.

Dunn, Read P., Jr. *Cotton in Egypt*. Memphis, TN: National Cotton Council, 1949.

Dupree, Louis. "Medieval European Feudalism and the Contemporary Middle East: A Clarification of Terms." *Report on Current Research: Survey of Current Research on the Middle East* (Spring 1957): 47–55.

Al-Duri, Abdul Aziz. "The Origins of 'Iqtāʿ in Islam." *al-Abḥāth* 22, nos. 1 and 2 (June 1969): 3–22.

Economic Commission for Africa, United Nations Economic and Social Council. "Cairo Declaration of Developing Countries," (September 14, 1962). Accessed November 23, 2023. https://repository.uneca.org/handle/10855/7151#:~:text=The%20Conference%20affirms%20that%20the,of%20international%20cooperation%20and%20assistance.

Economou, G. D., and Co. *Some Information About the Egyptian Cotton Market* (1926).

Edwards, Francis M. "The Egyptian Rural Problem." *Contemporary Review* 140 (August 1931): 191–199.

Egypt. No. 1 (1935). *Correspondence with the Egyptian Mission of Economic Enquiry Regarding Trade Relations*. London: H. M. Stationery Office, 1935.

Egypt. No. 1 (1901). *Reports by His Majesty's Agent and Consul-General on the Finances, Administration, and Condition of Egypt and the Soudan in 1900*. London: Harrison and Sons, 1901.

Egyptian Government. *Rapport de la Commission du Commerce et de l'Industrie*. Cairo: Imprimerie Nationale, 1918.

Egyptian State Railways, Telegraphs, and Telephones. *Annual Report on the Working of the Egyptian State Railways, Telegraphs, and Telephones, Financial Year 1943–44*. Cairo: E.S.R., T&T Printing and Stationery Department, 1944.

Egyptian State Railways, Telegraphs, and Port of Alexandria. *Report on the Egyptian State Railways and Telegraphs for 1907*. Cairo: Government Press, 1908.

Eichengreen, Barry, and Peter Temin. "The Gold Standard and the Great Depression." *Contemporary European History* 9, no. 2 (July 2000): 183–207.

Eisenhower, Dwight D. "Letter to Secretary Dulles Regarding Transfer of the Affairs of the Foreign Operations Administration to the Department of State, April 17, 1955." In Office of the Federal Register, National Archives and Records Service, General Services Administration, *Public Papers of the Presidents of the United States: Dwight D. Eisenhower, 1955*. Washington DC: U.S. Government Printing Office, 1959.

Ekbladh, David. "To Reconstruct the Medieval: Rural Reconstruction in Interwar China and the Rise of an American Style of Modernization, 1921–1961." *Journal of American-East Asian Relations* 9, no. 3/4 (Fall-Winter 2000): 169–196.

El-Biali, Abdul Mushin. "U.S.A and U.S.S.R. Styles in Economic Aid: A Case Study of Economic Aid to the United Arab Republic." MA thesis, The American University, 1965.

El-Gritly, Ali A. I. *The Structure of Modern Industry in Egypt*. Cairo: Government Press, 1948.

El Mallakh, Ragaei. "Economic Integration in the United Arab Republic: A Study in Resources Development." *Land Economics* 36, no. 3 (August 1960): 252–265.

El Mallakh, Ragaei W. "The Effects of the Second World War on the Economic Development of Egypt." PhD diss., Rutgers University, 1955.

El Shakry, Omnia. *The Great Social Laboratory: Subjects of Knowledge in Colonial and Postcolonial Egypt*. Stanford, CA: Stanford University Press, 2007.

Eman, André. *L'Industrie du Coton en Egypte*. Cairo: Imprimerie de L'Institut Francais, 1943.

Eman, André. "L'Industrie Égyptienne Sous la Dynastie de Mohamed Aly." In *Livre D'Or de la Fédération Égyptienne de* l'Industrie, 81–85. Cairo: Imprimerie Schindler, 1948.

Emmanuel, Arghiri. *Unequal Exchange: A Study of the Imperialism of Trade*. Translated by Brian Pearce. New York: Monthly Review, 1972.

Escobar, Arturo. *Encountering Development: The Making and Unmaking of the Third World*. Princeton, NJ: Princeton University Press, 1995.

Eshag, Eprime, and M. A. Kamal. "A Note on the Reform of the Rural Credit System in U.A.R (Egypt)." *Bulletin of the Oxford University Institute of Economics and Statistics* 29, no. 2 (May 1967): 95–107.

Esmeir, Samera. *Judicial Humanity: A Colonial History*. Stanford, CA: Stanford University Press, 2012.

Fajardo, Margarita. *The World That Latin America Created: The United Nations Economic Commission for Latin America in the Development Era*. Cambridge, MA: Harvard University Press, 2022.

Fatḥī, Ibrāhīm. "Ṭabī'at al-Sulṭa al-Burjwāziyya fī Miṣr," 1970. Accessed August 20, 2022. https://bel-ahmar.org/archives/4356.

Federici, Silvia. *Caliban and the Witch: Women, the Body, and Primitive Accumulation*. New York: Autonomedia, 2004.

Ferris, Jesse. "Guns for Cotton?" *Journal of Cold War Studies* 13, no. 2 (Spring 2011): 4–38.

Fishlow, Albert. "Comment." In *Pioneers in Development*, edited by Gerald M. Meier and Dudley Seers, 192–196. New York: Oxford University Press, 1984.

Foucault, Michel. "Governmentality." In *The Foucault Effect: Studies in Governmentality*, edited by Graham Burchell, Colin Gordon, and Peter Miller, 87–104. Chicago: University of Chicago Press, 1991.

Foucault, Michel. *Society Must Be Defended: Lectures at the Collège de France, 1975–76*. New York: Picador, 2003.

Frank, Andre Gunder. *Capitalism and Underdevelopment in Latin America: Historical Studies of Chile and Brazil*. New York: Monthly Review Press, 1967.

Fraser, Nancy. "Behind Marx's Hidden Abode: For an Expanded Conception of Capitalism." *New Left Review*, 86 (March/April 2014): 55–72.

Frieden, Jeffry A. *Global Capitalism: Its Fall and Rise in the Twentieth Century*. New York: W. W. Norton and Company Inc., 2006.

Friedmann, Harriet. "The Political Economy of Food: The Rise and Fall of the Postwar International Food Order." *American Journal of Sociology* 88 (1982): S260–S271.

Gallagher, Nancy Elizabeth. *Egypt's Other Wars: Epidemics and the Politics of Public Health*. Syracuse, NY: Syracuse University Press, 1990.

Gasper, Michael Ezekiel. *The Power of Representation: Publics, Peasants, and Islam in Egypt*. Stanford, CA: Stanford University Press, 2008.

Getachew, Adom. *Worldmaking After Empire: The Rise and Fall of Self-Determination*. Princeton, NJ: Princeton University Press, 2019.

Ghālī, Mirīt. *Al-Iṣlāḥ al-Zirā'ī: al-Milkiyya, al-Ījār, al-'Amal*. Cairo: Jamā'at al-Nahḍa al-Qawmiyya, 1945.

Ghālī, Mirīt. *Siyāsat al-Ghad: Birnāmij Siyāsī wa-Iqtiṣādī wa-Ijtmā'ī*. Cairo: Maṭba'at al-Risāla, 1938.

Ghonemy, Mohamed Riad. "Economic and Institutional Organization of Egyptian Agriculture Since 1952." In *Egypt Since the Revolution*, edited by P. J. Vatikiotis, 66–83. New York: Praeger, 1968.

Ghonemy, Mohamed Riad. "Resource Use and Income in Egyptian Agriculture Before and After the Land Reform with Particular Reference to Economic Development." PhD diss., North Carolina State College, 1953.

Ghurbāl, Muhammad Shafīq. *Muḥammad 'Alī al-Kabīr*. Cairo: Hindawi Foundation for Education and Culture, 2014. Reprint of 1944 edition.

Gilmore, Ruth Wilson. *Golden Gulag: Prisons, Surplus, Crisis, and Opposition in Globalizing California*. Berkeley and Los Angeles: University of California Press, 2007.

Ginat, Rami. *Egypt's Incomplete Revolution: Lutfi al-Khuli and Nasser's Socialism in the 1960s*. London: Frank Cass & Co. Ltd., 1997.

Ginat, Rami, and Odelya Alon. "En Route to Revolution: The Communists and the Free Officers—Honeymoon and Separation." *British Journal of Middle Eastern Studies* 43, no. 4 (October 2016): 590–612.

Goldberg, Ellis. "Marketing Commodities Does Not Happen on Commodity Markets: The Egyptian Bursat Al-'Uqud and Oil Futures Markets." In *The Politics of Islamic*

Finance, edited by Clement M. Henry and Rodney Wilson, 81–103. Edinburgh: Edinburgh University Press, 2004.

Goldberg, Ellis. *Trade, Reputation, and Child Labor in Twentieth-Century Egypt*. New York: Palgrave Macmillan, 2004.

Goldberg, Ellis, and Joel Beinin, "Egypt's Transition Under Nasser," *Middle East Report*, no. 107 (July/August 1982): 23–31.

Goldfinch, Gary. *Steel in the Sand: The History of Egypt and its Railways*. Dorset: Dorset Press, 2003.

Gordon, Joel. *Nasser's Blessed Movement: Egypt's Free Officers and the July Revolution*. New York: Oxford University Press, 1992.

Gran, Peter. *Islamic Roots of Capitalism: Egypt, 1760–1840*. Syracuse, NY: Syracuse University Press, 1998.

Greaves, Julian I. "Competition, Collusion, and Confusion: The State and the Reorganization of the British Cotton Industry, 1931–1939." *Enterprise & Society* 3, no. 1 (March 2002), 52.

Grubbs, Donald H. *Cry from the Cotton: The Southern Tenant Farmers' Union and the New Deal*. 1971; reissued Fayetteville: University of Arkansas Press, 2000.

Gruliow, Leo, ed. *Current Soviet Policies—II: The Documentary Record of the 20th Communist Party Congress and Its Aftermath*. New York: Praeger Publishing Company, 1957.

Hahn, Peter L. *The United States, Great Britain, and Egypt, 1945–1956: Strategy and Diplomacy in the Early Cold War*. Chapel Hill: University of North Carolina Press, 1991.

Al-Ḥakīm, Tawfīq. *Yawmiyyāt Nā'ib fī al-Aryāf*. Cairo: Dār al-Shurūq, 2004.

Haleh-Davis, Muriam. *Markets of Civilization: Islam and Racial Capitalism in Algeria*. Durham, NC: Duke University Press, 2022.

Hammad, Hanan. *Industrial Sexuality: Gender, Urbanization, and Social Transformation in Egypt*. Austin: University of Texas Press, 2016.

Hamrūsh, Aḥmad. *Thawrat 23 Yūlyū*, Vol. 1. Cairo: Al-Hay'a al-Miṣriyya al-'Āma li-l-Kitāb, 1992.

Hanna, Nelly. *Artisan Entrepreneurs in Cairo and Early-Modern Capitalism (1600–1800)*. Syracuse, NY: Syracuse University Press, 2011.

Hansen, Bent. "Income and Consumption in Egypt, 1886/1887 to 1937." *International Journal of Middle East Studies* 10, no. 1 (1979): 27–47.

Hansen, Bent. *The Political Economy of Poverty, Equity, and Growth: Egypt and Turkey, A World Bank Comparative Study*. New York: Oxford University Press, 1991.

Hansen, Bent, and Karim Nashashibi. *Foreign Trade Regimes and Economic Development: Egypt*, Special Conference Series on Foreign Trade Regimes and Economic Development, National Bureau of Economic Research, Vol. 4. New York: Columbia University Press, 1975.

Ḥarb, Muḥammad Ṭal'at. *Majmū'at Khuṭab Muḥammad Ṭal'at Ḥarb*, Vol. 1. Cairo: Imprimerie Misr, n.d.

Harvey, David. *Cosmopolitanism and the Geographies of Freedom*. New York: Columbia University Press, 2009.

Harvey, David. *Spaces of Capital: Towards a Critical Geography*. Edinburgh: Edinburgh University Press, 2001.

Hāshim, Zakī. *Al-'Umam al-Mutaḥida*. Cairo: Al-Maṭba'a al-Ālamiyya, 1951.

Hasanayn, Magdī. *Al-Ṣaḥrā'—Al-Thawra wa-l-Tharwa: Qiṣṣat Mudīrīyat al-Taḥrīr*. Cairo: al-Hay'a al-Miṣriyya al-'Āmma li-l-Kitāb, 1975.

Ḥassūna, Muḥammad Amīn. *Kifāḥ al-Sha'b min 'Umar Makram ilā Jamāl 'Abd al-Nāṣir*, 2 vols. Cairo: Maṭābi' al-Sabāḥ, 1955.

Ḥassūna, Muḥammad Amīn. *Jumhūriyyat Miṣr fī 'Āmaha al-Awwal*. Cairo: Maṭba'at al-Taḥrīr, 1954.

Ḥassūna, Muḥammad Amīn. *Jumhūriyyat Miṣr fī 'Āmaha al-Thānī*. Cairo: Maṭba'at al-Taḥrīr, 1955.

Hatem, Mervat. "Economic and Political Liberation and the Demise of State Feminism." *International Journal of Middle East Studies* 24, no. 2 (1991): 231–251.

Heydemann, Steven, and Robert Vitalis. "War, Keynesianism, and Colonialism: Explaining State-Market Relations in the Postwar Middle East." In *War, Institutions, and Social Change in the Middle East*, edited by Steven Heydemann, 100–145. Berkeley and Los Angeles: University of California Press, 2000.

Heyworth-Dunne, James. "Rifā'ah Badawī Rāfi' aṭ-Ṭahṭāwī: The Egyptian Revivalist (Continued)." *Bulletin of the School of Oriental Studies* 10, no. 2 (1940): 399–415.

Heyworth-Dunne, James. Review of *Feudalism in Egypt, Syria, Palestine and the Lebanon, 1250–1900 by A. N. Poliak*. *Bulletin of the School of Oriental Studies* 10, no. 2 (1940): 532–534.

Higher Committee for Agrarian Reform. *Silent Struggle Between the Egyptian Fellah and Mohamed Aly Dynasty*. Cairo: H.C.A.R Press Department, 1954.

Hobsbawm, Eric. *The Age of Empire: 1875–1914*. New York: Pantheon Books, 1987.

Hobsbawm, Eric. *Nations and Nationalism Since 1780: Programme, Myth, Reality*. Cambridge: Cambridge University Press, 1992.

Hobson, J. A. *Imperialism: A Study*. New York: James Pott & Company, 1902.

Hoskins, Halford L. *Soviet Economic Penetration in the Middle East: A Special Study Prepared at the Request of Senator Hubert H. Humphrey*. Washington, DC: U.S. Government Printing Office, 1959.

Howell, Leander D. *Cotton Prices in Spot and Futures Markets*. Washington, DC: United States Department of Agriculture, 1939.

Hubbard, W. Hustace. "Hedging in the Cotton Market." *The Annals of the American Academy of Political and Social Science* 155, Part 1: Organized Commodity Markets (May 1931): 23–38.

Ḥusayn, 'Ādil. *Al-Iqtiṣād al-Miṣrī min al-Istiqlāl ilā al-Taba'iyya, 1974–1979*, 2 vols. Beirut: Dār al-Kalima li-l-Nashr, 1981.

Ḥusayn, Ṭaha. *Musṭaqbal al-Thaqāfa fī Miṣr*. Cairo: Maṭba'at al-Ma'ārif, 1938.

Hussein, Mahmoud. *Class Conflict in Egypt, 1945–1970*. New York: Monthly Review, 1974.

Ikeda, Misako. "Sociopolitical Debates in Late Parliamentary Egypt, 1944–1952." PhD diss., Harvard University, 1998.

Al-'Imarī, Ādil. *Al-Nāṣiriyya fī al-Thawra al-Muḍāda*. Cairo: Dār al-Maḥrūsa li-l-Nashr wa-l-Khadamāt al-Saḥafiyya wa-l-Ma'lūmāt, 2009.

Injilz, Fridrīk. *Al-Tafsīr al-Ishtirākī li-l-Tarīkh: Mukhtārāt min Fridrīk Injilz*. Translated and introduced by Rāshid al-Barrāwī. Cairo: Maktabat al-Nahḍa al-Miṣriyya, 1947.

Institution of Civil Engineers. "Obituary." In *Minutes of the Proceedings* 240 (January 1, 1935): 789–790.

International Federation of Master Cotton Spinners' and Manufacturers' Associations. *Official Report of the International Cotton Congress*, 1927.

International Institute of Agriculture, Statistical Service. *International Yearbook of Agricultural Statistics 1909 to 1921*. Rome: Imprimérie de L'Institut International D'Agriculture, 1922.

International Institute of Agriculture. *World Cotton Production and Trade*. Rome: Printing Office of the Chamber of Deputies, 1936.

Ismāʿīl, Muḥammad Ḥāfiẓ. *Amn Miṣr al-Qawmī fī ʿAṣr al-Taḥadiyyāt*. Cairo: Markaz al-Ahrām li-l-Tarjama wa-l-Nashr, 1987.

Ismael, Tareq Y., and Rifa'at El-Said. *The Communist Movement in Egypt, 1920–1988*. Syracuse, NY: Syracuse University Press, 1990.

Issawi, Charles. "Asymmetrical Development and Transport in Egypt, 1800–1914." In *Beginnings of Modernization in the Middle East: The Nineteenth Century*, edited by William R. Polk and Richard L. Chambers, 83–400. Chicago: University of Chicago Press, 1968.

Issawi, Charles. *Egypt: An Economic and Social Analysis*. London: Oxford University Press, 1947.

Issawi, Charles. *Egypt at Mid-Century: An Economic Survey*. London: Oxford University Press, 1954.

Iyer, Samantha. *Agrarian Superpower*. New York: Columbia University Press, forthcoming.

Iyer, Samantha. "Colonial Population and the Idea of Development." *Comparative Studies in Society and History* 55, no. 1 (January 2013): 65–91.

Jacob, Wilson Chacko. *Working Out Egypt: Effendi Masculinity and Subject Formation in Colonial Modernity, 1870–1940*. Durham, NC: Duke University Press, 2011.

Jakes, Aaron G. "Boom, Bugs, Bust: Egypt's Ecology of Interest, 1882–1914." *Antipode* 49, no. 4 (February 2016): 1035–1059.

Jakes, Aaron, and Ahmad Shokr. "Capitalism in Egypt, not Egyptian Capitalism." In *A Critical Political Economy of the Middle East and North Africa*, edited by Joel Beinin, Bassam Haddad, and Sherene Seikaly, 123–142. Stanford, CA: Stanford University Press, 2021.

Jakes, Aaron G. *Egypt's Occupation: Colonial Economism and the Crises of Capitalism*. Stanford, CA: Stanford University Press, 2020.

Jakes, Aaron G. and Ahmad Shokr. "Finding Value in *Empire of Cotton*." *Critical Historical Studies* 4, no. 1 (Spring 2017): 107–136.

Jakes, Aaron George. "The Scales of Public Utility: Agricultural Roads and State Space in the Era of the British Occupation." In *The Long 1890s in Egypt*, edited by Marilyn Booth and Anthony Gorman, 57–86. Edinburgh: University of Edinburgh Press, 2014.

James, C.L.R. *Black Jacobins: Toussaint L'Ouverture and the San Domingo Revolution*, 2nd ed. New York: Vintage Books, 1963.

Jessop, Bob. "From Micro-powers to Governmentality: Foucault's Work on Statehood, State Formation, Statecraft, and State Power." *Political Geography* 26 (2007): 34–40.

Jirjis, Fawzī. *Dirāsāt fī Tārīkh Miṣr al-Siyāsī Mundhu al-'Aṣr al-Mamlūkī*. Cairo: Al-Dār al-Miṣriyya li-l-Ṭibā'a wa-l-Nashr wa-l-Tawzī', 1958.

Johnson, Amy Jo. *Reconstructing Rural Egypt: Ahmed Hussein and the History of Egyptian Development*. Cairo: American University in Cairo Press, 2004.

Jumhūriyyat Miṣr. *Al-Majlis al-Dā'im li-Tanmiyyat al-Intāj al-Qawmī*, 1955.

Kanet, Roger E. "Soviet Attitudes Toward Developing Nations Since Stalin." In *The Soviet Union and the Developing Nations*, edited by Roger E. Kanet, 27–50. Baltimore: John Hopkins University Press, 1974.

Kanet, Roger E. "The Soviet Union and the Developing Countries: Policy or Policies," *The World Today* 31, no. 8 (August 1975): 338–346.

Kanovsky, Eliyahu. *The Economic Impact of the Six Day War: Israel, the Occupied Territories, Egypt, Jordan*. New York: Praeger, 1970.

Karbell, Zachary. *The Leading Indicators: A Short History of the Numbers That Rule Our World*. New York: Simon & Schuster, 2014.

Kardouche, George. *The U.A.R in Development: A Study in Expansionary Finance*. New York: Praeger Publishers, 1966.

Kardouche, George K. *United Arab Republic: Case Study of Aid Through Trade and Repayment of Debt in Goods or Local Currencies*. United Nations Conference on Trade and Development, 1966.

Karl, Rebecca E. *The Magic of Concepts: History and the Economic in Twentieth-Century China*. Durham, NC: Duke University Press, 2017.

Keynes, John Maynard. *Indian Currency and Finance*. London: Macmillan and Co. Ltd, 1913.

Keyder, Çağlar. *State and Class in Turkey: A Study in Capitalist Development*. London: Verso, 1987.

Khan, Noor-Aiman. *Egyptian-Indian Nationalist Collaboration and the British Empire*. New York: Palgrave Macmillan, 2011.

Kholoussi, Samia. "Fallāḥin: The 'Mud Bearers of Egypt's 'Liberal Age.'" In *Re-Envisioning Egypt, 1919–1952*, edited by Arthur Goldschmidt, Amy J. Johnson, and Barak A. Salmoni, 277–314. Cairo: American University in Cairo Press, 2005.

Kindleberger, Charles P. *The World Depression, 1929–1939*. Berkeley: University of California Press, 2013. Reprint of 1973 edition.

Klat, Jules. *Les Opérations de Bourse En Egypte*. Alexandrie: 1933.

Krugman, Paul. *The Conscience of a Liberal*. New York: W. W. Norton & Company, 2007.

Kupferschmidt, Uri M. "Who Needed Department Stores in Egypt? From Orosdi-Back to Omar Effendi." *Middle Eastern Studies* 43, no. 2 (March 2007): 175–192.

Labīb, Fakhrī. *Al-Shīyū'iyyūn wa-'Abd al-Nāṣir: Al-Taḥāluf wa-l-Muwājaha, 1958–1965*, 2 vols. Cairo: Sharikat al-Amal li-l-Ṭibā'a wa-l-Nashr wa-l-Tawzī', 1990–1992.

Lacouture, Jean. *Nasser*. Paris: Editions de Seuil, 1971.

Ladejinsky, Wolf Isaac. *Agrarian Reform as Unfinished Business: The Selected Papers of Wolf Ladejinsky*, edited by Louis J. Walinsky. New York: Oxford University Press, 1977.

Lambton, Ann K. S. "The Evolution of the 'Iqṭā' in Medieval Iran." *Iran* 5 (1967): 41–50.

Laqueur, Walter. *The Struggle for the Middle East: The Soviet Union and the Middle East, 1958–1968*. London: Routledge and Kegan Paul, 1969.

Linīn, V. I. *Al-Isti'mār A'lā Marāḥil al-Ra's Māliyya*. Translated by Rāshid al-Barrāwī. Cairo: Maktabat al-Nahḍa al-Miṣriyya, 1945.

Lenin, Vladimir Il'ich. *Imperialism, The Highest Stage of Capitalism*. New York: Pathfinder Press, 2002.

Lewis, W. Arthur. "Economic Development with Unlimited Supplies of Labor." *The Manchester School* 22, issue 2 (May, 1954): 139–191.

Lewis, W. Arthur. "Reflections on South-East Asia." *District Bank Review*, no. 104 (December 1952): 3–20.

Link, Stefan J. *Forging Global Fordism: Nazi Germany, Soviet Russia, and the Contest over the Industrial Order*. Princeton, NJ: Princeton University Press, 2020.

Liu, Andrew B. "Production, Circulation, and Accumulation: The Historiographies of Capitalism in China and South Asia." *Journal of Asian Studies* 78, no. 4 (November 2019): 767–788.

Liu, Andrew B. *Tea War: A History of Capitalism in China and India*. New Haven, CT: Yale University Press, 2020.

Lockman, Zachary. "British Policy Toward Egyptian Labor Activism, 1882–1936." *International Journal of Middle East Studies* 20, no. 3 (August 1988): 265–285.

Lorenzini, Sara. *Global Development; A Cold War History*. Princeton, NJ: Princeton University Press, 2019.

Love, Joseph. "Raúl Prebisch and the Origins of the Doctrine of Unequal Exchange." *Latin American Research Review* 15, no. 3 (1980): 45–72.

Love, Joseph L. "The Origins of Dependency Analysis." *Journal of Latin American Studies* 22, no. 1 (February 1990), 143–168.

Luhayṭa, Muḥammad Fahmī. *Tarīkh Fu'ād al-Awwal al-Iqtiṣādī*, vols. 1–3. Cairo: Maktabat Al-Nahḍa al-Miṣriyya, 1945–1946.

Lukàcs, Georg. *History and Class Consciousness*. Translated by Rodney Livingstone. Cambridge, MA: MIT Press, 1971.

Luxemburg, Rosa. *The Accumulation of Capital*. Translated by Agnes Schwartzchild. London: Routledge, 2003. Reprint of 1913 edition.

Mabro, Robert. "Egypt's Economics Relations with the Socialist Countries." In *Economic Relations Between Socialist Countries and the Third World*, edited by Deepak Nayyar, 55. London: Macmillan Press Ltd., 1977.

Mabro, Robert. *The Egyptian Economy, 1952–1970*. London: Oxford University Press, 1974.

Mabro, Robert, and Samir Radwan. *The Industrialization of Egypt, 1939–1973*. London: Oxford University Press, 1976.

Macaulay, Thomas Babington. "Minute on Indian Education (2 February 1835)." In *Macaulay: Prose and Poetry*, edited by G.M. Young, 719–730. London: Rupert Hart-Davis, 1861.

Macdonald, Murdoch. *Nile Control*. Cairo: Ministry of Public Works, 1920.

Magdy, Rana. "The People Want—But Do They Have a Chance?" Interview by Gilbert Achcar. *openDemocracy*, February 21, 2014. Accessed May 9, 2023. https://www.opendemocracy.net/en/author/rana-magdy/page/2/.

Maier, Charles. *In Search of Stability: Explorations in Historical Political Economy*. Cambridge: Cambridge University Press, 1988.

Maklad, Shahenda, Yasmine M. Ahmed, and Reem Saad. "Interview with Shahenda Maklad." *Review of African Political Economy* 38, no. 127 (March 2011): 159–167.

Manela, Ezra. *The Wilsonian Moment: Self-Determination and the International Origins of Anti-Colonial Nationalism*. New York: Oxford University Press, 2007.

Mansour, Fawzy. "Third World Revolt and Self-Reliant Auto-Centered Strategy of Development." In *Toward a New Strategy for Development: A Rothko Chapel Colloquium*, 198–239. New York: Pergamon, 1979.

Marei, Sayyid. *Agrarian Reform in Egypt*. Cairo: Imprimérie de L'Institut Francais d'Archéologie Orientale, 1957.

Marʿī, Diāʾ. *Tarīkh al-Sīnimā al-Tasjīliyya fī Miṣr*. Alexandria: Bibliotheca Alexandrina, 2003.

Martin, Jamie. "The Global Crisis of the Commodity Glut During the Second World War." *International History Review* 43, no. 6 (2021): 1273–1290.

Martinez-Matsuda, Veronica. *Migrant Citizenship: Race, Rights, and Reform in the U.S. Farm Labor Camp Program*. Philadelphia: University of Pennsylvania Press, 2020.

Marx, Karl. *Capital: A Critique of Political Economy*, Vol. 1. Translated by Ben Fowkes. London: Penguin Books, 1976.

Marx, Karl. *Capital: A Critique of Political Economy*, Vol. 3. Translated by David Fernbach. London: Penguin Books, 1981.

Marx, Karl. "The 'First' Draft." In *Late Marx and the Russian Road: Marx and the "Peripheries of Capitalism,"* edited by Teodor Shanin, 105–117. New York: Monthly Review Press, 1983.

Mārks, Kārl. *Raʾs al-Māl: Al-Juzʾ al-Awwal*. Translated by Rāshid al-Barrāwī. Cairo: Maktabat al-Nahḍa al-Miṣriyya, 1948.

Mau, Søren. *Mute Compulsion: A Marxist Theory of the Economic Power of Capital*. London: Verso, 2023.

Al-Māwardī, Abu al-Hasan ʿAlī Ibn Muḥammad Ibn Habīb al-Baṣrī. *Al-Aḥkām al-Ṣulṭāniyya*. Cairo: Dār al-Hadīth, 2006.

Mayer, Arno J. *Wilson vs. Lenin: Political Origins of the New Diplomacy, 1917–1918*. Cleveland, OH: World Publishing Company, 1964.

Mayer, Thomas. *The Changing Past: Egyptian Historiography of the 'Urabi Revolt, 1882–1983*. Gainesville: University of Florida Press, 1988.

McKillop, Arthur T. *Note on the Readjustment of the Land Tax in Egypt 1895–1907*. Cairo: National Printing Department, 1907.

McMichael, Philip. *Development and Social Change: A Global Perspective*, 2nd ed. Thousand Oaks, CA: Pine Forge Press, 2000.

McNeill, John Robert. *Something New Under the Sun; An Environmental History of the Twentieth Century*. New York: W. W. Norton & Company, 2000.

Meek, Ronald L. "Smith, Turgot, and the 'Four Stages' Theory." *History of Political Economy* 3, no. 1 (1971): 9–27.

Meijer, Roel. *The Quest for Modernity: Secular Liberal and Left-Wing Political Thought in Egypt, 1945–1958*. London: Routledge Curzon, 2002.

Mies, Maria. *Patriarchy and Accumulation on a World Scale: Women in the International Division of Labor*. London: Zed Books, 1986.

Ministère des Finances, Département de la Statistique Générale. *Annuaire Statistique de l'Egypte 1920*. Cairo: Imprimerie Nationale, 1921.

Ministère des Finances, Département de la Statistique Générale. *Annuaire Statistique de l'Egypte 1921–22*. Cairo: Imprimerie Nationale, 1923.

Ministry of Finance, Statistical and Census Department. *Population Census of Egypt*, 1937.

Ministry of Finance, Statistical and Census Department. *Population Census of Egypt*, 1947.

Ministry of Finance, Statistical Department. *Statistical Yearbook of Egypt for 1909*. Cairo: National Printing Department, 1909.

Ministry of Social Affairs. *Co-operative Societies in Egypt*. Cairo: Government Press, 1948.

Ministry of Social Affairs, Fallah Department. *Note on Questions Relating to Agriculture, presented to the I.L.O. Mission*. Cairo, 1945.

Mintz, Sidney W. "Caribbean Society." In *International Encyclopedia of the Social Sciences*, Vol. 2, edited by David L. Sills, 306–319. New York: Macmillan, 1968.

Mishra, Pankaj. *From the Ruins of Empire: The Intellectuals Who Remade Asia*. New York: Farrar, Straus and Giroux, 2012.

Mikesell, Raymond F. "Sterling Area Currencies of the Middle East." *Middle East Journal* 2, no. 2 (April 1948): 160–174.

Mitchell, Timothy. *Colonizing Egypt*. Berkeley: University of California Press, 1991.

Mitchell, Timothy. *Rule of Experts: Egypt, Techno-Politics, Modernity*. Berkeley: University of California Press, 2002.

Moore, Jason W. *Capitalism in the Web of Life: Ecology and the Accumulation of Capital*. London: Verso, 2015.

Moore, Jason W. "Sugar and the Expansion of the Early Modern World Economy: Commodity Frontiers, Ecological Transformation, and Industrialization." *Review (Fernand Braudel Center)* 23, no. 3 (2000): 409–433.

Moulton, Mo. "Co-opting the Cooperative Movement? Development, Decolonization, and the Power of Expertise at the Cooperative College, 1920s–1960s." *Journal of Global History* 17, no. 3 (2022): 418–437.

Muḥī al-Dīn, Khālid. *Wa-l-'Ān Atakallam*. Cairo: Markaz al-Ahrām li-l-Tarjama wa-l-Nashr, 1992.

Mulattam, Munā. *Al-Ḥizb al-Shīyū'ī al-Miṣrī, 1921–1952*. Cairo: Al-Hay'a al-Miṣriyya al-'Āma li-l-Kitāb, 2020.

Al-Mulla, Aḥmad Salāḥ. *Al-Yasār al-Miṣrī Bayn 'Abd al-Nāṣir wa-l-Sādāt: Majallat al-Ṭalī'a, 1965–1977*. Cairo: Maṭba'at Dār al-Kutub wa-l-Wathā'iq al-Qawmiyya, 2014.

Mursī, Fu'ād. *Taṭawwur al-Ra'smāliyya wa-Kifāḥ al-Tabaqāt fī Miṣr*. Cairo: Al-Dār al-Miṣriyya li-l-Ṭibā'a wa-l-Nashr wa-l-Tawzī', 1949.

Mūsā, Muḥammad al-'Azab. *Awwal Thawra 'Alā al-Iqṭā'*. Cairo: Al-Hay'a al-Miṣriyya al-'Āma li-l-Kitāb, 2013.

Mūsā, Salāma. *Ghandī wa-l-Ḥaraka al-Hindiyya*. Cairo: Kalimāt 'Arabiyya li-l-Tarjama wa-l-Nashr, 2011. Reprint of 1934 edition.

Najīb, Muḥammad. *Kuntu Ra'īsan li-Miṣr*, 2nd ed. Cairo: Al-Maktab al-Miṣrī al-Hadīth, 1984.

Naḥḥās, Yūsuf. *Al-Fallāh: Hālatihi al-Iqtiṣāḍiyya wa-l-Ijtimā'iyya*. Cairo: Maṭba'at al-Muqtaṭaf wa-l-Muqaṭṭam, 1926.

Naḥḥās, Yūsuf. *Al-Quṭn fī Khamsīn ʿĀm*. Cairo: Dār al-Nīl, 1954.

Naḥḥās, Yūsuf. *Juhūd al-Niqāba al-Zirāʿiyya al-Miṣriyya al-ʿĀmma fī Thalāthīna ʿĀman*. Cairo: Dār al-Nīl li-l-Ṭibāʿa, 1952.

Al-Najjār, Aḥmad al-Sayyid. "Al-Thawra wa-Muwājahat Muʿḍilāt al-Iqtiṣād al-Miṣrī." Al-Ahram Center for Political and Strategic Studies, *Korāsāt Istrātījiyya*, Vol. 217, 2nd ed., 2011.

National Bank of Egypt, *National Bank of Egypt, 1898–1948* (for private circulation).

Al-Nūr, Ṣaqr ʿAbd al-Ṣādiq Hilāl. *Al-Arḍ wa-l-Fallāḥ wa-l-Mustathmir: Dirāsa fī al-Masʾala al-Zirāʿiyya wa-l-Fallāḥiyya fī Miṣr*. Cairo: Dār al-Marāya li-l-Intāj al-Thaqāfī, 2017.

Nutting, Anthony. *Nasser*. New York: E. P. Dutton, 1972.

O'Brien, Patrick. "The Long-Term Growth of Agricultural Production in Egypt: 1821–1962." In *Political and Social Change in Modern Egypt: Historical Studies from the Ottoman Conquest to the United Arab Republic*, edited by P. M. Holt, 162–195. London: Oxford University Press, 1968.

O'Brien, Patrick. *The Revolution in Egypt's Economic System: From Private Enterprise to Socialism, 1952–1965*. London: Oxford University Press, 1966.

Olsson, Tore C. *Agrarian Crossings: Reformers and the Remaking of the U.S. and Mexican Countryside*. Princeton, NJ: Princeton University Press, 2017.

Omar, Hussein A. H. "The Arab Spring of 1919." *London Review of Books Blog*, April 4, 2019. Accessed April 18, 2023. https://www.lrb.co.uk/blog/2019/april/the-arab-spring-of-1919.

Omar, Hussein. "The Irish Were Egyptians Long Ago." *Irish Independent*, November 28, 2020.

Osterhammel, Jürgen. *The Transformation of the World: A Global History of the Nineteenth Century*. Princeton, NJ: Princeton University Press, 2014.

Owen, Roger. *Cotton and the Egyptian Economy, 1820–1914: A Study in Trade and Development*. Oxford: Clarendon Press, 1969.

Owen, Roger. "Egypt and Europe: From French Expedition to British Occupation." In *Studies in the Theory of Imperialism*, edited by Roger Owen and Robert Sutcliffe, 195–209. London: Longman Publishing Group, 1972.

Owen, Roger. "Egypt in the World Depression: Agricultural Recession and Industrial Expansion." In *The Economies of Africa and Asia in the Inter-war Depression*, edited by Ian Brown, 137–151. London: Routledge, 1989.

Owen, Roger. "The Economic Consequences of the Suez Crisis for Egypt." In *Suez 1956: The Crisis and Its Consequences*, edited by Wm. Roger Louis and Roger Owen, 363–376. New York: Oxford University Press, 1991.

Owen, Roger. "The Ideology of Economic Nationalism in its Egyptian Context: 1919–1939." In *Intellectual Life in the Arab East, 1890–1939*, edited by Marwan Buheiry, 1–9. Beirut: American University of Beirut, 1981.

Owen, Roger. *The Middle East in the World Economy, 1800–1914*. London: I. B. Tauris & Co., 2009.

Owen, Roger. "The Rapid Growth of Egypt's Agricultural Output, 1890–1914, as an Early Example of the Green Revolutions of Modern South Asia: Some Implications for the Writing of Global History." *Journal of Global History* 1 (2006): 81–99.

Palacios, Guillermo. "Postrevolutionary Intellectuals, Rural Readings, and the Shaping of

the 'Peasant Problem' in Mexico: *El Maestro Rural*, 1924–1934." *Journal of Latin American Studies* 30, no. 2 (May 1998): 309–339.
Patel, Kiran Klaus. *The New Deal: A Global History*. Princeton, NJ: Princeton University Press, 2016.
Patnaik, Utsa, ed. *Agrarian Relations and Accumulation: The "Mode of Production" Debate in India*. Bombay: Oxford University Press, 1990.
Peck, David. "Mortgage Banking and Tenure Security in Egypt, 1900–1939." PhD diss., University of Utah, 2003.
Petrie, Ian. "Village Visions: Science and Technology in the Bengal Countryside, 1860–1947." PhD diss., University of Pennsylvania, 2004.
Piketty, Thomas. *Capital in the Twenty-First Century*. Translated by Arthur Goldhammer. Cambridge, MA: Belknap Press, 2014.
Polanyi, Karl. *The Great Transformation: The Political and Economic Origins of Our Time*, 2nd ed. Boston: Beacon Press, 2001.
Pollard, Lisa. *Nurturing the Nation: The Family Politics of Modernizing, Colonizing, and Liberating Egypt, 1805–1923*. Berkeley: University of California Press, 2005.
Poliak, Abraham Nahum. *Feudalism in Egypt, Syria, Palestine, and the Lebanon, 1250–1900*. London: Royal Asiatic Society, 1939.
Politi, Elie I. *L'Egypte de 1914 à "Suez."* Paris: Presses de la Cité, 1965.
Postone, Moishe. "Anti-Semitism and National Socialism: Notes on the German Reaction to the 'Holocaust.'" *New German Critique* 19, Special Issue 1: Germans and Jews (Winter 1980): 97–115.
Postone, Moishe. *Time, Labor, and Social Domination: A Reinterpretation of Marx's Critical Theory*. New York: Cambridge University Press, 1993.
Prebisch, Raúl. *The Economic Development of Latin America and Its Principal Problems*. Lake Success, NY: United Nations Department of Economic Affairs, 1950.
Primel, Casey. "Calculating Futures: Debt, Markets, and the Science of Prices in Colonial Egypt, 1882–1912." PhD diss., Columbia University, 2016.
Pursley, Sara. *Familiar Futures: Time, Selfhood, and Sovereignty in Iraq*. Stanford, CA: Stanford University Press, 2019.
Radwan, Samir. *Agrarian Reform and Rural Poverty: Egypt, 1952–1975*. Geneva: International Labour Office, 1977.
Rafaat, Samir. "The Rise and Fall of Alexandria's Cotton Exchange." *Egyptian Mail*, November 1, 1997.
Al-Rāf'ī, 'Abd al-Raḥmān. *Miṣr al-Mujāhida fī al-'Aṣr al-Hadīth*, 3 vols. Cairo: Dār al-Hilāl, 2016. Reprint of 1957 edition.
Ramaḍān, 'Abd al-'Aẓīm. *Al-Fikr al-Thawrī fī Miṣr Qabl Thawrat 23 Yūlyū*. Cairo: Silsilat Maktabat al-'Usra, 2004.
Rashad, Ibrahim. *An Egyptian in Ireland*. Privately printed for the author, 1920.
Rashād, Ibrāhīm. *Kitāb al-Ta'āwun al-Zirā'ī*. Cairo: Al-Maṭba'a al-Amīriyya, 1926.
Rashād, Ibrāhīm. *Mashrū' al-Mazāri' al-Ta'āwuniyya*. Maṭba'at Miṣr Sharika Musāhima Miṣriyya, n.d.
Rashād, Ibrāhīm. *Mudhakkirāt Mujāhid Ta'āwunī*. Cairo: Dār al-Taḍāmun li-l-Ṭibā'a wa-l-Nashr, 1970.

Rashād, Ibrāhīm. "Mudhakkira 'an Bank al-Taslīf al-Zirā'ī wa-l-Ta'āwunī wa-Iqrāḍ Kibār al-Muzāri'īn," May 1952. In *Al-Dā'iya Duktūr Ibrāhīm Rashād*, 'Abd al-Hakīm Shaṭā, 195–197. Isma'iliyya: Markaz 'Umar Luṭfi li-l-Tadrīb al-Ta'āwunī al-Zirā'ī, 1989.

Rashād, Ibrāhīm. *Wājibnā al-Ta'āwunī ba'd al-Mu'āhada*. Cairo: Al-Maṭba'a al-Amīriyya, 1937.

Rashād, Muḥammad. *Sirrī Jiddan: Min Malafāt al-Lajna al-'Ulyā li-Taṣfiyyat al-Iqṭā'*. Cairo: Dār al-Ta'āwun li-l-Ṭab' wa-l-Nashr, 1977.

Rejwan, Nissim. *Nasserist Ideology: Its Exponents and Critics*. New York: Halsted Press, 1974.

Reynolds, Nancy. *A City Consumed: Urban Commerce, the Cairo Fire, and the Politics of Decolonization in Egypt*. Stanford, CA: Stanford University Press, 2012.

Reynolds, Susan. *Fiefs and Vassals: The Medieval Evidence Reinterpreted*. Oxford: Clarendon Press, 1994.

Riad, Hassan. *L'Égypte Nassérienne*. Paris: Les Editions de Minuit, 1964.

Richards, Alan, and John Waterbury. *A Political Economy of the Middle East: State, Class, and Economic Development*. Boulder, CO: Westview Press, 1990.

Richards, Alan. *Egypt's Agricultural Development, 1800–1980: Technical and Social Change*. Boulder, CO: Westview Press, 1982.

Richards, Alan. "Egypt's Agriculture in Trouble." *Middle East Report*, no. 84 (January/February 1980): 3–13.

Richards, Alan. "Land and Labor on Egyptian Cotton Farms, 1882–1940." *Agricultural History* 52, no. 4 (October 1978): 503–518.

Richards, Alan R. "Primitive Accumulation in Egypt, 1798–1882." In *The Ottoman Empire and the World-Economy*, edited by Huri İslamoğlu-İnan, 203–243. Cambridge: Cambridge University Press, 2004.

Rifaat, Mohammed Ali. *The Monetary System of Egypt*. London: George Allen and Unwin Ltd., 1935.

Roberts, Charles Kenneth. *The Farm Security Administration and Rural Rehabilitation in the South*. Knoxville: University of Tennessee Press, 2015.

Robinson, Cedric J. *Black Marxism: The Making of the Black Radical Tradition*. London: Zed Press, 1983.

Rodgers, Daniel T. *Atlantic Crossings: Social Politics in a Progressive Age*. Cambridge, MA: Harvard University Press, 1998.

Rosenstein-Rodan, Paul N. "Problems of Industrialization of Eastern and South-Eastern Europe." *Economic Journal* 53, no. 210/211 (June–September 1943): 202–211.

Ro'i, Yaacov, and David Ronel, "The Soviet Economic Presence in Egypt and Its Political Implications." Research Paper No. 9, Soviet and East European Research Centre, Hebrew University of Jerusalem, September 1974.

Roy, Manabendra Nath. "An Indian Communist Manifesto." In *Selected Works of M. N. Roy*, Vol. 1, *1917–1922*, edited by Sibnarayan Ray, 161–168. Delhi, New York: Oxford University Press, 1987.

The Royal Government of Egypt, Ministry of Social Affairs. *The Fallāḥ Department*. Cairo: Société Orientale de Publicité Press, 1950.

The Royal Government of Egypt, Ministry of Social Affairs. *Social Welfare in Egypt.* Cairo: Société Orientale de Publicité Press, 1950.

Sa'd, Aḥmad Ṣādiq. "Ḥawl al-'Alāqa Bayn Namaṭay al-Intāj: Al-Kūlūnyālī wa-l-Asyāwī." In *Al-Naẓariyya wa-l-Mumārasa fī Fikr Mahdī 'Āmil, Al-Qiṣm al-Awwal*, 133–154. Beirut: Dār al-Farābī, 1989.

Sa'd, Aḥmad Ṣādiq. *Mushkilat al-Fallāḥ*. Cairo: Dār al-Qarn al-'Ishrīn li-l-Nashr, 1945.

Sa'd, Aḥmad Ṣādiq. *Ṣafaḥāt min al-Yasār al-Miṣrī fī A'qāb al-Ḥarb al-'Ālamiyya al-Thānya, 1945–1946*. Cairo: Maktabat Madbūlī, 1976.

Sa'd, Aḥmad Ṣādiq. *Tarīkh Miṣr al-Ijtimā'ī—al-Iqtiṣādī fī daw' al-Namaṭ al-Asyāwī li-l-Intāj*. Beirut: Dār Ibn Khaldūn li-l-Ṭibā'a wa-l-Nashr, 1979.

Saad, Reem. *Social History of an Agrarian Reform Community in Egypt*. Cairo Papers in Social Science 11, Monograph 4. Cairo: American University in Cairo Press, 1988.

Saad, Reem. "The Two Pasts of Nasser's Peasants: Political Memories and Everyday Life in an Egyptian Village." In *History and the Present*, edited by Partha Chatterjee and Anjan Ghosh, 127–148. New Delhi: Permanent Black Press, 2002.

Sadat, Anwar. *In Search of Identity*. New York: Harper and Row, 1977.

Salem, Sara. *Anticolonial Afterlives in Egypt: The Politics of Hegemony*. Cambridge: Cambridge University Press, 2020.

Ṣāliḥ, Ṣāliḥ Muḥammad. *Al-Iqṭā' wa-l-Ra'smāliyya al-Zirā'iyya fī Miṣr min 'Ahd Muḥammad 'Alī ilā 'Ahd 'Abd al-Nāṣir*. Beirut: Dār Ibn Khaldūn li-l-Ṭibā'a wa-l-Nashr, 1979.

Ṣāliḥ, Aḥmad Rushdī. *Krūmar fī Miṣr: Ṣafaḥāt min Tarīkh Miṣr al-Hadīth*. Cairo: Dār al-Qarn al-'Ishrīn li-l-Nashr, 1945.

Sanchez-Sibony, Oscar. *Red Globalization: The Political Economy of the Soviet Cold War from Stalin to Khrushchev*. New York: Cambridge University Press, 2014.

Sandberg, Lars. *Lancashire in Decline: A Study in Entrepreneurship, Technology, and International Trade*. Columbus: Ohio State University Press, 1974.

Ṣaqr, Bashīr. *Al-Fallāḥūn wa-l-Iqṭā': Qiṣṣat Kifāḥ Qaryat Kamshīsh*. Cairo: Dār al-Marāya li-l-Thaqāfa wa-l-Funūn, 2022.

Saul, Samir. *La France et l'Égypte de 1882 à 1914: Intérêts Économiques et Implications Politiques*. Paris: Comité Pour l'Histoire Économique et Financière de la France, 1997.

Al-Sayyid-Marsot, Afaf Lutfi. *Egypt's Liberal Experiment, 1922–1936*. Berkeley, Los Angeles, and London: University of California Press, 1977.

Schewe, Eric. "State of Siege: The Development of the Security State in Egypt During the Second World War." PhD diss., University of Michigan: 2014.

Schmelzer, Matthias. *The Hegemony of Growth: The OECD and the Making of the Economic Growth Paradigm*. Cambridge: Cambridge University Press, 2016.

Schumpeter, Joseph. *Imperialism and Social Classes: Two Essays by Joseph Schumpeter*. Translated by Heinz Norden. New York: Meridian Books, 1955.

Scott, David. "Colonial Governmentality." *Social Text*, no. 43 (Autumn 1995): 191–220.

Selim, Samah. *The Novel and the Rural Imaginary in Egypt, 1880–1985*. London: Routledge Curzon, 2004.

Selous, G. H. *Economic Conditions in Egypt*, prepared for the Department of Overseas Trade. London: H. M Stationery Office, 1933.

Sewell, Jr., William H. *Logics of History: Social Theory and Social Transformation*. Chicago: University of Chicago Press, 2005.
Sewell, William H., Jr. "The Temporalities of Capitalism." *Socio-Economic Review* 6 (2008): 517–537.
Al-Shāfi'ī, Shuhdī 'Aṭiyya. *Taṭawwur al-Haraka al-Waṭaniyya al-Miṣriyya, 1882–1956*. Cairo: Al-Dār al-Miṣriyya li-l-Ṭibā'a wa-l-Nashr wa-l-Tawzī', 1957.
Shalabī, 'Alī. *Azmat al-Kasād al-'Ālamī al-Kubrā wa-In'ikāsuhā 'alā al-Rīf al-Miṣrī, 1929–1934*. Cairo: Dār al-Shurūq, 2006.
Sharaf al-Dīn, Aḥmad, Ilhāmi al-Mirghanī, and Ṣābir Barakāt. "Kifāḥ 'Ummāl al-Sikka al-Ḥadīd fī Thamānīn 'Āman, 1906–1986." Kurrāsāt Ṣawt al-'Ummāl 1 (n.d.).
Sharikat Miṣr li-l-Ghazl wa-l-Nasīj. *Taqrīr Majlis al-Idāra*. Cairo: Maṭba'at Miṣr, 1939.
Al-Sharqāwī, 'Abd al-Raḥmān. *Al-Arḍ*. Cairo: Dār al-Shurūq, 2017. Reprint of 1954 edition.
Al-Shāṭi', Bint. *Al-Rīf al-Miṣrī*. Cairo: Maktabat wa-Maṭba'at al-Wafd, 1936.
Al-Shāṭi', Bint. *Qadiyyat al-Fallāh*. Cairo: Maktabat al-Nahḍa al-Misriyya, 1938.
Shaṭā, 'Abd al-Hakīm. *Al-Dā'iya Duktūr Ibrāhīm Rashād*. Isma'iliyya: Markaz 'Umar Luṭfi li-l-Tadrīb al-Ta'āwunī al-Zirā'ī, 1989.
Shaw, Bernard. *The Letters of Bernard Shaw to The Times, 1898–1950*. Collected and annotated by Ronald Ford. Dublin: Irish Academic Press, 2007.
Shenker, Jack. *The Egyptians: A Radical Story*. London: Allen Lane, 2016.
Al-Shirbīni, Aḥmad. *Tijārat Miṣr al-Khārijiyya, 1914–1939*. Cairo: Al-Hay'a al-Miṣriyya al-'Āma li-l-Kitāb, 2021.
Shiroyama, Tomoko. *China During the Great Depression: Market, State, and the World Economy, 1929–1937*. Cambridge, MA: Harvard University Press, 2008.
Shokr, Ahmad. "Reflections on Two Revolutions." *Middle East Report*, no. 265 (Winter 2012): 2–12.
Al-Sibā'ī, Bashīr. "Ṣāḍiq Sa'd: Biyūājrāfyā Mūjaza." *Adab wa-Naqd* 44 (February 1989): 30–33.
Sidky, Aziz. "Industrialization of Egypt and a Case Study of the Iron and Steel Industry." PhD diss., Harvard University, 1951.
Sidky, A. R. *The Agricultural Policy in the New Era*. Cairo: Government Printing Press, 1955.
Sidqī, Ismā'īl, *Mudhakkirātī*, 2nd ed. Cairo: Maktabat Madbūlī 1997.
Société de Crédit Foncier Égyptien. *Crédit Foncier Égyptien, 1880–1930*. Draeger, 1930.
Springborg, Robert. *Family, Power, and Politics in Egypt: Sayed Bey Mar'i—His Clan, Clients, and Cohorts*. Philadelphia: University of Pennsylvania Press, 1982.
Stiglitz, Joseph E. "The Myth of America's Golden Age." *Politico Magazine*, July/August 2014. Accessed May 9, 2023. https://www.politico.com/magazine/story/2014/06/the-myth-of-americas-golden-age-108013/.
Stokes, Eric. *The English Utilitarians and India*. Oxford: Clarendon Press, 1959.
Strange, Susan. *Sterling and British Policy: A Political Study of an International Currency in Decline*. London: Oxford University Press, 1971.
Ṣufayr, Anṭūn. *Muḥīṭ al-Sharā'i' 1856–1952*, Vol. 3. Cairo: Al-Maṭba'a al-Amīriyya, 1953.
Al-Ṭahṭāwī, Rifā'a Badawī Rāfi'. *Kitāb al-Jughrāfyā al-'Umūmiyya*. Bulāk, 1841.

Tanksy, Leo. *U.S. and U.S.S.R Aid to Developing Countries: A Comparative Study of India, Turkey, and U.A.R.* New York: Praeger, Inc., 1976.

Takriti, Abdel Razzaq, and Hicham Safieddine. "Arab Socialism." In *The Cambridge History of Socialism*, edited by Marcel van der Linden, 474–516. Cambridge: Cambridge University Press, 2023.

Taylor, Henry C., and Ann Dewess Taylor. *World Trade in Agricultural Products.* New York: Macmillan Co., 1943.

Thompson, Malcolm. "The Birth of the Chinese Population: A Study in the History of Governmental Logics." PhD diss., University of British Columbia, 2013.

Thompson, Warren S. "Population." *American Journal of Sociology* 34, no. 6 (1929): 959–975.

Tignor, Robert L. "Dependency Theory and Egyptian Capitalism, 1920–1950." *African Economic History*, no. 9 (1980): 101–118.

Tignor, Robert L. "The Economic Activities of Foreigners in Egypt, 1920–1950: From Millet to Haut Bourgeoisie." *Comparative Studies in Society and History* 22, no. 3 (July, 1980): 416–449.

Tignor, Robert L. "The Egyptian Revolution of 1919: New Directions in the Egyptian Economy." *Middle Eastern Studies* 12, No. 3, Special Issue on Middle East Economy (October 1976): 41–67.

Tignor, Robert L. *Egyptian Textiles and British Capital, 1930–1956.* Cairo: American University in Cairo Press, 1989.

Tignor, Robert L. "The Introduction of Modern Banking into Egypt, 1855–1920." *Asian and African Studies* 15 (1981): 103–22.

Tignor, Robert L. *State, Private Enterprise, and Economic Change in Egypt, 1918–1952.* Princeton, NJ: Princeton University Press, 1984.

Tignor, Robert L. *W. Arthur Lewis and the Birth of Development Economics.* Princeton, NJ: Princeton University Press, 2005.

Todd, John A. *The Cotton World.* London: Sir Isaac Pitman & Sons Ltd., 1927.

Todd, John A. *The Marketing of Cotton: From the Grower to the Spinner.* London: Sir Isaac Pitman and Sons Ltd., 1934.

Todd, John A. *The World's Cotton Crops.* London: A. and C. Black, 1915.

Tomich, Dale. "Rethinking the Plantation: Concepts and Histories." *Review (Fernand Braudel Center)* 34, no. 1/2 (2011): 15–39.

Tooze, Adam. *The Deluge: The Great War and the Remaking of Social Order, 1916–1931.* London: Penguin Books Ltd., 2014.

Toth, James. *Rural Labor Movements in Egypt and Their Impact on the State, 1961–1992.* Cairo: American University in Cairo Press, 1999.

Tripp, Charles. "Ali Maher and the Politics of the Egyptian Army, 1936–1942." In *Contemporary Egypt: Through Egyptian Eyes: Essays in Honour of Professor P. J. Vatikiotis*, edited by Charles Tripp, 45–71. London; New York: Routledge, 1993.

Truman, Harry S. "Inaugural Address." Speech, Washington, DC, 1949. "Harry S. Truman Presidential Library and Museum." National Library and Records Administration. Accessed April 20, 2023. https://www.trumanlibrary.gov/library/public-papers/19/inaugural-address.

Tucker, Judith. *Women in Nineteenth-Century Egypt*. Cambridge: Cambridge University Press, 1985.

'Ukāsha, Tharwat. *Mudhakkirātī fī al-Siyāsa wa-l-Thaqāfa*, 3rd ed. Cairo: Dār al-Shurūq, 2000.

United Nations Conference on Trade and Development. *The History of UNCTAD, 1964–1984*. New York: United Nations, 1985.

United Nations, Department of Economic Affairs. *Instability in Export Markets of Under-Developed Countries*. New York: United Nations Publication, 1952.

United Nations, Department of Economic and Social Affairs. *The Development of Manufacturing Industry in Egypt, Israel and Turkey*. New York: United Nations Publication, 1958.

United States, Central Intelligence Agency, Directorate of Intelligence. *Special Report: Egyptian Economy Approaching Another Crisis* (August 26, 1966). https://www.cia.gov/readingroom/document/cia-rdp79-00927a005400050003-7.

United States, Department of State. *Land Reform, A World Challenge*. Washington DC, 1952.

United States, Department of State. *The Sino-Soviet Economic Offensive in the Less Developed Countries*. Washington DC, 1958.

United States International Trade Commission. *The History and Current Status of the Multifiber Arrangement*. Washington DC, 1978.

'Uthmān, 'Abd al-Salām. *Al-Bitrūl wa-Iqtiṣādunā al-Qawmī*. Cairo: Maṭba'at Miṣr, 1948.

Vatikiotis, P.J. *Nasser and His Generation*. London: Croom Helm, 1978.

Vaughn, Mary Kay. *Cultural Politics in Revolution: Teachers, Peasants, and Schools in Mexico, 1930–1940*. Tucson: University of Arizona Press, 1997.

Vitalis, Robert. "On the Theory and Practice of Compradors: The Role of Abbud Pasha in the Egyptian Political Economy." *International Journal of Middle East Studies* 22, no. 3 (August 1990): 291–315.

Vitalis, Robert. "The End of Third Worldism in Egyptian Studies." *Arab Studies Journal* 4, no. 1 (Spring 1996): 13–32.

Vitalis, Robert. *When Capitalists Collide: Business Conflict and the End of Empire in Egypt*. Berkeley: University of California Press, 1995.

Wadia, Pestonji Ardesir, and Gulabbhai Naranji Joshi. *A Plea for an Effective Gold Standard in India*. Bombay: Bombay Chronicle Press, 1924.

Wahba, Mourad Magdi. *The Role of the State in the Egyptian Economy, 1945–1981*. Reading: Ithaca Press, 1994.

Waḥīda, Subḥī. *Fī 'Uṣūl al-Mas'ala al-Miṣriyya*. Cairo: Maṭba'at Dār al-Kutub wa-l-Wathā'iq al-Qawmiyya, 2010. Reprint of 1950 edition.

Wallerstein, Immanuel. *The Modern World-System*, vols. I–IV. New York: Academic Press, 1974.

Walsh, Maurice. *Bitter Freedom: Ireland in a Revolutionary World*. New York and London: Liveright Publishing Corporation, 2015.

Warriner, Doreen. *Land Reform and Development in the Middle East: A Study of Egypt, Syria, and Iraq*, 2nd ed. London: Oxford University Press, 1962.

Waterbury, John. *The Egypt of Nasser and Sadat: The Political Economy of Two Regimes.* Princeton, NJ: Princeton University Press, 1983.

West, Consul George. "Report by Consul George West on the Trade and Commerce of the Port of Suez for 1872." In *Commercial Reports, Accounts, and Papers*, LXIV, 1873.

Westad, Odd Arne. *The Global Cold War: Third World Interventions and the Making of Our Times.* New York: Cambridge University Press, 2007.

White, Richard. *Railroaded: The Transcontinentals and the Making of Modern America.* New York: W. W. Norton & Company Inc., 2011.

Wiener, Lionel. *L'Egypte et Ses Chemins de Fer.* Brussels: M. Weissenbruch, 1932.

Williams, Eric. *Capitalism and Slavery.* Chapel Hill: University of North Carolina Press, 1944.

Wilmington, Martin W. *The Middle East Supply Center.* Albany, NY: State University of New York Press, 1971.

Wizārat al-Māliyya, *Mizāniyyat al-Dawla al-Miṣriyya.* Cairo: Al-Maṭba'a al-Amīriyya (multiple years from 1919 to 1939).

World Cotton Conference. *Official Report of the World Cotton Conference.* Liverpool, June 13–15, 1921; Manchester, June 16–22, 1921.

Wright, Arnold, ed., *Twentieth Century Impressions of Egypt: Its History, People, Commerce, Industries, and Resources.* London: Lloyd's Greater Britain Publishing Company Ltd., 1909.

Yūnis, Sharīf. *Nidā' al-Sha'b: Tarīkh Naqdī li-l-'Īdyūlūjiyyā al-Nāṣiriyya.* Cairo: Dār al-Shurūq, 2012.

Yousef, Tarik M. "The Political Economy of Interwar Egyptian Cotton Policy." *Explorations in Economic History* 37 (2000): 301–325.

Yaqub, Salim. *Containing Arab Nationalism: The Eisenhower Doctrine and the Middle East.* Chapel Hill: University of North Carolina Press, 2004.

Zahra, M. A., and M. El-Darwish. *A Statistical Study of Some of the Factors Affecting the Price of Egyptian Cotton.* Cairo: Government Press, 1930.

Zannis, Joseph. *Le Crédit Agricole en Egypte.* Paris: La Librairie Technique et Économique, 1937.

INDEX

Abaza, 'Abdullah Fikri, 106
Abaza, Mona, 31, 34–35
Abbasid caliphate, 180, 181
'Abbud, Ahmad, 60, 247n115
'Abd al-Fattah, Fathi, 272n167
'Abd al-Karim, Muhammad, 165, 166
'Abd al-Rahman, 'A'isha, 144
Abdel Wahab, Ahmad, 94, 102, 105, 108, 114–117, 122, 134, 135; memorandum, 95
Abdel-Fadil, Mahmoud, 28, 202
Abdel-Malek, Anouar, 161, 221, 222
Abu al-Futuh, Muhammad, 63, 64
Abu Qurqas, Egypt, 106
Achcar, Gilbert, 176
activism, 4, 157, 172, 173, 229; communist, 222; George Bernard Shaw, 74; labor, 119, 120, 121; nationalist, 60, 156; rural, 200; Salah Husayn, 224; Sayyid Mar'i, 198
Adams, Richard, 201
Al-'Adawi, Zuhdi, 85f
Adly, Amr, 229
Administration of State Domain (Maslahat al-Amlak al-Amiriyya), 131, 163
'afandiyya (urban, middle-class intellectuals/professionals), 83
'Afifi, Hafiz, 145, 167
Africa, 4, 20, 36, 91, 195, 216; Africans, 239–240n48; Algeria, 263n91; East, 68; North, 159, 160; Sudan, 38, 240n56
agrarian production, 83, 247n120
agrarian reform, 79–80, 197–199; Free Officers' land policies, 24, 221; Higher Committee for Agrarian Reform (HCAR), 198; peasant cooperatives, 200, 218. *See also* land distribution/redistribution
agrarian reformers, 14, 24, 82, 170, 173, 176, 178, 205; Free Officers, 221; Husayn on, 128; Irish, 72, 74; Mirit Ghali, 172, 199; post-World War I, 79; Sayyid Mar'i, 199
agrarianism, 74
agricultural banks, 17, 23, 24, 129, 134, 142; Agricultural Bank, 33, 136
Agricultural Club (Al-Nadi al-Zira'i), 70
Agricultural Credit and Cooperative Bank, 198, 202. *See also* Crédit Agricole
Agricultural Ministry, 77
agricultural rent, 81, 131–133, 163, 164, 238n2
agricultural surplus, 68, 267n51; American, 212; appropriating, 80, 85, 141, 175, 196, 208; extraction, 26, 187; funds, 160

Ahmad, Muhammad, 131
al-Ajhuri, Ahmad Sadiq, 121
Alexandria, Egypt, 113, 118, 125; banks in, 46, 47, 158; British exporters in, 42; British Institute, 206; cotton exporters in, 46, 116; cotton market in, 22, 26, 33, 41, 159; cotton shipments to, 36, 106, 110, 203, 208; cotton storage in, 114; cotton trade in, 82, 111; cotton weighing in, 119f; Egyptian Delta Light Railways Company office in, 35; exchanges in, 88; export houses in, 43, 68, 70, 111, 117, 122; foreign-resident merchants based in, 56; futures markets in, 66, 207; governorate, 121; landholders, 146; merchants in, 15, 39, 65, 126, 247n115; Mixed Courts in, 98; police, 120; railway lines connecting, 34; spot market in, 69, 121; subgovernor of, 120; trading houses in, 17, 70, 89, 115; westernized elite, 147
Alexandria Bourse, 46, 69, 82, 91, 115; board of directors, 68; commodity trading, 44; consolidation of, 45; people registered on, 71, 72; price of cotton on, 32, 53; Wafd restrictions on, 67
Alexandria General Produce Association (AGPA), 252n115; cotton trade monopoly, 16, 26, 44, 83, 111–113, 115–122; large landowners against, 71, 83; Nahhas condemns, 68; presides over spot market, 41, 43–45; requires railways and roads, 16; subordination to national government, 127; A. W. Jessop, 70; Wafd restrictions on, 67, 95
Algeria, 263n91
Ali, Mehmed, 18, 153, 181, 182, 183; feudalism under, 222; military and, 170; modernization under, 15, 27, 178
Allam, Mahmoud, 133–134
Alliance for Progress, 194
Allied troops, 24, 160, 161, 202
American South (U.S.), 27, 52, 88, 90, 214
Americas, 239–240n48; Latin America, 91, 194, 195, 216, 232, 266n18, 273n14; North America, 46, 194; South America, 104
Amin, Samir, 232
'Amir, Ibrahim, 30, 222
Ammar, Abbas Mustafa, 146
'Anan, Husayn, 151
Anglo-Egyptian Condominium, 38
Anglo-Egyptian Oilfields Ltd., 202
Anglo-Egyptian Treaty of 1936, 202, 259–260n4, 261n44
Anglo-Iranian Oil Company, 206
Anis, Muhammad, 224, 262n63
anti-colonialism, 2, 19, 21, 53–56, 73, 76, 166, 223. *See also* colonialism
anti-communist containment, 211
anti-feudalism, 224
anti-imperialism, 6, 12, 229
anti-landlordism, 24, 177
anti-privatization, 229
anti-Soviet containment, 212
Arab intellectuals, 180
Arab oil exporters, 220
Arab socialism, 223, 235–236n16
Arab Socialist Union (ASU), 223, 224
Arab solidarity, 6, 12
Arabic (language), 3, 42, 73, 179
Argentinians, 194
Arrighi, Giovanni, 48, 123
al-'Ashmawi, Muhammad, 146
Ashmouni (cultivar), 95, 102, 206
'Ashur, Muhammad Badrawi, 80–81, 177
Asia, 195, 200; Asiatic mode of production, 186; Bengal, 142; capital destruction in, 230; China, 88, 90, 142, 199, 216, 217; communists, 4; cotton consumption in, 92; cotton transport to, 159; East, 91, 197; impoverishment of, 36; Indonesia, 220; in International Railway Congress Association, 104; Korea, 164, 175, 176, 206, 266n22; non-communist states in, 216; North Vietnam, 216; Pakistan, 211; political movements in, 20; South, 152, 239–240n48, 273n11. *See also* India; Japan

Associated Cotton Ginners of Egypt Ltd., 247n109
Association Committee, 45
Association of Produce Brokers, 44
Aswan Dam, 60, 169, 214–216
Asyut province, 66, 139, 208
'Atf, Egypt, 107
'Atiyya, Shuhdi, 222
Austrians, 19, 72
Avaro, Maylis, 210
Avigdor, Samuel, 99
Axis powers, 159, 160
a'yan (notables), 100
Ayrout, Henri, 146–147
Ayyubid Empire, 181

backwardness, 13, 77, 142, 144, 170, 191, 193; agrarian, 165; al-Barrawi's theory of, 182; economic, 2, 4, 24, 187; revolution against, 221, 223, 227
Badrawi 'Ashur, Muhammad, 80–81, 177
Baghdad Pact, 211
Baguriyya canal, 107
baling, 114. *See also* cotton processing
Bandung conference, 212, 214
Banha, Egypt, 247n109, 252n102
Bani Mazar, Egypt. *See* Minya Province
Bani Swayf, Egypt, 140, 208, 247n109
Bank Misr, 123, 125, 167, 183; in Egyptian institutionalization, 55; financial crisis, 261n44; funds Crédit Agricole, 135; investors affiliated with, 161; Misr Spinning and Weaving Company, 59, 165; Muhammad Rushdi of, 166; policies, 178; provides advances to cooperatives, 77; subsidiary firms under, 111
Bank of England, 47, 49, 210, 211
Bank of Rome, 249n25
Barclays Bank, 117, 137
barges, 106, 107, 108, 109f, 204. *See also* shipping
al-Barrawi, Rashid, 1–5, 178–182, 190, 221, 271n162; on farming, 175; on July Revolution, 13; landownership ceiling law, 197; Revolutionary Command Council meetings, 188; on Truman's Point Four program, 191–192
Beattie, Kirk, 7
Beckert, Sven, 55
Belgium, 38, 240n56, 251n81
Ben Bella, Ahmed, 263n91
Bengal, 142
Berque, Jacques, 257n60
Bey, Fitzpatrick, 120
Bey Radi, Mustafa, 100
bourgeoisie, 60, 106, 183, 232; industrial, 8, 135, 170; intellectuals, 173; mercantile, 27, 159; national, 7, 55, 215, 230, 266n18; reformers, 167; writers, 154
Bourse de Mina al-Basal, 41, 44, 69, 111, 117, 121
Brazil, 27, 68, 88, 90, 96, 194
Bresciani-Turroni, Constantino, 94, 123, 249n25
Bretton Woods system, 58, 191, 192, 233
British Empire, 5, 18, 38, 210; imperial geography of, 46; independence from, 73; industrial engine, 88; inspectors, 32, 239n24; international monetary network of, 47; monetary nationalism, 125; resistance against, 72; weakening of, 124; world economy, 48. *See also* United Kingdom/Great Britain
British Government Cotton Buying Commission, 159
British India, 52, 88, 90, 96, 153. *See also* India
British occupation, 27, 29, 152, 182; agrarian reformers against, 170; al-Barrawi condemns, 2; cotton expansion under, 62, 174, 184; creates mortgage sector, 99–100; Egypt's overpopulation under, 143; modern subjectivities efforts, 153–154; Nationalist Party opposes, 73; policies, 243–244n38; Sa'd Zaghlul criticizes, 64; Tal'at Harb criticizes, 58
British Residency, 99, 111, 125, 140, 246n83

British rule, 20, 49, 83, 123, 152, 243–244n38
Brussels, Belgium, 240n56, 251n81
Buhayra province, 35, 131, 149f, 247n109
Buhut, Egypt, 176
Bulgaria, 216
bureaucracy, 10, 45, 142, 160, 198, 205, 208, 232; AGPA appeals to, 117; agrarian, 24, 201; bureaucratization, 200; Mar'i empowers, 199; under Nasser, 127; Rashad on, 148, 200; system of railway administration, 38

Cairo Declaration of Developing Countries, 195
Cairo University, 168, 178, 258n73
Caisse de la Dette Publique, 38
Cambridge, England, 72, 73
canals, 16, 31, 152; Baguriyya, 107; Isma'iliyya, 107; Mahmudiyya, 41, 107, 252n93; Manchester Ship Canal, 252n90; Suez Canal, 12, 36, 159, 210; Suez Canal Company, 119, 215, 220, 222; Suez Canal Consultative Working Commission, 252n90
capital accumulation, 38, 92, 104, 237n53
capitalism, 14, 22, 37, 126, 226, 272n167; development, 8, 74, 174, 183, 232; domination, 9; Egyptian, 75, 161, 166, 178–188, 247n115; growth, 179; monopolies and, 1, 2, 4, 5, 7, 22, 176, 271–272n164; social relations, 184, 247–248n121; systems of, 184; temporality, 9, 10; Western European, 74, 231
capitalization, 165
Carver, Herbert, 42–43, 116
Carver Brothers & Co., 43, 70, 140, 160
Carver family, 111
cash crop production, 15, 21, 29, 30, 37, 162, 207; devastation of, 11, 171; during Great Depression, 90; under Mehmed Ali, 222
Central Navigation, 106
centralization, 21, 22, 224
cepalinos, 194, 266n18, 273n14
Chamber of Deputies (Majlis al-Nuwwab), 83
Chamber of Inland Navigation of Egypt, 105
Chayanov, Alexander V., 75
Chile, 138, 194
China, 90, 142, 199, 216, 217; civil war, 88
Chinese, 92, 247n120; communists, 186, 247n120, 265n129
Choremi (company), 43, 160
Chorémi, Constantin J., 116, 160
Cleland, Wendel, 257n60
cloth (*khadi*), 166, 246n97
Cold War, 194; demographic transition theory, 143; Egypt's cotton industry during, 209–220; geopolitics of, 18, 227; Nasserism's national development project compromised, 13; postcolonial states emerge during, 4; superpowers during, 202, 232
collectivization, 75, 175, 198, 263n88
colonialism, 155, 191, 227, 232, 235–236n16; agrarian foundation under, 21; capitalist system under, 184; dependence under, 226; development under, 5, 8; economic life under, 177; feudalism allied with, 2; Free Officers against, 187; national bourgeoisies under, 215; no industrialization under, 55, 181; Scott on, 152; struggles against, 76; workers under, 168. *See also* anti-colonialism
Comintern, 75
commodities, 26, 34, 53, 56, 63; agreements, 194; agricultural, 74, 90, 212; exportable, 114; fetishism of, 247n121; frontier, 18, 159, 237n53; Hamadi on, 207; monocrop, 18; production, 9, 10, 31, 132, 237n53; raw, 14, 96, 184, 196; trading, 44, 46; transport of, 16, 35, 108
communism, 75, 197, 199, 223; Egyptian, 182; international, 204
communists, 7, 171–173, 215, 222, 223, 231, 272n167; anti-communism, 211; Chi-

nese, 247n120, 265n129; Communist Bloc, 216; Communist Party of Egypt, 183; Communist Party of France, 265n141; Communist Party of the Soviet Union, 215; Curiel, 188; Egyptian, 7, 230, 265n141; Egyptian Communist Party, 157; parties, 272n167; Sadiq Sa'd, 173; Second Congress of the Communist International, 75; United Communist Party of Egypt, 222
companies: American, 205; banking, 17, 247n120; ginning, 59, 247n109; insurance, 247n120; joint-stock, 104, 161, 207–208; land, 61, 79, 176; mortgage, 17, 70, 79, 99, 102, 104; navigation, 105–106, 108–110; pressing, 114; real estate, 79; trading, 45, 79, 115, 229; transport, 79; truck, 203; wagon, 118
compradors, 7, 55, 232, 247n115
concessionary accumulation, 15, 18–22, 23, 212
constitution (1923), 94
constitution (1956), 5, 67, 221
contract market. *See* futures market
Cook, Edward, 88, 125, 127
cooperative societies, 23, 77, 137, 139, 142, 147, 150, 199; agricultural, 148; help reorganize cotton management, 20; as national institutions, 205
cooperatives movement, 147, 148, 263n88
cotton buying campaigns, 20, 66–68, 91, 94, 95, 132, 135
cotton exporting, 53, 95, 140, 196, 211, 217; exporters, 43, 45, 46, 96, 110, 248n18, 249n31; transportation, 109, 110, 205, 252n97
cotton growing, 1, 25, 28, 36, 52, 215, 238n2
cotton merchants, 44, 206; agricultural syndicate against, 70; in Alexandria, 65; as *compradors*, 247n115; in cotton transport, 63; interest in price volatility, 69; in navigation companies, 109; small cultivators borrow from, 34, 103, 133, 135; under state control, 46
cotton prices, 54f, 238n2, 245n64
cotton processing: ginning/pressing, 42f, 114, 115, 117, 237n46, 238n2; spinning/weaving, 27, 28, 92–93, 111, 165, 170, 246n97, 248n18; transportation, 109, 110, 205, 252n97; weighing, 43, 118–119, 119f, 121, 160, 254n138. *See also* ginneries/ginners; spinners
cotton production, 15, 34; British investments expand, 27, 28; children work in, 31; during Cold War, 209; during Great Depression, 89; Nasser increases, 214; Nile Valley depends on, 61; organizing, 32; peasant cultivators, 34, 103, 133, 135; Rashad's three step process, 78; Sakelleridis, 53; world, 91f, 96; World Cotton Conference, 242n1
cotton quality, 43, 67, 112, 115, 122, 245n74
Cotton Research Board, 44, 65, 76, 113
cotton trade, 14, 140, 193, 206; Abu al-Futuh's proposal for, 64; AGPA's role in, 44, 45, 83, 120; from Alexandria, 82; Egyptian merchants in, 89; export houses/trading firms, 111, 159; export policies, 59, 111, 214; Free Officers' intervention, 116, 207–209; global, 14; during Great Depression, 96, 126; licensed weighers in, 254n138; merchant capital invested in, 117; migrants in, 43; Mina al-Basal strike, 120; Misr Cotton Ginning and Trading Company in, 59; small cultivators and merchants, 72, 116; wartime regulations, 160–161; World Cotton Conference, 242n1
cotton traders, 84, 116, 140, 207; AGPA, 16, 83; Muhammad Farghali, 111, 206
Council of Agricultural Trade (Lajnat al-Tijara al-Zira'iyya), 63
Craig, James I., 93, 94
Crédit Agricole, 125, 134–139, 140–141, 147–148, 150, 151, 198, 200
Crédit Foncier Égyptien, 17, 53, 79, 98, 99, 102–104, 135, 145; Litigation Department of, 138

Crédit Hypothécaire d'Egypte, 138
Cromer, Lord (Evelyn Baring), 39, 143; administration of, 33, 136, 183
Cuba, 194, 195, 220
Curiel, Henry, 182, 188
currency, 192, 210; Egyptian pound, 33, 50, 123, 124, 125, 126, 218; foreign, 208; gold, 46–49, 53, 123–126, 210; hard, 193–196, 209–210, 212–213, 216–217, 219; imperial, 212; local, 46, 212; national, 48, 123, 126, 192, 193; paper, 47, 50
Czechoslovakia, 216, 217

al-Daghashi, Muhammad Subhi, 166, 170
dahabias (small wooden sailboats), 106
daira (royal estate), 25, 51
daira saniyya (foreign loans), 15, 213
Damanhur, Egypt, 43, 138, 247n109
Daqahliyya province, 1, 35, 132, 176, 185, 200, 247n109
Dayrut, Egypt, 247n109
Decauville (railway), 35
decolonization, 5, 6–14, 190, 215, 222; in Egyptian Nile Valley, 14; global, 4; long, 12, 13
defense, 65, 103, 125, 261n44. *See also* military
deficits, 124; balance of payments, 123, 219, 267n51; budget, 159; trade, 47, 196
Delta Light Railways, 35, 203
Democratic Movement for National Liberation (DMNL), 182, 187–188, 222
Department of Agriculture, Egypt, 44, 63, 76, 113
Department of Agriculture, U.S., 212
dependence, 13, 61, 132; on cotton exports, 196; on foreign markets, 22, 57, 88, 170; on global superpowers, 191, 220, 227; on imports, 168, 171, 199; market, 22, 51, 54; on Soviet Union, 218; technological, 24, 220; on trade, 211, 219
dependentistas, 195, 273n14
Derr, Jennifer, 142
despotism, 220, 235–236n16
destabilization, 22, 51, 56, 87, 89, 192. *See also* price stabilization
developing countries, 193, 194, 213; Cairo Declaration of Developing Countries, 195; Egypt as, 200, 214, 218. *See also* Third World
development, 246n97, 266n21, 272n167
development economics, 24, 58, 158, 168, 171
developmentalism, 3, 8, 178
al-Din, Fu'ad Siraj, 177, 206
distribution, 147, 150, 161, 198, 247–248n121; of advances for cotton cultivation, 149f; cotton, 117; of goods and services, 248n121; social, 2, 190, 223; water, 65; of wealth, 173; of working population, 162
Dudgeon, Gerald, 63
Dulles, John Foster, 214, 215
Dunn, Read, Jr., 163, 164, 185

Economic Commission for Latin America and the Caribbean (CEPAL), 194
economic democracy, 4
economic determinism, 145
economic growth, 11, 17, 124, 168, 191, 192
economic nationalism, 22, 58, 82; in interwar period, 56; post-World War I, 54, 164–165, 170, 177; pre-World War I, 242n11; Rashad and, 77, 79; views on large landholders, 83, 158
Economic Peasant (*Al-Fallah al-Iqtisadi*), 149, 150
economic specialization, 2
Edwards, Francis M., 32, 90, 91, 239n24
Egyptian Association for Social Studies (EASS), 146, 150, 178
Egyptian capitalism, 75, 161, 178–188
Egyptian communism, 7, 182, 222, 265n141; movement, 173, 230; parties, 157, 183, 188, 222
Egyptian Cooperative Association, 71
Egyptian Cotton Commission (ECC), 160, 207, 208

Egyptian Delta Light Railways Company, 35
Egyptian Federation of Industries. *See* Federation of Egyptian Industries
Egyptian General Cotton Organization, 208
Egyptian Socialist Party, 157, 263n91
Egyptian Star Navigation, 106
Egyptian State Railways (ESR), 38, 39, 107, 203, 240n65; cotton carried by, 35, 36; dieselization of, 202, 205; monopoly of, 16, 26, 40; navigation companies and, 108, 109, 110
Egyptian state revenue, 62f
Egyptian Sugar Company, 63–64
Egyptian-Czechoslovak arms deal, 212, 216
Eichengreen, Barry, 124
Eisenhower, Dwight D., 204, 212, 214, 215
El Shakry, Omnia, 12, 142, 143
El-Darwish, Mahmoud, 93, 94
El-Gritly, Ali, 168–169
Eman, André, 167
Emmanuel, Arghiri, 266n16
empires, 19; Austro-Hungarian, 20; Ayyubid, 181; European, 19; Fatimid, 180, 181; Muslim, 179; Ottoman, 64, 181; Russian, 20. *See also* British Empire
Engels, Friedrich, 3
engineers, 35, 247n120; civil, 252n90; E. W. Slaughter, 110; Henry Ashman Reed, 107; irrigation, 143; Muhammad Shafiq Jabr, 138
England, 35, 37, 72, 74, 125; agricultural revolution, 181–182; Bank of England, 47, 49, 210, 211; Cambridge, 72, 73; cotton consumption, 92–93; Egyptian Nile Valley tied to, 60; El-Gritly in, 168; Farghali in, 111; labor disputes in, 88; leads international railway commission, 16, 39; Liverpool, 52, 67, 88, 93, 241n87; Manchester, 52, 55, 58, 71, 72, 88, 111, 210–211; officials, 70; Rashad in, 73; Royal Agricultural College, 73; spinning, 67, 94, 96, 115, 116; textile manufacturers, 14, 18; trade union movement, 248n18; Utilitarians, 153. *See also* Europe, Western; Lancashire, England; United Kingdom/Great Britain
Entente Cordiale, 40
Europe, 76, 147, 158, 247n120, 258n73, 259–260n4; Austria, 19, 72; Austro-Hungarian Empire, 20; Bulgaria, 216; Central, 19, 169; cotton manufacturers, 45, 115; Czechoslovakia, 216, 217; Eastern, 19, 169, 217; Egyptian cotton prices to, 68; Egyptian cotton shipped to, 41; feudal, 184; Holland, 199; Hungary, 216; International Railway Congress Association session, 104; Italy, 27, 61, 72, 94, 159, 199, 202, 249n25; loan repayment to, 37; maritime transport with North Africa, 159; mechanized production in, 183; medieval, 180; Poland, 216; political atmosphere in, 48; price of clothing from, 52–53; Rashad in, 72; reformers, 74; Romania, 216; Sweden, 210; Switzerland, 210; telegraph to Egypt, 241n87; textile manufacturers, 63; wage-laborers in, 239–240n48; Warsaw Pact countries, 196, 209
Europe, Western, 187, 193, 240n56; Belgium, 38, 240n56, 251n81; capitalism, 74, 231; as center of international trade, 213; cotton exports to, 22, 26, 217; economy, 221; Egyptians get graduate degrees in, 168; gold standard, 124; history of, 179; Holland, 199; Ireland, 72, 73, 74, 120; landownership model, 186; manufacturing interests in, 52; post-World War II, 191, 230; railway-related imports from, 38; raw materials exported to, 34; spinners, 46; Switzerland, 210; trading partners in, 57. *See also* England; France; Germany; United Kingdom/Great Britain
exporters, 69, 114, 115, 117, 194; Alexandria-based, 116, 122; British, 42, 124; cotton, 43, 45, 46, 96, 110, 248n18; merchant, 33; oil, 220

exports, 121; agricultural, 205; cotton, 18, 53, 95, 159, 196, 209; of developing countries, 194; from Egypt, 249n31; Farghali's, 111; imports vs., 123; manufactured, 214; primary, 56, 57; raw materials, 90; returns on, 217; seed, 66; to socialist countries, 216; to United Kingdom, 211; wheat, 213

extra-economic coercion, 9, 15, 239–240n48

Fabian socialism, 3, 166

factionalism, 7

Fajardo, Margarita, 194

al-Fajr al-Jadid (New Dawn), 173, 183

Fallah Department, 128, 146, 151, 162, 163, 178, 185

Farghali, Muhammad, 111, 206

Farouk, King, 158

Farrer, Lord, 240n65

Fatimid Empire, 180, 181

al-Fayyum, Egypt, 99, 146, 247n109

Federation of Egyptian Industries, 55, 60, 105, 170

fellaheen, 71, 128, 141, 147, 151

feluccas (small wooden sailboats), 106

fetishism, 247–248n121

fetishization, 83, 84, 85, 226, 227, 233

feudalism, 223, 225f; abolition of, 188, 221, 231; al-Barrawi on, 2, 4, 271n162; Egyptian communists' view of, 7; elimination of, 5; feudalists, 225f, 271n162; *iqta'iyya*, 179, 180; *'izba* owners in, 21, 158, 230; July Revolution and, 14; large landowners in, 186; under Mehmed Ali, 222; in Middle East, 273n11; Muhammad Anis on, 224; Nahhas on, 180; *nizam al-iqta'*, 158, 179, 180; per classical political economists, 179; Poliak on, 181; Rashad on, 200; rentier accumulation as, 187; Schumpeter on, 19; semi-feudalism, 182, 184, 265n129; serfdom, 37, 180, 182; to socialism, 22, 183;

filyarat (contracts), 69

financial institutions, 47, 123, 125, 134, 137, 249n25; Agricultural Bank, 33, 136; Bank of England, 47, 49, 210, 211; Bank of Rome, 249n25; Barclays Bank, 117, 137; Crédit Foncier Égyptien, 17, 53, 79, 98, 99, 102–104, 135, 145; Crédit Hypothécaire d'Egypte, 138; International Bank for Reconstruction and Development, 193, 249n25; Land and Mortgage Company of Egypt, 17, 79, 98, 99; Land Bank of Egypt, 17, 98, 99, 104; Mortgage Company of Egypt, 17, 103; Société Foncière d'Égypte, 98; World Bank, 192, 214. *See also* agricultural banks; Bank Misr; Crédit Agricole; National Bank of Egypt

financiers, 26, 97, 147; AGPA as, 43; convene World Cotton Conference, 52; Egypt ruled by, 180; foreign, 34, 37, 124, 177, 178; merchant, 14, 18, 69, 82, 83, 84, 247n120; support Crédit Agricole, 136

Five Feddan Law, 34, 134, 135

Fordist industrial production, 166

Fordist-Keynesian accumulation, 231

foreign exchange, 193, 194, 195, 196, 202, 209, 214, 217; reserves, 123, 210, 218

Foreign Operations Administration (FAO), 204, 268n66

Foucault, Michel, 259n116

Foulon, M. E., 104

France, 39, 158, 181, 211, 215; banks, 17; Communist Party of France, 265n141; cotton markets, 159; in Egyptian cotton consumption and trade, 92, 93; Entente Cordiale, 40; French people, 16, 27, 35, 72, 98, 230, 266n16; French Revolution, 179; French School of Law (Cairo), 64, 90, 167; manufactures, 38; Paris, 57, 64, 95; School of Law in Cairo, 90; wartime policies, 210; weapons, 212

Free Officers, 155, 225, 271n162; abide by rules of international order, 12–13; Beattie on, 7; DMNL supports, 222; against economic backwardness, 4; economic

policies/reforms, 191, 196, 201, 205, 209, 215, 216; leaders, 1, 187, 189; legitimization of, 220, 226; national development under, 5, 21, 155; phases under Nasser, 6; program to abolish feudalism, 188; as progressive force, 231; role in Egyptian history, 230; seek assistance from Soviet Union, 212; seize power, 11, 17, 127; view of small farmers, 176
Free Officers' Revolt, 28, 151, 200, 203; collectivization and, 198; cotton nationalization and, 207; Egypt's transportation system and, 204; as fascist coup, 265n141; Hassuna on, 221
Fu'ad, King, 98, 245n74
Fu'ad I University, 2, 12, 178. *See also* Cairo University
fuel, 105; coal, 37, 38, 52, 202; diesel, 202, 203, 205; oil, 202, 203, 206, 220; petroleum, 111, 202, 203, 220
futures market, 66, 115, 206, 241n87; affects spot market, 45; of Alexandria, 41, 44; effects on cotton prices, 69, 71, 92; government eliminates, 207; in Great Depression, 67; state interventions into, 46. *See also* Alexandria Bourse

G77, 266n21
Gandhi, Mohandas Karamchand, 166, 246n97
Gaza Strip, Palestine, 212
General Agreement on Tariffs and Trade (GATT), 214
General Egyptian Agricultural Syndicate, 55, 64, 94, 98, 100, 101
General Motors, 205
Germany, 259–260n4; East Germany, 216, 217; Egyptian cotton markets for, 138; Germans, 138, 247n120; industrialization, 58; manufacturers, 38, 111; markets, 158, 159; Mediterranean military presence, 202; Nazis, 158, 159; war reparations, 94; warships and submarines, 49
Ghali, Mirit Butrus, 145, 167, 172, 173, 174, 176, 185
Gharbiyya province, 35, 101, 176, 247n109
Ghonemy, Mohamed Riad, 146, 162, 164, 260n25
ginneries/ginners, 26, 46, 117, 203, 208; Associated Cotton Ginners of Egypt Ltd., 247n109; cooperative, 78; cotton transport to, 35, 43, 109, 110; Misr Cotton Ginning and Trading Company, 59, 252n102
ginning, 42, 80, 111, 114, 203; costs of, 65; managers, 113; moneylenders' role in, 134; monopolies on, 237n46; regulations, 160; steam power in, 238n4
Girga Province, 66
Giza, Egypt, 91, 95, 139
global depression. *See* Great Depression
Global North, 266n16
Global South, 55, 192, 200, 212, 226, 266n16
global superpowers, 13, 18, 24, 190, 191, 213, 226; bipolarity, 215; during Cold War, 202, 232; discipline nationalist leaders, 214; Egypt's dependence on, 220, 227; Egypt's trade agreements with, 196; Soviet Union as, 211
globalization, 19, 126
gold standard, 46–49, 53, 123–126, 210
Goldberg, Ellis, 67
Gordon, Joel, 8–9
governmental accumulation, 18–22
governmentality. *See* rural governmentality
governmentalization, 259n116
Graves, R. M., 119
Great Depression, 17, 20, 23, 68, 71, 86, 90, 124; Alexandria export houses during, 111; cotton production during, 89; Crédit Agricole creation, 134–139; effects in Egyptian Nile Valley, 87; effects on landholders, 137; effects on traders, 87; futures market during, 67; Minost on, 157; monopolistic domains change during, 126–127; mortgage crisis during, 99; Sidqi government policies

Great Depression (*cont.*)
for, 95; welfare states help overcome, 229
Greeks, 16, 27, 43, 72

HADITU. *See* Democratic Movement for National Liberation (DMNL)
al-Hakim, Tawfiq, 144
halaqas (local markets), 43, 118
Halim, ʿAbbas, 120
Halton, W. F., 38
Hamadi, M. M., 206, 207
al-Hamid, Ahmad Nazmi ʿAbd, 177, 178
Hamrush, Ahmad, 188
Harb, Talʿat, 54, 58–60, 106, 111, 135, 205
Hartley, H. Clayton, 61
Harvey, David, 230
Hasanayn, Magdi, 198
Hashim, Zaki, 193, 265n12
Hassuna, Muhammad Amin, 221
Heaps, W., 116
Higher Committee for Agrarian Reform (HCAR), 198, 221
Higher Committee for the Liquidation of Feudalism, 224
Higher Council for Cooperatives, 77
Higher Council for Social Reform, 146
Hirdan, ʿUthman, 139
Hobsbawm, Eric, 19
Holland, 199
housing, 9, 144, 145, 165, 167, 172, 261n45
Hungary, 216
Husayn, Ahmad, 128–129, 146, 150, 151
Husayn, Salah, 224–225
Husayn, Taha, 145

Ibrahim, Yahya, 70
imperialism, 4, 5, 8, 187, 232, 271n162; age of, 192; agents of, 247n115; anti-imperialism, 6, 12, 229; British, 19, 34, 183, 211; Chinese employees, 247n120; collaborators, 247n120; of *compradors*, 247n115; economic, 179; Free Officers and, 271n162; New Imperialism, 47; Western, 48, 157, 215, 221
import-substitution industrialization (ISI), 54, 57, 62, 196
India, 36, 142, 211; colonialism, 152, 153; cotton exports, 52, 90, 211; cotton fields in, 88; cotton harvest in, 46; cotton prices, 96; cotton season, 47; cultivators, 27; Indians, 75, 125, 152, 166, 246n97
individualism, 78, 79
Indonesia, 220, 247n120
industrial societies, 76, 184, 246n97
industrialists, 61, 68, 86, 135, 166, 171, 247n120
industrialization, 213, 216, 242n11; centrally planned, 6; under colonialism, 181; domestic, 55; ethos, 168; five-year plan for, 217; foreign exchange and, 193, 209; of Germany, 58; in Ghali's and Saʿd's treatises, 172; import-substitution, 54, 57, 62, 195, 196; indigenous, 55; industry without, 57–63; land reform and, 8, 24, 157, 178; machine-driven, 170; Minost on, 157; Nasser's program of, 17, 169, 218; in national development, 21; state-led, 11, 166, 169, 190, 194, 223; textile, 167; transport needed for, 204; of United Kingdom/Great Britain, 72; Western-style, 76, 192
inflation, 23, 47, 83, 160, 164, 206; of cotton prices, 69, 96, 226n22; land value, 100; of reserve funds, 102
Inspection Office. *See* London Inspection Office
inspectors, 32, 76, 113, 114, 128, 239n24
institutionalization, 77, 134, 195
International Bank for Reconstruction and Development, 193, 249n25
International Cotton Congress, 71, 95
International Federation of Master Cotton Spinners' and Manufacturers Association, 115–116

international financial system, 19, 48, 249n25, 266n21
International Institute of Agriculture, 92
International Monetary Fund (IMF), 192, 218, 220
International Railway Congress Association, 104–105, 251n81
international trade and monetary systems, 57, 79, 80, 123, 212, 266n21; Bretton Woods system, 58, 191, 192, 233; British Empire international monetary network, 47; centers of trade, 213; devaluation, 218; Free Officers' trade policies, 17, 21; gold standard, 46–49, 53, 123–126, 210; IMF, 192, 218, 220; postwar global order, 191, 193; Short- and Long-Term Arrangements Regarding International Trade in Cotton Textiles, 214; sterling exchange standard, 123, 126, 210; trade agreements, 124, 196, 216, 218. *See also* monetary system
*iqta*ʿ, 179–180, 181
*iqta*ʿ*iyya*. *See* feudalism
Iran, 206, 211
Iraq, 153, 211
Ireland, 72, 73, 74, 120
Islam, 171, 176, 179, 228
Ismaʿil, Khedive, 38, 178
Ismaʿiliyya canal, 107
Israel, 212, 215, 219, 220
Istanbul, Turkey, 73
Italy, 61, 159, 199, 202, 249n25, 259–260n4; Italians, 27, 72, 94, 247n120, 258n73
ʿ*izba* (large private estates), 15, 17; attempts to abolish private ownership, 157; extent of cultivated land as, 28, 30; foreclosures on, 101–102; during Great Depression, 89; laborers on, 16, 31, 34, 80, 81, 130; Mehmed Ali's introduction of, 222; owners as feudal lords, 21, 230; owners as rentiers, 164, 175; owners critiqued, 146, 147, 158, 173, 176–177, 184; undermining of system, 162
Jabr, Muhammad Shafiq, 138
Jacob, Wilson Chacko, 154
Jakes, Aaron, 152, 242n11, 243–244n38
Japan, 46, 48, 92, 96; cotton exports, 211; Japanese Marxists, 186; postwar boom in, 230; reforms, 197; textiles, 248n15, 261n44
Jessop, A. W., 70, 117, 120, 121, 137
Jews, 16, 173, 181
Jirjis, Fawzi, 222
journalism, 6, 96, 111, 144, 194, 228
July Revolution, 12, 191, 197, 218, 221, 227; al-Barrawi on, 2, 13; Curiel supports, 188; Egyptian Marxist on, 7, 231; feudalism and, 14; Gordon on, 8–9; ideological legacy of, 233; Nasser on, 5

Kafr al-Zayyat, Egypt, 43, 101, 247n109
Kafr Rabiʿ, Egypt, 100
Kafr Salim, Egypt, 149f
Kafur Nijm, Egypt, 176
Kamal, Yusuf, 177
Kamshish, Egypt, 224
Karim, Muhammad, 148
Karl, Rebecca, 186
Kennedy, John F., 194
Keynes, John Maynard, 46, 47, 48, 124, 229, 231
Khattab, Muhammad, 172
Khedival Agricultural Society, 65
khedival government, 14, 16, 17, 39
Khrushchev, Nikita, 215–216, 222
Kitchener, Lord, 34
Korean War, 164, 175, 176, 206, 266n22
Krugman, Paul, 229

La Fluviale (company), 106
labor, 29–32, 37, 80–82, 112, 144, 165, 167; activism, 119, 120, 121; agricultural, 30, 161, 171; child, 32, 163; contractors, 118, 121; costs, 92, 248n18; disputes, 88, 118; forced, 31, 37; Labor Conciliation Board, 121; leaders, 120; organization,

labor (cont.)
29; of peasants, 21, 26, 83–85, 130–134, 162, 171, 202; rural, 74, 130, 167, 171, 174, 185; seasonal, 31; strikes, 19, 25, 117–118, 120–121; wage, 28, 81, 130, 184, 185, 201, 239–240n48
Ladejinsky, Wolf, 200
Lampson, Miles, 63
Lancashire, England, 18; Egypt supplies cotton to, 36, 68, 92; exports, 248n15; factories, 63, 67, 167; spinners, 66, 71, 91, 92, 93, 125; trade, 28
Land and Mortgage Company of Egypt, 17, 79, 98, 99
Land Bank of Egypt, 17, 98, 99, 104
land distribution/redistribution, 200, 221; al-Barrawi law on, 197; Ghali on, 172, 173; inequality in, 80, 156; land reform law, 1; Minost on, 157; to peasants, 24, 198, 208; political project for, 156; Sadiq Sa'd on, 175
land leasing, 23, 28, 32, 84, 162, 163, 164, 186
land reform, 21, 172, 197; Free Officers' program of, 24, 190, 199, 201, 210, 221; industrialization and, 8, 24, 157, 178; law, 1; Mexico's, 142; *Misr al-Fatat*'s proposal, 176; peasants on, 81; productivity and, 200; proposals for, 171
Land Tax Department, 32
land tenure system, 24, 79, 85, 146, 157, 183
landholders, 158, 198, 199, 245n64, 247n115; among ruling class, 21, 79, 156; Crédit Agricole aids, 141; debt burden of, 98; foreclosures on, 101; Great Depression's effects on, 137; land privatization effects on, 15; mortgage bankers cater to, 17; peasants' arrangements with, 30; reformers critique, 146; settlement laws affect, 103; wealth of, 97; during World War I, 28
landholding, 156, 171, 172, 173, 187, 242n11
landholding class, 15, 21, 127, 146, 177, 197, 243–244n38
landlord absenteeism, 23, 147, 173, 176
landlordism, 184
landownership, 28, 175, 176, 183, 186, 197
landowning, 8, 27, 28, 64, 72, 80, 127, 224
large estate owners, 33, 113, 176; against AGPA, 71, 83; as agrarian capitalists, 81; in feudalism, 186; Free Officers seize property of, 21; during Great Depression, 23, 89; harmful role of, 156; in *'izba* system, 30; land redistribution of, 1; Yusuf Nahhas speaks for, 29
Latin America, 91, 216, 232, 266n18, 273n14; Cuba, 194, 195, 220; Mexico, 141, 142. *See also* South America
League of Nations, 97
Lebanon, 147
Legislative Council, 254n138
Lenin, Vladimir, 3, 4, 19, 20, 75, 183
Levantine immigrants, 16, 64
Levi, Isaac G., 60, 61, 93
Lewis, W. Arthur, 168–169
liberalism, 124, 125, 145, 194
Lindemann family, 111
Lippman, Walter, 194
Little, Arthur D., 204
Liverpool, England, 52, 67, 88, 93, 241n87
livestock, 30, 141, 163, 213, 240n65; cattle, 148, 238n2
Lloyds Bank, 70
London Inspection Office, 38, 39, 50, 203, 240n56
London Monetary and Economic Conference, 96
long decolonization, 6–14
long/extra-long-staple cotton, 27, 28, 64, 209, 213, 214, 217; American, 93; Sakelleridis, 95
Lower Egypt, 107, 203, 247n109
Luhayta, Muhammad Fahmi, 178
Lutfi, 'Umar, 73
Luxemburg, Rosa, 36–37
Luxor, Egypt, 186

Maghagha, Egypt, 247n109
Mahalla al-Kubra, Egypt, 43, 247n109

Mahallawi, Egypt, 165
Mahir, Ali, 158, 159
Mahmudiyya Canal, 41, 107, 252n93
Mahran, Zakariyya, 166, 167
Maʿmal al-Qazzaz, Egypt, 221
Mamluk *iqtaʿ* system, 180, 181
al-Manayil, Egypt, 150
Manchester, England, 52, 55, 58; manufacturers, 111; merchants, 72; spinners, 71; textile factories, 88; trade, 210, 211
Manchester Cotton Association, 116
Manchester Ship Canal, 252n90
Mansura, Egypt, 35, 43, 98, 203, 247n109
manufacturers, 26, 72, 84; Alexandria exports to, 89; British, 67, 111, 124; continental, 240n56; in Egypt, 209; English textile, 14, 18, 27, 88; European, 45, 47, 63, 111, 115; foreign, 65; German, 38, 111; industrial, 92; Liverpool, 68; textile, 52; Western, 53, 116
al-Manzalawi, Ali, 122
Maqlad, ʿAbd al-ʿAziz, 91
Marʿi, Sayyid, 198–199
Marshall Plan, 191
al-Mawardi, Abu al-Hasan, 180
Marx, Karl, 3, 10, 16, 36, 74, 75, 231, 239–240n48; on fetishism of commodities, 247–248n121
Marxism, 12, 182, 183, 221, 222; Chinese, Soviet, and Japanese, 186; European, 31; Latin American, 273n14
Marxists, Egyptian, 12, 182, 197, 221–223, 273n11; Ahmad Sadiq Saʿd, 156, 172; al-Fajr al-Jadid (New Dawn), 173; Free Officers and, 220, 231; Ibrahim ʿAmir, 30; interest in production modes, 232; on July Revolution, 7; on Nasserism, 6; Sadiq Saʿd on, 230
McKillop, Arthur T., 76–77
McNeill, John, 12
mechanization, 27, 175; agricultural, 175; of boats and trains, 106; of industry, 161, 170, 179; of production, 183; rural, 167
Mediterranean Sea, 27, 41, 49, 125, 159
merchant families, 15, 23, 89
Messrs. John Birch and Co., 35
Mexico, 141, 142
Middle East, 20, 153, 160, 204, 211, 212; agricultural development, 151; feudalism in, 273n11; imperialism in, 8; Iran, 206, 211; Iraq, 153, 211; Israel, 212, 215, 219, 220; Lebanon, 147; Levant, 16, 64; Middle East Supply Center, 160; Misr Spinning and Weaving Company, 165; North Yemen, 214, 218; Palestine, 180, 187, 212; Persian Gulf, 202; postcolonial states in, 4; Sinai Peninsula, 220; Soviet influence in, 216; Syria, 64, 223; United Arab Republic, 205
military, 49, 158, 180, 196, 228; alliances, 211, 215; British, 18, 47, 162, 202, 259–260n4; conscription, 153; defeat by Israel, 219; Egyptian rebuilding, 220; equipment from the Soviet bloc, 217; Free Officers, 216; leaders, 1, 6; Mehmed Ali and, 170; Nasser's arsenal, 212; occupation of 1882, 34, 36, 78; supplies, 160, 212; support to Middle East, 204
Mina al-Basal, Egypt, 41–44, 67–69, 90, 159, 241n87; symbols and standards in, 111–122
al-Minya, Egypt, 247n109
Ministry of Agriculture, 65, 76, 77, 149, 151
Ministry of Communications, 203
Ministry of Culture, 224
Ministry of Education, 57
Ministry of Endowments, 181
Ministry of Finance, 41, 45, 49, 93, 94, 122, 133, 239n24
Ministry of Religious Endowments (Wizarat al-Awqaf), 131, 132, 139
Ministry of Social Affairs, 12, 128, 150, 163
Minost, Emile, 99, 145, 157, 258n73
Minsha (firm), 35
Minya province, 59, 66, 78, 106, 140
Misr Cotton Ginning and Trading Company, 59, 252n102
Misr Group, 59

Misr Spinning and Weaving Company, 59, 165
Misr Transport and Navigation Company, 59
Mitchell, Timothy, 152, 224, 259n115
Mixed Courts, 33, 41, 98, 101, 138, 254n138
mixed economy, 4, 229
mobilization, 112, 128, 232; anti-colonial, 2, 73; imperial, 143; nationalist, 78; peasant, 26, 177; political, 53
model villages, 23, 142
modernization, 10, 191, 232; agricultural, 176, 188, 190, 231; intellectual, 224; under Mehmed Ali, 15, 27, 178; of Mexico, 141; under nationalism, 155; political-economic, 224; state-led, 2
monetary system: Britain's imperial, 123, 124, 126; Egypt's, 46, 48, 49, 50, 89, 126, 158. *See also* currency; international trade and monetary systems
monopolies, 21, 23, 89; abolition of, 221; AGPA, 45, 68, 111, 112, 115, 117, 121; Association of Produce Brokers, 44; British, 205; capitalism, 2, 5, 7, 22, 176, 271–272n164; Carver, Moss, and Lindemann families, 111; in Egyptian Nile Valley, 14–18, 26, 51; ESR, 40; Great Depression's effect on, 126; July Revolution, 14; means of production, 173; mechanized industry, 161; Nasser, Gamal Abdel, 18, 37, 122; National Bank of Egypt, 123; provision of military supplies, 212; provision of seeds, fertilizers, and credit, 208; of railways, 39, 108, 204; in Ricardian theory, 262n83; Western, 4
monopolistic domains, 15, 17, 21, 22, 26, 51, 89, 126
monopoly capitalism, 1, 4, 5, 7, 176, 271–272n164
Montreux Convention, 130
Moore, Jason, 237n53
Mortgage Company of Egypt, 17, 103
Moscow, Russia, 75
Moss family, 111
Mubarak, Hosni, 228
Muhammad, Prophet, 180
Muhi al-Din, Khalid, 187, 188
Muhi al-Din, Zakariyya, 219
Munufiyya province, 25, 66, 100, 208, 224
Mursi, Fu'ad, 183, 265n141
Musa, Muhammad al-'Azab, 224
Musa, Salama, 166
Muslim Brotherhood, 176, 228
muta'ahidun (labor contractors), 118
mutamassir, 161, 166

Naguib, Muhammad, xxx
Nahhas, Yusuf, 68–72, 94, 170, 177, 205, 245n64; Abdel Wahab and, 122; on AGPA, 68, 127; on cotton prices, 100; criticizes Alexandria Bourse, 82; on cultivators, 84; on feudalism, 180; history of, 64; on Mina al-Basal spot market, 116; mocks mass production, 95; on smallholdings protection, 29; on sovereignty, 53; at World Cotton Conference, 52
nahiya (subdistricts), 136
al-Najjar, Ahmad al-Sayyid, 229
al-Nasr, Ahmad Hamdi Sayf, 52, 53
Nasser, Gamal Abdel, 1, 5, 7, 189, 230, 232, 235–236n16; agrarian bureaucracy under, 127; agrarian reform, 221; American government extends loan to, 205; appoints Magdi Hasanayn, 198; cooperatives, 201; cotton production, 214; development strategy, 216; Free Officers' regime, 6; ginneries decree, 208; global superpowers, 24; growth rates under, 218; Higher Committee for the Liquidation of Feudalism, 224; as independence leader, 229; industrialization under, 169; July Revolution, 5, 197; national development under, 10; nationalist movement, 187; nationalizes Suez Canal Company, 215, 222; political base, 6; positive neutrality,

212; rapprochement with communist states, 215; regime, 272n167; social gains under, 228; Soviet Union link, 218
Nasserism, 18, 271–272n164; al-Sinnawi on, 228; appeal of, 225; developmentalist diffusionism, 8; end of, 219; historiography of, 226; ideals of, 229; industrialization, 17; leaders of, 12, 13; long decolonization and, 6–14; material and ideological underpinnings, 190, 191; origins of, 3, 5; proponents of, 230–233
Nasserist state, 232; al-Barrawi as precursor of, 3; character of, 9; in cotton marketing, 208; cotton production in, 24; dependence on global superpowers, 220; development project, 196; El Shakry on, 12; ideological control, 7; legitimization of, 188, 224, 230; national development in, 226–227; peasant labor and, 202; political transfers of value, 210; socialism and, 223; United Communist Party of Egypt on, 222
National Bank of Egypt, 88, 125, 127, 135; buys/sells cotton, 66, 206; cotton prices, 51; loans to landowners, 33, 136; London Office, 50; manages national money, 193; monetary system, 49; paper currency, 47, 123
national banks, 20, 58, 85, 147, 154, 160, 205
National Charter (1962), 5, 221, 223
National Cotton Council, 163
national income, 50, 169, 189, 192, 218, 262n63
national wealth, 58, 59, 69, 77, 79, 190
nationalism, 55, 152–155; activism, 60, 156; mobilization, 78; monetary, 125; nationalist leaders, 20, 54, 155, 177, 214, 226; Nationalist Party (al-Hizb al-Watani), 73; sovereignty and, 82, 187, 229; Wafd Party, 20. *See also* economic nationalism
nationalization, 205–209, 223; of foreign assets, 196; of Omar Effendi, 229; of Suez Canal Company, 215, 222
Naus, Henry, 63–64, 135
navigation, 252n93; companies, 105–110; congresses, 252n90; inland, 40; regulation, 111; tolls, 16
nazir (steward), 146
Nazis, 158, 159
neoliberalism, 228, 229, 232, 233
neo-Malthusianism, 142
New Deal, U.S., 95–96, 141
New Imperialism, 47
New International Economic Order (NIEO), 266n21
New Orleans, Louisiana, 88
new society, 4
New World, 239–240n48
New York, New York, 88, 207
Nile Delta, 110, 144, 224, 238n4; bridges and locks, 109; cotton acreage, 93; cotton cultivation, 62; cotton prices, 130; cotton production, 27, 36, 53; crop seizures, 140; Daqahliyya province, 1; ginning factories, 247n109; landowners in, 33, 66, 136; large private estates (*'izbas*), 15, 30; local markets (*halaqas*), 43, 118; railways, 34, 203; river navigation, 107; rural unrest in, 25; unpaved agricultural roads, 35; Zaqaziq, Egypt, 64
Nile River, 14, 39, 107, 109f, 144
nizam al-iqta' (feudal system), 4, 158, 179, 180, 181, 182, 183, 221. *See also* feudalism
Non-Aligned Movement, 266n21
North America, 46, 194; American South, 27, 52, 88, 90, 214
North Atlantic Treaty Organization (NATO), 211
North Vietnam, 216
North Yemen, 214, 218

Ogg, Frederic Austin, 182
oligarchies, 17, 21; landed, 15, 18, 26, 156, 158, 174, 176
Omar Effendi (department store), 154, 228, 229

Orientalists, 273n11
Ottoman Empire, 64, 181
Overland Route, 34, 36
Owen, Roger, 8, 28, 37, 46, 54, 245n64

Pakistan, 211
Palestine War, 187
Palestinians, 180
Paris, France, 57, 64, 95
Paris Peace Conference, 57
paternalism, 77, 144
paved roads, 202, 203, 204
peasant farming, 259n115
peasant smallholders, 34, 175, 184, 185, 199, 243–244n38; Agricultural Bank provides loans to, 33, 136; borrow from Crédit Agricole, 141; traditionalism of, 78
Peasant's Companion (*Zimil al-Fallah*), 148–149
Peel & Co. Ltd., 43, 160
Permanent Council for the Development of National Production (PCDNP), 1–2
Persian Gulf, 202
Peru, 68
pests, 28, 52, 53, 113, 186; boll weevil/worm, 102, 132, 150; caterpillars, 31, 153; control of, 65; leafworms, 31, 32, 140, 218
Piketty, Thomas, 230
Plizaious (firm), 35
Plunkett, Horace, 74
Plunkett's Irish Agricultural Organization Society, 74
Point Four program, 191, 204, 211
Poland, 216
Polanyi, Karl, 47, 48
Poliak, Abraham Nahum, 181
Polier, Léon, 45
political leaders, 4, 6, 19, 97, 166, 176, 197; American, 212, 247n120; German, 247n120; Italian, 247n120; Soviet, 215, 247n120
political legitimacy, 1, 6, 21, 24, 226
political transfers of value, 195, 210, 214, 220
population growth, 143, 167, 169, 190, 261n45
Prebisch, Raúl, 194, 195, 266n16
pressing, 42f, 114–117. *See also* cotton processing
price stabilization, 96, 194, 206, 207. *See also* destabilization
primitive accumulation, 36, 239–240n48
privatization, 15, 17, 229
productivism, 23, 175, 185
protectionism, 62, 142
provincial district (*markaz*), 136, 252n115
Pursley, Sara, 153

Qalyubiyya province, 35, 163, 247n109
Qanatir, Egypt, 247n109
Qasr al-ʿAini hospital, 151
Qattawi (firm), 35

R & O Lindemann, 43
Radwan, Samir, 267n51
al-Rafʿi, ʿAbd al-Rahman, 221
railways, 22, 26, 88, 104, 106, 117, 252n90; administration, 15, 23, 38, 40, 89, 106; Decauville, 35; Delta Light Railways Company, 35, 203; department, 252n97; development and improvement, 251n81; light, 35, 36; petroleum-fueled, 202; in state revenue, 62f, 63; system, 34, 205
railways, state, 17, 34–40, 105, 108–110, 119, 202–205, 240n65; as monopolistic domain, 15, 16, 89, 126. *See also* Egyptian State Railways (ESR)
Rashad, Ibrahim, 72–82, 148, 170, 177, 200, 205; on collectivization, 175, 263n88; institutionalizes rural credit and cooperation, 127
raw materials, 190, 193, 209, 216; agricultural, 141; British, 39; cotton's value as, 90, 174; Egypt's access to, 204; export of, 3, 27, 34; glut of, 159; in industrialization, 195; prices of, 194, 266n16; production of, 19, 73, 170, 178; as source of foreign exchange, 214

al-Raya (The Banner), 183, 265n141
Reed, Henry Ashman, 107, 252n90
Rejwan, Nissim, 224
rentierism, 11, 21, 164, 172, 175, 187, 229, 247n120
revisionism, 220, 224
revitalization, 74, 142, 231
Revolutionary Command Council, 188
revolutions: agricultural, 181; Chinese, 265n129; Cuban Revolution, 194; Egyptian (1919), 54, 57; Egyptian (2011), 229; *First Revolution Against Feudalism/Awwal Thawra 'Ala al-Iqta'*, 224; French Revolution, 179; green, 28; Industrial Revolution, 27, 76, 179; national, 215; national-bourgeois (1920s), 7; national-democratic, 183, 222; Russian Revolution, 14, 19; socialist, 183, 265n141. *See also* July Revolution
Reynolds and Gibson (firm), 67–68
Ricardian theory of rent, 174, 263n83
Ricci, Umberto, 258n73
Richards, Alan, 28, 201
Rif'at, Muhammad 'Ali, 125
Romania, 216
Roosevelt, Franklin D., 95–96
Rosenstein-Rodan, Paul, 169
Roussin, L. G., 45, 49
Roy, Manabendra Nath, 75
Royal Society for Political Economy, Statistics, and Legislation, 60
rural Egypt, 22, 26, 116, 181, 184; capital accumulation in, 104; class disparities in, 66; feudalism of, 180, 182; landownership concentration, 28; social hierarchies in, 79; unequal landholding system, 171
rural governmentality, 23, 142, 147, 152–155, 156
rural reconstruction, 79, 129, 141, 146, 151
rural social centers, 23, 128, 142, 150, 151
rural tenancy, 260n25
Rushdi, Muhammad, 166
Russia, 36, 180, 182, 183. *See also* Soviet Union
Saad, Reem, 200
Sa'd, Ahmad Sadiq, 156, 173–175, 183–185, 230, 231, 263n83
Sa'dist Party, 198
Sakelleridis (cultivar), 53, 64, 66, 68, 93, 95, 102
Salih, Ahmad Rushdi, 183
Salvador, Isidor, 163, 173. *See also* Sa'd, Ahmad Sadiq
Sa'udi, Muhammad 'Abd al-Latif, 146
Schumpeter, Joseph, 19
Scott, David, 152
Second Congress of the Communist International, 75
semi-feudalism, 235–236n16, 265n129. *See also* feudalism
Senate (Majlis al-Shuyukh), 83, 172, 206
Sewell, William, Jr., 9
Shafiq Jabr, Muhammad, 138
Shafiq, Muhammad, 109
Sha'rawi, Huda, 60
Sharp, Walter Rice, 182
al-Sharqawi, Abd al-Rahman, 221
Sharqiyya province, 35, 74, 131, 176, 247n109
Shatanuf, Egypt, 150
al-Shati,' Bint, 144, 180
Shaw, George Bernard, 74, 263n88
shipping, 38, 109, 111; to Alexandria, Egypt, 36, 106, 108, 110, 203, 208; crisis, 158, 161; to Europe, 41; to Mina al-Basal, Egypt, 114; shippers, 43, 125, 247n120; statistics, 122; to Western Europe, 22, 26; during World War II, 158, 159
Shukri, Mahmud, 137
shunas (warehouses), 114, 140, 203
Sidky, 'Abd al-Razzaq, 189–190
Sidky, Aziz, 169
Sidnawi, Sam'an, 61
Sidqi, Isma'il, 54, 57, 94, 131, 135, 168
Sidqi Commission, 57, 58, 62, 178
Sinai Peninsula, 220
al-Sinnawi, Abdullah, 228
Siraj al-Din, Fu'ad, 177, 206

Slaughter, E. W., 110
Smith, Adam, 179
social justice/injustice, 12, 189, 228, 229, 233, 235–236n16
social welfare, 6, 11, 18, 151, 172, 218
socialism, 1, 7, 76, 216, 220–224, 230; Arab, 235–236n16; Egyptian Socialist Party, 157, 263n91; Fabian, 3; peasant commune, 198; socialist laws, 272n167; socialist revolution, 183, 265n141
Société Egyptienne de la Bourse Commerciale de Mina al-Basal, 41
Société Foncière d'Égypte, 98
Société Khédiviale d'Économie Politique de Statistique et de Legislation, 94
Société Misr Pour le Transport et la Navigation, 106
Société Misr pour L'Exportation du Coton, 111, 117
Society for National Renaissance, 145, 172
South America, 104; Argentinia, 194; Brazil, 27, 68, 88, 90, 96, 194; Chile, 138, 194; Peru, 68. *See also* Latin America
sovereignty, 13, 16, 20, 51, 53, 54, 56, 166; control and, 125; economic, 22; economic life, history, and, 179; in economic nationalist discourse, 82; monetary, 126; under Nasser, 212; nationalist understanding of, 187, 229; political authority and, 3; power of, 153, 154
Soviet Union, 90, 196, 199, 211, 212, 215–220, 263n88; aid, 216–217; trade, 210, 215, 216, 217, 218; West's containment of, 205, 212. *See also* Russia
specialization, 2, 73, 77, 111, 118, 213
spinners, 33, 44, 70, 112, 114; Asian, 92; foreign, 33, 46, 69, 86
spinners, British, 61, 63, 67, 68, 69, 94, 96; International Federation of Master Cotton Spinners' and Manufacturers Association, 115–116; Lancashire, 66, 91, 92, 93, 125; Manchester, 71
spinning. *See* cotton processing
stagism, 23, 56, 171, 187, 227; of capitalist development, 232; Egyptian communists' view of, 7; of fertility/mortality, 143; of modern Egypt, 5; Sidky's theory of, 169
Stalin, Joseph, 75, 215, 263n88
standardization, 115, 117; of cotton types, 114, 116, 122; of seeds, 65
state capitalism, 14, 272n167
steam power, 65, 111; in ginning, 238n2; in pressing, 114, 115; of trains, 105, 202, 205
stocks/stock exchanges, 46, 70, 71, 88, 102, 121; joint-stock companies, 104, 161, 207–208. *See also* Alexandria Bourse; Bourse de Mina al-Basal
Stoppani, Pietro, 97
Suares (firm), 35
Sudan, 38, 240n56
Suez, Egypt, 34
Suez Canal, 12, 36, 159, 210
Suez Canal Company, 119, 215, 220, 222
Suez Canal Consultative Working Commission, 252n90
Suhag province, 208
Supreme Railway Board, 40, 108
Sweden, 210
Switzerland, 210
Syria, 64, 223

tabaqa ʿaqariyya (real estate class), 156, 158
Tahrir Province (Mudiriyyat al-Tahrir), 198
al-Tahtawi, Rifaʿ, 180
Talkha, Egypt, 101
tamaliyya (resident workers), 30, 31, 80, 101, 162
Tanta, Egypt, 35, 43, 101, 133
tarahil (seasonal migrant workers), 30, 31
tax collection, 98
tax collectors (*sarrafs*), 113, 130, 136, 140; village-level, 253n115
Temin, Peter, 124
temporalization of difference, 186
territorialization, 82, 86, 157, 205–209

textiles, 61, 209, 219; Bank Misr and, 165; British, 67; English manufacturers of, 14, 18, 27, 88; European manufacturers of, 63; factories, 78, 213; industrialization, 167; Japanese, 248n15, 261n44; manufacturing, 52, 91, 92, 96; sales to Western countries, 214; workers, 196
Teymur, Hussein, 45
Thabit, Thabit, 150
Third World, 191, 215, 216, 218, 266n21
Third Worldism, 195
Tignor, Robert, 8, 60, 249n31
trade deficits, 47, 196
traders, 46, 51, 72, 110–114, 117, 121, 159, 207; AGPA, 83; in Alexandria, 91, 116; cotton markets for, 44; cotton processing monopolies of, 237n46; create AGPA, 16; currency, 125; drive cotton prices down, 69; economic nationalists against, 84; forbidden to use pseudonyms, 71; foreign, 177; General Egyptian Agricultural Syndicate against, 68; government officials work with, 122; under Great Depression, 87; Greek-speaking, 27; Hussein Teymur, 45; Lancashire, 67; linked to other parts of world, 10; report on peasants, 140–141; stores managed by, 43; wealthy, 18
traditionalism, 78, 80
Tripartite Aggression, 214, 222
Truman, Harry, 191, 204, 211
Tucker, Judith, 29
Turkey, 73, 211

'Ubayd, Makram, 116
'Ukasha, Tharwat, 1
'Ulaysh, Muhammad Hamza, 178, 179, 181
'umara' al-ard (princes of land), 158
'umdas (village mayors), 136, 140
U.N. Food and Agriculture Organization, 199
Unilateral Declaration of Egyptian Independence, 22, 53, 77, 239n24
Union of Agriculturalists, 61
United Arab Republic, 205
United Egyptian Nile Transport, 106, 107, 108
United Kingdom/Great Britain, 125, 126, 209, 210, 211, 214, 215; goods, 60, 246n97; trade union movement, 92, 248n18. *See also* England
United Nations, 193, 194, 199, 265n12
United Nations Conference on Trade and Development (UNCTAD), 195, 266n21
Upper Egypt (Sa'id), 43, 78, 247n109; landowners, 65–66; malaria epidemic in, 161; migrants from, 31; rail transport from, 110; river transport from, 106, 109
'Urabi, Ahmad, 221
U.S. Civil War, 18, 36
U.S. Department of Defense, 197, 203, 204, 215, 268n66
U.S. food aid program, 196, 199, 204, 205, 211, 212, 213; Egypt's growth rate, 218; halted, 220; influences Nasser's policies, 214; pillar of Free Officers' project, 215
U.S. State Department, 268n66
U.S. Technical Cooperation Administration, 204
'Uthman, 'Abd al-Salam, 202

valorization, 173, 179, 190
violence, 3, 9, 16, 19, 26, 36–37, 81, 153
Vitalis, Robert, 8, 55, 60, 247n115
volatility, 56, 85, 94, 99; American crop induced, 95; cotton merchants' interest in, 69; of cotton prices, 22, 32, 64; in flows of foreign finance, 242n11; of foreign markets, 3, 127; of goods/capital/prices, 60, 171; of imperial world economy, 24; in international markets, 51; national institutions to deal with, 205; price, 20, 25, 53, 80, 82, 83, 87, 192

Wafd Party, 66–67, 77, 94, 95, 119; Ali Mahir, 158; Bint al-Shati,' 144; Fu'ad Siraj al-Din, 206; Isma'il Sidqi, 57; Muhammad Badrawi 'Ashur, 80; nationalism, 20; Sa'd Zaghlul, 64; Sayyid Mar'i, 198
Wafdist Women's Central Committee, 60
wage labor, 28, 81, 130, 184, 185, 201, 239–240n48
Wahida, Subhi, 170
wakil (agent), 146
Warsaw Pact countries, 196, 209
Wasta, Egypt, 247n109
Waterbury, John, 191
weaving, 59, 111, 165, 170. *See also* cotton processing
weighing/weighers, 43, 118, 119f, 160; Weighers' Syndicate, 119, 121; Weights and Measures Law, 254n138
Wells, Sidney H., 57
West, George, 37
Western civilization, 75, 166
wheat, 27, 30, 80, 131, 212, 213; as weapon, 214
Wiḥdat al-Shīyū'iyyīn (communist group), 272n167
Wilson, Woodrow, 19, 20
Wissa, Esther Fahmy, 60
women, 101, 144, 151, 261n45; laborers, 29, 162, 165; Wafdist Women's Central Committee, 60
Workers Vanguard (al-Fajr al-Jadid), 173, 183
World Bank, 192, 214
World Cotton Conference, 52, 242n1
world economy, 4, 5, 201; British-centered imperial, 14, 19–20, 47; capitalist, 126, 226; imperial, 23–24, 48, 79, 82, 85, 87, 157, 171
World War I, 22, 26; agrarian reform after, 79–80; cotton value during, 90; demographic watershed after, 168; dominant currency before, 126; economic nationalism after, 54; Egyptian Nile Valley after, 56; Egypt's historical dynamics after, 18; Egypt's monetary system beginning in, 48; global cotton crisis after, 52; gold standard before, 123; imperial arrangements erode after, 87; Jakes on years before, 242n11; landholders during, 28; leads to Mina al-Basal strike, 120; money measurement before, 192; navigation competition after, 105; Owen on period before, 46; price volatility after, 25; Rashad relocates after, 72
World War II, 90, 111, 148, 155, 156, 158, 207, 230
World-Systems Analysis, 273n14

Yahya, Amin, 54, 70
Yahya, Hashim, 54, 93
yarns, 28, 213, 214, 248n18. *See also* spinning
Yemen, 214, 218
Yunis, Sharif, 9
Yusuf Bey, Amin, 71

Zaghlul, Sa'd, 57, 64, 67, 80
Zahra, M. A., 93, 94
Zannis, Joseph, 138
Zaqaziq, Egypt, 35, 64, 247n109
zarbias (stores), 43
Zasulich, Vera, 74, 231
Ziada, Mai, 180
Zifta, Egypt, 35, 203, 247n109

The authorized representative in the EU for product safety and compliance is:
Mare Nostrum Group
B.V Doelen 72
4831 GR Breda
The Netherlands

www.ingramcontent.com/pod-product-compliance
Lightning Source LLC
Chambersburg PA
CBHW031756220426
43662CB00007B/429
* 9 7 8 1 5 0 3 6 4 2 7 9 9 *